ADVERTISING
CAMPAIGN
STRATEGY

A Guide to Marketing Communication Plans

Fourth Edition

ADVERTISING CAMPAIGN STRATEGY

A Guide to Marketing Communication Plans

Fourth Edition

Donald E. Parente

Middle Tennessee State University

THOMSON
™
SOUTH-WESTERN

Australia · Brazil · Canada · Mexico · Singapore · Spain · United Kingdom · United States

THOMSON
SOUTH-WESTERN

Advertising Campaign Strategy: A Guide to Marketing Communication Plans, 4th Edition
Donald E. Parente

VP/Editorial Director:
Jack W. Calhoun

VP/Editor-in-Chief:
Dave Shaut

Sr. Publisher:
Melissa S. Acuña

Executive Editor:
Neil Marquardt

Developmental Editor:
Leslie Kauffman
LEAP Publishing Services, Inc.

Marketing Manager:
Nicole Moore

Sr. Production Project Manager:
Emily S. Gross

Sr. Manufacturing Coordinator:
Diane Lohman

Production House:
Interactive Composition Corporation

Printer:
Transcontinental Printing, Inc.
Louiseville, QC

Art Director:
Stacy Jenkins Shirley

Internal Designer:
Lisa Albonetti

Cover Designer:
Lisa Albonetti

Cover Images:
© Getty Images

Photography Manager:
Deanna Ettinger

Photo Researcher:
Susan Van Etten

Library of Congress Control Number: 2005931612

For more information about our products, contact us at:

Thomson Learning Academic Resource Center

1-800-423-0563

Thomson Higher Education
5191 Natorp Boulevard
Mason, OH 45040
USA

How do you develop professional skills that are much in demand but so scarce in the market? Skills that are widely admired yet understood by few? Skills essential for success, yet hard to develop? This book offers a solution to this puzzle. Specifically, it addresses the ability to think and plan holistically in what is becoming a marketplace of ever more narrowly sliced skill sets.

Conceptual thinking is ultimately what drives great marketing ideas-always has, always will. From the early days of mass marketing to today's highly segmented, fragmented, and not always well-integrated marketing, the ability to conceive and execute in complete propositions is what separates the extraordinary from the ordinary. It is what makes icons of brands like McDonald's, Nike, and Target. In a time where there is excess production capacity in virtually every industry, rapid parity in product performance, and an exponential increase in the number of ways of reaching consumers, never has insightful, well-planned marketing been more important.

On a sustained basis, consumers are not moved and brands are not built by loosely conceived tactics that are not much more than a series of one-shot ads. Consumers respond to strategic marketing campaigns—great campaigns that are conceived holistically and executed in a truly integrated manner where the motivations of consumers, the dynamics of markets, and the strengths and vulnerabilities of competitors have been understood and the end game is to have specific objectives, strategies that create sustainable competitive advantage, and inspired execution across all disciplines.

However, developing the skills to think and create at the broadest level is difficult nowadays. There are two key reasons. First, because of the general emphasis on efficiency in business, most firms, client, or agency, don't have the time or resources to develop people at the foundational conceptual thinking and strategy level. Second is a change in the way that marketing services are bought and sold, especially the unbundling of disciplines (creative, media, brand identity, interactive, promotion, etc.) and the development of specialists in each one of these disciplines. There are logical and beneficial reasons behind specialization, but it has made it harder to get experience at the whole-picture level. And this counts, because at some point, in some way, the whole picture—the entire marketing campaign—must come together. How well that happens is largely based on the quality of the thinking up front and throughout the process.

That is where this book comes in. It is valuable both as a strategic grounding in all of the campaign plan components and as a reference for those who will spend their careers working in specialized disciplines. The more you know about marketing and campaign planning at the broad level, the more effective you will be at having your piece of the puzzle fit best and work its hardest.

I have kept a copy of the earlier editions on my reference shelf. Even after 25 years in the business, and a lot of campaigns, I find the principles here to be great thought starters or "templates" when beginning to organize my thinking. For example, because a problem well defined is a problem half-solved, the preparation of a situation analysis covered in Chapters 2 and 3 is a strong grounding for creating a campaign. I think the structure for making choices in message strategy outlined in Chapter 6 is particularly valuable, because all great campaigns have a clear "point of view" that reflects choices of how to approach the marketing issue. This chapter provides a path for those choices to be more deliberate. Lastly, because contemporary marketing must often "touch" an inclusive range of targets across a broad range of contact points, Chapters 7 through 9 are an excellent overview of the modern media and marketing tools landscape.

When I studied under Don Parente, he emphasized two things that would allow a person to have the best chance at advertising career success and fulfilling professional potential: taking advertising seriously and learning to think conceptually.

This book is a chance to do both.

John Phifer
Managing Director
Moroch/Leo Burnett USA
Former Managing Director Leo Burnett-Mexico

How much is enough? How much is too much?

Students often tell me that there is a lot of detail in this book (and they really mean too much). Usually, they're more than eager to start putting together an ad campaign—especially if they have already taken four or five ad courses. But are they ready? That depends mostly on the philosophy or approach of the instructor teaching the course. Some faculty, especially part-time adjuncts, are particularly impressed with ideas and executions. Students are usually more than able to meet their expectations—often with considerable creativity and flair.

If, on the other hand, the course focuses on the advertising campaign process (or the conceptual elements that link one part of the campaign to another), I don't think students are ready. Of course, it's just my opinion. But my students forget quite a bit from one class to another. And adoption reports conclusively indicate that U.S. students are selling back virtually all their books (much less so overseas). As the advertising business becomes increasingly complex, it is difficult to integrate many of the new practices and ideas into the curriculum and still teach the basics. At many schools, accreditation standards preclude expanding the number of ad courses. At an American Academy of Advertising conference a few years ago, several members of a panel suggested that students really need a "fifth year" to help prepare them for the business. The portfolio schools provide that extra opportunity for creative students. But students interested in other areas don't have many options, short of graduate school—which for a variety of reasons is not a viable option for some students.

In my experience, unless I provide considerable focus and detail to students, they often come up short in a number of areas. First, they have a hard time setting objectives. Frequently they're too simplistic and don't provide a clear focus on what a specific area is designed to accomplish. This problem can lead to a somewhat disjointed effort where one area doesn't flow easily into another.

Second, unless I provide considerable attention to the elements that make up a particular strategy, students will sometimes confuse the conceptual underpinnings of their recommendations with their executions. In the media area, students will sometimes state their media objectives and immediately follow up by telling you their choices for media and vehicles. Ask students to state their creative strategy in a sentence or two, and for some it's not easy.

Third, most students don't go into advertising because they like to do research. Without a research aptitude or a research course or two in their background, the research that students conduct to develop a campaign is often fairly unsophisticated and lacks the insight, sensitivity, and validity that is common among professionals. Of course, information on research and design and methodology can easily be found in the library, but because of other demands on students' time, they often don't check it out. (Now, if they've kept their texts from a research class. . .) I've always found it helpful to spend time talking about research design and examples of tests they can use. Otherwise, students may spend a lot of time getting information that is only moderately helpful at best or misleading at worst.

Fourth, students don't generally understand the complexity of a modern marketing communication campaign—all the little things that practitioners do to give themselves an edge over the competition. This book is designed to be a comprehensive guide, but I know that it could cover a lot more. In the last edition, I began the book with the following words, much of which still seems applicable.

So little time. So much to learn.

Yes, we are in the middle of a communications revolution. New media. New technology. All things we've heard about many times. But it's more than that. The advertising agency business has changed significantly in the last several years shaking up the role agencies play and the mindset of the players. And the forecast is for more change, especially for large national companies.

Welcome to the unbundled world of advertising. Increasingly, big advertisers are developing the communication strategy and using agencies to execute their ideas. Traditional full-service agencies continue to offer a variety of services, but what many clients now want is simply a creative vendor. In other words, many clients now expect as the primary deliverable the "creative expression" of the marketing strategy, and not advertising, creative, media, or marketing strategy. Other marketing services, such as media, sales promotion, direct marketing, public relations, and e-commerce, are purchased à la carte, sometimes from an agency, sometimes not. Advertisers have become the integrators of all communication messages, particularly with large companies. Previously, an agency account supervisor would oversee the development and execution of the entire marketing communication campaign. Now that role is often much more limited. For small clients and small advertisers, work proceeds as it often has in the past, but for big companies, it is a new marketing environment. Consumers too are changing: their values, expectations, lifestyles, media habits, and consumption patterns.

For students trying to learn the business, the big picture is getting bigger—and more difficult. Part of the problem is that part of the business operates the way it has for many years—analyze problems and opportunities, set objectives, develop strategy, and execute like crazy—very logically. Another part of the business *appears* to ignore the above process, striving to entertain consumers, getting them to like the ad, and seemingly secondarily, making a compelling point about the brand. One approach is analytical and research based; the other is intuitive and dependent on talent. This second approach may only involve a small portion of the thousands of ads that are run every day, but often these ads are the most visible, reach the largest audience, and win a disproportionate share of advertising awards.

The implication for advertising education is simple: *teach what you can*. Can you teach creativity? Intuition? Talent? The question is arguable. But you can teach students how to use a process to think analytically or in an inspired way so that their creative abilities are used to solve problems and exploit opportunities.

The educator's dilemma involves balancing the amount of time to devote to the numerous details that are part of a contemporary marketing communication campaign and still allowing students the time to do a campaign (to gain experience). In a campaigns course, students are notoriously impatient to get started, especially when they see many of their favorite ads seemingly created out of not much more than a brainstorming session. However, even in comprehensive advertising programs, students forget what they have learned from one semester to another. (Repetition helps in education as it does in advertising.) One solution is to use this book as a manual, allowing students to consult it when the need arises. But remember, students are eager to get started on the campaign and likely will bypass any section of the book they feel isn't directly relevant to what they are working on (i.e., media, creative, or sales promotion). If they do skim over sections in the book, they may miss out on their chance to see how all the parts of a campaign are developed and fit together because it's unlikely they will get this exposure in the business world, in either an internship or full-time employment.

We offer no easy solutions. Our approach is to offer a detailed examination of the campaign process with a special emphasis on the analytical and strategic elements that are likely to lead to effective campaigns. We know there will always be advertising that works for reasons that resist analysis. But we do believe that if you understand the concepts that underlie successful advertising, when changes occur in the marketplace you will be in position to better understand and exploit them.

In the first three editions of this book, we were sensitive to titling the book *Advertising Campaign Strategy* even though it was clear to us the book was all about *marketing communication strategy*. We pointed out then that the advertising emphasis in the title was more a reflection of tradition than a belief that advertising can or should be prepared apart from other marketing communication tools such as sales promotion or public relations. We believe that the title and the orientation of the book have been well received. We continue to stress that smart companies begin with the premise that they are planning a marketing communication campaign, not an advertising campaign. This assumption not only helps companies avoid any overreliance on advertising, but it also helps them proactively consider other promotional options as part of a unified selling strategy. Far too often, communication tools, such as sales promotion, direct marketing, and public relations, are merely combined with an advertising program rather than integrated together to produce a seamless selling effort.

Our challenge as educators is to provide conceptual information in a form that is both useable and practical. To accomplish this task, we included numerous examples of the tests, techniques, principles, and procedures that are used in marketing communication, as well as a number of checklists and tips appropriate for a specific area. We recognize there are many ways to achieve a desired end. We know that as situations change, it may be appropriate to also change the approach or the organization.

■ HIGHLIGHTS OF ADVERTISING CAMPAIGN STRATEGY

The goal for this edition is to strengthen the way strategy is understood and developed to produce superior marketing communication campaigns. We continue to try and make this information easier to grasp and apply.

CHAPTER 1

This chapter introduces the reader to the purpose and scope of the book. After some discussion of the new marketing environment, including postmodern advertising, we present some of the core concepts that should be part of the mindset of students as they prepare for the campaign, including market segmentation, the marketing concept, the communication concept, integrated market communications, process orientation, and a campaign concept. We also present the essential elements in a strategic plan and explain how they relate to a marketing communication campaign. To close the chapter, we present a general outline for the campaign.

CHAPTERS 2 AND 3

These chapters cover what many people refer to as the situation analysis. Chapter 2 begins with a discussion of how to get ready for the campaign. This chapter focuses on analyzing the company and the consumer. It includes a thoroughly revised section on searching for information, online and in a typical university library, and an extensive discussion of syndicated research sources. We also provide broad coverage of the tests and techniques that can be used to complete the analyses. Chapter 3 essentially is a continuation of Chapter 2 but focuses on the market, product, and competitive analyses. Both Chapters 2 and 3 provide the principles and tools to make a thorough situation analysis.

CHAPTER 4

This chapter is basically about understanding problems and opportunities as a prelude to setting objectives. We emphasize that setting objectives should evolve logically out of the research foundation. Critical to our discussion of objectives is the importance of brand equity, which we also discuss in greater detail in the next chapter. To lay a foundation for setting objectives, we discuss the nature of problems and opportunities, and how to uncover them. Most of this chapter focuses on setting objectives, including the decision on how to segment the market. To discuss objectives we follow the principles associated with management-by-objectives (MBO) philosophy.

CHAPTER 5

This chapter is about the development of marketing communication strategy, but mostly it focuses on building the brand. We look at five interrelated elements: the determination of the selling focus, the management of brand equity, the marketing communication expenditure, the positioning of messages, and the targeting and delivery of messages. We devote most of this chapter to an extensive discussion of brand equity. We cover the communication expenditure only briefly, taking the position that this variable is not something students usually can change. We rely on the next three chapters to cover the positioning and targeting aspects of strategy in greater detail.

CHAPTER 6

This chapter is organized so that the first part of the chapter covers both essential and optional elements in a message strategy. The second part of the chapter focuses on execution, including how to evaluate the creative opportunity, an examination of strategic approaches for message strategy, an approach to developing creativity, and new and traditional approaches to creating advertising.

CHAPTER 7

This chapter parallels the organization of Chapter 6 in that it also begins with a brief examination of the elements that make up a media plan including objectives, strategy, and tactics. The chapter then proceeds to explain how to implement the basic media decisions: first, by examining what is involved with setting both quantitative and qualitative media objectives; second, by breaking down media strategy into its essential elements. This chapter finishes with an explanation of how to execute the media strategy.

CHAPTER 8

From an organizational point of view, we considered merging this chapter with the previous one on media, calling it integrated marketing communications. It obviously would have been too long, so we separated advertising media from other types of marketing communication using Chapter 8 to cover sales promotion, public relations, and direct marketing. We know that most advertising students do not get in-depth exposure to these areas, especially sales promotion and direct marketing, so we provided an extensive discussion of the techniques and tools common to the trade.

CHAPTER 9

We have made substantial changes to this chapter. We wanted to put in this chapter the extra things that advertisers increasingly are including in their campaigns to give them an edge over the competition. This chapter includes four major sections: (1) special market segments including global, African American, Hispanic, Asian American, and gay/lesbian markets; (2) special message strategies including multitiered advertising, cause-related marketing, green marketing, and cross promotions; (3) special media strategies including an updated look at advertising on the Internet, nontraditional media options, and examples of creative media approaches such as ambush marketing and fresh TV; and (4) strategies that are a meld of media and creative, such as buzz marketing and branded entertainment, including branded content and product placement.

CHAPTER 10

Evaluating the effectiveness of the campaign is the focus of this chapter. We present a comprehensive view of the many tests and techniques that are used to measure a campaign's effectiveness, briefly covering many of the commercial research companies that are involved in this type of testing. Unlike many of the chapters in other books on this topic, this chapter is organized correspondent to when the need for a particular type of research would arise in a campaign. First, we discuss concept testing, then move to in-depth discussions of copy testing, concurrent testing, and posttesting. This chapter was originally written with the assistance of Michael P. Kalasunas, director of research and planning, J. Walter Thompson.

CHAPTER 11

This chapter covers the task of putting a plans book together, largely focusing on interpreting and presenting the material covered in the previous chapters. For this edition, we expanded our suggestions about specific points to cover in the plans book, especially in the situation analysis. We have tried to use and integrate the ideas and advice of various educators around the country who either teach an advertising campaigns course or work with the AAF competition. New to this edition is Dennis Martin's "Top Ten Tips on Putting Together a Plans Book."

CHAPTER 12

This chapter focuses on putting together the presentation. This presentation is a comprehensive approach to the most taxing of areas. We are especially appreciative of having Tom Duncan and Sandra Moriarity's outstanding book, *How to Create and Deliver Winning Advertising Presentations,* as a model. This chapter also includes an extensive discussion of the special problems associated with the National Student Advertising Competition sponsored by the AAF. For this last section, we borrowed heavily from the advice of AAF competition veterans. We especially appreciate the contribution of Lynda Maddox and Tom Groth on how to compete in the National Student Advertising Competition (NSAC).

ACKNOWLEDGMENTS

This book is the result of the collective efforts of many people, including my family and colleagues. I would especially like to acknowledge the warm and friendly people at Thomson/South-Western: Leslie Kauffman, the developmental editor, who was always readily available to help me solve problems; Emily Gross, the production project manager who helped keep this project on track; Interactive Composition Corporation, the copy editing group that often helped redirect, if not challenge my thinking; and Amy Rose, project manager at ICC.

I would also like to thank the many educators who provided advice, often sharing their own particular approach to doing a campaign. Edd Applegate, Middle Tennessee State University, read most of the book and offered much valuable insight. Bruce Vanden Bergh, Michigan State University, reviewed and critiqued chapters in earlier editions. Leonard Reid, University of Georgia, thoroughly reviewed Chapters 2 and 3 in the first edition, and the effects of his suggestions continue in this edition. Arnold Barban and Helen Katz reviewed the chapter on media and made important suggestions on its organization when this chapter was first developed. Sharon Parente provided important professional assistance throughout the book, but especially in the section on using the library. A number of faculty shared with us their views on how to write a plans book for the first edition: Louise Gainey, University of Miami; Roger Lavery, University of Oregon; Howard Cogan, Ithaca College; Tommy Smith, University of Southern Mississippi; Carolyn Stringer, Western Kentucky University; and Jim Gilmore, Michigan State University. I am also appreciative of the assistance I received from my research assistants on all editions: Lisa Parente, Michigan State University; and Ryan Hale, Sheri Morris, and Evie Hartman of Middle Tennessee State University.

We also received a great deal of assistance from the following practitioners:

From Leo Burnett Co.: Mike Allen, Jane Spittler, Colin Hall, Cathy DeThorne, Mike O'Neal, Jack Phifer, Carol Fletcher, Rishad Tobaccowala, Josh McQueen, and Lisa Lager

From SRI International: Carrie Hollenberg, Rebecca Hollenbeck, and Kristen Thomas

From Hull Marketing Research: Bill Hull

From Foote, Cone & Belding: Dana Anderson and Karen Randolph

From Claritas, Inc.: Stephen F. Moore

From Standard Rate and Data Service: Lindsay H. Morrison

From Executive Recruiter: Susan Sedler

From Helen Curtis: Ralph Blessing

From McDonald's Corporation: Roy Bergold and Elizabeth MacAdams

From Mediamark Research, Inc.: Steve Ellwanger

From Quaker Oats: John Blair, Barb Marusarz, and Scott Hughes

From Nielsen Media Research: Ted Duff

From Nielsen North America: Dan Sarullo, Meredeth Spector, and Connie Milbourne

From Burke Marketing Research: Dan Evarrs

From Information Resources, Inc.: Kevin Bender and Jennifer Norris

From Competitive Media Reports: Symone Mangaroo

From Lintas Marketing Communications: Lou Schultz

From Tatham Euro RSCG: Michael Robinson

SPECIAL ACKNOWLEDGMENTS TO FORMER COAUTHORS

Throughout this book I use the pronoun *we* liberally. Part of the reasoning for this is stylistic, but a large part is my awareness of the contributions my former coauthors, Arnold Barban, University of Alabama; Bruce Vanden Bergh, Michigan State University; and Jim Marra, Temple University, have made to this book. Although much of their work has been rewritten, their ideas and influence is profoundly felt.

I am especially indebted to Arnold Barban for his help and encouragement with both the first and second editions. He has been a good mentor and a special friend.

Don Parente
May 2005

CONTENTS IN BRIEF

CONTENTS

CHAPTER 2

The Research Foundation Part One: Understanding Clients and Consumers 29

CHAPTER 3

The Research Foundation, Part Two: Market, Product, and Competitive Analyses 65

CHAPTER 4

Appraising Opportunities and Setting Objectives 95

CHAPTER 9

Enhancing the Marketing Communication Mix   255

CHAPTER 10

Evaluating the Effectiveness of the Campaign 293

CHAPTER 11

Preparing the Plans Book 317

CHAPTER 12

Preparing a Winning Presentation 349

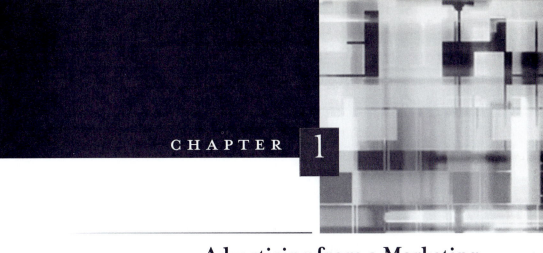

CHAPTER 1

Advertising from a Marketing Communications Perspective

"Advertising" works. The amount of investment in marketing communications has never been greater. Figuring out how to make it work really well has become the hard part. Are consumers paying attention? The more ads consumers see, the less they *choose* to see. Competing in the new marketing environment of parity products, advertising overload, hectic lifestyles, VCRs, TiVos®, remote controls, and mute buttons is challenging. Ads today are more creative than ever. New technology and new attitudes are helping spawn spectacular advertising. Writers and art directors are limited only by their imagination. Special effects wizards can translate the dreamable into the doable. What cool stuff will we see tomorrow? Maybe today?

Super Bowl Sunday has become a showcase for new ads and new campaigns. The advertising is so interesting it is talked about before *and* after the game. One point of debate among ad people is whether the ads are examples of great advertising or merely good film. What is beyond debate is that the ads are usually highly entertaining. Each year seems to showcase new technology or creative techniques. But some ask, "Do these ads really help sell the product?" Even though others counter that sales are not the ads' primary objective, many wonder: Has the role of advertising changed, at least for megabrands?

Discussions about an ad's effectiveness can get complicated. Effectiveness can be difficult to achieve and hard to measure. Because of the increasing sophistication of the market and the nature of the advertising task, running some of these ads requires a good measure of faith. The public has become advertising savvy and, perhaps, a bit jaded. Not only is the public exposed to countless ads, it is also inundated with promotional messages virtually everywhere it goes—from classrooms and ball fields to the restroom at the local pub. Moreover, many companies sell products that have no distinguishing intrinsic qualities, nothing to set them apart from the competition other than, perhaps, an image or a personality. In the top agencies, people in every discipline are continually challenged to think creatively to produce advertising that is better and more creative than earlier work—not to mention that of the competition. Writers, art directors, media planners, sales promotion experts, and all others are encouraged to think "out of the box," or to be "disruptive." There's a lot of pressure, but when the pieces all come together in the right way, the feeling is exhilarating. The last thing great ad people want to be is mediocre or dull.

Truly creative work often exists at the edges of common thinking. The more common the ideas, the less creative or different the work. Creative thinking involves expanding, contracting, or reshaping the boundaries of the way people normally think. Creative work often reflects insights about human behavior, nature, or current society and relates them to the product in a fresh way. The important thing is to be fresh while relevant. Different while accessible. Maybe even original. If people expect one thing, surprise them with another. The forces that lead to creative thinking may produce advertising that is entertaining, but not necessarily ads that sell. Among management, similar thinking often leads to changes in philosophy or procedures. As businesses and markets evolve, changes are inevitable. But the changes may not be for the better. ROI, MBO, TQM, IMC, CRM, EVA, SVA, reengineering, disruption, and under-the-radar are only some of the ideas that have changed the lexicon in the marketing and advertising business. It's likely these concepts do not hold as much promise today as when they were first introduced (or do they?). It's great to be an instrument of change. But for most people, it's enough to be able to evaluate change, to figure out what works, what doesn't—how to survive and thrive in a changing environment. Evaluating change can be as difficult as anticipating change. Telling people how to evaluate and anticipate change can be almost as difficult as bringing about change—but we do have a few suggestions.

▮ PROCESS ORIENTATION

It can be helpful to think about change as something that occurs within a **process**—something that occurs over time, usually involving many steps. A good manager **adapts to change** by learning what those steps are and how they interrelate. Otherwise, if you merely concentrate your attention on producing end results, such as an ad, you may wind up seeing what you want to see, or believing what you would like to believe about the ad's likely success. And if you pay scant attention to *how* you get results, as markets change, you may not be flexible enough to keep up. Instead, by understanding how all the parts in a process interrelate, when the environment changes, you can better manage change. Whether your understanding is rigorously analytical or based on intuition, when change comes you can better anticipate it, evaluate it, and be an agent for it.

In developed markets, changes have become so widespread and massive that they appear to be coming from all directions simultaneously. Still, there is often an underlying order in even the most complex situations. What makes change so difficult to manage in today's sophisticated market, as opposed to a textbook, is that the process is *circular*. In textbooks, the steps in a process often occur along a linear time line, so that a campaign might have a beginning and an end. In a dynamic market, especially one characterized by massive change, conclusions and decisions have to be reevaluated seemingly all the time. Markets today change far more quickly than they did as little as 10 or 15 years ago. We think the steps in the campaign process should be viewed as taking place along a spiral path rather than a straight line. This means that by the time you finish analyzing background information and make decisions, it is often time to gather more information and do more analysis. Viewed this way, the campaign development process strives for continuous improvement. We recommend that you think of the campaign as an evolving work, even though for some people (say, students), the process must have a beginning and an end.

We've organized this book as follows:

- Chapter 1 explores the mindset necessary to develop and execute a marketing communication campaign.
- Chapters 2 and 3 examine the principles and tools to analyze the background information.
- Chapter 4 covers turning problems and opportunities into campaign objectives.
- Chapter 5 discusses the development of campaign strategy.
- Chapters 6, 7, and 8 address ways to execute the campaign strategy through the development of message, media, and integrated communication plans.
- Chapter 9 looks at the extra, but often substantial, things that can be done to enhance a marketing communication campaign.
- Chapter 10 shows how to evaluate a campaign.
- Chapter 11 examines the way to put together a comprehensive plans book.
- Chapter 12 discusses various ways to put together a winning presentation.

Critical to the understanding of this book is the knowledge that each of these chapters is inextricably linked together in what we call the **campaign process.** The purpose of this process is to develop a **marketing communication plan.** This plan outlines the activities, ideas, and executions that take place in order to achieve campaign objectives. In marketing plans, objectives are usually defined in terms of sales or market share. In an advertising plan, the goals may be the same, or the objectives may be set in terms of communication criteria, such as awareness or image. The best plans are strategic in nature, but it doesn't necessarily follow that all plans are strategic. Plans, like strategy, usually take place over an extended period.

DEVELOPING STRATEGY WITHIN THE PROCESS

Generally, the objective of strategy is to give the company a competitive advantage. The key to strategic thinking involves anticipating consumer and competitive responses to a variety of alternative actions and planning accordingly. Strategic thinkers plan for the current time frame and *at least* the foreseeable future. So, a plan that focuses on price deals or coupon offerings is not particularly strategic because most of its effect is likely to be felt only in the short term. On the other hand, an effort to improve or strengthen the image of a brand is likely to have a much more lasting effect. Strategic plans consist of actions that tend to be general in nature as opposed to tactics that are more specific. Another key to effective strategy is to devise a plan that integrates all the activities, ideas, and executions so that they are directed toward achieving common goals. In an integrated plan, the effect of all the actions taken together is greater than the sum of the individual parts. To develop such a plan, think of the campaign as a series of steps or operations, focusing on the interrelationship of the various elements. This is what we call **process orientation.**

OPPORTUNITY AND THE COMMUNICATION REVOLUTION

The field of advertising is in a state of continuous change. A troubling economy, rapidly changing technology, constantly evolving business models, and new media put pressure on people to change the way they conduct business. Over the last decade, corporations tightened their belts through layoffs and other staff reductions to operate leaner and, some would say, meaner. The downsizing of the last decade, and a slow economy following the turn of the century, has resulted in a sizable opportunity for beginners to advance their advertising careers. The traditional progression of junior executives coming up through the ranks into middle management positions no longer works as it did in the past. As a result, there is greater opportunity for people who understand the way things really work.

However, advertising operations, whether in an agency or in a department, are relatively small businesses. Opportunities to learn on the job in an informal or formal training program are much fewer today than they used to be. New hires, especially recent graduates, need a solid conceptual understanding of the advertising process—from day one. Procedures and techniques—the kinds of knowledge students often learn through internships—are less important in a dynamic changing market. Learning the way things are done today is no guarantee the same procedures will be used next year. People in the forefront of this new era understand that the changes taking place in business are more a function of new attitudes and new ways of looking at advertising than a result of new hardware, emerging technology, or new media.

Yet for many brands, the business and its purpose are fundamentally the same as they were a decade ago. This book strives not only to provide a transition between new and more traditional ways of thinking but also to indicate where a traditional approach is still valid. Over the years, advertising practitioners have referred to advertising as a *problem-solving* business. Typically, the problem involves selling a product, although it can also encompass a service or an idea. Very often these problems are solved through an advertising campaign. Today, advertisers are increasingly aware of the full range of promotional tools from which to choose: from advertising and public relations to sales promotion, infomercials, product placement, and event marketing. This book has been titled *Advertising Campaign Strategy* more out of a sense of tradition than as a reflection of the view that advertising can or should be prepared apart from other types of marketing communication. Consumers tend to view all contacts they have with promotion elements as advertising. From our perspective, advertising is simply one of the various marketing communication tools businesses use to get their messages to consumers. However, an advertising campaign will usually include other types of marketing communication along with advertising.

Advertising is, of course, a business. Practitioners are keenly aware of this fact; their customers, clients, and business associates seldom let them forget it. Intellectually, students and people starting out in advertising are aware that advertising is a business, but their lack of work experience sometimes causes them to lose sight of this fact. Some may even think of advertising as an art—a kind of applied art. Professionals understand that there is an art to using advertising creatively, but it is still a business, an important tool of marketing. Its usual goal is to help sell products and services. This book, and particularly this chapter, looks at how advertising interrelates with other aspects of marketing. The challenge to the student of advertising is to reconcile the differences between any new advertising practices or thinking and the principles and procedures that have proven effective over a period of years.

THE NEW MARKETING ENVIRONMENT

To fully appreciate how advertising can solve problems, it is helpful to understand the relationship of advertising to other activities in a marketing program. As many authors have noted, to sell a product effectively, it must be the right product, at the right price, at the right place, and with the right promotion. Each element must be in harmony with the others. The marketing environment has changed quite a bit during the past decade. The forecast for the immediate future: *more change*. To be effective in this new environment, a planner needs to reevaluate exactly what it means to have the right product, price, place, or promotion. To be successful, a company should strive to gain a competitive edge. The alternative is to simply "get by"—which in today's business environment is an invitation for a company to get "passed by." The reality of the marketplace is that even when the elements may not be quite "right," the company still has to figure out a way to capitalize on what it is doing right or it will be forced out of business.

THE RIGHT PRODUCT

Getting this piece of the marketing mix right has become increasingly more complicated in recent years. At a time when different product and size introductions are on the rise, retailers are trying to streamline operations to get a better grasp on the profitability of everything they sell to improve the bottom line. Scanner data systems allow managers to assess the movement of every product variation, or stockkeeping unit (SKU), in a store. But getting the right product to the store requires an understanding of how consumers and the marketplace are changing.

Traditionally, marketing-oriented companies either asked consumers what they wanted or drew an inference from their behavior. Today, when researchers ask consumers what they want, consumers often don't know. Products in many generic categories have become so sophisticated that they do at least a fair job of satisfying consumers' needs or wants. Because it is often easier for consumers to focus on what they feel they lack rather than on what they want, researchers usually get more information if they ask consumers about their gripes or complaints. So researchers are focusing less on consumers' needs and wants and more on their dissatisfactions with current choices (i.e., the consumers' problems).

As consumers become more sophisticated, they seem to be making more decisions based on microissues. Ten or 15 years ago, car manufacturers seemed ambivalent about where consumers set cups or cans in an automobile. Today, this feature often receives prominent attention in automobile ads, whether the car is inexpensive or pricey. Today, researchers and developers focus hard on consumers' problems, no matter how small or seemingly insignificant. Anything to get an edge.

Many consumers report they do not have any problems. When this happens, researchers often shift the focus from consumers' problems to consumers' interests. It's perhaps a sign of relative affluence, but today consumers buy many products not because they want or need them, nor because they help them solve problems. Instead, consumers will sometimes buy something even though their interest is minimal. Many consumers are recreational shoppers. If researchers can't find any interests worth promoting, advertisers may try to build psychological value into a product, by developing a personality or brand image for the product. For example, Tommy Hilfiger promotes itself as multicultural, Ralph Lauren encourages an image of American sophistication, and Calvin Klein pursues an edgy, hip image.

However, regardless of the category, the "big" product ideas (e.g., iPod®, FUBU apparel) are often the result of combining a knowledge of an industry or technology with an "intuitive" understanding of consumers to create a great leap forward in one step.

THE RIGHT PRICE

Increasingly, the right price seems to mean the right lower price. The success of Wal-Mart, Home Depot, Target, and other mass-merchandise retailers continues to exert downward pressure on prices as value-conscious consumers patronize low-price retailers in ever-increasing numbers. Brand-name manufacturers are no longer able to dictate to retailers suggested retail prices. Eastman Kodak, for example, tried suggesting a "minimum advertised price" (MAP) on its premium-priced Royal Gold film, backing it with dealer rebates for all vendors who held the line on the MAP. The idea was to build a generous margin into the price of each roll of film and thus encourage retailers to do more in-store promotions of Kodak film. However, Wal-Mart disregarded the MAP, gave up the dealer rebate, and priced the product lower than the suggested retail price.[1] Wal-Mart competes on the basis of low prices—and competes very well. In the new marketing environment, there seems little companies can do to stem a retailer's inclination to operate on narrow profit margins.

A landmark date in the trend toward operating on a narrower price margin occurred in the spring of 1993. Philip Morris, the consumer products giant, put a 40-cents-per-pack price cut on its full-price brands of cigarettes. By doing so, the company tacitly acknowledged that the consumer trend toward craving lower prices was here to stay. On what some observers refer to as Marlboro Friday, the response on Wall Street was a drop in the share prices of many consumer product companies, from Procter & Gamble and Sara Lee to Coca-Cola and General Mills. Traders seemed to be saying that if Philip Morris could not maintain its price margins with Marlboro, the number-one brand in the world at the time, then other consumer product companies would also be vulnerable. Today, companies continue to relentlessly pursue cost-cutting measures.

THE RIGHT PLACE

A revolution in the marketplace has also affected the way marketers view strategies of place—the right place. An aggressively competitive marketplace has led many companies to get the product to the consumer in ways that would not have been considered in earlier times. McDonald's, long a staunch advocate of the freestanding store, now places restaurants in gas stations, convenience stores, universities, hospitals, and other nontraditional locations. Consumer product companies are also steadily losing control over decisions within the channel of distribution to the giant retailers. Wal-Mart is legendary for exacting stringent requirements on its suppliers regarding inventory control and shelf facings.

Many companies are also opting to market their products directly to consumers. With the increasing ease and widespread use of computers in business, many companies are amassing sizable databases that enable them to target narrowly defined consumers with a minimum of waste.

Although the Sears general merchandise catalog is dead, the success of specialty merchandise catalogers, such as Lands' End, L.L. Bean, and Victoria's Secret, suggests there will be even more material in the mailboxes of the future. Now that the success of home shopping networks is well established, the prospect of greater interactive shopping, especially through the Internet, promises to ensure that changes in the distribution system will continue in a dramatic fashion.

Today, all kinds of products are sold over the Internet. Even groceries are sold on the Web, with online grocers like Peapod, NetGrocer, Albertsons, and Grocer Online vying for virtual customers. Some may question how many consumers will really pay extra to have their groceries delivered. It's merely a matter of time and habits; many already do for pizza.

THE RIGHT PROMOTION

Coming up with the right promotion in the new marketing environment continues to pose many more questions than we can now answer. Some industry analysts attribute the changes in the advertising business to the splintering of the mass media into narrower interest segments. Much of this effect is the result of developments in the creation of new databases, the growing use of ZIP code target marketing, and the use of checkout scanners in retail stores to analyze product movement. Simultaneously, there is a proliferating array of new media delivery options. The dizzying activity taking place within the media appears to be driving many of the changes in advertising. But advertisers are also more worried than ever that consumers are ignoring their advertising. Television playback systems like TiVo™ allow viewers to zip through commercials. Consumers are also suffering from advertising overload and prone to tune out ads that they perceive are blatantly persuasive (whatever that means). A key advertising challenge is to develop messages consumers can't ignore by placing them within a program as they do with product placement, or that they don't want to avoid by simply creating more interesting and entertaining advertising (translation: it's good to be cool).

Another viewpoint is that the changes in the advertising business are more a reflection of a powerful but natural evolution of the marketplace as it becomes increasingly sophisticated. Changes within the media aren't causing change so much as they reflect the new marketing environment. Building brand equity has become more difficult, yet perhaps more important, as products in many generic categories approach parity and consumers change their priorities about the importance of various products in their lives. Companies cope with this difficulty in numerous ways. To reach narrower consumer segments, advertisers experiment with new media delivery systems. The motivation to use these options is a function of both the need to fine-tune the message to the specific needs or wants of the consumer and to reach the target efficiently. Some ZIP code marketing systems, such as PRIZM, allow a marketer to zero in on the geographic location of its prime prospects with a minimum of waste. They also enable an advertiser to custom-tailor the message to the target market's values and lifestyles. In the new marketing environment, advertisers are increasingly rethinking their message strategy.

Advertisers now frequently size up the differentiating characteristics of their products and conclude that there is not enough opportunity to promote the product based on "functional" benefits alone. They are aware that consumers believe there are no significant differences among products in many categories and, because of active or hectic lifestyles, it may not matter much if there were. As a result, companies strive to "build the brand." Their approach is to add value—largely intangible—to the brand name so that consumers buy the brand for what they believe it represents. Done right, this approach can lead to powerful brand identities. Done poorly, this approach often ends up prioritizing entertainment values that drive awareness of the ad alone versus providing any lasting consumer equity for the brand.

In late 1992, Coca-Cola jarred the advertising business by announcing that it would use the Hollywood-based Creative Artists Agency (CAA) to create the bulk of its television commercials. This news left its longtime advertising agency, McCann-Erickson, unclear about its future role. Michael Ovitz, chairman of CAA at the time, and one of the most powerful people in the field of entertainment, had easy access to some of the more renowned directors in Hollywood. Many in the advertising community wondered if Coca-Cola would set an example for other major advertisers to focus more on entertainment and less on selling its product. CAA created numerous spots often without copy, jingle, or any unifying theme other than the tagline "Always Coca-Cola."

Advertising Age commissioned two separate studies to gauge the effectiveness of the campaign. The first study attempted to measure "likeability"[2] and the second, "persuasibility."[3] Not surprisingly, the campaign scored high on likeability, especially a computer-generated spot featuring polar bears; and ranked below average on persuasibility. Was this an effective campaign? It's hard to measure. Large consumer-goods companies like Coca-Cola are able to reach consumers with various messages or imagery at numerous times through traditional media advertising as well as through packaging and signage. Because of this massive exposure, it is extremely difficult to isolate and measure the true effects of a campaign on sales.

One could argue, however, that the campaign's sales-building effectiveness based the trade-off on likeability versus persuasibility. Surprisingly, it's not an easy question to answer. Because of the prominence of Coca-Cola's advertising in the media and the attention it has received in the trade press, this campaign sent mixed signals to advertising practitioners and educators.

One position might be called the David Ogilvy School of Advertising after the legendary advertising great. This position holds that there are factors that make some campaigns succeed and others fail. Advertising educators often favor this approach because it acknowledges that there are principles and guidelines to sound advertising. Another approach to advertising is loosely associated with the West Coast. It features unconventional, highly creative approaches and techniques, often dramatizing a relationship between people and the product. Many advertisers are increasing the executional creative content of their ads in the belief it will forge a stronger relationship between a brand and consumers. Success with this approach is more a function of talent or inherent creativity than with what one might read about advertising techniques in a book. Although the notion of having advertising created by entertainment professionals has faded, the importance of integrating marketing and entertainment has grown dramatically. For many national brands, there has been a convergence between advertising and entertainment—what some call "advertainment." Although academicians might admire "West Coast" advertising, it's a lot harder to teach.

POSTMODERN ADVERTISING

For lack of a better term, this unconventional approach to creativity might be called **postmodern advertising.** Like postmodernism in art or architecture, it too challenges rationality or convention in its field. Bob Kuperman, former president-CEO of TBWA Chiat-Day North America, believes that "persuasion is an art." This is the kind of advertising that "moves people." Unlike science, "its success is dependent on a complex mix of qualities that can be neither measured nor predicted."[4] Steve Hayden, creative director on the IBM account at Ogilvy and Mather Worldwide believes that most consumer buying decisions are based on irrational processes and require irrational advertising. On the other hand, a rationalist's position is that these ads are "creatively self-indulgent and grossly inefficient."[5] Not surprisingly, ad people have very different ideas about the value of postmodern advertising.

A second landmark campaign is still cited today, over a decade later, as an example of this new kind of advertising—advertising that is highly creative, yet perhaps unable to produce results. In the summer of 1996, TBWA Chiat-Day produced a highly popular campaign for Nissan Motor Corp. featuring a quirky, smiling Asian character called Mr. K. The advertising, "Life is a journey. Enjoy the ride," hardly showed the product, but instead focused on characters such as dogs, birds, and Barbie Doll characters. Many critics and creatives loved the campaign.[6] *Time* magazine ranked it number one in the category, "Best Advertising of 1996."[7] However, by spring 1997, the company had drastically changed its campaign, prodded by dealers who complained that the campaign did little to stimulate sales despite advertising expenditures of over $200 million. Reportedly, there was also pressure from the parent company in Japan, which was concerned about a decline in sales despite an increase in sales for the overall category.[8] Eventually, the campaign, and its apparent lack of results, is thought to have cost both the marketing director and the president-CEO their jobs.

In retrospect, there appeared to be two major problems with the campaign. First, the advertising barely showed what the cars looked like and conventional wisdom suggests that people like looking at cars. Second, the campaign tried to associate a funny, exciting, hip image to a line of cars and trucks that many people felt were somewhat conservative—often visualizing a Nissan car in the color black. As this line of thinking goes, the advertising promise did not reflect perceived product characteristics.

There have been many successful examples of both the postmodern approach and the more conventional approach throughout the history of advertising. A big question today is whether advertising needs to be more entertaining, creative, and different to break through a seemingly ever-increasing number of multimedia messages, or whether the principles and techniques that have evolved over the years are still effective. To answer some of these questions, it is helpful to look at what we call the right attitude.

THE RIGHT ATTITUDE

For a company to have the right product, price, place, and promotion, its employees need the right mindset. We call this the **right attitude.** Companies can be successful even though they appear to do many things wrong. The marketplace can be forgiving; a company need not operate at optimum efficiency or effectiveness to make a profit. But the marketplace can be brutal in the price it exacts on companies that have to compete against rivals who understand *how to compete*. Some of the concepts beginners should keep uppermost in their minds as they prepare an advertising or marketing communication campaign include:

- The marketing concept
- The communication concept
- The integrated marketing communication concept
- The advertising campaign concept
- A strategic orientation

▌THE MARKETING CONCEPT

After World War II, many firms adopted what became widely known as **the marketing concept.** Basically, this is a philosophy of how to do business. The marketing concept provides decision makers with a framework for the planning and development of strategies for the right product, price, place, and promotion. Of all the principles associated with this philosophy, consumer orientation is the most important. Implementing this principle can range from a simple focus on the needs, wants, and problems of specific market segments, to organizing the entire marketing effort to appeal to a single market segment, or niche.

CONSUMER ORIENTATION

A consumer orientation emphasizes the importance of planning all marketing activities to satisfy the needs and wants of consumers. The notion that planning should start with the consumer evolved as the marketplace began to change after World War II. Before the war, firms in the United States were production oriented. The population was rapidly expanding, and the Great Depression had left many Americans hungry for products. The demand for goods exceeded the supply, and the main concerns of businesses were to produce products quickly, efficiently, and inexpensively. Because of burgeoning consumer demand, products generally sold well. During the war, much of industry shifted from the production of consumer goods to wartime matériel, suppressing consumer demand artificially. Nevertheless, because of the tremendous demands of war, industry expanded considerably along with increases in technology. Following the war, American firms realized that they had the capacity and the technology to produce more than consumers would demand. The result was rugged, aggressive marketing competition.

The firms that competed best were those that catered to the specific needs and wants of consumers. Developing products became more important than manufacturing. At first, the idea was simply to give consumers what they wanted rather than what the engineers, designers, chemists, or chefs had in mind when they developed a product. This new orientation produced results, but it became apparent that a firm could neither quite satisfy all potential consumers with one or two products—nor did it have to in order to make a profit. Product diversification increased as firms vied with one another to satisfy the growing sophistication of consumers' needs and wants.

MARKET SEGMENTATION

Increasingly through the 1970s, many firms realized that to satisfy the growing sophistication of consumers' needs and wants, they had to compete through product diversification. Market segmentation, aimed at specific segments of the overall market, became widespread as firms developed, priced, distributed, and promoted a heterogeneous variety of products to heterogeneous groups of consumers (i.e., groups that differ from one another on the basis of some common demographic characteristic such as age, income, or ethnicity). This segmentation happened in many products and industries, such as shampoo, cigarettes, beer, coffee, and, at a much later date, automobiles. Firms realized they would be more competitive by dividing up the overall market for the generic product into smaller markets, or segments, often targeting each segment with its own separate brand. Each of these markets represented relatively homogeneous groups whose members were similar based on a characteristic, such as age, income, or lifestyle. Often, they had the same selective tastes and preferences. Companies appealed to these segments by differentiating their product to cater to these special tastes. The combination of increased brand competition, increasing risks associated with new product introductions, and increasingly involved channels of distribution caused these firms to reevaluate their marketing philosophy.[9]

Other firms understood that segmenting the market was not simply a better way to compete, it was the *only* way to compete. Increasingly, companies began to target smaller and narrower segments of the broad market, often by creating a database of current and prospective customers. To reach narrow target audiences firms sometimes used direct marketing.

At the retail level, stores have for many years offered a fairly narrow product line. Take clothing stores, for example. Shops such as For Petites Only, 5-7-9, and Lane Bryant cater to a certain-size woman. In the 1980s and the 1990s, this kind of segmented selling would be increasingly referred to as "niche marketing."

NICHE MARKETING

Niche marketing usually means more than merely segmenting the market. Niche marketers typically offer only products within a narrow range, but within that range they offer a fairly deep selection. Sometimes they will compete against a more broadly based company, such as a department store, on the basis of quality, as Victoria's Secret does, and other times they will compete on the basis of price, as Office Depot does.

Many of the new breed of retailers, such as Toys "R" Us, are able to compete on the basis of price, quality, and selection. As a broad-based retailer, Interstate Department Stores nearly went bankrupt. When it decided to focus its concentration on the toy business with which it had been successful, it changed its name to Toys "R" Us and became a multibillion-dollar company. Unfortunately for Toys "R" Us, the company has been unable to compete with Wal-Mart and likely will leave the toy field and concentrate on its Babies "R" Us division where it competes much better. Still, category killers, as they are sometimes called, are generally enjoying spectacular growth and will likely branch out into other areas in the future.

Bed Bath & Beyond is typical of the new specialty retailers offering domestic goods such as housewares and linens in the home furnishings market. Its stores are all superstores, with each retail outlet averaging more than 35,000 square feet. Department stores and small retailers like Linens 'n Things and the Pottery Barn are its main competition. Its products are a cut above those of mass merchandisers like Wal-Mart and Kmart in terms of selection and look of the store. By focusing on "Everyday Low Prices" (EDLP), Bed Bath & Beyond has enjoyed tremendous success.

MASS CUSTOMIZATION/PERSONALIZATION

The marketing concept puts a high value on satisfying consumers. This philosophy has progressively led companies to develop and provide products to smaller and narrower segments of the market, and in many cases to individuals. Although individuals have always been able to custom-order some products to their own unique specifications, many companies now offer customized products on a *mass* basis. Gilmore and Pine note how companies can take four different approaches to mass customization:

- Create a customized product after a dialogue with individual consumers to learn their specific needs and wants (e.g., Mustang car interiors, computers, clothes, and shoes).
- Offer a standardized product that can be modified to some extent by its users (e.g., Burger King—"Have it your way," Amazon.com, faceplates on cell phones).
- Market a standardized product differently to different users (e.g., office furniture and lighting).
- Provide individual customers with unique products without letting them know that they have been customized for them (e.g., Kroger, Food Lion; the A&E television network tracks the behavior of registered users and sends them personalized pitches).[10]

In many cases, the products are not exactly unique nor is the message. Still, many marketers are having success micromarketing their products to smaller and smaller segments. Toyota Scion vice president Jim Farley talks about the importance of this trend, saying, "The youth market is all about personalization and specialization."[11] The personalization trend includes more than customized products, methods of delivery, and selling messages; it may also lead to more variation in pricing. Coca-Cola is experimenting with "smart" vending machines that are linked to its internal computer network, thus allowing the price of a can of Coke to vary by time of year or temperature.[12]

FIGURE 1-1	THE MARKETING CONCEPT ERA

1950s	1960s	1970s	1980s	1990s	2000s
Consumer Orientation	Market Segmentation		Niche Marketing		Mass Customization/ Personalization

Figure 1-1 provides a rough approximation of the development of the marketing concept over the past 50 years. There are, of course, wide differences in the way companies within an industry apply the marketing concept and, similarly, there are great differences among industries. For example, the cigarette industry applied the principles of market segmentation much earlier than the beer industry. Though it seems that companies will be forced by market pressures to apply marketing concept principles, it does not mean they will end up as niche marketers. The opposite may in fact be the case. As niche marketers become more successful, they will likely broaden their product line. Already this seems to be happening with Bed Bath & Beyond and Office Depot. Nor does it necessarily follow that companies that offer personalized products will continue to provide this customization in the future. There is some evidence that too much variety and complexity can *decrease* consumer satisfaction. For some consumers, simplified choices can lead to increased satisfaction.[13]

Marketing concept notions, such as "the consumer is always right" or "give the consumers what they want," have been around for many years. What is different in the new marketing environment is that consumers have access to much more information than ever before. Many car buyers shop online before visiting a dealership. When they do, they're arming themselves with information on dealer costs.

MARKETING INTEGRATION

To implement marketing concept principles effectively, firms coordinate decisions within their major areas, such as production and finance, with those of marketing. All activities then become part of a total system to produce want-satisfying products and services. In the process, marketing decisions usually take precedence over those of finance or production. Within marketing, product planning precedes decisions on pricing and distribution for the determination of product policy. The marketing concept philosophy encourages executives in and out of marketing to integrate their decisions and activities for the achievement of common goals. Decisions about product quality, pricing, and distribution are often beyond the authority of advertising planners even though decisions made in nonadvertising areas have a direct influence on the effectiveness of an advertising campaign. Many firms recognize this relationship and involve advertising specialists in marketing decisions at the planning stage.

OTHER EMPHASES

The basic principle of the marketing concept is that a firm should marshal its activities toward producing products or services that satisfy existing needs and wants of the consumers. Rather than emphasizing its own resources as its first priority, a company will instead establish giving consumers what they want as its top priority, or as Ford Motor Company likes to say, "Job One." Ford concluded that what consumers want most in a car is quality or durability, and, in the slogans "Quality is Job One," or "Built Ford tough," Ford is telling consumers that it understands what they want, and their needs are the company's highest priority. In this kind of environment, certain other philosophies, or ways of doing business, become common.

Firms tend to be research oriented. Product development evolves out of consumer research. The needs, wants, and problems of the consumer are ascertained through an evaluation of factual data and rigorous observations. Focus groups, one-on-one interviews, attitude and opinion surveys, lifestyle and ethnographic studies, product-usage observations, sales analyses, consumer complaint feedback, and test marketing are but some of the ways a research-oriented firm gets information about the consumer. In contrast, new product ideas in many firms come from the president or the research-and-development (R&D) staff. They are often intuitive and frequently reflect the views of manufacturing or engineering.

In fields that are driven by technology, it often makes more sense to allow technical people to lead the way because consumers may not be sufficiently sophisticated to know which kind of features are possible in a new product line. In this environment, the focus is less on satisfying needs and wants and more on *exceeding* needs and wants. Computers, telecommunications, consumer electronics, and automobiles are some examples of product categories where in recent years technical people are producing innovations faster than consumers can articulate their want for them.

Another principle associated with the marketing concept is the policy that activities should be planned. With the growing sophistication and competitive nature of the marketplace, firms need to anticipate problems, uncover opportunities, and forecast demand. Planned activities are an efficient and effective way to deal with a complex marketplace. A marketing campaign is the execution of a marketing plan. Plans provide direction for all those involved in the marketing effort. It is common for marketing plans to be written. In advertising, the larger agencies deem it almost mandatory in the planning of an advertising campaign.

The advertising firm Batten, Barton, Durstine, and Osborn Worldwide Inc. (BBDO) gives the following reasons a written plan is necessary:[14]

1. It encourages clear and logical thinking.
2. It demonstrates a management approach to advertising by relating media, copy, and art to marketing facts and goals.
3. A written plan offers a factual basis for advertising direction, execution, performance, and appropriation.
4. It provides a complete guide in writing for everyone working on the account, as well as a ready source of information for new personnel joining the client or BBDO.

5. It registers what needs to be done for future improvement and provides an annual benchmark of accomplishment.
6. A plan informs BBDO's top management of an account's goals and progress.
7. It serves as an as-needed policy document for client advertising management to use with other departments, corporate management, and directors.
8. It promotes understanding of, and agreement on, objectives and tactics among both client and BBDO organizations.

THE COMMUNICATION CONCEPT

It is not enough to have the right product; a company has to communicate what is right about the product, even if it's simply an image or identity. Like the marketing concept, the communication concept suggests that all planning begin with consumers. This concept requires the originator of the message to encode information, whether in words or pictures, *in terms of the consumers' needs, wants, interests, or problems.* To be effective, the message creator has to have a solid understanding of the social and psychological makeup of the target market. In other words, the writer has to understand what makes consumers tick so that he or she can better relate to them—the audience. One reason ad agencies have so many young people working for them is to help the agency relate to the very important youth market. For many older adults, talking to your own kids in terms of what's cool, current, or meaningful is hard enough. Talking to others can be mystifying. For some it's like trying to speak a foreign language. Even when you get the words right, there is often the lingering feeling that one of the parties doesn't quite get it.

Failure to interpret a message in terms of consumers' needs or wants may mean the ad fails to communicate. Consumers will either ignore the ad, not understand it, or may simply feel that the message is not meaningful. Moreover, because of hectic consumer lifestyles and the vast number of messages consumers are exposed to every day, a message may communicate well enough, but may be forgotten unless it is attached to a distinctive advertising property. Motel 6 and Red Roof Inns both offer budget-priced rooms. Part of what makes Motel 6 sound economical is its name—some people still remember when it had rooms priced at six dollars per night. Red Roof Inns gets across its message in a memorable way with a simple slogan: "Sleep Cheap."

The above proposition seems fairly straightforward and sensible. Yet it appears that many ads are developed more from the perspective of the advertiser than from that of the consumer. When this happens, the advertising tends to focus more on the qualities of the product that the advertiser thinks are important but not, unfortunately, on those the potential consumer thinks are important when considering buying the product.

A related and potentially more serious problem occurs when advertising is created without focusing on consumers' needs or problems but is created instead to look or sound good. Sometimes this is called creativity for technique's sake. An advertisement can be very entertaining, but it may not help sell the product. Every year after the advertising award shows, people in the industry talk about how the best ads did not win. In fact, advertisers often indulge in a sardonic humor contest trying to predict the first award-winning agency that will lose the account for which it had won the award.

Along with a focus on consumers' needs, wants, and problems, the communication concept implies an understanding of what communication can or cannot accomplish. Specifically, communication affects the way people think, believe, or feel. By itself, it is seldom enough to sell the product. Communication, especially advertising, needs to operate in harmony with the other elements in the marketing mix. It is crucial that planners understand precisely the role advertising needs to assume to influence consumer behavior. Because advertising is a form of persuasive communication, its role is often best defined in terms of communication criteria that have the ability to stimulate purchasing behavior, such as awareness, comprehension, attitude, or image.

For example, when Gillette was ready to introduce its revolutionary Sensor razor, it knew that its advertising would have to do more than tell consumers that it was a better razor; it would have to explain to consumers that the razor was better because the blade was mounted on flexible coils that float along the contours of a person's skin. The approach was so successful that the Gillette Sensor became the number-one nondisposable razor in the world.

Gillette learned from its experience in introducing double-edged razor blades in 1971 that sometimes you have to get consumers to understand how something works before they will believe a product claim. Before double-edged razors came along, it is doubtful that many consumers ever gave much thought to the idea of using more than one blade at a time. Gillette worked hard to get consumers to understand why double-edged razors provide a closer shave. The Gillette message was that "the Gillette Trac II gives you a closer shave, because the first blade lifts each hair, the second blade cuts it off at the skin line." In 1998, Gillette introduced the Mach3 triple-blade razor. Once again Gillette found it necessary to explain how the product delivered on the advertising promise of offering the consumer "a closer shave in fewer strokes." In 2003, the Mach3Turbo was marketed as a "revolutionary blade [that] lets you shave both up and down." In 2004, Gillette introduced the battery-powered M3Power razor with pulsing action that "stimulates hair upward and away from the skin, making it dramatically easier to shave more thoroughly in one easy power stroke."

Deciding on an appropriate role for advertising is of course not easy. The advertising planner has to project what the effects of each possible strategy might be on consumers' behavior. For example: Would establishing or increasing brand awareness lead to greater sales? Would it be more effective to reinforce or change the attitude of the consumers? Should advertising try to improve or intensify the image of the product?

It is easier to establish awareness than it is to change consumers' attitudes or get consumers to understand how a product operates. Moreover, there are no guarantees that if these tasks are achieved, they will result in increased sales. Not surprisingly, many advertisers opt for the conceptually simpler tasks of increasing awareness or working with a brand's image. With those approaches, however, advertisers run the risk that the copy-writer or art director will become misguided and focus more on the creativity or the technique in the advertisement and less on what would be an appropriate selling message.

■ INTEGRATED MARKETING COMMUNICATION

The idea that a firm should coordinate, or integrate, all of its communication or promotional activities has been around for more than two decades. What is different in the past 20 years is that firms better understand that to compete in an increasingly sophisticated marketplace, the messages they disseminate must blend together to achieve interrelated objectives. In the past, companies were often content to let an ad agency take care of its advertising, a public relations agency handle the PR, and its own marketing department manage the sales promotion. Very often the advertising would go off in one direction, the public relations program in another, and the sales promotion in still another. Although the efforts might produce interrelated results, a marketer might question whether this is the most efficient and effective way to operate. The integrated concept embodies the idea that all parties involved in a campaign blend their efforts into producing seamless marketing communications.

Propelling the new emphasis on integrated marketing communication are marketers who understand that the old ways of doing business no longer work. Today's marketplace has become increasingly sophisticated. Although academicians have discussed integrating and coordinating elements of the marketing and promotion mixes since at least the 1960s, especially by using what was then referred to as a "systems approach," it has been only relatively recently that the concept has caught on.[15]

As the physical distinctions among brands in many categories become negligible, the role advertising plays in creating a psychological difference has become more important. At the same time, other types of communication may become even more important in stimulating short-term sales, such as sales promotions and direct marketing. Increasingly, the strategy for many large advertisers is to surround consumers with as many points of contact with the brand as is economical. As a result, nontraditional media and other marketing communication tools often take on added importance.

As firms apply the lessons of market segmentation and product differentiation, they target smaller parts of the overall market. As firms speak to consumers with an increasing number of voices, locating the sources of all of a company's communication within the same organization can be more efficient. Typically, there is better communication within an organization than between organizations.

Because of the tremendous increase in communication technologies, marketers need to be flexible to revise strategies and tactics to meet changing situations. It can be more efficient and quicker for all of a firm's messages to come from one organization. *Whether it is more effective is a matter of some debate.*

For some people, the concept of integrated marketing communication sounds better as theory than it works in practice. Locating the sources of a firm's message in one marketing communication company will only make the operation more efficient and effective if each specialized area of that group works harmoniously with the others and avoids the political infighting that sometimes occurs as each unit vies for a piece of the promotional budget. Moreover, advertisers may want more expertise than an ad agency typically possesses. The solution is to go elsewhere. If a frozen food company wants a sales piece for a new product launch, does it want an agency's creative person or someone who is an expert in frozen food? The expert may have 20 years experience at Kroger. The expert will likely know from experience what is likely to motivate the trade people—a key to many new product launches. The agency creative person's experience is generally with consumers.

Not only are advertisers telling agencies they don't want them to handle other types of marketing communication, but frequently they want them to handle only parts of their advertising as well. Agencies are **"unbundling"** their services and offering them à la carte. So an agency may get the media assignment on an account, but not the creative and vice versa. It's also common these days for an advertiser to give creative assignments for the same brand to *different* agencies. The Budweiser frogs were created by DDB Needham in Chicago, but the Budweiser lizards were created by Goodby, Silverstein and Partners in San Francisco. Although agencies may suggest that the combined effect of all the messages work best when one source handles everything, ad managers within the company retort that it is *their* job to see to it that all messages are compatible (not the agency's).

Ad agencies, especially the big ones, are also at a disadvantage in terms of cost-effectiveness. Advertisers can often outsource promotional work to suppliers who operate with a lower overhead, particularly in terms of real estate and health benefits. Other advertisers find that they can maintain direct control at a lower cost over promotional elements, such as direct marketing, sales promotion, and packaging, by locating these specializations within the company. Ad agencies are often located in some of the priciest locations—at least in major cities.

Regardless of the source of each promotional element, the effect of all activities should be synergistic; that is, each individual or unit's activity should be coordinated so that the combined effect of all contributions is greater than the sum of its parts.

◼ THE ADVERTISING CAMPAIGN CONCEPT

The key to successful advertising is planned advertising. One of the better ways to plan promotional activities is through a campaign that interrelates all activities. Advertisements that are interrelated have greater retentive value than a series of different one-shot ads. Consumers remember advertising longer when each advertisement helps support, reinforce, or even intensify the others.

There are both highly visible and unseen aspects to an advertising campaign. To the average consumer, an advertising campaign is simply a series of ads that look or sound alike. To the student or the practitioner, a campaign may involve all the activities that help produce advertisements designed to achieve interrelated goals, such as consumer surveys, brainstorming, or media analyses. Considering this broader range of activities, we define an **advertising campaign** as **a series of advertisements, and the activities that help produce them, which are designed to achieve interrelated goals.**

This definition works in situations where the advertiser relies exclusively on advertising. However, in many cases the advertiser will broaden its promotional focus to include other types of marketing communication, such as sales promotions, publicity, and direct marketing. A broader focus requires more than a new definition; it also requires a new way of looking at a campaign. Therefore, it may be more accurate to think of an advertising campaign as a marketing communication campaign even though it relies exclusively on advertising as its promotional tool. Notwithstanding, it is likely that the label advertising campaign will stick. Whether you think of it as a marketing communication campaign or the more common advertising campaign, the definition above specifies what it does, but it does not tell what an effective campaign is or does.

CHARACTERISTICS OF AN ADVERTISING CAMPAIGN

The written form of the advertising plan is usually called either the campaign plans book or simply the **plans book.** Planning is the process by which one establishes the objectives, strategy, and tactics. *The main quality that distinguishes a campaign from merely a collection of ideas and ads is unity.* Upon seeing or hearing an ad from a unified campaign, people can tell that it belongs to a family of other ads that have preceded it. *To unify a series of ads, there should be some element that weaves a thread of continuity throughout the campaign that ties all the ads together.* To be effective, campaigns should be strategic in nature, thereby recognizing that campaigns take place over time and are adjusted and modified to take into consideration a changing situation. Nike used to talk about its shoes; now, much of its advertising is image oriented.

CAMPAIGN CONTINUITY

In a sense, all ads for the same product are interrelated inasmuch as they generally try to achieve the same ultimate objective—sell the product. What separates a campaign from a collection of ads is the degree to which each execution is connected. *In a campaign, the general plan is to put something in each ad that leaves a similar impression with consumers so that they feel one ad is a continuation of the others.* These elements can be something observable (i.e., physical) or something one thinks about or feels (i.e., psychological).

Many advertising launches start out as cohesive, coherent campaigns, but somewhere in development the advertising loses its focus because of weak leadership, poor planning, or executional problems. Inadequate execution can result from a variety of problems, such as changes in leadership, lack of talent, deficient work habits, personality problems, or insufficient motivation. Problems with leadership or planning often stem from the wrong kind of orientation. The best campaigns are oriented and executed strategically.

STRATEGIC ORIENTATION

If creative ideas are the heart and soul of a campaign, then strategy is the brain. Strategy is the general plan designed to give the campaign its competitive edge. It is more like an outline than a blueprint. The guidelines that are a part of the plan provide direction over the course of the campaign period. Strategy provides the framework within which all those involved in the campaign should operate. Strategy implies that all members of an organization work as a team toward common goals. Strategic plans result from team members who can anticipate the future and who are able to develop the ideas, operations, and procedures to achieve the organization's goals. A major problem with some strategic plans is that they simply take too long to develop, especially when they are put together by a committee. As part of the strategic-planning process, companies need to build into their operations a strict time schedule and a way of limiting discussion of the items in a plan, or they run the risk of what is sometimes called paralysis by analysis. Ten or 20 years ago, it was common for firms to talk about contingency plans to describe the course of action a company would implement if the situation changed. Today, markets change so quickly and frequently that one can be sure the situation will change and in ways that are often difficult to anticipate. It is therefore imperative that firms integrate options into their strategic plans that provide sufficient flexibility so firms can respond to changing situations in a timely manner.

Although it is easy to talk about strategic plans, it is another thing to deliver them. Advertisers often demand highly creative campaigns—the kind of out-of-the-box thinking that sometimes resists strategic or conceptual analysis. To deal with this potentially conflicting situation, advertisers sometimes assign their advertising requirements to an agency and their strategic planning to a management consultant, such as Booz, Allen, & Hamilton.

A CORPORATE STRATEGIC PLAN

To understand corporate thinking, you need to understand upper-level management. Because upper-level managers are not always available, the next best place to start is with the corporate strategic plan (assuming one exists). There are a number of elements common to all strategic plans, although different disciplines may call them by different names.[16] Among these elements are:

- Organization mission
- Strategic analysis
- Long-term objectives
- Strategy

- Integrated programs
- Financial projections
- Executive summary

Although the above elements are part of a typical strategic corporate plan, they should be an integral part of all ad campaigns. In an advertising or marketing communication plan, they will likely appear in various sections of a plans book. Listed below is a description of each of these elements, with an explanation of how they might be handled in an advertising plan.

1. ***Organization Mission.*** An organization mission statement embodies what the organization is concerned with, the purpose of its existence, and, perhaps, why the business was started. It is the logical starting point of a strategic plan. In advertising plans, the purpose is to solve marketing and communication problems and to take advantage of opportunities. These points are usually discussed in an analysis of the company that is typically found in a larger section titled "Situation Analysis." Often a company's mission is fairly broad, straightforward, and implied. General Motors' mission is to sell a lot of cars. The Chevrolet division's mission is to provide affordable cars for families. The mission of the Oldsmobile division was unclear for a long time. Not surprisingly, the company did not survive.

   A mission becomes an important aspect of the company analysis insofar as it influences the company's ability to solve its problems or capitalize on opportunities. In some markets the problems may not be easily or readily solved, and the company may be better advised to veer off in a new direction to capitalize on different opportunities. In the 1980s, IBM concentrated on solving the problems associated with its mainframe computer business. As a result, it failed to appreciate fully the market potential of the personal computer and lost its preeminent position in the computer business to other companies that were quicker and more adept at capitalizing on new opportunities.

2. ***Strategic Analysis.*** The strategic analysis is the research foundation of a strategic plan. In an advertising plan, the strategic analysis identifies the critical issues, and the strategic focal points that will be addressed by the advertising and marketing communications' strategy. It is normally covered in the situation analysis, which usually consists of an analysis of background information on the company: consumer, market, product, and competition. The purpose of the strategic analysis (or a situation analysis) is to give the company a competitive advantage in information.

3. ***Long-Term Objectives.*** Goals, or objectives, are statements about what each unit involved in the campaign would like to accomplish. A corporation's strategic plan tends to be written more for the organization as a whole than for the marketing function, and so they tend to be broadly based and to reflect what the company wants to accomplish over an extended period. In contrast, marketing and advertising goals are typically written for no more than a year and

are specific. As the marketplace becomes increasingly dynamic, complex, and fast changing in the twenty-first century, it is likely that objectives, whether short term or long term, will be set for periods shorter than one year.

4. *Strategy.* To understand strategy is to understand the importance placed on the interrelationship, or interconnectedness, of all the activities planned to achieve a goal. Strategists understand the linkages among actions, between actions and a reaction, or, as is sometimes the case in advertising, between an action and no response. This linkage is what differentiates a strategy from merely a list of ideas or actions. Moreover, a strategist understands that actions, reactions, and responses take place over time. Like a master chess player, a marketing strategist has to forecast each move and countermove in the marketplace. In an advertising plan, there might be marketing, advertising, creative, and media strategies, as well as various strategies associated with other types of marketing communication. The purpose of a strategy is to achieve a goal. The best strategies are competitive in nature, designed to give the company an advantage. Even when a company is content to follow the brand leader and profit on what it leaves behind, unless the company finds some advantage, small or large, it runs the risk that it will be forced out of business as consumers determine there is not enough value in what the company sells.

5. *Integrated Programs.* This aspect of a strategic plan details the cross-functional actions required to implement the strategy and achieve the objectives. In an advertising campaign, these actions are often referred to as tactics or executions, and they usually appear in major sections pertaining to the media, creative, or sales promotion strategy. The emphasis on integrated programs underscores the team concept in which each program or activity is designed to work harmoniously with other units in the company.

6. *Financial Projections.* Financial projections typically involve the financial expectations and the measures used to evaluate the company's performance. In advertising and marketing communication plans, the projections are covered in a number of different ways and places. Actual expenses are normally handled in a section of the plans book dealing with the budget. Sales projections are normally covered under marketing objectives. Profit projections typically are not covered in marketing plans. Measures to assess the financial projections of a marketing communication program may appear if an advertiser prepares the plan. If the plan is prepared by an agency, it is typically omitted. Since around the mid-1980s, agencies have become decreasingly involved in measuring the effectiveness of advertising programs. That function has largely gone over to the advertiser or to outside research firms. Some agency people are delighted to see this responsibility taken over by their clients. As one agency vice president told the author, "It was sort of like grading your own paper."

7. ***Executive Summary.*** Although many corporate strategic plans
    have an executive summary or overview at the beginning, many
    advertising plans put one at the beginning and frequently the
    end of major sections, such as the situation analysis, the creative
    strategy, or the media strategy.

■A CAMPAIGN OUTLINE

There are many different ways to outline a campaign, especially if it is for a
marketing communication plan. Essentially, a plan serves as a guide for those
who work on the campaign and as a proposal for those who have to have it
approved. As a proposal, there are often a number of different approaches
to get someone to approve spending what is usually a substantial sum of
money. (Generally, it is a good idea to consider any expenditure substantial.)

At the J. Walter Thompson (JWT) agency, planning begins with the
answers to five basic questions:

- Where are we?
- Why are we there?
- Where could we be?
- How could we get there?
- Are we getting there?

When the agency gets the answer to the last question, the process starts
all over again. At JWT, employees refer to the process as a planning cycle
because the process is ongoing. There is a beginning but no real end to
the way they plan for an account.

In academic circles, the above questions receive a fair amount of attention, but they usually get labeled differently. Exhibit 1-1 shows how these
basic questions tend to be handled in an advertising campaigns class.

EXHIBIT 1-1 TWO APPROACHES TO PLANNING A CAMPAIGN

J. Walter Thompson Asks	A Typical Advertising Class Response
Where are we?	Develop a situation analysis.
Why are we there?	Identify problems.
Where could we be?	Identify opportunities.
How could we get there?	Develop message, media, and marketing communication strategy and tactics.
Are we getting there?	Develop a plan to measure or track the effectiveness of the campaign.

Listed in Exhibit 1-2 is the type of outline someone would prepare before undertaking a campaign. This plan lists the steps a company would take in developing a marketing communication campaign. Not all organizations would pursue every step. For example, some companies might not have a direct marketing or public relations plan. These steps will be described in greater detail in following chapters.

EXHIBIT 1-2 AN OUTLINE FOR A MARKETING COMMUNICATION PLAN

I. Introduction or Overview
II. Situation Analysis
    A. Company analysis
    B. Consumer analysis
    C. Market analysis
    D. Product analysis
    E. Competitive analysis
    F. Problems and opportunities (optional)
III. The Target Market Profile
IV. Objectives
    A. Marketing
    B. Communication
    C. Advertising
V. Marketing Communication Strategy
    A. Advertising Strategy
        1. Creative or message strategy
           a. objectives
           b. strategy
           c. tactics or executions (often put at the end of the plan)
        2. Media strategy
           a. objectives
           b. strategy
           c. tactics or vehicles
           d. cost estimates
           e. continuity schedule
    B. Sales Promotion
        1. Objectives
        2. Strategy
        3. Tactics or executions
    C. Public Relations
        1. Objectives
        2. Strategy
        3. Tactics or examples
    D. Direct Marketing
        1. Objectives
        2. Strategy
        3. Tactics or examples

EXHIBIT 1-2	CONTINUED

   E. Other (Such as Event Marketing, Infomercials)
      1. Objectives
      2. Strategy
      3. Tactics or examples
  VI. Communication Assessment Measures (Optional)
 VII. Budget
VIII. Summary

CAMPAIGN PROGRESS CHECKLIST

At this point in the campaign you should have a solid understanding of the following points:

1. To be successful in a changing environment, you need to understand how advertising works at the conceptual level.

2. Understanding how the elements in a process interrelate increases the likelihood that the end results will be successful.

3. To understand the new marketing environment, you need to know how having the right product, price, place, and promotion has changed in recent years.

4. To produce effective advertising, you need the right attitude or mindset.

5. The marketing concept suggests that all planning be geared toward meeting consumers' needs, wants, interests, or problems.

6. The communication concept suggests that messages should interpret the want-satisfying qualities of the product in terms of consumers, needs, wants, interests, or problems.

7. The integrated marketing communication concept suggests that a firm should coordinate and integrate all of its communication and promotional activities so that they present a unified, seamless message to consumers.

8. The advertising campaign concept suggests that unified, interrelated ads will have a greater effect than the sum of a series of unrelated ads.

9. Successful campaigns are strategic in nature. They provide a general plan, competitive in nature, involving a series of interrelated actions to take place over time. A strategic plan anticipates responses in the marketplace and plans accordingly.

10. Corporate strategic plans are similar to advertising campaigns and should be studied to prepare better campaigns for an advertiser.

Notes and References

[1] G. Khermouch, "Kodak, Wal-Mart Price Stand-off is a Royal Rumble," *Brandweek,* 18 April 1994, p. 6.

[2] A.W. Fawcett, "CAA Ads Make Big Splash with Youth, Women," *Advertising Age,* 12 April 1993, p. 1.

[3] A.W. Fawcett, "CAA's Coke Ads Fall Flat on Persuasion," *Advertising Age,* 10 May 1993, p. 4.

[4] A. Vagnoni, "Creative Differences," *Advertising Age,* 17 November 1997, p. 28.

[5] Ibid.

[6] Dottie Enrico, Bruce Horovitz, and Melanie Wells, "Ads Hit Hot Buttons for Some, Leave Others Cold," *USA Today,* 9 December 1996, p. B3.

[7] "The Best Advertising of 1996," *Time,* 23 December 1996, p. 77.

[8] James R. Healey, "Nissan's 'Mr. K' Takes a Back Seat," *USA Today,* 3 March 1997, p. B2.

[9] These ideas were first presented to the author by Professor Nugent Wedding at the University of Illinois and exist in John D. Leckenby and C. Nugent Wedding, *Advertising Management: Criteria, Analysis, and Decision Making* (Columbus, Ohio: Grid, 1982), ch. 1.

[10] H. Gilmore and B.J. Pine, "The Four Faces of Mass Customization," *Harvard Business Review* 75:1 (January/February 1997), pp. 91–101.

[11] Mark Rectin, "Is Honda Losing Its Cool among Youths?" *Automotive News,* November 2004, p. 30.

[12] For more information on mass customization and personalization see Ronald E. Goldsmith, "The Personalized Marketplace: Beyond the 4 Ps," *Marketing and Intelligence & Planning* 17:4 (1999), pp. 178–185; and Ronald E. Goldsmith and Jon B. Frieden, "Have It Your Way: Consumer Attitudes toward Personalized Marketing," *Marketing Intelligence & Planning* 22:2 (2004), pp. 228–239.

[13] C. Huffman and B.E. Kahn "Variety for Salle: Mass Customization of Mass Confusion," *Journal of Retailing* 74:4 (1998), pp. 491–513.

[14] *The Advertising Plan at BBDO, A Handbook for Account Managers* (New York: Batten, Barton, Durstine & Osborn, n.d.).

[15] D.P. Robin and C.E. Harris, Jr., "An Integrated Approach for Applying Marketing Strategy," *Business Ideas and Facts* (Winter 1973), pp. 35–40.

[16] These seven elements are found in P.J. Below, G.L. Morrissey, and B.L. Acomb, *The Executive Guide to Strategic Planning* (San Francisco: Jossey-Bass), pp. 9–10.

CHAPTER 2

The Research Foundation Part One: Understanding Clients and Consumers

To prepare for a campaign, get a pad of paper. Think about the kind of information you'll need for the campaign.

Professionals are sensitive about how they manage their time. When they search for information, they usually know exactly what they are looking for—even though they may not actually find it. General or undefined searches take up unnecessary time that could be better spent on other assignments. Practitioners seldom have the luxury of "extra time." You need a plan.

▮ DEVELOPING A RESEARCH PLAN

You should work from an **outline;** it will help you manage your time. A plan will help you understand both the information you need and how to acquire it. As you accumulate information, you should be well on your way to building a research foundation. Professionals usually have their own way of working, but if you are a beginner or a student, consider using the following topics as a rough outline:

- Where to begin the search for information
- How to separate the search into sections
- How to obtain the information
- How to process the information

THE SEARCH FOR INFORMATION STARTS WITH THE COMPANY

Most professionals can actually start anywhere. Their experience gives them the kind of judgment that allows them to process information in *any* order without biasing the information or ideas that follow. On the other hand, with beginners, first impressions are often lasting impressions. In the classroom, it is not uncommon to hear students generate creative ideas only minutes after receiving a copywriting assignment, and well before they have completed any analysis of background information. Despite being cautioned by the instructor to defer their ideas until they complete

a **copy brief (or platform),** the same ideas frequently show up in the finished ads. Not surprisingly, the ideas are often off target and off strategy.

At the Batten, Barton, Durstine & Osborn Worldwide Inc. (BBDO)
advertising agency, it has long been the practice to defer the search for
product information until after the prime prospects and their problems
have been determined. BBDO's concern is that eager staffers too often
immerse themselves in product information before they understand the
consumers' needs and wants. By talking first to the designers, engineers,
or chemists, they run the risk of assuming that the reasons the R&D people developed the product are the same reasons why consumers buy the
product. Companies hope this is true, but frequently it is not.

The BBDO people are applying what academicians refer to as the **marketing concept;** that is, all planning begins with the consumer. However,
although we agree with the marketing concept in principle, it is usually
more efficient to focus first on the company's problems and opportunities
because a firm simply may not want to proceed in certain directions,
regardless of what consumers might want.

Separating the Search into Sections

At this stage, it is usually a good idea to divide the search into separate
areas. Even though much of the information that is uncovered will apply
in several areas, it helps to split up the work so that certain areas are not
overlooked. It is much better to get most of the information on the first
go around than to have to go back repeatedly and fill in missing pieces of
information. We suggest beginning the search with an analysis of the background information, usually referred to as a **situation analysis.**

We suggest you begin your search in the following areas:

Company analysis
Consumer analysis } Do these
Market analysis   } together

The order in which you search for information after the company and
the consumer/market analysis is not very important. Neither should it be
necessary to complete the above analyses before you begin to search for
information in the areas listed below:

Product analysis   } Do these
Competitive analysis } together

Gathering the Information

Information on the company's mission, finances, products, and other
matters usually comes from primary sources, such as company executives
and staff; and secondary sources, such as magazine articles. It is generally
best to start with secondary sources. The information you find can help
you develop questions to pursue through primary research. Often, you
can anticipate some of your needs for primary research quite early. If so,
you should start developing a plan as early as you can.

There are many ways to get information. To get the research foundation off on the right footing, it helps if the information is from an

objective source. You will probably be tempted to check out the company on its Web site or in the marketplace through observation and interviews. Although these techniques have value, they may be biased. Similarly, you will want to talk to consumers, but it is better to hold off until you can determine the current users of the product objectively. Typically, this means you will start your active search for information in the library.

Processing the Information

Adopting a Competitive Attitude.   Getting the information is only half the task. You must also process the findings to provide advantages for the people working on the campaign. This requires the right kind of attitude. The marketplace is very competitive. Copywriters work hard to develop big ideas—approaches that stand out from the competition. Media planners look for unique or special opportunities to deliver selling messages. Buyers look for the most efficient way to send the messages. It's all very competitive. Researchers need to be every bit as competitive as creative and media personnel.

How Much Information Is Enough?   You don't have enough information until you can provide campaign planners with information that's better than what the competition is receiving. In many mature product categories, sales increases come primarily from the competition's market share. Competitive researchers strive to furnish planners with an edge by providing information that is current, comprehensive, and insightful.

Analysis versus Description.   Comprehensive analyses usually take time, effort, and money. Not all companies (or students) have the resources of their rivals. Therefore, it is worth reemphasizing the importance of searching for information efficiently. Generalized searches often waste time; they tend to be more descriptive than analytical. Descriptive information usually tells people what they already know or could easily find out. An analyst breaks down background information into components, examining the nature and function of each topic to be analyzed and the interrelationships among sections, as you'll see later. Beginners should think like an analyst. For example, as you look for information on the company, you should have a clear understanding of the function of the company analysis, and how this analysis interrelates with the consumer, market, product, and competitive analyses. We will cover these ideas shortly.

Insight Rather Than in Sight.   The problem with a descriptive analysis is that it usually tells only the obvious. We refer to this treatment as *putting the information in sight.* Even when an analysis is especially comprehensive, most adequate researchers will eventually discover the information. Descriptive information puts the burden of finding value or meaning on the reader (assuming it is a report). The key to doing good research is to interpret the information that is in sight, to provide **insight.** Researchers only gain insight when they clearly understand the inner nature of the object being analyzed. For example, it is not enough to identify the prime prospects and the competition. It is also important to determine why consumers buy the brands they do. This usually requires the researcher to probe beyond what is obvious. To connect with consumers, you must first understand them.

Consider: Why do consumers clip coupons? shop at superstores? drive miles out of their way to buy the lowest price gas? The obvious reason would be to save money. In the case of Home Depot, it might also be to have access to a wide array of merchandise. Although these reasons may be some of the most important, other obscure, but more profound reasons may be operating. For many homemakers and do-it-yourselfers, saving money is less important for economic reasons than because of how it makes the saver feel. For some consumers, clipping coupons may be less about saving money and more about reinforcing their self-image of being a thrifty homemaker. Similarly, for many do-it-yourselfers, doing home projects is as much about testing one's abilities as it is about saving money. For these people, shopping at Home Depot may help to reinforce an image that the consumer is a smart person. This is an example of what's sometimes called the BOBO (i.e., bourgeois/bohemian) phenomenon. BOBOs will buy a Viking oven, but shop at SAM'S, or drive a Range Rover and pump their own gas.

These suppositions are merely hypotheses. But if you are developing a campaign for Home Depot or a similar advertiser, they might be worth pursuing. The obvious reasons (price, quality, or availability) why consumers buy a product are often the things companies can do very little to change. If the company does not have a clear price or quality advantage, then the company may be lost about how to strategically direct its promotion. Often, it is the obscure or secondary reasons why consumers buy a product that offer the more creative and effective ways to sell it.

Viewed objectively, a Saturn automobile does not look significantly different from many other cars. But it is clear that Saturn has tapped into a special consumer motive for buying. In the summer of 1994, 40,000 Saturn owners came to the semirural area around the small town of Springhill, Tennessee, to attend a Saturn homecoming celebration.[1] Was it possible in the short span of a couple of years that Saturn had achieved the kind of cult status that has been true for cars like Jaguar, Porsche, Jeep, or even Mustang? Probably not. What the Saturn owners bought was the Saturn experience. The company correctly identified that many consumers simply wanted, as its slogan said, "a different kind of car" from "a different kind of company," even if that difference came primarily in the form of a change in attitude. Ten years later, these differences don't seem so meaningful. Not surprisingly, sales have fallen from an earlier peak.

THE SITUATION ANALYSIS

The situation analysis consists of the background information that will be used to develop the campaign. The information should be **organized, structured, detailed,** and **focused.** Typically, the information is typed into a document and then used to develop strategy and tactics. In the business world, this document, or report, is usually put into a loose-leaf binder, signifying that the analysis is ongoing and subject to continual change. Enlightened companies view analyses as part of a research system, instead of the result of a research project. In a class project, the situation analysis is simply the beginning section of a more comprehensive **plans book.**

CHARACTERISTICS OF BACKGROUND INFORMATION

Organization.   There is more than one way to organize a campaign. We recommend organizing in an outline format along simple lines. We delineate campaigns by using sections that cover broad topics like the company, consumer, market, product, and competition. By using broad topics, you can include within a section any analysis that makes sense for that particular situation.

Structure.   The situation analysis should be *structured* so that *it is clear that the company's problems and opportunities are uppermost in the minds of the people who are performing the analysis.* Remember, although you could make a case to conduct the consumer analysis first, company representatives usually feel more comfortable if the company is first.

For each of the sections in the situation analysis, you should assume an *inside-outside* perspective. With an **inside perspective,** you should strive to understand the company's problems from its point of view. However, sometimes company executives are too close to the situation to have an objective viewpoint. Therefore, viewing the company's situation from an **outside perspective** may provide different and valuable information. Similarly, as the analyst, you want to understand, if not empathize—from an inside perspective—how consumers think and feel. If you only view things from the consumer's perspective, however, you may not get an accurate picture of why they buy or do not buy a product. There are fewer subjects about which people are less objective than themselves.

Consider consumers who drink Samuel Adams beer. If you ask them why they choose that particular brand, they will likely give you some paraphrase of the answer "because I like it." If you probe further, they may tell you specifically why their beer choice is superior to other brands, especially the drinkers of Samuel Adams, the best-selling craft-brewed beer. However, in the beer business there is a common saying, "People don't so much drink a brand's beer, as they drink its advertising." This implies that people consume a certain brand of beer more for psychological reasons than physical ones. If so, then the key task of a researcher often involves moving beyond obvious reasons to uncover motives that are more deeply seated. In the case of Samuel Adams, you would want to know how much of the brand's popularity is due to taste, and how much of it is a reflection of the various images consumers have of the brand. In some instances, an inside approach—trying to think like the consumer—works, and in other cases, taking a more detached approach, or an outside perspective, will provide a more objective and accurate answer. We suggest in each analysis you take both an inside and an outside approach.

Detail.   The purpose of the situation analysis is to provide a research foundation that can be used to develop strategy and tactics. Because tactics are detailed executions of the overall strategy, it is important to provide creative and media personnel with sufficient detail to fully exploit their opportunities as well as keep their work on target and within the strategy. It is not usually enough to learn that consumers value low prices, fast service, and quality food when they choose a fast-food restaurant. This information does not provide enough useful detail. Research questions should be posed to elicit specific information—how low a price, how fast the service—preferably in quantitative terms. If this information is difficult to obtain, then the questions might be stated to provide information of a relative or comparative nature, such as Company A has higher-quality food than Company B.

Focus.   It is important that the detail in the situation analysis focuses on identifying problems and opportunities. Detail without focus is merely padding, or information without meaningful significance. For example, the history of the company is an important part of the company analysis, *but only insofar as it sheds light on the firm's current problems and opportunities.* When and how the company was founded is relevant only if it helps to explain recent or current problems and if it helps make clear why the company can take advantage of an opportunity. Problems and opportunities form the basis for setting objectives. All analyses should focus on identifying the particular aspect of the situation that could either prevent the company from achieving its objectives or enable it to exploit a marketing advantage. These aspects are the company's problems and opportunities, and will be discussed in greater detail later.

CHOOSING THE ANALYTICAL FORMAT

There are a number of ways to process the information you collect. Three of the most common are the **SWOT** analysis, **brand audit,** and **problems and opportunities** focus. Each approach works well. We don't have a strong preference as to which format you use. Briefly, let's look at the major sections in a **SWOT** analysis:

Strengths	a firm's marketing, financial, manufacturing, and
Weaknesses	organizational competencies
Opportunities	a situation, actual or potential, in which a firm can operate profitably
Threats	forces within the environment that threaten profitable operations

Although the SWOT acronym suggests that the analysis begins with an examination of the company's strengths and weaknesses, usually it's the other way around. Typically, the firm analyzes the external environment for threats to its market position and for opportunities it can exploit. These are then evaluated in terms of the company's internal resources, looking at both its strengths and weaknesses. SWOT analyses' findings are then often displayed in chart format. For example, threats may be classified according to their seriousness and the probability that they will occur. Similarly, opportunities may be classified as strong, medium, or marginal.

A **brand audit,** like a SWOT analysis or a problems and opportunities focus, is another way of providing background information.[2] In a brand audit, the emphasis is clearly on brands, in a SWOT analysis the emphasis is often on the company. For example, a SWOT analysis might look at a *company's* success in introducing brands in the marketplace; a brand audit will usually take a slightly different perspective and examine the *brand's* history, especially for national branded products. Although the word *audit* implies a more formal examination, brand audits frequently are not. Sometimes it's merely a difference in perspective or semantics. Still, a brand audit suggests an attitude, namely that the brand is all important, not the company or the "product." Many "brand auditors" are mindful of the saying, "products exist on shelves in the marketplace, brands exist in consumers' minds." A brand audit sometimes leads to a **brand contact audit:** an identification of the ways in which consumers come into contact daily, weekly, or monthly with an impression of the brand.

We use a simple **problems and opportunities** approach because it helps identify where the company is going to have a problem (which is somewhat similar to a threat) or an opportunity. We divide our analysis into the areas mentioned earlier: company, consumer, market, product, and competition. These areas, of course, are part of the situation analysis. The analysis of an area should begin by examining the **critical issues** within the area. For example, the critical issues for most companies are sales and profits. However, for companies breaking into a market, the critical issue may be market share, or more ominously, survival. Sometimes survival is viewed as a temporary hurdle to overcome. For example, civic construction projects can depress a retail store's sales, but the effects are usually short-lived.

A critical issue can also depend on one's perspective. Each fall, a common problem at many division 1A universities is inadequate attendance at football games. At many of these schools, the football program operates very much like a business. From the athletic director's perspective (an inside perspective), the critical issue often involves getting the public to support the team. Entreaties to support the team—"we need your help"—are common. From the public's point of view (an outside perspective), attending a game is not usually about support or school loyalty. It's about enjoyment or satisfaction, something that is likely to be influenced by the quality of the team, the festive atmosphere, or the quality and quantity of restrooms. The athletic administration would like people to attend games because of school or civic loyalty. It's just not very realistic.

In the problems and opportunities approach, the analyst starts by examining critical issues and moves toward uncovering the problems and identifying the opportunities associated with the various critical issues. In Chapter 4, we'll discuss how to turn these problems and opportunities into objectives. The process looks something like this:

Examine Critical Issues → Uncover Problems → Identify Opportunities → Set Objectives

■ THE COMPANY ANALYSIS

We believe the situation analysis should begin with an analysis of the company. This analysis should consist of some basic ideas of what the company is concerned with and what it represents. The focus in the analysis should be on the company's major problems and opportunities. Whether you are working for the company directly, are with its agency, or are doing this project as a class assignment, it is imperative that you operate on the same "wavelength" as the company. To help you formulate the kind of questions you will ask in your research, try to imagine you are in a marketing staff meeting to review the past year and to make preliminary plans for the upcoming one. What problems would be discussed? What opportunities will the staff talk about? A good company analysis provides a benchmark to keep you from going off on a tangent, pursuing opportunities the company will never consider.

SALES AND PROFITS: A GOOD PLACE TO START

Generally, the problems and opportunities discussed in this type of meeting focus on money, in the form of either sales or profits. For many companies, these are the only issues. Usually money problems are symptomatic of more fundamental problems, especially if you look at sales (or profits) over a period of years. **Trend analyses** often uncover problems that barely show up in a static time frame. A company can have an off year for many reasons. If sales problems persist for more than a couple of years, it usually points to a weakness in any or all of three categories: the company itself, the industry, or the overall economy. If you start with the money and ask enough questions, the more deeply rooted problems usually emerge, *especially if you look at the company's problems over time.* Exhibit 2-1 presents how you can use an extended line of questioning to uncover a company's fundamental problems and to evaluate whether they can become opportunities.

As the decade of the eighties opened, things were not going well at General Motors (GM). Foreign imports had made steady inroads in the automobile industry, and GM was having difficulty competing, especially against the Japanese automobile manufacturers. Exhibit 2-1 is a simplistic view of how GM might have determined its opportunity to develop the Saturn automobile.

This line of questioning is, of course, simplistic. It merely demonstrates the value of extending a line of questioning to uncover hidden problems and opportunities. In an actual discussion, the participants would need more information both to pose the questions and to answer them. To ask and answer questions intelligently, your research should include information that is both internal and external to the firm.

Internal Information

Essentially, internal information comes from within the firm, although the company may not be forthcoming with the information you need. In some instances, it must be inferred from outside sources. Consider asking the following questions:

- What is the company's mission?
- What is the company's culture like? (laid-back? conservative? progressive?)

EXHIBIT 2-1 GENERAL MOTORS: PROBLEMS AND OPPORTUNITY ANALYSIS

Question	Answer
What is the basic problem?	Declining sales, eroding share of market, weak profits.
Why?	Consumers increasingly prefer imported cars, especially Japanese.
Why?	Japanese cars have a higher quality image.
Would consumers buy more GM cars if the quality improved?	Not significantly in the short run.
Why?	The problem is as much perceptual as it is real.
Would it help with the image if GM built a completely new car in a newly formed division?	Only if consumers could be convinced the car was made completely different from the old GM ways by a new kind of company.

- How ambitious is the company?
- How much risk is it willing to incur?
- What is the state of the company's financial, technological, and managerial resources?
- What are the sales trends over the past several years?
- How profitable has the company been?
- Has the company's share of market been going up? down?

External Information

This type of information covers the factors or forces outside the firm that influence its problems and opportunities. Consider asking the following questions:

- What has been the sales trend in the industry over the past several years?
- What is the general economic climate? (recession? boom times?)
- Are there any social, cultural, or political conditions detrimental to the future of the company? (changing dress codes? new political administration?)

At this point, the analysis should not be in depth, or you will run the risk that the company's perception of its problems and opportunities will bias the way you view the consumer. To evaluate the company's problems and opportunities fully, you need to complete the situation analysis, by examining the consumer, market, product, and competition.

STARTING THE LIBRARY SEARCH

A general search on the company is a good place to start. You will be looking primarily for articles on the company, but information on the industry or generic category can also be useful. After you have acquired and digested general information, the next step is to focus on specific information about the company. The most informative articles usually come from trade publications, newspapers, and popular periodicals.

Using the Library

1. Begin your search by looking for articles about the company's advertising and marketing problems. It is preferable to perform this search using a database that just indexes business articles. Go to the section of your library's Web site dedicated to research databases, and look for sources like:

   - ABI/Inform (Research, Global, Select)—This valuable source indexes and abstracts articles from 1971 to the present appearing in up to 1,600 management, marketing, and business journals, including articles on advertising.
   - EBSCO's Business Source (Elite, Corporate, Premier)—This scholarly business database indexes and abstracts over 1,000 peer-reviewed marketing, management, economics, finance, accounting, and international business journals and over 1,200 trade and general business magazines. Bonus features include numerous countries' economic, industry, and market research reports.
   - Gale's General Business File ASAP (International)—This database provides access to a variety of sources including full-text journal and magazine articles, local business titles, investment reports, company directory listings, PR Newswire releases, and several major newspapers. Also look for Gale's Business and Company Resource Center.
   - LexisNexis® Academic—The academic version of LexisNexis provides subscribers with unlimited Web access to full-text news, business, legal, medical, and reference resources.

   These business databases index articles from thousands of business publications and often provide full-text access to the articles remotely 24/7 with student login. Most online periodical indexes have both basic and advanced search levels. The basic search level will allow you to enter one or more keywords, which will be searched anywhere in the article citation.

2. A basic keyword search on the company's name combined with advertising or marketing is a good place to start. If sufficient results are found, try narrowing your search to include articles on sales of specific brands. In cases where you find no or too little information, broaden your search to include the company, generic category, or the industry as a whole. You will be looking for obvious trends and will probably be happiest with articles retrieved from trade publications like *Advertising Age, Brandweek, Beverage World, Supermarket News,* and *Automotive News* and from newspapers like the *New York Times* and the *Wall Street Journal.*

3. Next, try to learn more about the company, especially its marketing background. The most comprehensive and detailed company information will be found in financial investment information services subscribed to by your library such as Mergent Online, Standard & Poor's Compustat® or NetAdvantage, Hoover's Online, and Disclosure's Compact D/SEC. A company name search in Mergent Online will provide you with detailed financial information, company history, news, business, subsidiaries, annual reports and more. In-depth company information is also available through the government's EDGAR database (http://www.sec.gov/edgar.shtml). Databases that package articles along with directory information such as Gale's Business and Company Resource Center, LexisNexis Academic, and Factiva® will allow you to perform both searches using just one source. A visit to the company's Web site should also be helpful; just remember that the information contained therein is likely biased.
4. Check out other supplementary sources of information. Use your library's online catalog to search for books about a certain brand, company, or industry. However, be sure to check the publication date to avoid using information that is too dated. Look for regularly updated reference series such as the *International Directory of Company Histories* and *Standard & Poor's Industry Surveys.*
5. You will also need to obtain information concerning consumers and the brand or product category. Although articles will also be helpful, check your library specifically for *Simmons Study of Media and Markets, Choices 3,* or *Mediamark Reporter (MRI)*. Both sources survey large numbers of U.S. consumers in order to provide demographic data concerning the users of broad and specific product categories and to highlight what media they use. Please note that the most recent information available using either source will likely be at least five years old.
6. When you are finished with the above search you likely will need to continue searching in a similar fashion for specific information on consumers and competitors (see sources in step 3).

For assistance with library resources, check database help features and look for librarian-provided online tutorials and guides. Direct support is also available from librarians in person at the reference desk and by phone, e-mail, or chat.

WORDS OF ADVICE

Many students will be tempted to ignore the above sources. It's certainly easier to do a LexisNexis search or to type some brands and company names in Google™, sit back, and click on the hits. If you're achievement oriented or competitive, you should realize that the quality and quantity of information can give you the edge to do great advertising. For example, the financial sources often provide a different perspective and insight than one finds in more journalistic sources. Sometimes doing an extensive search is like doing one more revision.

MOVING FORWARD IN THE ANALYSIS

Once you have a good feel for the company's situation, it's time to begin the consumer analysis. Later, as you begin to understand the consumer, you may want to complete the company analysis by observing or interviewing company personnel and getting sales data from within the company. It may seem awkward or contrived to begin the company analysis, then move on to the consumer analysis, and then come back again to complete the company analysis. Keep in mind that doing research is every bit as much an art as it is a science. The idea is to discover information in such a way that you remain as objective as possible. Once you listen to what company personnel have to say, your thinking may become biased.

▌CONSUMER ANALYSIS

The distinguishing feature of successful advertising is a persuasive, memorable message. The message can be spoken, printed, or simply implied. The key to developing these kinds of messages is not so much to understand words and ideas, but to understand people. Leo Burnett, like many advertising greats, intuitively knew how to talk to the average person. He was often described as a man of average appearance and voice who could instantly grasp the "inherent drama" in a product and relate it to consumers in a way that talked neither up nor down to people. In the twenty-first century, the marketing task will be far more complex and competitive than it was as little as 10 to 15 years ago. More than ever, marketing and advertising people need to understand consumers. A good consumer analysis boils down to about five general questions:

1. **Who are the consumers?** What characteristics do they have in common?
2. **How do they use the product?** How much? Where? When?
3. **What motivates them to buy?** How do they think or feel about buying things in general, and the generic product or the brand in particular?
4. **What do they look for in a product?** What are their needs, wants, problems, and interests?
5. **How do they look at life?** What are their values? What do they like? What are their passions? How do they go about their daily life routines? How does the product fit into their lives? How are they influenced by others?

WHO ARE THE CONSUMERS?

The prime prospects for most products are usually the people who have consumed the product in the past. Although this is not an ironclad rule, it is a guideline that most companies follow. Even though one market segment may be comparable to another in terms of demographic and psychographic characteristics, there may be other factors that influence product usage that are difficult to pinpoint. The simplest way to predict future usage is to look at product usage data. The best place to fish is not necessarily where the fish are, but where the fish are "biting" (feeding).

For example, more hot dogs are sold per capita in the city of Chicago than in any other major metropolitan city in the United States. Hot dogs have long been part of the culture in Chicago and have been big sellers there for more than 40 years. The hot dog of choice is a kosher-style, all-beef product, and is usually sold in a small building specializing in take-out service. The most popular brand is Vienna. Over the past 20 years, entrepreneurs have taken this concept to cities as diverse as Albuquerque, Atlanta, Tuscon, St. Louis, Denver, Nashville, and Panama City, Florida. Although these businesses survive, they seldom thrive as they do in Chicago. Why? Because these cities are not Chicago. Apparently, the hot dog does not have sufficient want-satisfying qualities to have anything more than limited appeal. In Chicago, people go out of their way to eat hot dogs because it is something many of them have grown up with. The original reasons why they consumed hot dogs no longer really matter.

PRODUCT USAGE

Information on product usage is an important way to determine who the users are. Even though you may be able to get information on product usage from trade publications, information will likely be more comprehensive and objective if you consult either *Simmons Study of Media and Markets* published by the Simmons Market Research Bureau (SMRB) or *Mediamark Reporter* published by Mediamark Research, Inc. (MRI). *Simmons* and *MRI*, as they are often called, are the two major syndicated research sources of product-usage information. Each of these services reports on the usage of brands, products, and services in approximately 800 categories. Usage is typically cross-referenced according to various demographic characteristics, including gender, age, education, occupation, geographic location, race, income, and marital status. Figure 2-1 is an example of data that might be found in *Simmons* or *MRI*. How to use (read) the information included in this figure follows.

How to Read Columns A, B, C, and D
Column A refers to the total number of people who bought or used the product that fall into the demographic segment to the left (e.g., there are 6,166,000 adults 18–24 years of age who are heavy users of regular cola drinks).

Column B indicates the percentage of the *demographic segment to the left* that fall into the user category at the top (e.g., 22.43% of all adults 18–24 years of age are heavy users of regular cola drinks).

Column C indicates the percentage of people *who bought or used the product* that fall into the demographic segment to the left (e.g., 20.14% of all adults who are heavy users of regular cola drinks are 18–24 years of age).

The number in column D compares how the demographic segment to the left uses the product to the average usage for all adults. The index number for average usage is 100 and any number above or below 100 indicates above or below average usage (e.g., an index of 155 means that adults 18–24 years of age are 55% more likely to be heavy users of regular cola drinks).

To understand consumers, it helps to look at current users. The goal of the analysis is to describe consumers based on common characteristics.

FIGURE 2-1 | MRI PRODUCT USAGE DATA

REGULAR COLA DRINKS, NOT DIET

Drinks or Glasses/Last 7 Days

Base: All 2004 Spring Mediamark Research weighted Pop. (000) *Projections relatively unstable, use with caution	Total Population 18 Plus				HEAVY USERS (MORE THAN 7)				MEDIUM USERS (3-7)				LIGHT USERS (0-2)			
	A (000)	B Across	C Down	D Index	A (000)	B Across	C Down	D Index	A (000)	B Across	C Down	D Index	A (000)	B Across	C Down	D Index 0
All	211845	100.00	100.00	100	30617	14.45	100.00	100	39767	18.77	100.00	100	49550	23.39	100.00	100
Men	101655	100.00	47.99	100	18368	18.07	59.99	125	21377	21.03	53.76	112	22859	22.49	46.13	96
Women	110190	100.00	52.01	100	12249	11.12	40.01	77	18390	16.69	46.24	89	26691	24.22	53.87	104
Parents	73494	100.00	34.69	100	12237	16.65	39.97	115	14787	20.12	37.19	107	18387	25.02	37.11	107
HH status: head of household	130137	100.00	61.43	100	18974	14.58	61.97	101	23898	18.36	60.09	98	30360	23.33	61.27	100
HH status: homemakers	130274	100.00	61.50	100	16730	12.84	54.64	89	22660	17.39	56.98	93	30383	23.32	61.32	100
HH status: prof/mgr	42793	100.00	20.20	100	4434	10.36	14.48	72	7458	17.43	18.75	93	10812	25.27	21.82	108
HH status: sole parent	11993	100.00	5.66	100	2059	17.16	6.72	119	2512	20.94	6.32	112	3023	25.21	6.10	108
Educ: graduated college plus	51950	100.00	24.52	100	4507	8.68	14.72	60	8100	15.59	20.37	83	13065	25.15	26.37	108
Educ: attended college	57213	100.00	27.01	100	8344	14.58	27.25	101	11352	19.84	28.55	106	13456	23.52	27.16	101
Educ: graduated high school	67355	100.00	31.79	100	11518	17.10	37.62	118	13104	19.45	32.95	104	14660	21.77	29.59	93
Educ: did not graduate HS	35327	100.00	16.68	100	6248	17.69	20.41	122	7211	20.41	18.13	109	8368	23.69	16.89	101
Educ: post graduate	17196	100.00	8.12	100	1320	7.68	4.31	53	2417	14.06	6.08	75	4261	24.78	8.60	106
Educ: no college	102682	100.00	48.47	100	17766	17.30	58.03	120	20314	19.78	51.08	105	23029	22.43	46.48	96
Age 18-24	27492	100.00	12.98	100	6166	22.43	20.14	155	7004	25.48	17.61	136	6676	24.28	13.47	104
Age 25-34	39096	100.00	18.45	100	7039	18.00	22.99	125	8283	21.19	20.83	113	10244	26.20	20.68	112
Age 35-44	44333	100.00	20.93	100	7140	16.11	23.32	111	8689	19.60	21.85	104	11310	25.51	22.83	109
Age 45-54	40026	100.00	18.89	100	5018	12.54	16.39	87	7044	17.60	17.71	94	8995	22.47	18.15	96
Age 55-64	26743	100.00	12.62	100	2796	10.45	9.13	72	4120	15.41	10.36	82	5621	21.02	11.34	90
Age 65+	34155	100.00	16.12	100	2459	7.20	8.03	50	4627	13.55	11.64	72	6703	19.62	13.53	84
Employment: working full time	112161	100.00	52.94	100	17694	15.78	57.79	109	22383	19.96	56.29	106	26187	23.35	52.85	100
Employment: working part time	23062	100.00	10.89	100	3106	13.47	10.14	93	4471	19.39	11.24	103	5912	25.63	11.93	110
Employment: not working	76622	100.00	36.17	100	9818	12.81	32.07	89	12913	16.85	32.47	90	17451	22.78	35.22	97
Occupation: professional	22111	100.00	10.44	100	2130	9.63	6.96	67	4026	18.21	10.12	97	5560	25.14	11.22	108
Occupation: executive/admin/mgr	20682	100.00	9.76	100	2304	11.14	7.53	77	3432	16.59	8.63	88	5253	25.40	10.60	109
Occupation: clerical/sales/tech	38455	100.00	18.15	100	5673	14.75	18.53	102	7342	19.09	18.46	102	9056	23.55	18.28	101
Occupation: precision/crafts/repair	14379	100.00	6.79	100	3177	22.09	10.38	153	3477	24.18	8.74	129	3125	21.73	6.31	93
Occupation: other	39596	100.00	18.69	100	7517	18.98	24.55	131	8577	21.66	21.57	115	9105	22.99	18.37	98
HHI $150,000+	14089	100.00	6.65	100	1368	9.71	4.47	67	1952	13.85	4.91	74	3547	25.18	7.16	108
HHI $75-149,999	51008	100.00	24.08	100	5921	11.61	19.34	80	9474	18.57	23.82	99	12237	23.99	24.70	103
HHI $60-74,999	24052	100.00	11.35	100	3404	14.15	11.12	98	5144	21.39	12.94	114	5054	21.01	10.20	90
HHI $50-59,999	18915	100.00	8.93	100	2863	15.14	9.35	105	3470	18.34	8.73	98	4590	24.27	9.26	104
HHI $40-49,999	21142	100.00	9.98	100	3290	15.56	10.75	108	4147	19.61	10.43	104	4715	22.30	9.52	95
HHI $30-39,999	23479	100.00	11.08	100	4038	17.20	13.19	119	4652	19.81	11.70	106	5088	21.67	10.27	93
HHI $20-29,999	24114	100.00	11.38	100	4217	17.49	13.77	121	4531	18.79	11.39	100	5527	22.92	11.15	98
HHI <$20,000	35046	100.00	16.54	100	5517	15.74	18.02	109	6398	18.26	16.09	97	8792	25.09	17.74	107
Census Region: Northeast	40543	100.00	19.14	100	4928	12.16	16.10	84	6826	16.84	17.16	90	9283	22.90	18.73	98
Census Region: South	76644	100.00	36.18	100	12988	16.95	42.42	117	15615	20.37	39.27	109	18171	23.71	36.67	101
Census Region: North Central	47979	100.00	22.65	100	7297	15.21	23.83	105	8699	18.13	21.88	97	10729	22.36	21.65	96
Census Region: West	46680	100.00	22.04	100	5405	11.58	17.65	80	8627	18.48	21.69	98	11367	24.35	22.94	104
Mktg Region: New England	10604	100.00	5.01	100	1205	11.36	3.93	79	1694	15.98	4.26	85	2082	19.64	4.20	84
Mktg Region: Mid Atlantic	33891	100.00	16.00	100	4144	12.23	13.54	85	6039	17.82	15.19	95	8183	24.15	16.51	103
Mktg Region: East Central	27407	100.00	12.94	100	4578	16.70	14.95	116	4936	18.01	12.41	96	6304	23.00	12.72	98
Mktg Region: West Central	31986	100.00	15.10	100	4507	14.09	14.72	98	5614	17.55	14.12	94	7306	22.84	14.74	98
Mktg Region: Southeast	42304	100.00	19.97	100	7706	18.22	25.17	126	8214	19.42	20.65	103	10135	23.96	20.46	102
Mktg Region: Southwest	24728	100.00	11.67	100	3860	15.61	12.61	108	5611	22.69	14.11	121	5641	22.81	11.38	98
Mktg Region: Pacific	40925	100.00	19.32	100	4617	11.28	15.08	78	7659	18.71	19.26	100	9898	24.19	19.98	103
County size A	86941	100.00	41.04	100	10774	12.39	35.19	86	16289	18.74	40.96	100	20913	24.05	42.21	103
County size B	63405	100.00	29.93	100	9813	15.48	32.05	107	11922	18.80	29.98	100	14595	23.02	29.45	98
County size C	30730	100.00	14.51	100	4812	15.66	15.72	108	6173	20.09	15.52	107	7095	23.09	14.32	99
County size D	30770	100.00	14.52	100	5218	16.96	17.04	117	5384	17.50	13.54	93	6947	22.58	14.02	97
Marital status: single	51782	100.00	24.44	100	10202	19.70	33.32	136	11425	22.06	28.73	118	12629	24.39	25.49	104
Marital status: married	119963	100.00	56.63	100	15250	12.71	49.81	88	21875	18.23	55.01	97	28260	23.56	57.03	101
HH size: 1	29319	100.00	13.84	100	3322	11.33	10.85	78	4500	15.35	11.32	82	6492	22.14	13.10	95
HH size: 2	69030	100.00	32.59	100	7860	11.39	25.67	79	11826	17.13	29.74	91	15674	22.71	31.63	97
HH size: 3-4	80800	100.00	38.14	100	13733	17.00	44.85	118	15976	19.77	40.17	105	19384	23.99	39.12	103
HH size: 5+	32696	100.00	15.43	100	5703	17.44	18.63	121	7466	22.83	18.77	122	8000	24.47	16.15	105
Children: any	89093	100.00	42.06	100	15275	17.15	49.89	119	18453	20.71	46.40	110	21998	24.69	44.40	106
Race: White	165206	100.00	77.98	100	22832	13.82	74.57	96	28859	17.47	72.57	93	37096	22.45	74.87	96
Race: Black/African American	24003	100.00	11.33	100	4054	16.89	13.24	117	5361	22.34	13.48	119	6714	27.97	13.55	120
Race: American Indian or Alaska Native	2770	100.00	1.31	100	677	24.43	2.21	169	628	22.66	1.58	121	475	17.16	0.96	73
Race: Asian	4534	100.00	2.14	100	587	12.94	1.92	90	934	20.61	2.35	110	1241	27.38	2.51	117
Race: Other	16480	100.00	7.78	100	2705	16.41	8.84	114	4198	25.47	10.56	136	4345	26.37	8.77	113
Spanish speaking (in an english language capable HH)	27987	100.00	13.21	100	4196	14.99	13.71	104	6553	23.42	16.48	125	7160	25.58	14.45	109
Spanish or Hispanic Origin or Descent	25608	100.00	12.09	100	3903	15.24	12.75	105	6103	23.83	15.35	127	6516	25.45	13.15	109

*This work is comprised of confidential and copyrighted material and is the property of Mediamark Research Inc. on loan to its subscribers for their exclusive and confidential use persuant to a written agreement with Mediamark Research Inc.

Source: From 2004 Fall *MRI*.

These characteristics can then be used to define or delineate a **market segment.** A market segment then becomes the **target audience,** or **target market,** if it is the segment at which the advertising is to be directed. *The targeting decision is a key element of the campaign strategy and should* *be deferred until all the individual analyses have been completed.* Users are typically described according to the following characteristics:

- demographic criteria
- psychographic criteria
- degree of product/brand usage
- degree of brand loyalty

Demographic Criteria. Demographic criteria describe the consumer in terms of variables such as age, gender, income, geographic location, marital status, education, race, and family life cycle. These criteria are easily the most widely used form for describing or defining the target market. This information is relatively easy to measure, and is available from a number of research sources, such as *Simmons* and *MRI.*

Although the value of using demographic criteria to segment the market is obvious for some products, for others it may not provide enough discriminatory power to distinguish between prime and only fair prospects. For example, two groups may be comparable in terms of age, sex, education, and income, but may not have the same propensity to buy ski equipment because they differ in ways that demographic criteria are not able to suggest. To better understand consumers, an analyst will often examine the psychological makeup and lifestyles of consumers to gain insight into other factors that can affect their predisposition to buy. However, when it comes to buying media, planners usually revert to demographic criteria.

Psychographic Criteria. Psychographic criteria include information that is both psychological in nature (such as personality, motivation, and attitude), and sociological in nature (such as lifestyles, activities, and the way people go about their daily routines). Although demographic criteria are relatively easy to measure, psychographic characteristics are not. The data are not likely to be as reliable or valid as demographic information because of the greater difficulty in defining and measuring psychological and sociological constructs. It is usually much easier to measure whether someone is male or female and a high school graduate than it is to measure whether someone is affectionate, liberal, or even something as simple as how often he or she dines out. As a result, much of the psychographic information used in advertising is customized to fit the specific needs of the advertiser. We will discuss two sources of information in this section: (1) *Simmons,* which is widely available, but of limited value, and (2) the VALS 2 system, which is widely used, *but not likely to be available in libraries.*

Simmons presents some psychographic information cross-referenced to demographic criteria and media exposure. This information is based on a respondent's self-concept and is collected via personal interview. Basically, interviewers ask consumers to rate themselves with respect to a group of adjectives according to a 5-point (Likert) scale. Each of the adjectives, such as affectionate, broad-minded, and egocentric, is then cross-referenced with demographic variables, such as age, income, and geographical location. This information is provided on CD-ROM, which is the way most advertisers and agencies access this data. The categories (four to a page) are as follows:

AFFECTIONATE	AMICABLE	AWKWARD	BRAVE
BROADMINDED	CREATIVE	DOMINATING	EFFICIENT
EGOCENTRIC	FRANK	FUNNY	INTELLIGENT
KIND	REFINED	RESERVED	SELF-ASSURED
SOCIABLE	STUBBORN	TENSE	TRUSTWORTHY

To use this information, an analyst first has to determine the demographic makeup of the product users, and then use the above descriptors to help define the market segment.

VALS™ is a consumer psychographic system developed by SRI International and currently run by SRI Consulting Business Intelligence (SRIC-BI) for segmenting U.S. consumers and predicting consumer behavior. VALS classifies consumers into eight basic groups based on their answers to a battery of 35 attitude items and several demographic questions. (Figure 2-2 presents the VALS typology). Integrating the VALS battery into commercial surveys (e.g., VALS is integrated into Mediamark Research, Inc.'s *Survey of American Consumers*), into custom questionnaires for focus group screeners allows new product developers and marketers a method for identifying appropriate targets for their products and services. VALS data also provide a method for an integrated marketing approach from new product development to brand positioning and from advertising to media selection. Media preferences are collected twice a year.

The VALS system is based on two concepts: primary motivation and resources. It was developed to segment the market and predict consumer behavior. According to VALS, consumers are motivated to pursue and acquire products, services, and experiences that provide satisfaction and give shape, substance, and character to their identities. They are guided by one of three powerful motivations:

1. **Ideals Motivated**—these consumers are guided in their choices by abstract, idealized criteria, rather than by raw emotion, events, or desire for approval and opinions of others.
2. **Achievement Motivated**—these consumers look for products and services that help them be more efficient, reach goals, or demonstrate the consumers' success to their peers.
3. **Self-Expression Motivated**—these consumers are guided by a desire for social or physical activity, variety, and risk taking.[3]

The VALS system is also based on the concept of resources, which includes income, education, energy level, willingness to take risks, and self-confidence.

Related VALS products include GeoVALS™, providing data on where to find concentrations of the desired target by ZIP code or block group, as discussed in Chapter 3, and Japan-VALS™, for understanding Japanese consumers.

Other sources of psychographic information are also available, especially on lifestyle. Most of these sources, such as Claritas, Inc., and *SRDS,*

FIGURE 2-2 | THE VALS™ FRAMEWORK

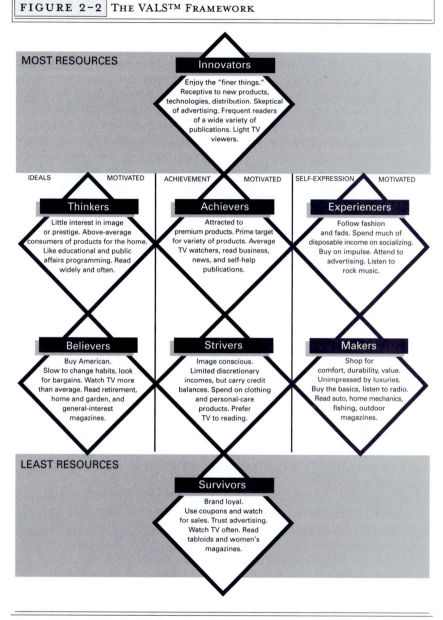

MOST RESOURCES

Innovators

Enjoy the "finer things."
Receptive to new products,
technologies, distribution. Skeptical
of advertising. Frequent readers
of a wide variety of
publications. Light TV
viewers.

IDEALS   MOTIVATED   ACHIEVEMENT   MOTIVATED   SELF-EXPRESSION   MOTIVATED

Thinkers

Little interest in image
or prestige. Above-average
consumers of products for the home.
Like educational and public
affairs programming. Read
widely and often.

Achievers

Attracted to
premium products. Prime target
for variety of products. Average
TV watchers, read business,
news, and self-help
publications.

Experiencers

Follow fashion
and fads. Spend much of
disposable income on socializing.
Buy on impulse. Attend to
advertising. Listen to
rock music.

Believers

Buy American.
Slow to change habits, look
for bargains. Watch TV more
than average. Read retirement,
home and garden, and
general-interest
magazines.

Strivers

Image conscious.
Limited discretionary
incomes, but carry credit
balances. Spend on clothing
and personal-care
products. Prefer
TV to reading.

Makers

Shop for
comfort, durability, value.
Unimpressed by luxuries.
Buy the basics, listen to radio.
Read auto, home mechanics,
fishing, outdoor
magazines.

LEAST RESOURCES

Survivors

Brand loyal.
Use coupons and watch
for sales. Trust advertising.
Watch TV often. Read
tabloids and women's
magazines.

Source: SRI Consulting Business Intelligence, http://www.sric-bi.com/VALS/.

---

use the information in coordination with data on specific markets, as will be discussed in Chapter 3 under "Market Analysis." *If these sources of information are not available, the researcher will have to collect the information using primary research techniques.* We will discuss some of these techniques later in this chapter.

Degree of Product/Brand Usage.   Another useful way to think of consumers is according to the amount of a product they use. The standard way to classify usage is to categorize consumers into *heavy, medium,* and *light* users. Both *Simmons* and *MRI* report their data on product usage in this manner. Although it may seem obvious that an advertiser would want to target heavy users, this is not an appropriate strategy for all marketers. Aiming at heavy users usually puts a company into direct competition with the market leader. In some categories, such as candy bars or appliances, advertisers can aim at the heavy users, and even if they sell much less than the brand leader, they can still carve out a satisfactory share of the market. In other categories, such as cigarettes, going after the heavy user will pit the company directly up against Marlboro and Newport, the two top brands of cigarettes in the United States. In the case of Marlboro, one of the two or three most powerful brand names in the world regardless of the product category, the competition is especially formidable. When new brands are introduced in the cigarette industry, they usually target the message strategy to the medium and light users. On the other hand, if you have the marketing muscle like McDonald's, you can do as it does and target a number of segments, including super heavy users (SHUs).

Degree of Brand Loyalty.   It is usually helpful to get some feel for the amount of brand loyalty in a product category. The amount of brand loyalty displayed by consumers can have a strong influence on both advertising strategy and tactics. Knowing the amount of brand loyalty in the market can help determine whether the brand's core equities are eroding. If so, then the planners have to decide whether to take steps to shore up a brand's equity (to be discussed in Chapter 4) or rely on various pricing and sales promotion tactics.

The most powerful type of brand loyalty measures is behavioral. Both ACNielsen and Information Resources, Inc. (IRI), measure the extent to which households buy the same brand in two successive periods. Customers are then divided into new and loyal customers. New customers are further classified according to whether they purchased on a deal or not.[4]

If the analyst does not have access to scanner data, then *an alternative approach is to collect information on consumer buying styles either through primary or secondary research.* One method developed by Leo Burnett is to categorize consumers into four different patterns of brand loyalty and buying strategies.

1. *Long loyals* are committed to one brand regardless of price or any other factor. These numbers are declining and are seen mostly when the purchase is "highly involving." Top-of-the-line cosmetics is a good example.
2. *Rotators* show regular patterns of shifting between preferred brands motivated by variety rather than price.
3. *Dealer sensitives* show a pattern of shifting between preferred brands determined by availability of special offers or incentives.
4. *Price sensitives* follow a decision rule to purchase the cheapest option, regardless of brand.[5]

Simmons reports information on buying style (based on the consumer's self-concept) in the following categories:

BRAND LOYAL   CAUTIOUS
ECONOMY-MINDED   EXPERIMENTERS
PLANNERS   STYLE-CONSCIOUS
CONFORMISTS   ECOLOGISTS
IMPULSIVES   AD BELIEVERS

When and How Often Consumers Buy

A common premise in advertising is to advertise in line with existing trends of consumer behavior. Two trends that are especially important to media planners are:

- How often consumers buy the product (i.e., the purchase cycle)
- When consumers buy the product (i.e., the seasonality)

Media planners use information pertaining to how often consumers buy and when they buy to help them schedule advertising impressions. The most accurate source of information on the purchase cycle and the seasonality of consumer purchases usually come from ACNielsen's or IRI's product usage audit. An analyst can also access information from trade articles and industry associations.

What Motivates Consumers to Buy?

After you have identified current users, it can be helpful to understand what motivates them to spend their money one place and not another. Do they have a "sweet spot" or "hot button" in their psychological makeup? Do grandmothers have a special feeling for their grandkids? Do teenage boys relate differently to performance automobiles than young girls? Determining how consumers feel about a product or brand can be the key to developing a persuasive message.

To understand consumers' motivations, you must first understand what factors influence them. Advertisers are always trying to understand why consumers behave the way they do. Over the years, numerous models have been developed to explain the consumer buying process. These models typically explain the process from a consumer's first exposure to an ad, to the actual purchase of the product. These models are explained in most consumer behavior texts, usually under the subheading of *learning hierarchy,* and are widely available in libraries. You may want to consult them.

Trade articles about consumers can provide some insight into what motivates people to buy a product. Other secondary research is unlikely to be of much help. Primary research will probably be your best source of information. We shall discuss some of the techniques later in this section, but first you need to determine which questions to pursue.

One way to organize your understanding of buyer behavior is to examine what consumers think and feel about the product and how they use it. This material in Exhibit 2-2 presents some of the questions you should

---

EXHIBIT 2-2	RESEARCH QUESTIONS TO CONSIDER

How consumers think about the product

1. To what extent are they aware of the product, especially the brand name?
2. Do they know about the brand's special features, ingredients, or hidden qualities?
3. Do they understand how the product or brand works?
4. Do they understand the brand's superior qualities?

How consumers feel about the product

1. What is their attitude toward the product category?
2. What is their attitude toward the specific brand?
3. To what extent do they like or desire the product or brand?
4. Do consumers trust the brand to deliver the promised benefits?
5. Do consumers have a preference for this brand?
6. What image or personality do consumers associate with the product or brand?
7. What do consumers feel is this brand's essence?

How consumers use the product

1. How do consumers use the product?
2. Where do consumers use the product?
3. When do consumers use the product?
4. Why do consumers use the product?
5. Are there alternative uses for the product?
6. Under what conditions would the consumer use more of the product?

---

consider when pursuing your secondary or primary research and will help you organize the kind of information you need to understand why consumers will or will not buy a product.

The information obtained from these questions will then be used to help determine the campaign's problems and opportunities. These, in turn, will provide the foundation for setting objectives after all the analyses are completed.

WHAT DO CONSUMERS LOOK FOR IN A PRODUCT?

In the course of conducting consumer interviews, there is often a subtle shift in the focus from how consumers think or feel about a product to *what they would like the product to do for them.* Although some consumers are able to identify quickly how they expect to benefit from using a product, it can take other consumers a while to make this identification. If they do not make this shift, you will have to lead them in this direction, whether you are using a structured questionnaire or conducting a **depth interview.** If you can pinpoint how consumers expect to benefit from a product, then the most direct and effective way to advertise is simply to interpret the want-satisfying qualities of the product in terms of the needs or wants of the consumer.

Determining consumers' needs and wants in the 1950s and 1960s was relatively easy; today it is a lot harder. Consumers may not be perfectly satisfied with a product, but it does not necessarily follow that they can articulate exactly what they are looking for. It takes some skill on the part of the interviewer to get consumers to reveal enough information to provide insight into why they might buy a product. Consumers typically buy products for the following reasons:

- The product satisfies needs or wants.
- The product helps solve problems.
- The product simply arouses curiosity or interest.
- The brand makes a statement about who the consumer is or who he or she aspires to be.
- The consumer likes the brand or its advertising.

Consumers may also buy a product because they like the values or lifestyle depicted in the advertising. However, this insight is more likely to result from an analyst's inference about consumers' values and lifestyles rather than from consumers' explanations of why they buy a product. Consumers may say they are buying the product because of the ads—after interviewers show consumers the advertising—but they don't usually offer that information before.

Needs and Wants. The difference between a need and a want is generally a matter of perspective. Consumers often confuse this difference. A young boy going to a basketball camp may feel he "needs" a pair of celebrity-endorsed shoes to fit in; a young girl may feel she "needs" to diet for similar reasons. Most people would not agree with the boy or the girl. To a researcher, the difference between a need and a want may be a semantic distinction with no practical implications.

Problems. Generally, people's needs and wants are fairly well satisfied. This makes it more difficult to get information from consumers. Even when people are dissatisfied with the results of using a product, they may not be aware of what they want in its place. However, if you ask consumers if they have any gripes about or problems with using the product, the information they reveal can provide just enough insight upon which you can base an advertising campaign or make product improvements. For example, consumer research for Gillette uncovered the useful information that when women cut themselves shaving, they blame themselves. Perhaps, not surprisingly, when men cut themselves, they blame the blade or the razor.

Consumer researchers have to be careful when designing questions that they move beyond simple questions that ask people what they need or want in a product. In the case of companies like Gillette, if researchers ask women what they want in a razor, it is very likely that the women would not know what to tell them. However, Gillette researchers know that women have problems shaving, so in their consumer research they questioned women about how they use their razors.

Researchers found that women usually shave their legs while showering, whereas men mostly shave at a sink. Researchers also knew that when men use a razor, the head of the razor is on top, and the stem is on the bottom. Conversely, when women are showering, the stem of the razor is usually on top and the head of the razor is facing down. As a result, the underside of the razor catches the water streaming down from the show-erhead, and women commonly complain the razor slips from their hands, especially if their hands are soapy.

Gillette used this information to redesign the Sensor razor expressly for women. Instead of a thin stem, the housing holding the razor was made to fit the palm of a woman's hand. A special rubbery grip, which Gillette obtained from its Parker Pen subsidiary, was attached to the hous-ing. Because Gillette relied heavily on consumer research to develop the product, its print ads are laden with copy reflecting how the Sensor for Women addresses women's problems.[6]

HOW DO CONSUMERS LOOK AT LIFE?

Although a substantial amount of information on consumer values and lifestyles is available from syndicated sources, it may not be specific enough to fit the given campaign. Also, the sources are not widely avail-able in libraries. A number of primary research techniques that can be used to get the above information will be discussed shortly. One of these tech-niques, based on observation, is widely used in advertising and goes by the name **ethnography.** This type of qualitative research is especially helpful in focusing on those aspects of consumers' lifestyle that directly affect the way consumers use a product.

Ethnography

The literal meaning of *ethnography* refers to the description and classifica-tion of various cultures and racial groups. In advertising, it pertains more to the observation of consumers as they go about their daily routines. Many of the techniques are borrowed from anthropology. Researchers try to put themselves in the place of consumers by getting as close to them as possible and by trying to simulate an actual purchase decision for a partic-ular product. To learn about consumer lifestyle characteristics and how they use a product, an interviewer goes to a consumer's environment, observes behavioral patterns, and asks questions. As part of the observa-tional process, the interviewer takes photographs.

When conducting research for a food product, for example, an inter-viewer would ask the consumer questions to reveal his or her eating phi-losophy and management: Is the family health oriented? To what extent do family members make trade-offs between foods that are good for them and food that simply tastes good? How does the family rationalize their choices? How much of a family's food intake is consumed on the run? How much is part of a regular sit-down meal? How often does the family dine out?

The interviewer may also accompany the consumer to a supermarket and observe the decision process up close and personal. This process provides the research effort a better understanding of the dynamics and trade-offs consumers make while shopping for a particular product. If an advertiser wants to know what consumers think of a certain restaurant chain, the researcher not only goes to the restaurant to observe con-sumers, but also goes to one of the restaurants *with* a consumer. This way the researcher can experience firsthand the problems, irritants, and satisfactions from the consumer's point of view. The researcher hopes to gain insight by looking for clues and relationships. The idea is to think like a consumer, but interpret like an analyst.

Euro RSCG Tatham, a major advertising agency in Chicago, used ethnographic research (see Exhibit 2-3) to learn how consumers make decisions about frozen entrees. The company learned that consumers have both rational and emotional needs connected to frozen entrees. Consumers classify brands in either a rational category (good for you) or an emotional category (tastes good). Consumers perceive all the nutritional

---

EXHIBIT 2-3 A DAY IN THE LIFE OF AN ETHNOGRAPHER

9:00 A.M.	The researcher arrives at the home of a consumer to discuss food. The appointment has been setup by a firm that specializes in recruiting people to participate in consumer research.
9:05 A.M.	After exchanging pleasantries, the interviewer engages the consumer in a discussion of the family's eating philosophy and the way she or he manages the cooking and the availability of food for the family. The interviewer asks about the role played by other members of the household in shopping and cooking.
9:15 A.M.	The interviewer asks to see the consumer's cookbooks and any special recipes. A photograph is taken of the books.
9:25 A.M.	The interviewer asks to look in the consumer's pantry and cupboards, carefully noting snack items, national brands, and the proportion of canned to soft-packaged goods. The interviewer photographs the products.
9:35 A.M.	The interviewer asks to look inside the refrigerator, noting the amount of fresh food, leftovers, and the prominence of national brands. More photos are taken.
9:45 A.M.	The interviewer checks the freezer and inquires about the length of time items have been in there. The proportion of entrées to single-item packages including desserts is noted. More photos are taken.
9:55 A.M.	The interviewer takes photos of the kitchen, especially of gadgets and other labor-saving devices. The interviewer asks to go shopping with the consumer and gives her or him $50.
10:10 A.M.	They arrive at the supermarket, get a cart, and walk down the aisles. The interviewer takes special note of the consumer's interest in fresh produce, bakery items, canned goods, meat, nonfood items, and frozen food. The interviewer observes the consumer's interest in price shopping and the relative importance of store brands to nationally advertised items.
10:40 A.M.	Prior to getting in the checkout lane, the interviewer takes a photograph of the cart. While in the checkout lane, the interviewer asks the consumer to explain the purchase decisions.
10:45 A.M.	The interviewer says good-bye and prepares to go to the next meeting. Later, back in the office, the consumer's statements will be compared to the photographs and the interviewer's notes.

brands, like Healthy Choice, Lean Cuisine, and Weight Watchers, as *nutritional frozen food*. Because these products satisfy rational needs, there was little emotional loyalty to any one brand.

The agency found that when consumers stand in front of a frozen-food case, they "taste bud" shop rather than "brand shop" for frozen entrees. Consumers chose the individual items they know taste good and meet their personal nutritional needs. The challenge for the agency and the advertiser was, first, to interrupt this kind of switching behavior and, second, to secure greater loyalty toward their brand through more emotionally based communications that were more relevant to consumers' needs and that differentiated the company's brand from the others.[7]

Other Qualitative Research Techniques

In addition to ethnography, there are a number of other techniques that can be used to gain insight on consumers. In many ways, the research that is done to develop campaigns is more an art than it is a science. It is quite common to hear advertising people refer to their research as "soft"—in other words, not technically rigorous. Usually, it simply means that the analysis is more qualitative than quantitative. The main purpose of qualitative research is to develop insights into how to talk to consumers. Among the heaviest users of qualitative research are agency account planners.

THE ACCOUNT PLANNING REVOLUTION

By the early 1980s, a number of U.S. agencies, notably Chiat/Day, adopted a system many British ad agencies were using to manage the flow of information used to develop marketing campaigns. This system is called **account planning.**[8] The account planner's main function is to develop and manage the flow of information using traditional and nontraditional research to uncover special consumer insights that could provide the basis for a message strategy. Account planners work directly with copywriters and art directors, often sharing responsibility for the creative ideas, instead of apart as traditional researchers have often done. Historically, copywriters have had an aversion to researchers bearing numbers. This, in part, led some agencies, such as Foote, Cone & Belding, to gradually develop their researchers into account planners. Although account planners use all kinds of information, much of the research effort they manage is qualitative, including **ethnographic studies, one-on-ones, focus groups,** and **projective tests.** The more traditional quantitative research such as surveys, observation, consumer panels, and experiments is likely to be done by the advertiser (or a research supplier).

Role of Qualitative Research

The key to successful qualitative research is to understand both the purpose and the limitations of the various techniques. Qualitative research is usually conducted to *develop* the campaign strategy. It is especially useful in gaining insight on consumers. However, this type of research should not be viewed as a substitute for more rigorous and systematic studies because of the limited size and representativeness of the typical sample, and the difficulty and subjectivity in coding lengthy conversation. Qualitative studies can be useful in providing ideas and in evaluating concepts, ads, and campaigns, but may not be as reliable or valid as a more traditional quantitative study. Still, the insights derived from qualitative studies typically drive the campaign's strategic approach. A quantitative study provides the "bones" to a body of research; a qualitative study provides texture or "flesh."

Asking Questions. The key to a good interview is to know when and how to ask questions. A good interviewer looks for insight on how the consumer thinks, feels, and acts. The most meaningful information is rarely on the surface. An interviewer must use sensitivity and judgment to ferret out the best pieces of information. Often this information will be used to develop **strategic** and **tactical focal points** (more about these later). Interviewers tend to get better with experience; however, if beginners pay attention to the tips in Exhibit 2-4, they should do fine.

One of the main advantages to qualitative research is the opportunity it provides to uncover consumers' underlying thoughts and feelings, including attitudes, prejudices, biases, and motivations. Although it helps to have an experienced interviewer conduct the research, there is a simple technique—called **laddering**—that beginners can use as a tool to link up a product's attributes, or qualities, with the values consumers place on using a particular product.

Laddering. This technique refers to a type of questioning used with depth interviews. An interviewer asks a series of questions designed to trace the relationship between a product's attributes and the value consumers get out of using a product. The technique is based on **Means–End Theory,** which loosely states that consumers use products as the means to achieve various ends. These ends get defined in terms of consumer values.[9] Most consumers respond to a question as to why they use a product, or what they look for in a product, with an answer that focuses on a product's qualities, or attributes. This is a relatively basic or "lower" form of knowledge. However, consumers do not buy products for their attributes as much as they buy a product for what it can do for them—how it makes them feel. If advertisers can uncover a person's feelings, or how consumers get value out of using a product, they can use this information to develop a message strategy based on emotions rather than on simple product characteristics.

The technique is called laddering because the interviewer keeps asking questions that gradually reveal the relationship between a product's attributes and the value it provides to a consumer. Because an attribute tends to be a physical property, and a value is psychological in nature, the interviewer is moving from a lower form of knowledge to a higher form. In a sense, the interviewer is moving up the "ladder of knowledge" about the product.

Conceptually, the element linking an attribute to a value is a **consequence.** As a result of using a product with certain attributes, consumers usually experience an effect (i.e., a consequence). The consumer then

| EXHIBIT 2-4 | TEN TIPS TO A PRODUCTIVE INTERVIEW |

1. Be yourself. It is important to make consumers feel as comfortable as possible. If they sense you are acting in a way that is very different from your normal personality, it could make them feel uneasy. So be yourself—your warm, friendly, serious self.

2. Briefly tell the consumer about the interview. Consumers are naturally curious, if not suspicious. Keep the information general but informative. Tell them you are developing an advertising campaign and want their opinions on the product (or category).

3. Tape record the interview. After a while interviewees tend to forget about the tape recorder. However, if they see you feverishly taking notes, they may slow down to let you catch up. They may also feel self-conscious.

4. Give consumers easy questions to start. The object is to get consumers talking easily and naturally. Though the first questions should be easy, they should be open-ended so the interviewee doesn't simply answer the question with a one-word answer.

5. Avoid leading questions. If interviewees sense how you might answer a question, they may tell you what they think you want to hear. Be sure to phrase questions without giving any verbal or nonverbal clues as to what your position might be.

6. Probe. Probe. Probe. Consumers don't always know why they think, feel, or act a certain way. You'll want to use the word why repeatedly to get at deeply seated thoughts and feelings.

7. Listen carefully to the answers. Many times inexperienced interviewers will be so busy planning their next question that they will fail to pay attention to details and miss an opportunity to follow up on an important line of questioning.

8. Make the interviewee work. Even conscientious interviewees get tired or lazy. After 15 minutes or so, be sensitive to a decrease in the interviewee's attention or interest. Be polite, firm, and persistent. Reward them periodically with positive acknowledgment.

9. Focus. Focus. Focus. Interviewers also wear down. Make sure you hear the last half of any sentence or phrase.

10. When finished, say thank you. It's important you maintain professional standards. Be sure to leave the interviewee feeling positive about the experience.

interprets this effect in terms of what it means to them (i.e., its **value**). These concepts can be further refined. An attribute can be something tangible, or physical (such as flavors, colors, sizes, nutritional ingredients, calories, shapes, and horsepower), or it can be something largely intangible, or psychological (such as *sexy* clothing, *funny-looking* toys, *prestigious-looking* automobiles, or *youthful* brand images). Interviewers usually begin their questioning by asking about a product or a brand's attributes.

Consequences can be either functional (more tangible in nature) or psychosocial (more subjective). When the advertising for Silkience shampoo suggests that using the product will leave hair soft, silky, and manageable, it is stressing **functional consequences.** If the advertising emphasizes how a woman's hair will make people admire her, it is stressing the **psychosocial consequences.** Consequences can also be described from both a negative and positive point of view. Advertisers seldom even imply that using their product will have undesirable consequences, but suggestions that using a competitive product will have negative consequences is a common practice. Advertisers, however, will play up the potential negative consequences of *not* using their product. For example, advertising for Hertz rent-a-cars plays up the negative qualities of a nameless a competitor when it uses the tagline, "There's Hertz, and not exactly." In a depth interview, a skillful interviewer will ask consumers why they want to avoid a specific "negative" outcome and then move "up" the means–end chain to questions about positive consequences and eventually about values.

Positive consequences are interpreted in terms of how a consumer **benefits** from using a product. Copywriters put a lot of emphasis on benefits in advertising copy. It is widely believed that consumers buy products more for their benefits than for their attributes. This belief leads some advertisers to *segment* their market, at least in part, in terms of the benefits consumers look for in a product. This approach, called **benefit segmentation,** influences both the message and media strategy. For example, the market for toothpaste consists mostly of consumers who hope to benefit from using a product that prevents cavities, freshens breath, or simply tastes good. Over the years, advertisers have consistently communicated the same general message regarding the benefit they hope to provide to toothpaste users. Some of the benefits and the advertisers that hope to provide them are as follows:

Benefit	↔	**Brand**
Prevents cavities	↔	Crest
Freshens breath	↔	Aquafresh
Tastes good	↔	Aim or Colgate

Students are probably much more familiar with the first two brand/benefit associations because benefit segmentation also influences media strategy. The target market for toothpaste that tastes good is mothers with small children—not college students (even though some college students have small children). Therefore, typical students are much less likely to be exposed to a media message about Aim than Aquafresh.

After the interviewer learns the benefits the consumers are looking for, the questioning can then focus on how the benefits will affect the consumers' state of mind, or **values.**

Some scholars further refine values according to whether they are **instrumental values** (i.e., they express preferred modes of conduct and behavior, such as being independent, loving, polite, responsible, or simply having a good time) or **terminal values** (i.e., they express end states of mind or being such as peacefulness, comfort, self-esteem, security, true friendship, or simply happiness).[10] An experienced interviewer will ladder the questions beginning with inquiries about a brand's attributes and ending with questions that elicit responses that identify the values the respondent hopes to obtain using the product. Figure 2-3 presents the different levels of meaning associated with product usage.

The laddering procedure works best when the interviewer is able to interact with a respondent in a one-on-one situation. With some modification, it can also be used with focus groups. Experienced interviewers use various techniques to elicit distinctions between one level of meaning and another. Respondents may not actually know the answer to a question, or the question may be probing a sensitive area. Sometimes the interviewer can simply redirect the question; other times it may be helpful to use silence to give the respondent time to think or displace tension. Sometimes it is helpful to change the context of the question from a question involving the interviewee's motives or values to one involving a third person. Sometimes the laddering procedure will not result in eliciting responses that go beyond consumer benefits.[11]

FIGURE 2-3 | LEVELS OF MEANING ASSOCIATED WITH PRODUCT USAGE

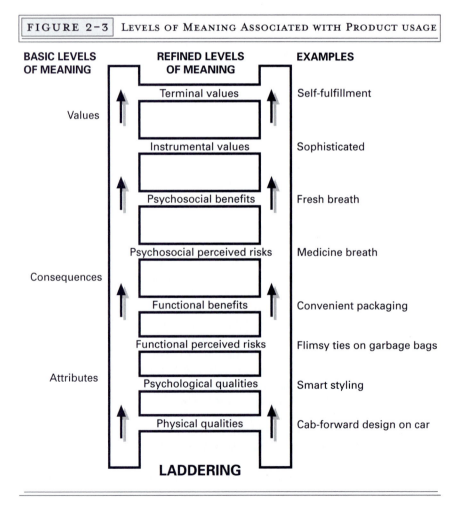

BASIC LEVELS OF MEANING	REFINED LEVELS OF MEANING	EXAMPLES
Values	Terminal values	Self-fulfillment
	Instrumental values	Sophisticated
	Psychosocial benefits	Fresh breath
Consequences	Psychosocial perceived risks	Medicine breath
	Functional benefits	Convenient packaging
	Functional perceived risks	Flimsy ties on garbage bags
Attributes	Psychological qualities	Smart styling
	Physical qualities	Cab-forward design on car

LADDERING

Often, it is enough to simply begin most questions with the word *why.* Why is that important? Why don't you like that? Why do you think other people will think that? How does that make you feel? What does that mean to you?

The dialogue below presents an example of a laddering technique that was used for a safety razor. The respondent is female.

Interviewer: What do you look for in a razor?
Respondent: One that won't saw my legs off.
Interviewer: What do you mean?
Respondent: I don't like the blades if they're too sharp.
Interviewer: Why?
Respondent: Because I end up cutting my legs up around my knees.
Interviewer: Why?
Respondent: I guess I'm just too impatient. I'm usually in a hurry and half the time I drop the razor and when I go to pick it up I get water in my eyes.
Interviewer: Why do you drop the razor?
Respondent: It just slips out of my hand. It's soapy.
Interviewer: Is it more important to have a razor that isn't too sharp, or would it be better to have a razor that wouldn't slip out of your hands?
Respondent: I guess a razor that won't slip out of my hands. Then I could take more time and do a better job with my legs.
Interviewer: Why is that important?
Respondent: I like the way my legs feel, and I like knowing they look good.
Interviewer: Why?
Respondent: Everybody wants good-looking legs.
Interviewer: Why is that important?
Respondent: It feels good. It just does.

One-on-Ones. The more academic name for this technique is the **depth interview,** but most people in advertising simply call this a one-on-one. This type of interview is generally used when information is going to be difficult to obtain using less costly techniques such as surveys and focus groups. In these sessions, a trained interviewer interacts with an individual through a variety of loose, unstructured questions. The intent of the interviewer is to uncover hidden meanings, problems, attitudes, motives, and the activities of consumers, while carefully avoiding influencing the respondent. This type of interview is especially appropriate when:

1. A detailed probing of an individual's behavior, attitudes, needs, or wants is required.
2. A highly detailed, step-by-step understanding of complicated behavior or decision-making patterns (such as planning the family vacation) is required.
3. The subject matter is of a sensitive or embarrassing nature (such as personal hygiene products).
4. The subject matter is likely to be of a highly confidential nature (such as personal investments).

5. Strong, socially acceptable norms exist (such as baby-feeding philosophy) and group interaction may influence responses.
6. The interviews are with professionals (such as finance directors).[12]

Focus Groups.   A focus group interview is one of the more useful forms of a depth interview. The typical group consists of from 8 to 12 persons, although some major ad agencies report they are using as few as 6 people. Group participants are selected and recruited to be representative of the consumer segment thought to be the target audience. The interview generally takes place in a comfortable room, with a trained moderator guiding the discussion. Meetings often last between one and three hours; an hour is fairly typical. The session is usually recorded and may even be viewed and videotaped from behind a two-way mirror.

The purpose of the focus group interview is to uncover some of the more hidden thoughts, feelings, and problems consumers have with respect to the product. The moderator follows a prepared rough outline of topical questions to keep the meeting focused on the topic. Moderators take great care not to inhibit discussion. Part of the value of a group interview comes from the interaction of the group's participants. In a productive focus group, participants often make points or ask questions that may not occur to the investigators. Frequently, consumers not only have more answers than investigators, but better questions as well. Although there is frequent criticism of the misapplication of focus groups—especially about the nonrepresentativeness of samples—focus groups are still widely used. It was estimated that over $1 billion was spent on this type of research in 2003.[13]

Student-directed focus groups sometimes encounter a problem that professionals usually are able to avoid. Experienced moderators know how to subtly steer a discussion to cover all the predetermined topics. Part of the technique involves interjecting a few words, phrases, or short sentences to redirect discussion so that it all appears very natural. This requires the moderator to listen carefully for the right moment to speak. Experience helps, but there is also some skill involved.

Because of a student's lack of experience, he or she is not likely to be as familiar as a trained moderator with the subquestions associated with a topic. This can come across as awkwardness, especially because there is usually some nervousness associated with moderating a focus group for the first time. This problem can be intensified if the student also begins to worry about when to introduce the next question, and how to phrase it so that the transition from one topic to another question is a smooth one.

One solution is to have two student moderators. The first student asks a question and then listens intently for the right moment to introduce appropriate prompting comments. Meanwhile, the other student is following the conversation and mentally preparing for the next general question. When the moment is right, the second student asks the next general question as well as makes the subtle comments that generate the freewheeling atmosphere characteristic of successful focus group interviews. From that moment on, the two students alternate questions.

Projective Tests.   This form of qualitative research is another good way to learn about the consumer, but it is also a powerful way to get information about the product, so it will be discussed in Chapter 3 under "Product/Brand Analysis."

Survey Research

Although qualitative research is very good at generating ideas and providing insight on the consumer, the analyst usually runs a risk that the research findings may not be generalizable to a larger population base. Primarily for this reason, a more rigorous study involving survey research is frequently appropriate.

Survey research tends to imply the use of a questionnaire. The research is usually very structured, quantifiable, and can be administered by less skilled personnel. This type of research is more likely to be administered by the advertiser or a private research company rather than an advertising agency. Among the most popular methods of acquiring data are telephone interviews, mall intercepts, self-administered questionnaires, and e-mail and mail questionnaires.

Telephone Interviews.   This technique is particularly useful in studies requiring a broad cross section of the population such as a national sample. Its relatively low cost is sometimes offset by the difficulty of keeping individuals talking on the phone longer than 15 minutes. This method has largely replaced door-to-door personal interviews. It is widely used in advertising tracking studies that are designed to assess awareness levels, attitudes, and product usage. Telephone interviewing, especially used in conjunction with a Wide Area Telephone Service (WATS) system, used to be one of the two most popular data collection techniques, the other being the mall intercept.[14]

Because of caller ID, answering machines, and surveys used as a ruse to sell products, response ratings have dropped from 40% a decade ago to 14% in 2000.[15] Today, the Internet is increasingly the data collection technique of choice because it is usually cheaper, quicker, and easier to use than virtually all other techniques.

Mall Intercepts.   This is the most popular form of the personal interview. Respondents are either interviewed on the spot or escorted to a private area within the mall. Students often use a variation of this technique and interview consumers outside the mall because it is usually time consuming and difficult to secure permission to go inside. Although personal interviews can take place anywhere, including the home, malls offer many advantages. This approach is especially useful when the testing procedure requires getting consumer reaction to visual stimuli such as packaging, name change alternatives, advertising concepts, and advertisements. The interviewer usually works from a questionnaire, and large numbers of consumers can be interviewed in a relatively short time. Less skilled personnel can administer the questionnaire.

The major disadvantage of this method is the representativeness of the sample. People who visit shopping malls are not necessarily representative of the rest of the population. On the other hand, mall shoppers are often precisely the cross section of the population many advertisers are interested in reaching. A variation of the mall intercept is the **after-purchase intercept** where consumers are interviewed after they have purchased a product. Web site intercepts are another variation, though still in their infancy.

Self-administered Questionnaires.   As a general rule, it is much better to have an interviewer fill out the questionnaire than the consumer. This puts the interviewer in control of the flow of information and reduces the likelihood of misunderstood questions. The interviewer can also control the pacing of questions and answers, thereby helping to ensure that the questions on the second half of a questionnaire receive the same consideration as earlier ones.

There are two basic types of self-administered instruments: a **leave-behind questionnaire** and a **hand-delivered questionnaire.** With the first type of questionnaire, consumers are invited to fill out a form at some central location, usually a retail store or a restaurant. To work well, some control should be maintained over which respondents fill the form out. The second type of self-administered questionnaire works much better.

With this method, a data collector personally delivers a questionnaire to the home of a preselected respondent who has been offered an incentive. The data collector informs the consumer that the questionnaire will be picked up after a period of time, usually a week. This second step helps improve the representativeness of the sample, a major problem with self-administered questionnaires. This procedure is the primary method the Simmons Market Research Bureau uses to collect data on product usage, and it is especially useful and cost-effective when a large amount of information is to be collected.

E-mail and Mail Questionnaires.   These methods of gathering data are used primarily because of their low cost. A questionnaire can be e-mailed or mailed to potential respondents, attached to a product in the marketplace, or included within the body of a magazine or newspaper. The main disadvantage of these methods occurs with both nonresponses and the representativeness of the respondents filling out the questionnaire. It is very difficult to determine the extent to which nonrespondents are similar to respondents on the variables that influence product usage, even if you match up both groups based on demographic and psychographic criteria.

The mail questionnaire is actually a variation of the self-administered questionnaire and has many of the same advantages and disadvantages. Some control over nonresponse is gained if the sampling units have been recruited to participate in a consumer panel. National Family Opinion, Research Inc. (NFO) is a leader in this area and uses the mail questionnaire successfully with an active panel base of more than 550,000 U.S. households. However, one recurring criticism of panels in general is that even if cooperation can be maintained over panel participants, it is often a more difficult task to get a representative cross section of the appropriate population to join the panel.

This method can be effective if the company offers the consumer a sufficient incentive to complete the questionnaire. To reduce nonresponses, some companies include a product sample with the questionnaire and offer to send the consumer additional coupons upon completion of the questionnaire. Other companies ask customers to fill out mail questionnaires when turning in their warrantee agreements for new product purchases. Companies use this approach as a major source of information in developing a database on their customers. A major variation of the mail questionnaire is the **diary,** which companies use to collect information on consumer purchases. Marketing Research Corporation of America (MRCA) uses the diary method to monitor the purchasing habits of its consumer panel consisting of 7,500 households.

E-mail, in addition to being cheaper, quicker, and easier than most other techniques, is also more likely to elicit honest responses. People are often more direct and frank online than they likely would be over the phone or in person. An online researcher reportedly asked the same question in a mall intercept survey and via the Internet: "How often do you bathe or shower each week?" The average via the Internet was 4.8 times and in the mall interview 6.2 times.[16] (Which do you think was more honest?) Internet panels are gradually replacing panel studies that were previously conducted by paper mail.

A RATIONALE FOR CONDUCTING THE RESEARCH IN SEQUENCE

There is really no rigid pattern to the order in which professionals conduct their research. However, there may be *some* rationale for students to do their research in the following order:

1. One-on-ones
2. Focus groups and other qualitative studies
3. Surveys
4. More studies as needed

We recommend starting your research with one-on-ones. If you don't have much experience with either the product category or the brand, one-on-ones can give you some depth on how consumers think and interact with the product or brand. The background you pick up here can then be used to develop questions for focus groups or other studies. And the best part for students is that they are much more convenient to conduct. After focus group studies are complete, the findings can be used to develop questions for a possible survey. The goal is to get information and ideas from the one-on-ones and focus groups, and then use surveys to assess the extent to which the findings exist among the target audience or the population as a whole. Remember, information obtained from one-on-ones and focus groups is fine for ideas, but it does not mean you can generalize from individuals or small groups to a larger consumer base, such as the target audience. Following the survey research, you will probably want to continue to do research as needed.

◼ COMPLETING THE COMPANY AND CONSUMER ANALYSES

Although this chapter is coming to a close, it does not mean that the company and consumer analyses are complete. Many of the analytical techniques to be discussed in Chapter 3 will shed additional light on the company and consumer. For example, many of the sources of information on the company can and should be used to gain insight on the competition, and many of the techniques recommended for the competitive analysis will be of value in analyzing the company. It is also worth noting that many of the tests used to evaluate the product say as much about the consumer as they do about the product. In short, although we have separated the situation analysis into distinct sections, the information-gathering efforts described in each section should be used to further the search for insight on the problems and opportunities facing the company. This means that in the event the research foundation is separated into sections and assigned to different members of a team, information should be shared so that each section benefits from the cross-fertilization of the information obtained from other areas.

CAMPAIGN PROGRESS CHECKLIST

At this point in the campaign you should generally be aware of the following points:

1. The most efficient way to begin a campaign is to prepare an outline of the research plan.

2. We suggest doing the background analysis in the following order: company and consumer analyses first, followed by those dealing with the market, product, and competition.

3. To be competitive, information should be **more than descriptive**—it should be **insightful.**

4. Whether you do a SWOT analysis, a brand audit, or focus on problems and opportunities, examine the critical issues in the analysis and relate them to problems and opportunities. These will provide the basis for the objectives you set later.

5. In a company analysis, the company's history is far less important than the history of the company's problems and opportunities.

6. In the company analysis, it's also helpful to look at industry or generic sales trends.

7. It's not only important to know who uses a product or brand, but also why and how they use it.

8. Laddering techniques help uncover how a product's attributes influence the value consumers get out of using a product.

9. One-on-ones and focus group research are good ways to get ideas for strategy and executions, but their findings are not generalizable to the population as a whole.

10. Survey research is a good way to assess the degree to which a finding exists in the overall population, but the results may only be as good as the sample from which the study is drawn.

Notes and References

[1]R. Serafin and B. Johnson, "Saturn-alia in Springhill Next Summer," *Advertising Age,* 18 October 1993, p. 55.

[2]The author is indebted to Jan Slater who shared her thoughts and material on brand audits.

[3]SRI International, *Values and Lifestyles* (Menlo Park, CA: SRI International, 1998).

[4]D.J. Curry, *The New Marketing Research Systems: How to Use Strategic Database Information for Better Marketing Decisions* (New York: John Wiley & Sons, 1993), p. 86.

[5]J.F. Engel, T.C. Kinnear, and M.R. Warshaw, *Promotional Strategy: Managing the Marketing Communications Process, 8th Ed.* (Burr Ridge, IL: Irwin, 1994), p. 14.

[6]R. Koselka, "It's My Favorite Statistic," *Forbes,* 12 September 1994, p. 162.

[7]This information is based on written material from Michael Robinson, research director, Euro RSCG Tatham.

[8]For more information, see Lisa Fortini-Campbell, *Hitting the Sweet Spot: The Consumer Insight Workbook, 2nd Ed.* (Chicago: Copy Workshop, 1992), pp. 159–170.

[9]J. Gutman, "A Means–End Chain Model Based on Consumer Categorization Processes," *Journal of Marketing* 46 (Spring 1982), pp. 60–72.

[10]Milton J. Rokeach as quoted in J. Paul Peter and Jerry C. Olson, *Consumer Behavior and Marketing Strategy, 2nd Ed.* (Homewood, IL: Irwin, 1987), p. 78.

[11]T.J. Reynolds and J. Gutman, "Laddering Theory, Method, Analysis, and Interpretation," *Journal of Advertising Research* (February/March 1988), p. 16.

[12]D.S. Tull and D.I. Hawkins, *Marketing Research: Measurement and Method, 4th Ed.* (New York: Macmillan, 1987), p. 311.

[13]Christoph Hitz, "Sharpening the Focus," *Brandweek,* 3 November 2003, p. 28.

[14]W.R. Dillon, N.H. Firtle, and T.J. Madden, *Essentials of Marketing Research* (Homewood, IL: Irwin, 1993), p. 154.

[15]John Rubin, "Online Marketing Research Comes of Age," *Brandweek,* 30 October 2000, p. 26.

[16]*Ibid.*

CHAPTER 3

The Research Foundation, Part Two: Market, Product, and Competitive Analyses

THE MARKET ANALYSIS

It is widely understood in the advertising business that the mass market is becoming increasingly fragmented. This change does not necessarily mean that the role of national advertising has diminished. Rather, it underscores the importance of giving extra attention to local markets. One common line used with many variations is "Think globally, but act like a retailer."

The basic purpose of the market analysis is to determine the geographic areas that warrant special attention, either because they are problems or because they are most likely to respond favorably to the company's marketing communication program. In a sense, this section is merely an extension of the consumer analysis. Advertisers treat this topic separately for two reasons: (1) to help organize additional sources of information that focus primarily on geographic data, although they may include demographic and psychographic data, and (2) to help media planners identify geographic areas where they should allocate media dollars. The second point is becoming an important consideration as marketers increasingly narrow the focus of their communication strategy and look for markets that need extra emphasis.

A word of clarification: The term *market* may be used both to indicate a geographic area and as a descriptive term to refer to a population segment, such as a Hispanic market. The words *target market* usually refer to both a population segment and a geographic area. In some plans, a market analysis would be referred to as a "geographic analysis." That is common and acceptable. We prefer using the word *market* for our section because it connotes a place where sales take place and where consumers live and buy.

PRODUCT-USAGE DATA

The importance of a market is usually determined by the amount of product usage and the number of current users in the area. If this information is unavailable or hard to come by, planners will usually select a market based on the demographic or psychographic characteristics of the consumers living in the area. Wherever possible, however, purchase behavior should be used as a predictor of future sales.

A good place to start the analysis is with sales data that are internal to the company. If the company has analyzed its sales geographically, this information is likely to be available from the marketing department. If not, then the task will be far more difficult to accomplish.

The amount and type of information will vary from company to company and usually depend on the research suppliers with whom the company works. For students, the information they can get usually depends on who is providing it and what the sources are willing to share. A student may be limited to what is available in a university library. Unfortunately, many important sources of market information, including share-of-market data and resource tools such as ACNielsen's SCANTRACK and Information Resources, Inc.'s InfoScan, are not likely to be found in libraries. If the information is available, a common use of the data is to construct index numbers that indicate the *relative* value of a market.

Index Numbers

Index numbers are widely used measures to indicate a market's sales potential. In this section, we briefly look at three types of indexes: (1) product-usage index numbers cross-referenced by the geographic areas reported by the Simmons Market Research Bureau (SMRB); (2) a buying-power index, usually developed from data in the Sales & Marketing Management *Survey of Buying Power;* and (3) a brand-development index and its companion, a category-development index.

Simmons Market Research Bureau (SMRB).   SMRB provides information on product usage for some 800 brands, products, and services and cross-references them by broad classifications of geographic areas. The areas include nine geographic regions of the country (such as Midwest), four classifications of county size (such as County Size A), three metropolitan categories (such as Metro Central City), and three areas of dominant influence (ADI) categories (such as Top 5 ADIs). The product-usage data are broken down by total usage and the percentage usage accounted for by the geographic segment. Of special interest are the index numbers for the geographic segments that indicate relative product usage. These numbers may be used as a rough predictor of sales potential. Mediamark Research, Inc. (MRI) provides data similar to those of Simmons'.

Buying–Power Index (BPI).   This index is another handy measure that can be used to help predict sales potential. It is typically developed from data provided by Sales & Marketing Management's *Survey of Buying Power,* but can also be compiled from data from a variety of sources. The BPI is a multiple-factor index that uses a number of statistics associated with a market to indicate sales potential. The *Survey of Buying Power* uses population, effective buying income (also called disposable income), and retail sales for its calculations. The *Survey of Buying Power* devotes a page in each issue to take readers step-by-step through the procedures for calculating a

BPI—including how to allocate weights (i.e., emphasis) to various factors. Another source for market statistics is SRDS.

Sales & Marketing Management (S&MM). This useful source is available in most libraries, in part because it is relatively inexpensive. It's published monthly, but the most useful issue for market information is the August issue's Survey of Buying Power (see Figure 3-1). This issue provides statistical information on each state, according to Metropolitan Statistical Area (MSA), counties, and many of the larger cities. Statistics are provided for population, age groups, number of households, effective buying income (EBI), and retail sales for six types of retail stores (food, eating and drinking, general merchandise, furniture/furnishings/appliances, automotive, and drug).

S&MM also produces a special *Survey of Media Markets.* This coverage provides statistics for geographical areas according to designated market areas (DMAs, which are Arbitron's designation for the 211 TV markets). Additionally, S&MM provides a ranking of metropolitan areas for each of

---

FIGURE 3-1 | A TYPICAL PAGE FROM THE *Survey of Buying Power*

METRO & COUNTY TOTALS

FLORIDA CON'T.

METRO AREA County City	Total Population (000s)	\% of Population by Age Group 18-24	25-34	35-49	50+	House-holds (000s)	Total Retail Sales	Food & Beverage Stores	Food Serv. & Drinking Estab.	General Merch.	Furnit. & Home Furnish. and Electron & Appliances	Motor Veh. & Parts Dealers
NAPLES	276.0	6.8	10.9	18.8	43.6	113.3	4,484,728	584,361	396,077	351,728	379,721	837,382
COLLIER	276.0	6.8	10.9	18.8	43.6	113.3	4,484,728	584,361	396,077	351,728	379,721	837,382
• Naples	22.3	2.3	5.0	15.1	66.9	11.5	995,069	88,572	123,402	100,960	89,801	98,172
OCALA	273.2	6.5	9.8	19.3	43.1	113.4	3,187,434	446,479	169,674	600,655	86,658	812,956
MARION	273.2	6.5	9.8	19.3	43.1	113.4	3,187,434	446,479	169,674	600,655	86,658	812,956
• Ocala	47.6	9.4	11.7	19.7	36.2	19.4	1,497,476	137,451	91,239	284,598	38,947	459,833
ORLANDO	1,739.1	9.8	14.6	23.4	27.5	660.7	25,093,787	3,196,045	2,846,081	2,406,478	1,084,884	7,348,457
LAKE	220.7	9.8	9.9	19.3	44.7	92.8	2,305,124	380,360	133,899	328,033	61,772	628,128
ORANGE	951.7	11.2	16.0	23.7	23.8	356.5	15,672,862	2,005,505	2,009,837	1,178,358	665,685	4,591,816
• Orlando	193.7	11.1	20.4	22.2	24.3	84.7	3,384,123	396,717	436,189	238,596	146,103	1,016,292
OSCEOLA	187.7	9.5	14.1	22.8	26.9	66.1	1,978,530	300,798	335,108	407,934	36,694	344,231
SEMINOLE	379.0	8.5	13.7	25.4	27.1	145.3	5,137,271	509,382	367,237	492,153	320,733	1,784,282
PANAMA CITY	152.4	8.8	12.8	23.7	30.8	61.7	1,975,939	173,637	277,939	382,099	66,878	475,418
BAY	152.4	8.8	12.8	23.7	30.8	61.7	1,975,939	173,637	277,939	382,099	66,878	475,418
• Panama City	36.9	9.8	13.5	22.5	31.3	15.1	860,000	66,345	86,794	151,828	35,373	276,997
PENSACOLA	426.9	10.9	13.0	22.8	29.0	161.7	4,160,913	526,568	339,304	767,983	155,141	1,128,104
ESCAMBIA	305.6	12.3	13.2	21.7	29.4	116.4	3,255,172	319,782	286,373	559,396	143,257	915,991
• Pensacola	57.8	9.2	11.7	22.0	34.3	25.5	1,073,537	74,141	124,153	248,696	70,888	123,157
SANTA ROSA	121.3	7.3	12.5	25.5	28.2	45.3	905,741	206,786	52,931	208,587	11,884	212,113
PUNTA GORDA	147.0	4.5	7.3	16.7	56.0	66.6	1,708,242	292,322	163,708	292,590	98,252	322,696

METRO AREA County City	Total EBI ($000)	Median Hsld. EBI ($)	\% of Hslds. by EBI Group A $20,000-$34,999	B $35,000-$49,999	C $50,000 & Over	Buying Power Index
NAPLES	8,099,309	47,548	20.4	20.5	46.6	.1327
COLLIER	8,099,309	47,548	20.4	20.5	46.6	.1327
• Naples	1,253,414	55,846	15.8	16.2	54.9	.0216
OCALA	4,005,349	27,582	32.8	19.1	17.2	.0832
MARION	4,005,349	27,582	32.8	19.1	17.2	.0832
• Ocala	734,041	27,261	29.6	16.2	20.9	.0226
ORLANDO	32,367,897	38,500	25.7	21.3	33.9	.6339
LAKE	3,145,438	27,056	34.3	19.1	15.8	.0641
ORANGE	18,037,281	40,241	24.6	22.0	36.0	.3660
• Orlando	3,642,949	34,870	27.8	21.9	27.9	.0758

METRO AREA County City	Total EBI ($000)	Median Hsld. EBI ($)	\% of Hslds. by EBI Group A $20,000-$34,999	B $35,000-$49,999	C $50,000 & Over	Buying Power Index
OSCEOLA	2,381,487	30,699	33.6	22.5	18.4	.0519
SEMINOLE	8,803,691	48,182	19.4	20.3	47.5	.1519
PANAMA CITY	2,460,257	31,961	28.1	20.6	24.0	.0501
BAY	2,460,257	31,961	28.1	20.6	24.0	.0501
• Panama City	552,236	29,454	25.2	20.8	20.0	.0149
PENSACOLA	6,468,006	32,232	27.9	20.0	25.2	.1252
ESCAMBIA	4,447,541	30,924	28.5	19.2	23.4	.0902
• Pensacola	1,135,351	32,244	25.8	17.0	29.0	.0236
SANTA ROSA	2,020,465	36,136	26.4	21.9	29.8	.0350
PUNTA GORDA	2,410,634	29,012	35.8	20.2	17.2	.0471

10 retail merchandise lines. Figure 3-1 presents part of a typical page from the *Survey of Buying Power.*

SRDS.   In the monthly volumes covering spot radio, spot television, and newspapers, SRDS publishes market information similar to the statistics in the *Survey of Buying Power.* Data are presented for population, households, and effective buying income for the United States, geographic regions, and each state.

Brand Development Index and Category Development Index.   The brand development index (BDI) and category development index (CDI) must be calculated using information from various sources. These indexes indicate how well a brand performs in a market relative to the number of people living in the area. So, in an average market, if that market accounts for 1% of the total population, it might be expected to account for 1% of a brand's or a category's total sales. The formula looks like this:

$$\frac{\% \text{ of a brand's total U.S. sales in a market} \times 100}{\% \text{ of total U.S. population in a market}} = \text{BDI}$$

If the index number is greater than 100, it means that the brand is doing above average in this market. If the number is less than 100, the brand is not doing as well proportionally in this market as it is doing in other areas. In either case, the reasons for success in one market or a below-par performance in another should be investigated, if possible. A major reason a brand does well is that sales in the generic category are high. To assess this effect, a CDI can be calculated. The formula is as follows:

$$\frac{\% \text{ of a category's total U.S. sales in a market} \times 100}{\% \text{ of total population in a market}} = \text{CDI}$$

If the index number is greater than 100, a preliminary judgment will be that the market is receptive to the product (i.e., the category). If the number is less than 100, it does not necessarily mean that the market is not receptive to the category, but only that the market does not use the product to the same degree as do other markets. This situation calls for further analysis. Is there sufficient distribution in the market? Do dealers in the market use low, medium, or high levels of promotional support in the market, especially sales promotion? How new is the product to the area? If marketing promotional levels have been weak, it may indicate a marketing opportunity that can be taken advantage of simply through an increase in promotional support. The essential point to understand is that CDIs and BDIs are a way to get you thinking about the *relative* importance of a market. They should not be used as the only justification for deciding the degree of promotional effort to use in an area.

The next important step is to compare the BDI number to the CDI number. If the BDI is lower than the CDI and both indexes are still greater than 100, that means that the brand and the category are doing well, but consumers are more receptive to competitive brands. This finding is generally perceived as an opportunity because it is usually much easier to get consumers to switch brands than to get them to use a product for the first time. However, it would be a mistake to assume that a high BDI and a higher CDI automatically mean a marketing opportunity. In all cases, the analyst should take a close look at the market and assess the amount of promotional support in a market as well as the history of the market's response to promotions.

DEMOGRAPHIC AND PSYCHOGRAPHIC DATA

Assessing market opportunities on the basis of product usage is the first step. The next step is to take the demographic and psychographic characteristics of current users and look for similar characteristics in geographic areas around the country. Generally, the smaller the area you can identify, the more useful the information. Simmons and MRI, for example, provide demographic information on a regional basis, whereas some so-called geodemographic companies, such as Claritas, Inc. (with its PRIZM program) and CACI Marketing Systems (with its ACORN® Clustering System), provide information on areas as small as block groups (250–550 households), blocks (25–50 households), and ZIP+4s (6–25 households).

Two sources of market information that fill the gap between geodemographic sources (PRIZM) and *Simmons* and *MRI* are increasingly available in libraries: The *Lifestyle Market Analyst,* published by SRDS, and the *Sourcebook of ZIP Code Demographics,* published by CACI Marketing Systems.

Lifestyle Market Analyst is a relatively new source of information. It is becoming increasingly available at university libraries. This resource provides demographic and lifestyle information on the DMAs, including county breakouts for the 10 largest DMAs. It includes a profile for each of 68 lifestyle interests, cross-referenced to the 211 DMAs. Figure 3-2 shows how demographic information is presented for the Lincoln & Hastings-Kearney, plus NE market, and Figure 3-3 presents the lifestyle information on Gainesville, Florida.

The *Sourcebook of ZIP Code Demographics* contains statistics on all residential ZIP codes in the United States. For each ZIP code, it provides information on population, gender, age distribution, race, people of Hispanic origin, various kinds of household information, and family and household income. The information comes primarily from the U.S. Census, but also includes CACI's own estimates. A statistical summary is provided for each state.

GEODEMOGRAPHIC DATA

Geodemographic analyses are based on the principle that people who live in the same neighborhood tend to have similar characteristics. There are three major geodemographic computer-programming systems: PRIZM by Claritas, ACORN Clustering System by CACI, and Claritas' MicroVision®. Each of these systems classifies geographical units of varying sizes according to information obtained from the U.S. Census Bureau. These areas are then delineated using demographic and behavioral data obtained from the

FIGURE 3-2 | DEMOGRAPHIC MARKET PROFILE FROM LINCOLN & HASTINGS-KEARNEY

Lincoln & Hastings–Kearney Plus, NE

Demographics
Base Index US ≈ 100

Total Adult Population 520,301

Occupation	Population	%	Index
Administrative	68,680	13.2	90
Blue Collar	77,005	14.8	129
Clerical	62,550	10.1	100
Homemaker	66,599	12.8	98
Professional/Technical	129,035	24.8	93
Retired	63,248	16.0	96
Sales/Marketing	26,535	5.1	90
Self Employed	10,406	2.0	133
Student	6,764	1.3	118

Education (2000 Census)

Elementary (0–8 years)	23,911	5.5	72
High School (1–3 years)	33,476	7.7	64
High School (4 years)	141,728	32.6	114
College (1–3 years)	137,380	31.6	115
College (4+ years)	98,688	22.7	93

Race/Ethnicity

White	472,433	90.8	133
Black	6,764	1.3	11
Asian	7,805	1.5	38
Hispanic	25,495	4.9	37
American Indian	2,081	0.4	50
Other	5,203	1.0	56

Total Households 272,696

Age of Head of Household	Households	%	Index
18–24 years old	20,452	7.5	150
25–34 years old	42,813	15.7	98
35–44 years old	50,721	18.6	87
45–54 years old	53,721	19.7	94
55–64 years old	36,269	13.3	89
65–74 years old	29,451	10.8	101
75 years and older	38,998	14.3	131
Median Age	**49.1 years**		

Sex/Marital Status

Single Male	53,721	19.7	95
Single Female	59,720	21.9	90
Married	159,254	58.4	106

Children At Home

At Least One Child	81,538	29.9	97
Child Age Under 2	10,908	4.0	105
Child Age 2–4	20,998	7.7	103
Child Age 5–7	21,270	7.8	107
Child Age 8–10	20,452	7.5	99
Child Age 11–12	15,544	5.7	98
Child Age 13–15	22,634	8.3	95
Child Age 16–18	22,634	8.3	101

Home Ownership

Owner	184,342	87.6	100
Renter	88,354	32.4	99

Stage in Family Lifecycle	Households	%	Index
Single, 18–34, No Children	31,905	11.7	114
Single 35–44, "	11,999	4.4	75
Single 45–64, "	24,815	9.1	80
Single, 65+ "	25,361	9.3	109
Married, 18–34, "	10,090	3.7	112
Married, 35–44, "	6,272	2.3	77
Married, 45–64, "	43,359	15.9	104
Married, 65+ "	37,632	13.8	120
Single, Any Child at Home	19,361	7.1	80
Married, Child Age Under 13	33,542	12.3	103
Married, Child Age 13–18	28,633	10.5	105

Household Income

Under $20,000	56,993	20.9	106
$20,000–$29,999	39,268	14.4	121
$30,000–$39,999	37,359	13.7	118
$40,000–$49,999	32,996	12.1	115
$50,000–$74,999	55,357	20.3	105
$75,000–$99,999	25,088	9.2	81
$100,000 and over	25,361	9.3	60
Median Income	**$40,778**		

Income Earners

Married, One Income	56,993	20.9	94
Married, Two Incomes	102,261	37.6	114
Single	113,442	41.6	93

Dual Income Households

Children Age Under 13 years	24,543	9.0	120
Children Age 13–18 years	22,634	8.3	117
No Children	55,085	20.2	111

Age By Income

18–34, Income under $30,000	28,360	10.4	127
35–44, "	11,181	4.1	89
45–64, "	20,452	7.5	93
65+ "	36,269	13.3	124
18–34, Income $30,000–$49,999	16,907	6.2	119
35–44, "	13,635	5.0	106
45–64, "	23,179	8.5	116
65+ "	16,634	6.1	124
18–34, Income $50,000–$74,999	11,181	4.1	105
35–44, "	13,907	5.1	108
45–64, "	21,816	8.0	104
65+ "	8,454	3.1	103
18–34, Income $75,000 and over	6,545	2.4	63
35–44, "	12,271	4.5	63
45–64, "	24,815	9.1	72
65+ "	6,817	2.5	78

Credit Card Usage

Travel/Entertainment	14,726	5.4	40
Bank Card	216,248	79.3	100
Gas/Department Store	61,357	22.5	87
No Credit Cards	50,721	18.6	111

Source: Reprinted from the 2004 edition of The Lifestyle Market Analyst® published by SRDS with data supplied by EQUIFAX.

FIGURE 3-3	LIFESTYLES MARKET PROFILE FROM GAINSVILLE, FLORIDA

Lifestyles
Base Index US = 100

Gainesville, FL

The Top Ten Lifestyles Ranked by Index

Science/New Technology	155	Boating/Sailing	123
Science Fiction	131	Wildlife/Environmental	121
Military Veteran in Household	127	Horseback Riding	119
Running/Jogging	124	Electronics	119
Improving Your Health	123	Tennis Frequently	116

Home Life	Households	%	Index	Rank
Avid Book Reading	42,505	35.8	97	131
Bible/Devotional Reading	30,751	25.9	105	106
Flower Gardening	38,943	32.8	93	183
Grandchildren	22,559	19.0	77	206
Home Furnishing/Decorating	25,527	21.5	84	208
House Plants	31,344	26.4	113	67
Own a Cat	39,537	33.3	115	59
Own a Dog	52,597	44.3	114	95
Shop by Catalog/Mail	58,177	49.0	95	178
Subscribe to Cable TV	64,589	54.4	92	145
Vegetable Gardening	26,951	22.7	92	177

Good Life	Households	%	Index	Rank
Attend Cultural/Arts Events	20,065	16.9	114	24
Cruise Ship Vacations	22,440	18.9	110	31
Fashion Clothing	23,865	20.1	103	57
Fine Art/Antiques	10,448	8.8	88	199
Foreign Travel	22,202	18.7	111	35
Frequent Flyer	28,614	24.1	98	56
Gourmet Cooking/Fine Foods	24,221	20.4	104	52
Own a Vacation Home/Property	8,786	7.4	67	163
Travel for Business	9,855	8.3	93	67
Travel for Pleasure/Vacation	48,323	40.7	103	46
Travel in USA	41,793	35.2	96	102
Wines	21,015	17.7	95	79

Hobbies & Interests	Households	%	Index	Rank
Automotive Work	17,928	15.1	101	159
Buy Pre-Recorded Videos	16,741	14.1	80	207
Coin/Stamp Collecting	9,380	7.9	89	200
Collectibles/Collections	16,266	13.7	88	194
Community/Civic Activities	12,704	10.7	88	184
Crafts	28,376	23.9	94	180
Current Affairs/Politics	11,398	9.6	104	66
Donate to Charitable Causes	50,697	42.7	88	175
Home Workshop	35,975	30.3	96	189
Military Veteran in Household	29,089	24.5	127	59
Needlework/Knitting	15,553	13.1	89	186
Our Nation's Heritage	8,667	7.3	107	74
Self-Improvement	25,171	21.2	101	75
Sewing	15,553	13.1	86	197

Sports, Fitness & Health	Households	%	Index	Rank
Bicycling Frequently	24,221	20.4	106	76
Dieting/Weight Control	33,719	28.4	104	56
Golf	18,403	15.5	81	162
Health/Natural Foods	29,326	24.7	105	39
Improving Your Health	43,099	36.3	123	1
Physical Fitness/Exercise	48,798	41.1	105	34
Running/Jogging	18,878	15.9	124	21
Snow Skiing Frequently	5,699	4.8	58	144
Tennis Frequently	9,380	7.9	116	24
Walking for Health	34,194	28.8	92	197
Watching Sports on TV	35,263	29.7	90	178

Investing & Money	Households	%	Index	Rank
Casino Gambling	11,517	9.7	56	196
Entering Sweepstakes	19,234	16.2	102	106
Moneymaking Opportunities	14,129	11.9	103	89
Real Estate Investments	13,535	11.4	113	33
Stock/Bond Investments	24,933	21.0	93	125

Great Outdoors	Households	%	Index	Rank
Boating/Sailing	16,860	14.2	123	38
Camping/Hiking	31,463	26.5	95	150
Fishing Frequently	37,756	31.8	107	145
Horseback Riding	9,023	7.6	119	66
Hunting/Shooting	18,997	16.0	89	174
Recreational Vehicles	11,517	9.7	92	161
Wildlife/Environmental	21,609	18.2	121	34

High Tech Activities	Households	%	Index	Rank
Electronics	22,677	19.1	119	7
Home Video Games	13,179	11.1	102	106
Listen to Records/Tapes/CDs	59,127	49.8	100	78
Own a CD Player	89,522	75.4	103	24
Own a CD Rom	72,900	61.4	111	14
Own a Camcorder	37,043	31.2	94	161
Own a Cellular Phone	82,517	69.5	102	50
Own a Personal Computer	73,493	61.9	108	27
Own an Apple/Macintosh	7,124	6.0	103	46
Own an IBM Compatible	71,475	60.2	109	22
Photography	29,445	24.8	109	35
Science Fiction	14,604	12.3	131	6
Science/New Technology	18,047	15.2	155	1
Subscribe to Online Service	68,863	58.0	105	34
VCR Recording	17,453	14.7	95	149

The Lifestyle Market Analyst 2005	**Market Profiles**	**267**

Source: Reprinted from the 2005 edition of The Lifestyle Market Analyst® published by SRDS with data supplied by EQUIFAX.

census, syndicated research sources such as *Simmons* and *MRI,* and the system's own proprietary data-gathering procedures. The systems group areas throughout the United States with similar characteristics into categories so that advertisers can target geographically only those areas that contain their target audience (e.g., affluent neighborhoods).

The newest generation of geodemographic systems can be linked to other research databases, including media consumption research, UPC scanner data, consumer panels, and lifestyle typologies (such as VALS). This kind of linkage means that an advertiser could define a target audience in terms of demographic and psychographic characteristics and then identify specifically where these consumers can be found geographically. The primary geographic unit is the postal ZIP code; hence, the use of these systems is often called **ZIP code marketing.** We'll examine the oldest and one of the most widely used systems: PRIZM.

PRIZM. This system has been around since the early 1970s and has evolved along with the increasing sophistication of the data in the U.S. Census. In the 1990s, Claritas factor-analyzed the dozens of demographic and lifestyle variables in the census into six broad categories that represent most of the variance among different neighborhood types. These categories are:

1. Social rank (income, employment, education)
2. Household composition (age, sex, family type, dependency status)
3. Mobility (length of residency by owner or renter, auto ownership)
4. Ethnicity (race, foreign birth, ancestry, language)
5. Urbanization (population and housing density, such as urban, suburban, small city, town, rural)
6. Housing (owner/renter status, home values, number of stories)

These six categories are then statistically analyzed to produce 62 so-called neighborhood types. Each of these neighborhood types has been assigned a nickname, such as blue-blood estates, executive suites, and pools and patios.[1] PRIZM uses maps and computer software to describe the location of these neighborhood types. The geographical areas are based on a comprehensive, computerized, digitized street map of the United States that was used in the 1990 census and known by the acronym TIGER (for Topographically Integrated Geographic Coding and Referencing System).

The 62 neighborhood types, or clusters, are also grouped into larger clusters called a social group. Figure 3-4 presents the 14 social groups that represent almost all of the households in the United States.

Each social group is described in words, such as Urban Uptown. The number under each social group indicates the number of the clusters in each category. For example, the Urban Uptown, social group U1, consists of five clusters, numbers 06 through 10. Figure 3-5 presents a summary of the demographic and lifestyle characteristics of each of the clusters in this social group. (Note that these are not the five wealthiest neighborhood types.)

The ability of the PRIZM system to deliver addressable names and mappable targets at the micromarket level has obvious advantages to advertisers, especially in the planning of media strategy within a larger market. The ability to analyze markets at the microlevel block group or less has also been widely used for fund-raising, site selection, and recruiting.[2] Exhibit 3-1 on page 75 presents the PRIZM neighborhood types.

GeoVALS™. SRI Consulting Business Intelligence developed GeoVALS to allow users of the VALS system, discussed in Chapter 2, to locate concentrations of specific VALS consumers by ZIP code or block group.

FIGURE 3-4 | PRIZM SOCIAL GROUPS

Social Groups

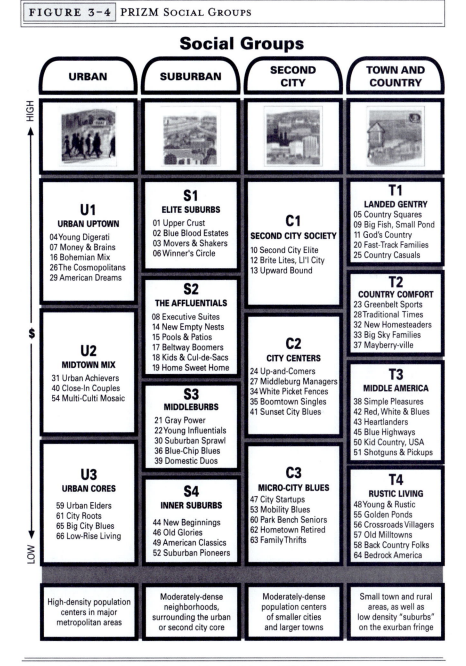

URBAN	SUBURBAN	SECOND CITY	TOWN AND COUNTRY

HIGH

U1
URBAN UPTOWN
04 Young Digerati
07 Money & Brains
16 Bohemian Mix
26 The Cosmopolitans
29 American Dreams

S1
ELITE SUBURBS
01 Upper Crust
02 Blue Blood Estates
03 Movers & Shakers
06 Winner's Circle

C1
SECOND CITY SOCIETY
10 Second City Elite
12 Brite Lites, Li'l City
13 Upward Bound

T1
LANDED GENTRY
05 Country Squares
09 Big Fish, Small Pond
11 God's Country
20 Fast-Track Families
25 Country Casuals

S2
THE AFFLUENTIALS
08 Executive Suites
14 New Empty Nests
15 Pools & Patios
17 Beltway Boomers
18 Kids & Cul-de-Sacs
19 Home Sweet Home

T2
COUNTRY COMFORT
23 Greenbelt Sports
28 Traditional Times
32 New Homesteaders
33 Big Sky Families
37 Mayberry-ville

$

U2
MIDTOWN MIX
31 Urban Achievers
40 Close-In Couples
54 Multi-Culti Mosaic

C2
CITY CENTERS
24 Up-and-Comers
27 Middleburg Managers
34 White Picket Fences
35 Boomtown Singles
41 Sunset City Blues

S3
MIDDLEBURBS
21 Gray Power
22 Young Influentials
30 Suburban Sprawl
36 Blue-Chip Blues
39 Domestic Duos

T3
MIDDLE AMERICA
38 Simple Pleasures
42 Red, White & Blues
43 Heartlanders
45 Blue Highways
50 Kid Country, USA
51 Shotguns & Pickups

U3
URBAN CORES
59 Urban Elders
61 City Roots
65 Big City Blues
66 Low-Rise Living

C3
MICRO-CITY BLUES
47 City Startups
53 Mobility Blues
60 Park Bench Seniors
62 Hometown Retired
63 Family Thrifts

S4
INNER SUBURBS
44 New Beginnings
46 Old Glories
49 American Classics
52 Suburban Pioneers

T4
RUSTIC LIVING
48 Young & Rustic
55 Golden Ponds
56 Crossroads Villagers
57 Old Milltowns
58 Back Country Folks
64 Bedrock America

LOW

High-density population centers in major metropolitan areas	Moderately-dense neighborhoods, surrounding the urban or second city core	Moderately-dense population centers of smaller cities and larger towns	Small town and rural areas, as well as low density "suburbs" on the exurban fringe

Source: Information courtesy of Claritas, Inc. Information based on 2000 Census data.

GeoVALS data is delivered in Excel files on a CD. It can be downloaded into mapping software, such as Scan/US. GeoVALS is used most often for direct mail purposes and is useful for site location applications. Figure 3-6 (see page 76) presents a diagrammatic view of the United States showing the percentage of the VALS types in Augusta, Georgia, ZIP code 30907.

FIGURE 3–5 CHARACTERISTICS OF PRIZM NEIGHBORHOOD CLUSTERS

Characteristics of PRIZM Neighborhood Types

	Winner's Circle	Money & Brains	Executive Suites	Big Fish, Small Pond	Second City Elite
Cluster Name					
Demographic Description	Executive-Level Suburban Families	Older, Upscale Urban Sophisticates	Upscale, Suburban Singles & Couples	Upscale, Older Exurban Couples	Executive Couples in Small Cities
Tenure/Housing Type	Owner/SFDU	Owner/SFDU	Owner/SFDU, Hi-Rise Multi	Owner/SFDU	Owner/SFDU
Cluster Number	06	07	08	09	10
Perdominant Age Ranges	25-54	45+	25-44	45+	45+
Key Education Level(s)	College Graduate+	College Graduate+	College Graduate+	College Graduate+	College Graduate+
Race/Ethnicity	White, Asian	White, Asian	White, Asian	White	White
Lifestyle Preferences	Go Downhill Skiing Own a Home Theatre System *Parents* Magazine *The Cartoon Network* TV Honda Odyssey	Shop at Nordstrom Support The Arts *Business Week* Magazine All-News Radio BMW 5 Series	Exercise At Health Clubs Research Internet Real Estate *GQ* Magazine *Will & Grace* TV BMW 3 Series	Go Cross-Country Skiing Own a Vacation/Wknd Home *Southern Living* Magazine Classical Radio Cadillac de Ville	Own Home Exercise Equipment Travel Domestically by Plane *Travel & Leisure* Magazine *Wall Street Week* TV Chrysler 300M

Source: Information courtesy of Claritas, Inc. Information based on 2000 Census data.

EXHIBIT 3-1	PRIZM NEIGHBORHOOD TYPES

Group	Cluster	Cluster Nickname	Group	Cluster	Cluster Nickname
Urban Uptown			Urban Cores		
U1	04	Young Digerati	U3	59	Urban Elders
U1	07	Money & Brains	U3	61	City Roots
U1	16	Bohemian Mix	U3	65	Big City Blues
U1	26	The Cosmopolitans	U3	66	Low-Rise Living
U1	29	American Dreams	Middleburbs		
Elite Suburbs			S3	21	Gray Power
S1	01	Upper Crust	S3	22	Young Influentials
S1	02	Blue Blood Estates	S3	30	Suburban Sprawl
S1	03	Movers & Shakers	S3	36	Blue-Chip Blues
S1	06	Winner's Circle	S3	39	Domestic Duo
2nd City Society			Micro-City Blues		
C1	10	Second City Elite	C3	47	City Startups
C1	12	Bright Lites, Li'l City	C3	53	Mobility Blues
C1	13	Upward Bound	C3	60	Park Bench Seniors
Landed Gentry			C3	62	Hometown Retired
T1	05	Country Squires	C3	63	Family Thrifts
T1	09	Big Fish, Small Pond	Middle America		
T1	11	God's Country	T3	38	Simple Pleasures
T1	20	Fast-Track Families	T3	42	Red, White, & Blues
T1	25	Country Casuals	T3	43	Heartlanders
Midtown Mix			T3	45	Blue Highways
U2	31	Urban Achievers	T3	50	Kid Country, USA
U2	40	Close-In Couples	T3	51	Shotguns & Pickups
U2	54	Multi-Culti Mosaic	Inner Suburbs		
The Affluentials			S4	44	New Beginnings
S2	08	Executive Suites	S4	46	Old Glories
S2	14	New Empty Nest	S4	49	American Classics
S2	15	Pools & Patios	S4	52	Suburban Pioneers
S2	17	Beltway Boomers	Rustic Living		
S2	18	Kids & Cul-de-Sacs	T4	48	Young & Rustic
S2	19	Home Sweet Home	T4	55	Golden Ponds
City Centers			T4	56	Crossroads Villagers
C2	24	Up-and-Comers	T4	57	Old Milltowns
C2	27	Middleburg Managers	T4	58	Back Country Folks
C2	34	White Picket Fences	T4	64	Bedrock America
C2	35	Boomtown Singles			
C2	41	Sunset City Blues			
Country Comfort					
T2	23	Greenbelt Sports			
T2	28	Traditional Times			
T2	32	New Homesteaders			
T2	33	Big Sky Families			
T2	37	Mayberry-ville			

Source: Information courtesy of Claritas, Inc. Information based on 2000 Census data.

FIGURE 3-6 | GEOVALS™ DATA FOR S AUGUSTA, GA

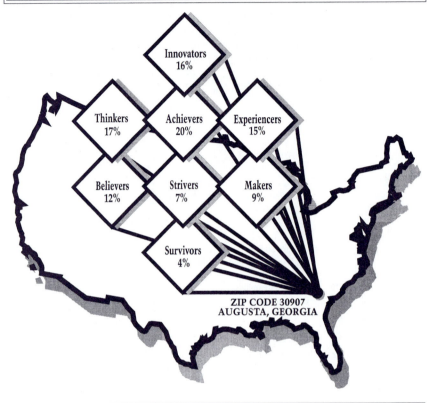

Source: SRI Consulting Business Intelligence, http://www.sric-bi.com/VALS/.

▋PRODUCT/BRAND ANALYSIS

In the product analysis, the basic questions address how the many aspects of the product match up with consumers' needs, wants, problems, and interests. A product consists of both physical and psychological attributes. Even simple products are surprisingly complex. Is this product the right size? Is it priced right? Is it in the right place? Consumers typically buy a product because of the whole package. They may say they are buying a product based on price, but that is only because they have implicitly accepted that the product has met their minimum standards of quality. The way a product is marketed can have a profound influence on whether consumers believe or feel the product addresses their needs and wants. Perception can be more important than reality. It is up to the analyst to determine both what a product is and how it is *perceived*. There is often a difference between the external and internal perception of the brand. Companies may think they understand how consumers think and feel about their products, but testing often proves otherwise.

As product categories become more mature, the strategic focus in marketing a product tends to shift from an emphasis on physical qualities to ones that are more *intangible* in nature. These intangible qualities are associated with the brand name, or simply, the *brand*. Although consumers buy the package, an insightful analyst will usually think of the product as a whole but break it down into its component parts. The key to organizing the analysis of a product is to look at both the brand, or its psychological qualities, and its physical qualities, which typically include the product's quality, price, distribution, and promotion. A number of questions must be considered:

1. Does the product package have the ability to give consumers what they want (or need, and so forth)?
2. Does the product package promise or address what consumers want?
3. Does the delivery of the product package match up with consumers' expectations?
4. Can the product package exceed consumers' expectations?
5. What is the essence of the brand?
6. Does this essence have value?
7. To what extent is this brand liked?
8. How strong is the brand?

The first three questions tend to focus on potential barriers to a successful marketing program. A product without substance or real want-satisfying qualities is unlikely to be successful over the long term. If a product has special qualities but does not promote them, special opportunities may be lost. Opportunities can be perishable. Promising consumers one thing but delivering another can also lead to a product's diminished effectiveness. Usually, perception is not only more important than reality, for consumers, perception is their reality. What is delivered to consumers is not nearly as important as what they believe they are receiving. For many brands, what consumers want is the right image, something that suggests something about the individual. Chanel No. 5 has been a popular perfume for over 50 years. For many it is an elegant fragrance, to others "it's the stuff my grandmother wears." Knowing which perception is more prominent is important, but it's also worth pursuing whether the association between grandma and Chanel is a classy, prestigious image or simply one that is old-fashioned.

The fourth question focuses more on what the product could be—either real or perceived. This question is the most difficult one to answer—both from the consumers' point of view and from the perspective of a marketing strategist. To get the answer requires imagination on the part of the researcher and the consumer.

The fifth, sixth, and seventh questions have always been important. But for many products, the physical distinctions between one brand and another are not what they used to be. Products are likely to be even more similar in the future than they are now. The day will come when some Coca-Cola knockoff will taste surprisingly like Coke! Companies are increasingly aware that the way to market success is by differentiating the product through the images, personalities, or values that are associated with the brand name. This is generally called **building the brand.** The analyst's job is to determine what makes this brand—*this brand* and not some other. The special mental connections that consumers make with a brand, taken as a whole, can be referred to as the **essence of a brand.** Some of the essence is intrinsic to the product—the way a BMW's performance characteristics influence the way people think of its drivability. These intrinsic characteristics can be thought of as the "DNA" of the brand. Other mental connections are the result of the way the brand has been promoted (e.g., Marlboro cigarettes) or the way people have experienced the brand (e.g., Harley-Davidson motorcycles).

Question eight (How strong is the brand?) is the logical conclusion of the preceding seven questions. The answer to this question will provide direction to the development of the *strategic focal point* of the campaign. Brands tend to exert varying degrees of loyalty on consumers. The following is a brand loyalty continuum:

Brand Awareness → Brand Acceptance → Brand Preference → Brand Insistence

Companies want to move consumers across the above continuum toward brand insistence—where consumers will accept no substitutes for the product. Somewhere along the continuum in the area of brand preference and brand insistence is the near ultimate status of the **power brand.** These brands are so powerful that the names alone are worth considerable money to the owners. Coca-Cola. Kodak. Marlboro. Intel. Microsoft. Budweiser. Smuckers. Clinique. The Gap. Steinway. Harley-Davidson. Mercedes Benz. Disney World. Heinz. McDonald's. Though companies may desire to own power brands, it is not realistic for most. The analyst's job is to determine the current status of the brand and at least a preliminary assessment of its opportunity to get stronger.

LOOKING AT THE PRODUCT

To get a full appreciation of what consumers think or feel about a product, it is often helpful to compare it to its competition. In doing a product analysis, it may be useful to perform some aspects of the competitive analysis at the same time. We separate these steps in this chapter primarily to help the reader see how the various parts of the situation analysis fit together and not because we feel they should be done sequentially. There are a number of useful ways to describe a product's qualities: concrete or abstract, physical or psychological, and tangible or intangible. In the advertising business, products are usually discussed in terms of their attributes, which tend to be physical; their functions, which are mostly physical and somewhat psychological; and their images or brand personalities and reputations, which are psychological.

Product Attributes
In evaluating a product, it is always helpful to understand how many of a product's want-satisfying qualities are tangible product attributes and how many are intangible. If a product comes up short in the attribute area, then the solution to the problem of how to market it is more likely to

come from research and development than from marketing. Problems concerning how to market intangible qualities, such as images and brand personalities, can be addressed with advertising and other marketing communication tools. In analyzing a product's more tangible qualities, consider the following:

- Product variety
- Special designs
- Differentiating features
- Qualities (hidden and obvious)
- Packaging
- Sizes
- Services
- Warranties
- Returns[3]

Product Functions

In many product categories, consumers are less interested in a product's attributes, which they don't understand or don't want to understand, than they are in what the product can do for them. In the 1970s, commercials for some antiperspirants said the product contained aluminum chlorohydrate—a technical word, but not beyond the ability of consumers to remember. Today, the active ingredient in Arrid XX® antiperspirant deodorant is aluminum zirconium pentachlorohydrexgly. Not surprisingly, all consumers want to know is that it keeps them "extra, extra dry."

Consider paper products. Charmin Ultra® bathroom tissue is promoted primarily on the basis of its "Squeezably Soft & Thick" attributes. In contrast, Bounty® paper towels have long been promoted based on their absorbency— "The Quicker Picker-Upper." In recent years, ads for Bounty emphasized the towel's strength—"Look! It's Quilted." Of course, it's also possible to emphasize both attributes and functions. Ads for Kleenex Ultra® facial tissues emphasize their "extra layer of softness" that provides a "soft, silky feel" to the skin.

For some products, the decision to emphasize an attribute or function may depend on the target audience. The package of Edge® Gel, a shaving preparation targeted for men with sensitive skin, prominently displays the message that the product is "for closer, more comfortable shaves!" Skintimate® Shaving Gel for women, like Edge Gel, is formulated for sensitive skin and contains aloe vera. Yet, the Skintimate brand only mentions how the brand functions on the back of the package and in small print. Apparently, women understand the effects of aloe on sensitive or irritated skin better than men. They do not need to be told what effect using the brand might have on their skin.

BRAND PERSONALITY

People have long projected onto inanimate objects qualities that are normally associated with human beings. This is true for products, and especially so for branded products. In fact, it is the history of a brand, and all its associations, that often gives a product its distinctive personality.

A brand name has value. It can be estimated subjectively through qualitative research or more rigorously in paired comparison tests.

In a research setting, a whole range of questions associated with the brand or the brand personality can be addressed, including those focusing on purchasing intentions and price sensitivity. The research question can be as simple as "Which one do you prefer?" Exhibit 3-2 presents a brand valuation test for a fast-food chicken restaurant using this question in a taste test.

Usually done with matched samples, this type of test is used to estimate the value of the brand name. Presumably, the increased preference shown for Brand A in the second sample (where the brands are named) can be attributed to identifying the chicken as Brand A. This valuation test (or a variation of this test) can be used to determine how much value the brand name adds to the product.

The next step is to understand how the product's attributes and brand personality contribute to its success (or lack thereof). To obtain this information, companies and agencies use a variety of techniques, including some already discussed, such as survey research, one-on-ones, and focus groups, as well as other techniques that we will discuss later in this chapter.

PRODUCT TESTING

One of the best ways to evaluate consumers' thoughts about a product is to give them a product under real-life conditions and ask them what they think of it. Consumer testing focuses on consumers and attempts to understand their wants. Similarly, product testing seeks to understand a product's ability to satisfy a want. For this situation, there are three basic types of testing procedures:

EXHIBIT 3-2 BRAND VALUATION: WHICH PRODUCT DO YOU PREFER?		
	1st Sample	2nd Sample
	Unnamed Chicken	Named Chicken
Brand A (our chicken)	50%	60%
Brand B (the competitor's chicken)	50%	40%

1. *Monadic testing* presents consumers with one product at a time and requires them to make an evaluation without using any other product for comparison. (When scales are used as the testing instrument, it is sometimes called a *noncomparative rating scale.*) Monadic tests are designed to mirror real-life situations where consumers do not have competitive products to use as a basis for making comparisons. The idea is that consumers implicitly compare the product undergoing testing with other products they have considered. These tests are widely used in advertising.
2. *Paired comparison testing* presents the consumer with two (or more) products simultaneously, and requires them to make an evaluation. Unlike monadic tests, which focus on the qualities and attributes of the product undergoing testing, paired comparison tests focus on the differences between products. These will be discussed in greater detail in the section on competitive analysis.
3. *Projective tests* involve a much different way of collecting information about the product. This type of testing comes from clinical psychology. These tests are designed to get respondents to reveal their inner feelings and beliefs by having them project their own feelings and beliefs onto some situation that is ostensibly about someone or something other than themselves. Naturally, this is often used to provide information about consumers. We include a description of these tests here because of their value in learning about brand personalities.

Monadic Tests

A wide variety of tests fall into this category. Most are some variation of a numerical rating scale and involve the measurement of respondents' predisposition to respond to the product, usually in a favorable or unfavorable way. Some of the more commonly used scales are described below.

Semantic Differential.   This is one of the most widely used tests in marketing research. The basic version consists of a series of bipolar adjectives usually separated by a 7-point rating scale. The test can be used to measure both a product's attributes and its image.

EXAMPLE	Brand X Roasted Chicken Restaurants*							
	Friendly	___	___	___	___	___	___	___	Unfriendly
	Clean	___	___	___	___	___	___	___	Messy
	Modern	___	___	___	___	___	___	___	Old-fashioned
	Expensive	___	___	___	___	___	___	___	Inexpensive

*A variation of this technique uses phrases instead of bipolar adjectives.

Stapel Scales.   This test is a variation of the semantic differential scale. In this technique, respondents are typically asked to rate a product or a retail outlet according to the intensity of their agreement or disagreement with a product or a phrase. This test is fairly easy to administer and is often used in telephone interviews.

Telephone Interview: Please rate Brand X Roasted Chicken on the following qualities ranging from +5 to –5. (Sometimes a 0 is included as a neutral point, but some researchers feel it is better to make respondents choose a positive or negative value.)

+5	+5	+5	+5
+4	+4	+4	+4
+3	+3	+3	+3
+2	+2	+2	+2
+1	+1	+1	+1
tasty food	nutritious food	good value	distinctive flavor
–1	–1	–1	–1
–2	–2	–2	–2
–3	–3	–3	–3
–4	–4	–4	–4
–5	–5	–5	–5

Likert Scales.   Respondents are requested to indicate their agreement or disagreement with a series of statements. This is a relatively easy scale to construct and administer. Care should be taken, however, to provide a balance in the number of favorable and unfavorable statements.

Brand X Roasted Chicken Restaurants

	Strongly Agree	Agree	Neither Agree nor Disagree	Strongly Disagree	Disagree
This store has great-tasting chicken.	_____	_____	_____	_____	_____
The counter personnel are unfriendly.	_____	_____	_____	_____	_____
The inside of the store is comfortable.	_____	_____	_____	_____	_____
Roasted chicken is good for you.	_____	_____	_____	_____	_____

Purchase Interest.   This test requires respondents to indicate on a 5- or 11-point scale the likelihood that they will buy a product or service. The correlation between actual consumer purchases of a product and consumers' indications that they intend to purchase it is less than perfect. Nevertheless, the technique is also called *purchase intent.*

Please answer the following question.

If roasted chicken were available in your area, how likely would it be that you would purchase it?

_____ Definitely would buy.

_____ Probably would buy.

_____ Might or might not buy.

_____ Probably would not buy.

_____ Definitely would not buy.[4]

Likeability Scales. These tests are often used when the brand in question is essentially a parity product. In these cases, it is often felt that consumers make brand decisions on how well they "like" a product. The following itemized rating scale is one of a number of tests that can be used to test likeability.

EXAMPLE

Please mark on the following scale how much you like Brand X Rotisserie Chicken.

_____ 100 Superior.   _____ 50 Neutral.
_____ 90 Excellent.   _____ 40 Do not like it very well.
_____ 80 Like it very much.   _____ 30 It's not so good.
_____ 70 Like it quite well.   _____ 20 Do not like it at all.
_____ 60 Like it fairly well. _____ 10 It's terrible.

Projective Tests

To uncover the more elusive aspects of a brand's personality, many advertising agencies use projective techniques. Trained interviewers coax responding consumers to reveal underlying attitudes, feelings, and motivations by having them project themselves into a situation. Examples of some of the more widely used tests follow.

Sentence Completion. This technique requires respondents to complete a series of incomplete statements with the first word or phrase that comes to mind.

EXAMPLE

The best-tasting pizza usually comes with _____.
The thing I like least about going out to eat pizza is _____.
The thing I like most about eating pizza is _____.

Story Completion. This technique is a variation of the sentence completion test. In this test, interviewers tell respondents the details of part of a story and ask them to fill in the rest.

EXAMPLE

A man and a woman are walking down the street with their nine-year-old daughter. They stop exactly midway between a Pizza Hut and a KFC restaurant to discuss which one to enter. What are they saying to each other and how does this scene end? _____ (Open-ended question)

Word Association. This technique requires respondents to say the first word that comes to mind when they hear a stimulus word. In free word association, only the first word is important. In successive word associations, a series of words is requested. Usually, a neutral word is inserted between the words in which the interviewer is most interested.

EXAMPLE	Stimulus Word	Word Association	Successive Word Associations		
	pizza	_____	_____	_____	_____
	stuffed crust	_____	_____	_____	_____
	inexpensive fast food	_____	_____	_____	_____
	hamburgers (neutral)	_____	_____	_____	_____
	healthy fast food	_____	_____	_____	_____
	tasty fast food	_____	_____	_____	_____

Role Playing.   Respondents are asked to assume the role of another person or an object. One common technique involves asking respondents to persuade reluctant customers to buy a product. The techniques that are used tend to reveal respondents' attitudes toward the product and potential customers.

Pretend Games.   Respondents are asked to imagine the product is an average person, movie star, sports figure, or relative. Typically, the interviewer asks questions about where the people live, the kinds of houses they live in, and their ages. The responses are then used to provide definition to the brand's image or personality.

Storytelling.   Another technique—popular among account planners—uses storytelling as a way of better understanding what consumers *really* want. It is based on the premise that much of what influences consumers occurs beneath their level of awareness. Storytelling is a way to get people to reveal their inner feelings and thoughts. One of the more popular techniques was developed by Jerry Zaltman at the Harvard Business School. His technique is based on the idea that people think in images, not in words. Product users are directed to collect images from photo albums, catalogs, magazines—virtually anything—and produce a collage of these images. These images serve as a metaphor for a person's inner thoughts and feelings. Below is a simplified outline of the steps used.

1. Product users are recruited and asked, "What are your thoughts and feelings about buying and using . . ." (the brand or product in question).
2. Users are asked to collect about a dozen pictures.
3. After a week, the subjects are interviewed in an intense two-hour session.
4. With the help of a technician, a collage is computer generated (i.e., a composition of images placed in an incongruous relationship, usually for their symbolic or suggestive effect). These new pictures then become windows into the consumers' minds.

Storytelling has been used by DuPont to learn how women *really* feel about panty hose. Previous research, especially focus groups, indicated women hate panty hose and wear them only because they feel they have to. DuPont, which has a vested interest in panty hose (it manufactures nylon), wondered if there wasn't more to it than that. The women in the study produced images of twisted telephone cords, steel bands strangling trees, and shrink-wrapped fence posts. (Apparently, these women really disliked wearing panty hose.) But there were also conflicting images of a vase of flowers in one collage and a garden hose against a backdrop of a silk dress in another. These images seemed to suggest that women had more of a "like-hate relationship" with panty hose. Subsequent interviews brought out that women liked the way panty hose made their legs look sexy to men—something they would be unlikely to say in a survey or a focus group. As a result of these findings, hosiery manufacturers and retailers changed their advertising to include images of sexiness, even to businesswomen.[5] Still, sexy or not, panty hose continues to be a hard sell for many women.

SEARCHING FOR PRODUCT/BRAND OPPORTUNITIES

With many of the above tests, the researcher is seeking to understand the extent to which the product's attributes and brand qualities address consumers' needs and wants. Products that match up well with consumers' wants offer many ideas to help shape the strategic and tactical focal points around which the strategy gets developed and executed. Researchers can use many of the above tests to predict strategic and tactical opportunities. To identify opportunities with an existing product, a description of the product is often compared to the actual product.

To set up this comparison test, consumers are intercepted in a shopping mall and given a series of tests (such as purchase interest test, likeability test, or measure of perceived value) asking them to rate the product described on the test (i.e., the product concept). Immediately following these tests, the respondents are given a sample of the product. About a week later they are contacted and asked the same set of questions. The **test-retest procedure** is used to diagnose problems and identify opportunities. If the product does not meet consumers' expectations (i.e., it underdelivers), then it may be sent back to research and development for further work. If the product exceeds their expectations (i.e., it overdelivers), then this situation is viewed as an opportunity to exploit. This procedure can also be used to compare what the consumer would most like to have in this kind of product (i.e., an idealized concept of the product) to the actual product.

EXAMPLE	Version One	Version Two
	Step 1 Rate a description of the product.	**Rate the idealized concept of the product.**
	Step 2 Try the product.	**Try the product.**
	Step 3 Rate the actual product.	**Rate the product again.**

. . .

Step 4 Is the product rating in Step 3 better than that in Step 1 (i.e., it overdelivers), or worse than that in Step 1 (i.e., it underdelivers)?

EVALUATING THE REST OF THE MARKETING MIX

To get a complete picture of how the product is matching up with the needs and wants of the consumer, it is necessary to evaluate the rest of the marketing mix: pricing, distribution, and promotion program.

Pricing.   Most of the information about consumers' sensitivity to price can be obtained while research is conducted on the product. Care should be taken that consumers' responses are not taken too literally. For example, consumers frequently indicate that a product's price is too high. The key question as to whether price is a disadvantage can best be answered by market tests. Companies routinely vary the price of the product in isolated markets while holding other factors constant to gauge the effects of a market's sensitivity to price. This procedure is greatly facilitated with the use of scanner (UPC) technology.

Distribution.   To understand a product's ability to match up well with consumers' needs and wants, analysis should focus on the extent to which the product is available, in a general sense, and conveniently available, in a specific sense. Judgments can be qualitative and based on simple observation, or quantitative and based on scanner data indicating the percentage of the all-commodity volume (i.e., the total amount of sales in a given category) that can be accounted for by the outlets handling the company's product.

Promotion.   Although it can be helpful to separate advertising from other forms of marketing communication, the distinction between advertising and sales promotion is increasingly blurred in consumers' eyes. Most of the evaluation in this area comes from consumer research. What do consumers think of the current advertising campaign? What do consumers think about coupons (a form of price discounting)? However, much of what consumers think and feel about the message strategy part of the campaign can be inferred from consumer and product testing, particularly those tests that focus on brand personality. In the past, large advertisers often used sophisticated tracking systems, such as ACNielsen's Monitor Plus, to monitor the timing, frequency, and content of television commercials. However, ACNielsen discontinued this service. As a result, advertisers and their agencies use their own proprietary systems to keep track of their rivals' promotional efforts.

Although most of the effects of the creative part of the campaign can be inferred, the media effects should be measured. To do this kind of calculation requires an understanding of how the media plan will deliver the desired audiences and markets. The success of the plan often depends on how much money is being spent on advertising and whether this amount is sufficient to achieve the advertising objectives. Naturally, companies know how much money they are spending, but if the analyst is a student, then the best source to consult is one of the syndicated sources reporting competitive media expenditures, such as *Competitive Media Report's (CMR's) Leading National Advertisers/Media Watch Multimedia Service.*

COMPETITIVE ANALYSIS

Consumers have a limited amount of purchasing power. What they do not spend on brand X, they will surely spend somewhere else. Even though this statement is not literally true, it is a good position to maintain to keep a company thinking competitively. In other words, a forward-thinking company should always be apprised of its competition, both direct and indirect. A company may be a weak competitor one day, and the next day undertake a course of action that can force its rivals out of business.

To begin a competitive analysis, it is important first to identify the options consumers consider in their purchasing decisions. These options include buying products *that directly compete with each other in the same generic category* and products that only *indirectly compete with each other because they are in different categories.* For example, the direct competition for wine coolers is other wine coolers, but the indirect competition may include wine, clear malt liquor, and specialty mixed drinks. The options also include not buying anything or postponing the purchase decision to a later time.

To do a thorough competitive analysis, rival companies and their brands should be understood in as much depth as the analyst's company. In practice, this may not be feasible or practical. At a minimum, companies usually try to get a basic understanding of their rivals' resources and the real and perceived comparative distinctions among the brands that compete with the company's own brands.

Many of the tests and procedures that were discussed in the company analysis (see Chapter 2) and in the preceding description of product analysis are also appropriate here. These procedures include one-on-ones and focus group interviews. Projective tests can also be useful to gain insight into the brand personalities of competitive products. Many of the monadic tests, especially the semantic differential and the Stapel scales, can be used to compare one product to another simply by repeating the test for each competitive brand. This section will emphasize the tests and techniques that are comparative in nature.

PRODUCT COMPARISONS

These evaluations often form the basis for the strategic decisions, especially positioning, that will follow as the campaign develops. We will examine two types of comparisons: perceptual mapping, which examines where a company or brand fits in consumers' perception of the product category, and attitude scales, which are used to compare one brand or company to another.

Perceptual Mapping

This technique can help the analyst understand how a product is positioned in consumers' minds. Tests to implement perceptual mapping range from a simple technique, which is what we shall discuss here, to more complicated multidimensional scaling techniques that require computer software to calculate.[6]

Perceptual mapping is often used to get a feel for a brand's image. A brand's image is the result of a number of factors, including the physical and functional aspects of the brand, psychological qualities associated with the brand's heritage, and the totality of all the images associated with competitive brands. A perceptual map helps define a brand's image by putting it into the context of how consumers perceive the brand with respect to competitive brands. An image takes on a finer shade of meaning when an analyst can see how respondents rate a brand compared to its competition.

A perceptual map shows these distinctions by rating various brands on two dimensions simultaneously. For example, a retail store can be evaluated based on both friendly-unfriendly service and high-quality–low-quality merchandise. Although not all of a brand's image or personality can be explained by two dimensions, this rating usually gives the analyst some feel for how consumers perceive the various brands with respect to each other. In perceptual mapping, the researcher will often choose which dimensions to use with respondents, based on his or her experience. In multidimensional scaling, the testing makes no assumptions with regard to the dimensions that are appropriate for the brands being examined. The dimensions are usually derived from judgments respondents make about the similarity of brands or their preference for the brands based on various attributes or qualities.

Figure 3-7 presents a perceptual map for various performers based on an informal test conducted in an undergraduate class on advertising

---

FIGURE 3-7 | PERCEPTUAL MAP OF PERFORMERS

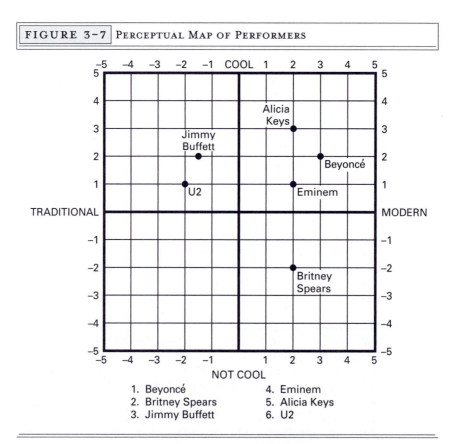

1. Beyoncé
2. Britney Spears
3. Jimmy Buffett
4. Eminem
5. Alicia Keys
6. U2

principles. Naturally, the map would likely look considerably different with an older age group.

Comparative Rating Scales

As we discussed in the section on product testing, one of the basic types of product tests that can be conducted to evaluate the competition is the comparative attitude rating scale.

Rank Order Rating Scales. In this test, respondents are asked to rank order a number of products (or retail stores) on the basis of some specific criterion. The ranking may be on the basis of overall quality, but the criterion is usually a specific attribute or quality.

EXAMPLE

Please rank the following restaurants from 1 to 5 according to which has the best-tasting chicken. Use a 1 to indicate the best.

_____ Boston Market Chicken

_____ Popeye's

_____ KFC

_____ Church's

_____ Brand X Chicken

Fractionation Rating Scale. This test requires respondents to rate several products on the basis of some criterion by comparing them to one specific product. Usually, the specific product is the brand leader or the company's brand. The objective of this test is to give the analyst an idea of how similar or different consumers consider the various brands.

EXAMPLE

If the Brand X Chicken restaurant is assumed to score 100 points on "fast service," how would you compare each of the following restaurants to it?

_____ Boston Market Chicken

_____ Popeye's

_____ KFC

_____ Church's

Paired Comparison Rating Scale. This test is simple in concept, but somewhat complicated to implement. It requires respondents to compare two products to each other and select one based on some criterion. If there are only two brands, then the testing procedure is a fairly simple one requiring respondents to indicate a preference for one brand over the other. A comparison is made for each attribute that is thought to be important in the product category. However, if the number of brands in the test is greater than 2, then the number of comparisons for each attribute goes up dramatically according to $[n(n2 - 1)/2]$. This means for 3 brands the number of paired comparisons would be 3 (4 brands = 6; 5 brands = 10); 6 brands would require 15 comparisons for each rated attribute. To set up this procedure, it might be helpful to consult a marketing research text.[7]

This test can be especially useful when a company is considering two or three versions or recipes of the same product. It is also used when a company believes it may position a brand against a specific competitor.

DOUBLE-CHECKING PRICES AND DISTRIBUTION

Analyzing the competition based on price and distribution is fairly similar to the way you analyze the product. You can obtain much of this information as you analyze the product. Because the information will often be obtained in the product analysis, it is usually a good idea to double-check each competitor's prices and distribution strengths and weaknesses as you would the company in the product analysis.

PROMOTION COMPARISONS

To be comprehensive, the competitive analysis should include an understanding of the competition's marketing communications activity. Data on some of the activity may be difficult to obtain; information on advertising is usually more readily available.

Competitive advertising can be divided into information about the message and about the media. Because advertisers no longer have access to the Ad Tracker database that provided information for ACNielsen's now defunct Monitor Plus service, most analysts (including students) usually construct their own albeit less-sophisticated database. One common method popular among students is to keep a file of all competitive advertising. Print ads can be tearsheets, and broadcast spots can be brief summaries. Usually it is helpful to do an informal content analysis of ads to track competitive positioning, themes, images, attributes, and objectives.

To get information on competitive media activity, it is possible to systematically monitor the major media. However, this is time consuming and not likely to be comprehensive. The most rigorous approach is to consult one of the syndicated sources of media expenditures, such as *CMR's Leading National Advertisers (LNA)*. Figure 3-8 presents a partial page from *LNA*.

The most effective use of this information was summarized by the staff of *Media Decisions* more than 25 years ago. Although there have been tremendous changes in the media world within the past decade, the information is still very much on target.

1. The expenditure figures can show you regionality and seasonality, and how these factors are changing for all competitive and potentially competitive brands.
2. The data can give you a market-by-market fix on ad budget size and media mix.
3. You can use the data to spot new product tests and to track new brand rollouts.
4. You can infer from where the money is being spent how competitors view their target audiences, how they profile their brands, and where they seek to position themselves in your marketplace.

| FIGURE 3-8 | LNA/MEDIAWATCH MULTI-MEDIA SERVICE |

$50 CMR Sample		Media vs Time Period Report					
	Report						
MEDIA	Total	Jan–Dec 99	Jan–Dec 00	Jan–Dec 01	Jan–Dec 02	Jan–Jun 03	% of Total
[Dominos Pizza]							
Magazines	873.4	735.7	0.0	0.0	0.0	137.7	0.2%
Newspapers	5,396.1	815.5	1,466.5	1,421.8	1,148.3	544.0	0.8%
National Newspapers	15.7	0.0	0.0	11.8	3.9	0.0	0.0%
Outdoor	1,547.0	488.8	356.0	209.5	286.4	206.3	0.3%
Network Television	192,878.5	45,012.1	47,255.0	41,959.8	38,441.0	20,210.6	28.2%
Spot Television	232,022.5	50,852.8	57,293.1	52,833.8	50,253.7	20,789.1	29.0%
Syndicated Television	381.8	73.5	201.3	73.8	33.2	0.0	0.0%
Cable TV Networks	84,669.0	15,129.2	15,588.7	16,535.0	24,948.1	12,468.0	17.4%
Network Radio	9,008.1	0.0	0.0	297.0	5,405.8	3,305.3	4.6%
National Spot Radio	5,596.5	1,134.8	1,493.0	840.1	1,779.8	348.8	0.5%
Internet						1,058.9	1.5%
Yellow Pages						12,506.3	17.5%
Subsidiary Total	532,388.6	114,242.4	123,653.6	114,182.6	122,300.2	71,575.0	100.0%
[Pizza Hut Inc.]							
Magazines	40.0	0.0	0.0	0.0	40.0	0.0	0.0%
Newspapers	1,329.7	492.3	356.0	150.6	165.8	165.0	0.2%
National Newspapers	513.5	101.0	180.8	0.0	231.7	0.0	0.0%
Outdoor	3,976.0	618.5	1,248.9	1,037.6	753.4	317.6	0.3%
Network Television	301,452.0	51,284.8	73,060.1	70,453.6	62,550.2	44,103.3	46.1%
Spot Television	257,422.6	54,142.3	53,042.1	55,055.4	68,942.7	26,240.1	27.4%
Syndicated Television	320.2	6.7	39.5	264.8	9.2	0.0	0.0%
Cable TV Networks	77,712.3	9,236.6	15,029.7	17,307.7	20,528.5	15,609.8	16.3%
Network Radio	174.6	45.0	104.4	25.2	0.0	0.0	0.0%
National Spot Radio	24,079.8	9,775.9	8,501.0	4,065.1	856.7	881.1	0.9%
Internet						0.5	0.0%
Yellow Pages						8,436.1	8.8%
Subsidiary Total	667,020.7	125,703.1	151,562.5	148,360.0	154,078.2	95,753.5	100.0%

Source: © 2005 Competitive Media Reporting, Inc. (d/b/a TNS Media Intelligence). All rights reserved.

5. You can watch spending patterns of the opposition—TV flighting, radio rotation, position practices in magazines, or day of week in newspapers.

6. Once you have complete knowledge of what your "enemies" are up to, you can make better decisions as to where to meet them head-on and when to outflank them.

7. In new-product and line-extension planning, expenditure data are essential to estimate how much it will cost to get into a market, who's already there, and which competitive product types are growing fastest in the new product's market segment.[8]

COMPLETING THE ANALYSIS

The title to this subsection is somewhat of a misnomer because an analysis should be an ongoing process. However, practically speaking, there are deadlines to meet and expense budgets to maintain—research can be expensive. Following the analysis of each of the major sections, there should be at least an informal sense of where the problems and opportunities lie. Frequently, this is a formal procedure. If so, following the completion of all the analyses, you will want to summarize the problems and opportunities. Similarly, if you follow the SWOT format, you'll want to lay out the strengths, opportunities, weaknesses, and threats to provide the basis for decision making, which usually follows soon after the above analyses. We begin to discuss these decisions in Chapter 4.

CAMPAIGN PROGRESS CHECKLIST

At this point in the campaign you should generally be aware of the following points:

1. The basic purpose of the market analysis is to identify and understand those geographical areas that are most likely to respond favorably to the marketing communication campaign.

2. A good way to evaluate the relative importance of a market is to look at the amount of product usage and the number of current users in the area.

3. Index numbers are a quick way to assess how a market compares to other markets based on product usage and other demographic variables.

4. Professionals can use geodemographic systems to define their targets in terms of various geographical sizes such as ZIP codes, postal carrier routes, and blocks.

5. The major purpose of the product analysis is to determine how the product characteristics match up with consumers' needs, wants, and interests.

6. Often, the most important product characteristics are the images, personalities, or values associated with the brand name.

7. To get a complete picture of how the product is matching up with the needs and wants of consumers, it is also necessary to look at a brand's pricing, distribution, and promotion.

8. In analyzing competition, it's important to analyze both the direct competition within the product category and indirect competition, which can come from many sources.

9. To thoroughly analyze the competition, rival companies should be understood in as much depth as the analyst's company.

10. An especially valuable way to analyze the competition is to compare media expenditures and creative themes.

11. Following the analysis of the background information, it's often helpful to summarize the problems and opportunities (perhaps in a SWOT format).

Notes and References

[1]Some of this information is from promotional material by Claritas, Inc.

[2]D.J. Curry, *The New Marketing Research Systems: How to Use Strategic Database Information for Better Marketing Decisions* (New York: John Wiley, 1993), p. 255.

[3]Adapted from Philip Kotler, *Marketing Management: Analysis, Planning, Implementation, and Control, 8th Ed.* (Englewood Cliffs, NJ: Prentice Hall, 1994), p. 98.

[4]For more information on 11-point scales, see William R. Dillon, Thomas J. Madden, and Neil H. Firtle, *Essentials of Marketing Research* (Homewood, IL: Irwin, 1993), p. 279.

[5]D.H. Pink, *Metaphor Marketing* (April/May 1998), pp. 214–229.

[6]T.C. Kinnear and J.R. Taylor, *Marketing Research: An Applied Approach, 3rd Ed.* (New York: McGraw-Hill, 1987), p. 536.

[7]D.S. Tull and D.I. Hawkins, *Marketing Research: Measurement and Method, 4th Ed.* (New York: Macmillan, 1987), p. 286.

[8]"Do You Know Your Competitive Brand Data?" *Media Decisions* (August 1975), p. 60.

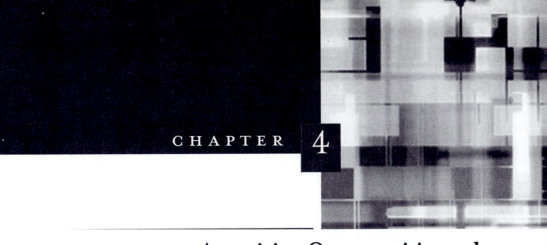

CHAPTER 4

Appraising Opportunities and Setting Objectives

When the background analysis is finished, it's time to reach conclusions and make decisions. Because information gathering is an ongoing process, all decisions should be revised whenever new information is received.

The first major conclusion to reach is the determination of how much value there is either in the company's name or in the brands it sells. The second and third conclusions are to determine problems and opportunities. These conclusions provide direction for the developing campaign.

The first decision is to define the target market. The discovery and identification of problems and opportunities form the basis for setting campaign objectives and influence the delineation of the target audience. The campaign objectives provide direction to the rest of the campaign. Organizationally, the campaign should proceed roughly as shown in Figure 4-1.

PURSUING BRAND EQUITY

Businesses do not want consumers to comparison shop. This statement is as true for large firms as it is for small retail operations. Companies may tell consumers they want them to shop around, but they don't really mean it. They want consumers to buy their products or shop in their stores because of what their name represents. These names have value, or equity, to a company in the same way that a firm has equity in the assets it owns. After reviewing the background analysis, the analyst should at least have a general idea of how much equity a company currently possesses, and how much it can acquire.

Companies put brand names on products to distinguish them from other products. Naming a product provides consumers with something tangible they can use to associate with thoughts, feelings, and images. If these associations are positive, the advertiser has gained some measure of control over consumers' future purchases. These associations provide advertisers with a value they can use to persuade consumers to buy their product. (This value is independent of the product's physical qualities and is called **brand equity.**)

FIGURE 4-1	FLOW CHART OF CAMPAIGN PROCESS

Situation Analysis

Determine Equity

Identify Problems

Uncover Opportunities

Define Target Market

Develop Strategy
(such as message and media)

Execute Tactics
(such as message and media)

For example, telling someone you own an expensive electric guitar says something about the kind of instrument you own. It might also suggest you are a cool individual if you go on to say the guitar is a leading brand such as Gibson instead of a minor brand like Silvertone (i.e., a legendary Sears brand). If you expand further and state you have a vintage Les Paul model, many music lovers and musicians would recognize immediately that you own the preferred brand of many legendary rock and blues guitarists and would extend you deferential acknowledgment. Consumers are usually willing to pay the premium price because of the extra value they derive from owning the Les Paul name. The name and its associations have become company assets.

AVOIDING PRICE COMPETITION

Companies want repeat business for their products. Most firms do not like to compete strictly on the basis of price. Price competitors often devote so much of their effort to being the low-cost producer that they have insufficient resources left over for product development. This situation can be profitable as long as the firm keeps its costs low. Invariably, firms lose their low-cost advantage because other companies find ways to operate more cheaply, or because competitors shift their manufacturing facilities to countries with lower labor costs. Advertisers invest in developing brand equity to avoid price competition, especially as competitive products approach parity. The more value a company can add to its brands, the less likely it will have to compete on a price basis. Building the brand can be as important to a company as improving a product's quality.

COMPETING ON THE BASIS OF QUALITY

Companies also strive to compete through product innovation. In many mature consumer-goods categories, this type of competition is difficult. Even when a firm is able to develop differentiating qualities for its products, it seldom takes long for the competition to duplicate the product. When Procter & Gamble developed the first soft, chewable cookies, it test-marketed them before distributing the product nationally. By the time the product went into national distribution, Nabisco, Keebler, and Frito-Lay all had comparable products in the marketplace.[1]

National brands also face formidable competition from private labels along a variety of fronts. General merchandise retailers, such as Wal-Mart, sell generic equivalents under their own labels. Private-label suppliers, such as Perrigo (which sells personal care and over-the-counter products) and Sovex Inc. (which specializes in cereal knockoffs), continue to encroach into product categories where traditional brands have been dominant. Major brands also compete against themselves as companies such as Ralston-Purina and Keebler introduce private-label products into markets in which they already compete with their own national brands. Apparently, they are willing to cannibalize the sales of their own brands because of the perception, "if they don't enter the private-label market, another company will."[2]

BRAND NAMES REMAIN IMPORTANT

The result of this multifaceted competition is a dynamic marketplace that replicates the status quo with unprecedented quickness. The traditional notion of carefully and deliberately building brand loyalty through heavy doses of consumer advertising, liberal amounts of sales promotion, and solid, intensive promotion work within the distribution channel has been largely refined by the idea that all of these activities will continue to be important in the twenty-first century—and beyond—but they will all have to be done much more quickly.

The traditional analogy of building brand equity as a mason builds a wall upon a strong foundation should be reconceived as a hunter sighting a target at point-blank range. The target is surprisingly difficult to hit because not only is the target moving quickly, so is the hunter. Still, the target can be hit.

Progressive companies understand that achieving brand equity will continue to be an important corporate goal, but they also appreciate that they cannot rest upon past achievements. Successful companies of the future will not build brand equity so much as they will pursue brand equity.

An important function of the situation analysis is to assess the company's brand equity. To both pursue and build brand equity, a successful campaign will have to solve problems and exploit opportunities.

█ DEFINING PROBLEMS AND IDENTIFYING OPPORTUNITIES

Problem solving seems to be a driving force in the management style of some firms who are constantly adapting to new problems or crises. These companies seem to be perpetually fighting fires. One of the qualities of a good strategic thinker is the ability to anticipate, so sound strategic planners try to avoid fires by focusing on prevention.

In marketing, **a problem is any barrier or situation that makes it difficult to achieve an objective, whether past, present, or future.** For a company to survive, it must be able to solve its problems and achieve its objectives. In marketing, problems are often discussed in terms of how they relate to sales or market share. A common cause of many marketing problems is communication, or its more commercial version, promotion. Of all the variables in the marketing mix, promotion is the easiest to manipulate and, frequently, the easiest to get wrong.

There are only so many things one can do with the price, distribution, or product line. It is impractical to keep changing these elements every week, month, or even year. Because of the complexity inherent in the promotion area, many of the marketing problems can be traced to communication or message problems. Is the company transmitting the most persuasive message? Is the chosen medium the most cost-efficient? To what extent are consumers aware of the products? Some of the marketing problems may be traced also to difficulties with distribution, pricing, or product development. The reader may want to consult a book on marketing management for more details.

If a company is very good at solving its problems, it can turn them into marketing opportunities. For a company to be a leader in its field, it must be able to consistently capitalize on its opportunities. **An opportunity is a situation or a circumstance that can potentially give the company a marketing advantage.** Opportunities are based on assumptions that a company both wants to take advantage of a situation and *can*. Listed in Exhibit 4-1 are some classic examples of companies that were able to transform a marketing problem into an opportunity.

Sometimes the difference between a problem and an opportunity depends on how one looks at a situation. The thick consistency of Heinz ketchup can be viewed as either a problem or an opportunity. Persons who correctly see opportunities where others see only problems are considered good leaders. When leaders see opportunity where others cannot, they get elevated to visionary status.

Not surprisingly, problems can't simply be transformed into an opportunity merely by taking an optimistic attitude. Factors internal and external to the firm can have a significant bearing on the extent to which a firm can capitalize on its opportunities.

EXTERNAL FACTORS

A number of conditions under which a firm has little control can often have a profound influence on its ability to take advantage of an opportunity. The political and legal environment, especially in foreign countries,

EXHIBIT 4-1 VIEWING A PROBLEM AS AN OPPORTUNITY

Product: Arm & Hammer baking soda
Problem: Its use for cooking limits its market potential.
Opportunity: Develop new uses for the product (for example, as a freshener in refrigerators and freezers, or as a deodorizer to sprinkle on rugs).

Product: Miller Lite beer
Problem: Male heavy drinkers perceive low-calorie products as not very masculine.
Opportunity: Associate the product with very masculine men.

Product: Heinz ketchup
Problem: Product pours too slowly for some users.
Opportunity: Associate slow pouring with richness.

Product: Smucker's jelly and jam
Problem: Has a funny sounding name.
Opportunity: Suggest that the quality must be especially good to overcome the funny name (With a name like Smucker's, it has to be good®).

can make it difficult and sometimes next to impossible for firms to get even the simplest venture started.

The cultural and social conditions of a state, region, or country are usually so pervasive as to make it inadvisable for firms to buck existing trends. McDonald's understood that when opening restaurants in India, a country where most people do not eat beef, it would have to operate significantly differently than it does in the United States. One difference in India is that McDonald's sells vegetable-based burgers. Similarly, what might sell well in Nashville may not do well in Seattle. It does not take a sophisticated market research study to predict that grits are not likely to do as well in the Northwest as they do in the Southeast, no matter how much promotion they receive.

It is also wise to look at economic conditions. Introducing an expensive product during a recession may be possible but probably not as easy as during a period of economic expansion.

INTERNAL FACTORS

In evaluating whether to pursue an opportunity, a firm needs to carefully differentiate between a vision and a dream. In marketing, the word *visionary* has come to refer to someone who sees an opportunity and understands whether the company has sufficient resources to take advantage of it. Dreamers also see opportunities, but they are unrealistic about a company's ability to develop and execute successful strategies to see the dream come to fruition. To pursue opportunities, firms usually need adequate resources in three major areas: finance, production, and marketing.

Financial Resources

To compete even on a local level, companies are often best advised to have sufficient capital resources to initiate action and to sustain the activity over time. Many small-business owners underestimate the cost of doing business. For example, restaurants selling pizza can get by with a relatively small overhead as long as they restrict their sales to within the store. If they expand their business to include home delivery, expenses can increase considerably. To speed up the baking of the pizza, which it will have to do to be competitive, the operation will probably require a conveyor oven (very expensive). To cover mounting costs, the company will have to draw business from an area larger than its current customer base.

With this kind of investment, the company runs the risk of getting in over its head, particularly when it faces the prospect of significant promotional expenses. The small pizza operation that thought it would be able to compete based on word of mouth is faced with financial demands it is unable to meet. Businesses like this can and do lose a lot of money. On a national scale, financial requirements become even more important.

Production Resources

Thinking up new product concepts or services is a lot easier than producing the product or implementing the service. As the saying goes, "The devil is in the details." In the fast-food business, many people will tell you that operational details doom more restaurants than the product concept. New product ideas do not become opportunities unless the company has sufficient resources to ensure that a quality product gets produced at a competitive cost. In the short run, the firm needs managerial expertise, technological competence, and physical facilities. In the long run, the firm can acquire or buy these things, but opportunities generally do not last over an extended period.

Marketing Resources

Ford Motor Co. was reputed to be one of the most dominant companies in the history of the world. Yet many of the readers of this book think of Ford as the number-two automobile company behind General Motors. The difference is that Henry Ford's genius was in his ability to marshal production resources to sell cars, and the genius of Alfred Sloan of General Motors was in marketing. Henry Ford's myopic view that the company only sell black automobiles regardless of consumer wants is nearly unthinkable today. It underscores the importance of having marketing-savvy people in decision-making positions.

▌OPPORTUNITIES

Following the analysis of the background information, it should be apparent where opportunities exist in each of the areas analyzed: the company and its resources, the consumer, the market, the product (including its price, distribution, and promotion), and the competition. Opportunities within the consumer area should receive prominence. The classic mistake is to confuse what the company would like to sell with what consumers want to purchase. When seeking out opportunities, the focus generally should be on ways to increase sales. There are four basic ways to increase sales:

1. Get current users to continue using the brand.
2. Get current users of the brand to use more of the product.
3. Find new uses for the product.
4. Find new users.

1. *Retaining Current Users.* Getting current users to continue using the brand should be the foundation on which all strategy aimed at stimulating demand is based. Generally, it's cheaper and easier to convince someone to buy something he or she is already using. This much is obvious. However, it is important to remember that competitors actively try to persuade consumers to switch brands. This is frequently accomplished by undermining a consumer's loyalty to a brand. Brand leaders especially will often remind consumers that they are making the right decision by purchasing their brand. For example, Hertz is the category leader in rental cars. It likes to remind its consumers that even though there are other rent-a-car companies that are cheaper, "There's Hertz, and 'not exactly'" (to quote a tagline it has used in recent years).

2. *Getting Current Users to Use More.* Increasing product use by current users is also a popular way to expand sales. The Hanes Her Way® sports bra is now promoted for everyday use following company research that showed that the surge in girls' athletics is causing the demo (short for demographic) to request the garment for everyday use. The National Fluid Milk Processor Promotion Board with its "Got milk?" campaign encourages people to drink three glasses of milk a day (knowing most adults do not). The Michigan Dental Association reminds the public, "Don't be six months late for your six-month checkup." Advertisers sometimes urge consumers to use more of a product by encouraging them with price deals such as buy one get one free (BOGO). Another way to get consumers to use more of a product is to find new uses for it.

3. *Finding New Uses for a Product.* This is accomplished relatively easily with a food product by developing new recipes. The pages of *Family Circle* and *Woman's Day* are filled with numerous ideas on how to use existing products in new, if only slightly different, ways. Arm & Hammer Baking Soda has successfully persuaded consumers to put this product, which was developed for use in baking, in refrigerators to absorb odors. Now it encourages consumers to sprinkle the powder on rugs before vacuuming and on cat litter boxes to prevent odors. By expanding the category, Arm & Hammer gets new users it might not have otherwise.

4. *Finding New Users.* Getting new users for the brand is a lot like prospecting for gold. A good place to begin is to look where you have already been successful. Next, you'll probably want to look where other companies have found success. At this point, you'll

want to evaluate how much profit you can make searching for gold where it has already been found, or whether it is economically justifiable to start looking for new places. In advertising, you prospect for new users by identifying characteristics that current users possess in common, such as demographic and psychographic variables. One problem with this approach is these variables may not have the same sales predictive power in a new market as they had in the old market.

When seeking ways to expand sales, consider opportunities associated with the following:

- Changing consumer needs, wants, or interests
- Changing consumer lifestyles
- Emerging markets in the United States
- Emerging markets overseas
- Established markets overseas
- Product or brand advantages
- Service strengths
- New technologies
- Pricing advantages
- Distribution strengths
- Marketing and promotional strengths[3]

One of the most important opportunities to identify is where the business is going to come from. This opportunity, of course, refers to the **target audience, or target market.** This decision helps provide the foundation upon which the campaign is built. *Note: some planners make the mistake of defining the target market immediately following the consumer analysis.* This decision should be deferred until all the analyses are complete to be sure the company has sufficient resources to satisfy the consumer's needs, wants, or interests.

THE TARGET MARKET DECISION

Engel, Warshaw, and Kinnear discuss three basic options with regard to this decision: undifferentiated marketing, differentiated marketing, and concentrated marketing.[4] The **undifferentiated market** essentially treats the audience as one mass market. A company must use sufficiently broad but still fairly dramatic creative appeals to be effective with so many diverse subgroups in this overall category. As the marketplace has become increasingly competitive, this approach has decreased in use because rival firms undercut it by targeting a subgroup in the market with a focused and usually more effective appeal. A variation of this option is to target only the largest segment of the overall market, usually the so-called heavy half.

The **differentiated market** is probably the most widely used option today. With differentiated markets, companies may (1) divide the market into segments (usually called primary, secondary, and tertiary markets); (2) identify a target audience, or market, and refer to target groups within that category; or (3) simply call all targets market segments. Cigarette companies have long used a segmented market approach, as do many companies that offer multiple brands in product categories where the products are similar. A good part of the early success of General Motors can be traced to its strategic decision to divide the overall car market into segments and to develop products that catered to the differentiated market segments.

The **concentrated market** option, also referred to as a **market niche,** assumes that a firm will achieve more success targeting a smaller segment in the overall market than by competing directly against the market-share leader in all segments. The niche marketer runs a risk by conceding the largest segment of the market to another, usually larger company. The market-share leader that has built up brand equity over a broader base may decide to confront the niche marketer head-on with a new product. The leader would be trading on its brand equity to acquire market share from the smaller market while maintaining the same market share in the larger segments. Gatorade, the leader in the sports drink market, undoubtedly realized that once Coca-Cola and PepsiCo decided to enter the sports beverage market, share erosion was all but inevitable because of the substantial brand equity associated with the Coke and Pepsi brand and their extensive distribution systems. On the other hand, PepsiCo, realizing the power of the Gatorade brand, purchased the brand for its own line of beverages, thus solving a problem for both brands.

DELINEATING THE TARGET MARKET

It is important to be sensitive to how information about the target market will be used. Creative people look for insight into the consumer to help them develop and craft persuasive messages; media planners and buyers look for some special piece of information that they can use to deliver these messages efficiently or creatively. Early in the campaign, the determination of the target market is done largely in outline form. Later, the creative and media personnel will use the information discussed in the consumer analysis and their own thinking to define the target audience in greater detail. Typically, the target market should be defined, or delineated, taking into account at least some of the following criteria:

- Demographic variables
- Psychographic variables (including lifestyle)
- Product usage (heavy, medium, or light)
- Brand loyalty
- Consumers' needs and wants
- Consumers' interests
- Consumers' problems
- Consumers' motivations

█SETTING OBJECTIVES

After the target market has been defined, the next step is to translate opportunities into objectives. Setting objectives is one of the key decisions in any campaign, and it is one of the hardest. First, planners should determine what advertising, or any other form of communication, can accomplish that will lead to sales. Increase brand awareness? Change an image? Increase consumer understanding of how the product works?

Next, they need to be specific about the desired level of awareness or understanding, or what kind of an image they want the change to portray.

Most businesspeople will tell you that their advertising objective is to sell the product. What they may not realize is that even though the ultimate goal may be to generate sales, to achieve this objective, some mental effect has to take place in the minds of consumers. For some brands, this intervening goal may be increasing awareness; for others, it may be to change consumer attitudes or upgrade a brand's image. These intervening goals are sometimes called communication effects.

One analogy looks at the football coach preparing his locker-room speech at halftime. The team is losing. What does he tell them? Try harder. Focus more. Most coaches know that this type of old-style motivational speech can actually produce counterproductive results with the team becoming overly tense or tight. Coaches know that they have to be prepared with a full analysis of the situation before they enter the locker room. If the basic problem is that the team is not completing enough passes, then the coach needs to determine the reason why and whether any coaching adjustments can be made to correct the situation. Is the offense too predictable? Are the offensive linemen not giving the quarterback enough time? The coach's message to the players must address the specific problem.

The solutions to the team's problems are a lot like the objectives one can set for an advertising campaign. There are many different goals one can try to accomplish, but individually the achievement of one objective is unlikely to guarantee winning or sales. So the coach might suggest that the offensive coordinator mix up the offense more, have the receivers run different patterns, change blocking assignments. Put in a new quarterback. Or the coach can do what a lot of advertisers do: Keep trying, keep the faith, and hope things work out.

Setting objectives is a discipline that presents many problems. In addition to trying to measure objectives, some people feel that the process of researching, determining, and writing the objectives takes more time than they can afford. Others worry that setting specific objectives may make them more accountable than they would prefer. Setting and writing objectives can be difficult. Aside from generating sales and sales leads, creating awareness, and improving images, executives often feel unsure about what else they can say. Some of the problems with understanding objective setting are due to semantic confusion, but most of the difficulty results from an inadequate understanding of the various principles that underlie the setting of objectives. Most of the principles in the following section have evolved out of George Odiorne's classic work on management by objectives (MBO).[5]

DEFINITION OF OBJECTIVES

An objective is the desired end of an action—what one expects to accomplish. In MBO terminology, an objective is an effectiveness standard. In an advertising or marketing campaign, all of the strategies and tactics—including creative ideas—are designed to achieve certain results. These results are the objectives, although a practitioner may not refer to them as such. Some people distinguish between an objective and a goal. We use the words interchangeably to represent a desirable, specific end.[6]

FUNCTION OF OBJECTIVES

Why set objectives? Some argue that they take time that is better spent elsewhere, like talking about strategy or ideas. Objectives provide direction so everyone is working toward the same end—with a minimum of detours. In the creative area, all messages should convey the same feel, information, or variation of the same idea. Media strategy and tactics should focus on the same audiences.

Setting objectives serves to communicate to all those charged with the responsibility of achieving the objectives exactly what is expected of them. Logically, the achievement of an objective should solve some problem or exploit an opportunity.

An objective is also established to provide for accountability. Objectives serve as standards against which the output or performance of a person or a unit can be evaluated. In the production area of a firm, setting objectives is a long-established practice. For example, in many factories, production goals (sometimes referred to as quotas) are established for individuals and departments. In the production area it is relatively easy to set objectives because the output is tangible.

In advertising, it is often difficult to establish a direct causal relationship between advertising and sales because advertising is only one of many variables influencing sales. People disagree about the nature of objectives in advertising. Some say objectives should be stated in terms of sales; others want objectives defined in terms of communication effects, such as awareness or attitude shift.

MARKETING VERSUS ADVERTISING GOALS

Most advertising is basically designed to sell a product or service. However, people do not automatically buy a product after they are exposed to an ad. First, they have thoughts or feelings about a product, and then they buy it (or don't buy it). Advertising and other types of marketing communication directly affect consumers' mental processes. Advertising can be thought of as a stimulus that produces a response or an effect.

If the objective is to provide direction to the strategist, then it must indicate specifically what thoughts or feelings an ad should evoke. These thoughts and feelings can be defined in terms of communication criteria, such as awareness and attitude. In other words, if advertising can stimulate an awareness or a favorable attitude in a consumer, then these effects may trigger a purchase response. Therefore, it makes little sense to set sales as an objective for advertising because these communication effects *precede* sales.

The effects that intervene between advertising and sales are usually the goals that advertising, or any other type of marketing communication, should strive to accomplish. These goals, indirect in nature, can be thought of as communication objectives. In most situations, advertising objectives should be formulated as communication objectives.

There are exceptions to this advice. New procedures are being developed and refined with scanner technology that increasingly allow a researcher to isolate the particular effect of advertising on sales. These procedures combine data from consumer panels with information from both in-home and retail scanners of UPC-coded items. The consumer data include information on broadcasting and print exposure, sales promotion activities, and price information. Because the data on media exposure, sales promotion, pricing, and product usage all come from the same sample, it is called **single-source data.** The two largest systems, SCAN-TRACK from ACNielsen and InfoScan from Information Resources, Inc., have been discontinued. These systems reportedly were expensive and time consuming. It will be interesting to see whether these systems or similar ones are used in the future, given the potential single-source data systems have in tying a direct causal relationship between advertising and sales. (Late-breaking information suggests that Arbitron has a new single-source measurement system in development.)

In some types of direct marketing, researchers are also able to trace a sale to a specific advertisement. However, unless an advertiser uses a single-source system, it is usually easier to evaluate the effectiveness of advertising by measuring the achievement of communication goals than by measuring sales.

Even with single-source data, there are still numerous unmeasured variables that can affect a sale. The effects of advertising frequently interact with a consumer's response to a product's quality, price, service arrangements, and distribution to produce a combined effect that stimulates a sale. Some uncontrollable variables are also at play, such as the economic and political environment, competitive activity, and even the weather. Thus, it is often difficult to isolate the effect of advertising on sales, particularly because advertising often affects sales over a lengthy period. Therefore, advertising objectives formulated in terms of communication criteria provide a better measure of accountability than objectives formulated in terms of sales.

Still, it is hard to convince many people that sales are not the relevant measure. Some advertisers would rather define advertising objectives in terms of sales because they have difficulty accepting the value of using communication criteria for their advertising objectives. We then suggest using communication criteria as the core elements in the creative objectives. Until measurement problems linking advertising to sales are overcome (including expense), planners should consider setting advertising objectives in terms of communication criteria. These criteria should be formulated to provide a critical link tying advertising to sales.

PLANNING THE OBJECTIVES

To devise an effective strategy, the planner must determine precisely the role that advertising and related communication play in the purchase decision. This role is sometimes called the **communication task.** Over the years, there have been a number of attempts to conceptualize the effects of communication and to relate them to consumer behavior. Implicit in these efforts is the notion that consumers pass through a number of stages on their way to a purchase decision.

Colley, in his so-called DAGMAR approach (Defining Advertising Goals for Measured Advertising Results), suggests five steps through which a brand must climb to gain acceptance: unawareness, awareness, comprehension and image, attitude, and action.[7] Robert Lavidge and Gary Steiner suggest six steps: awareness, knowledge, liking, preference, conviction, and purchase. Their model, which has received wide exposure, further examined the sociopsychological underpinnings of each of these steps.[8]

Each of these models discusses psychological constructs such as attitude, knowledge, and comprehension. These constructs exist within consumer's minds, where they are, of course, not directly observable and therefore difficult to measure. Just as Colley and Lavidge and Steiner do not see eye to eye on the abstract and complex nature of these concepts, there are other differing opinions about the importance of the various communication criteria discussed in these models and their effect on influencing sales. There are also differing opinions about whether consumers need to pass through each phase on the way from awareness to a purchase decision: Must consumers understand how a product operates before they make a purchase? How important is liking the product (or a commercial)? How important is the brand image versus the physical qualities of the product?

Answers to these questions are important because they provide the core elements of a campaign's objectives. Although these are difficult questions, the communication effects will be the impressions (i.e., the thoughts or feelings) that a campaign leaves with consumers. If the planner makes good decisions, the effects, if achieved, should stimulate sales.

Communication Tasks

Advertising plays an important part in stimulating sales. It may be helpful to think of each communication task as consisting of both a communication effect and an action word that indicates what is supposed to be done with respect to the effect. For example, awareness is a common communication effect. But simply saying that the advertising task is to generate awareness may not provide clear direction to creatives. It may also be a mistake if awareness is not the problem.

During the debate over the effectiveness of the Nissan "Enjoy the ride" campaign (as discussed in Chapter 1), comments in the trade papers indicated that the campaign was an awareness campaign. Was this a problem? Even if its top-of-mind awareness was low, do prospects for this type of car buy the first name they think of? Maybe for a soft drink, or a can of beer, people order the first brand that comes to mind, but for a $20,000 automobile probably not.

The first step in determining objectives is to figure out which communication effect is likely to predispose the target audience to buy. For Nissan, the campaign was also designed to give the car an exciting—perhaps even hip—image. However, it's similarly hard for cars and people to appear as something they are not, and more important, what people believe they are not. Think of a Nissan and you're likely to think of a black car (unless you own one of a different color). Though the "Mr. K" campaign was fun and entertaining, people still think of a Nissan as a practical car. Follow-up campaigns have focused more on product attributes that reflect the car's quality and engineering. However, perceptions can change, and they probably have for Nissan, but usually it takes some time.

Once you determine the particular effect you want the campaign to achieve, the next step is to determine what you would like to see happen with respect to the desired effect. Pepsi Cola has been fairly successful at getting across the idea that it is a modern, if not hip, drink for young-minded people. Pepsi sells a lot of soft drinks with this image, even if it is not as much as the company would like. Because this image works, the communication task shouldn't be to change this image (remember, Pepsi would like to sell more). Pepsi's task is to *intensify* its image. For other campaigns, words such as *establish, maintain, increase,* or *change* are action words that indicate the desired status of the effect the campaign is designed to achieve. So one might increase or establish awareness, change an image or attitude, maintain or increase brand preference. One could also set as a goal increasing the levels of trust or liking in a brand. Exhibit 4-2 includes some common communication effects and associated action words.

EXHIBIT 4-2 OBJECTIVES AND THEIR ACTION WORDS

Desired Communication Effect	Action Associated with Effect
Awareness (top-of-mind) (brand) (specific product qualities) (of ingredients) (the omission of ingredients)	Establish, maintain, or increase.
Comprehension or understanding	Establish, maintain, or increase.
Conviction or believability	Establish, maintain, increase, or reinforce.
Trust	Establish, maintain, increase, or reinforce.
Attitude	Establish, maintain, reinforce, or change.
Image	Establish, maintain, reinforce, change, or intensify.

WRITING THE OBJECTIVES

Communication objectives should be written down. This step facilitates communication by providing a common set of short-term, intermediate, and long-term goals to guide decision making. It also establishes standards that clearly indicate the basis on which a campaign will be evaluated. Writing the objectives reduces the likelihood of a misunderstanding or misinterpretation of what is expected. People get sick; executives leave. Having written objectives helps ensure that work continues along the correct path.

Writing objectives requires a thorough understanding of the principles that underlie the setting of sound objectives. Ten criteria to consider in planning and writing objectives follow.

A CONCEPTUAL FOUNDATION FOR SETTING OBJECTIVES

The principle that objectives should be specific and measurable is well established in advertising literature. However, students and practitioners may still encounter a number of problems unless they consider the following criteria.

Unit Oriented.   Objectives should be set for each unit in an organization that performs a task. In advertising, the relevant tasks generally are associated with the marketing, advertising, creative (message), and media areas, as well as other types of marketing communication, such as sales promotion and public relations. Even though one person or department may be responsible for decisions in more than one area, it is helpful to set separate objectives for each area. A typical campaign report should include marketing, advertising, creative, media, and marketing communication objectives as long as there are strategies and tactics in place to achieve the goals.

Objectives should not be set for a unit unless that unit (or department) can achieve the desired result independently. A common mistake is to confuse marketing goals with advertising goals. For example, "to sell X number of units" is clearly a marketing objective because selling a product requires a combination of various activities, such as those associated with product quality, price, distribution, and promotion, that are not normally under the control of the advertising unit. Objectives should be set so that the tasks necessary to achieve the goals are clearly the responsibility of a specific unit.

A staff member working within a unit or area deserves to be rewarded not only for his or her contribution to a unit but also for the unit's contribution to the organization even if the overall effort may be a failure. Formulating objectives that are unit oriented helps provide for each unit's accountability.

Unit Linked.   All efforts that are oriented toward goals should be linked with one another. Both the creative plan and the media plan in an advertising campaign have their own set of objectives, and these objectives should be compatible. These goals must be directly connected to an advertising objective that, in turn, is tied into a marketing objective. Similarly, marketing goals must be compatible with production goals and finance goals and directly linked to corporate goals. Suppose, for example, the firm Acme's New Age Drinks had recently introduced a beverage. Exhibit 4-3 illustrates how its corporate goals might be linked to advertising goals.

In an actual campaign, a number of objectives would be written for each unit; the examples in Exhibit 4-3 illustrate how objectives link together. From this perspective, one can see how the objectives of an advertising campaign are usually linked to sales even though a sales figure is not established as an objective of the advertising effort.

Linking objectives avoids overlap, a situation in which two units are responsible for accomplishing the same thing. **Overlap** often occurs when a goal like increasing sales is written as both a marketing and an advertising objective. **Underlap** occurs when no unit is assigned the responsibility of achieving a result, as sometimes occurs with sales promotion. The marketing unit may expect the advertising unit to develop the program and vice versa. Writing objectives that are unit linked should avoid overlap and underlap.

Output Oriented. Many written statements of the objective incorrectly focus on an activity, or input, rather than on the desired result, or output. In other words, the strategy and tactics are confused with the objective. To appeal to consumers' desires for safety can be part of the message strategy. An input-oriented objective might read, "to associate Brand X with safe or security-inspiring situations"; an output-oriented objective would

---

EXHIBIT 4-3	LINKING OBJECTIVES

1. *Corporate objective:* to increase the rate of profit from 5% to 7% of sales by the year 2006.
2a. *Financial objective:* to secure $10 million in capital to finance the construction of a new production facility within the next six months.
2b. *Production objective:* to produce 100,000 cases of Fruit Juicy by the end of the first quarter.
2c. *Marketing objective:* to increase sales of Fruit Juicy 300% compared to the previous year by the end of the year.
3. *Advertising objective:* to establish top-of-mind awareness in 70% of the target market by the end of October 2007.
4a. *Creative objective:* to establish in the minds of the target market an association between the trade character, JUICE MAN, and Fruit Juicy.
4b. *Media objective:* to reach 85% of the target market by the end of the year.
4c. *Sales promotion objective:* to get 20% of the target market to play the tropical sweepstakes game during the first quarter.

rephrase the statement to read, "to develop within the target market a feeling that Brand X is a safe product." Both statements have approximately the same meaning, but input-oriented statements focus on what the company is doing, which is part of the strategy, whereas an output-oriented statement focuses on the end results. Focusing on the desired result rather than the activity is a better indication of advertising effectiveness. Output-oriented statements are expressed in a way that lends them to evaluation.

Time Bounded.   An advertising campaign is usually completed within a specified period, frequently one year. The progress made in the campaign should be reviewed at various points during the campaign. Objectives should reflect an expectation that specific results will be achieved by specific dates. For example, one might set as an advertising objective "to achieve brand awareness for brand X fruit drinks in 50% of the target market within the first three months of the campaign" (or by a specific date). A second objective might be "to achieve 70% awareness by the end of the second three-month period." Time-bounded objectives establish benchmarks that allow a campaign to be evaluated, or tracked, over time. Increasingly, objectives are likely to be set for periods shorter than one year because of rapidly changing market conditions.

Realistic.   Objectives in this category should be neither overambitious nor underambitious—they should be attainable. Some executives may set their objectives at levels they do not expect to achieve but just to give them something to aim for. These are sometimes called **stretch objectives.** In MBO terminology this situation is an overload, a condition that presents definite problems when trying to evaluate the effectiveness of a unit. Unrealistic objectives only indicate what the planner would like to achieve, not what can be achieved. Even worse, if a firm is using the objective-and-task method of determining the size of the advertising budget, it will set the objectives and then figure out the cost of achieving them. Unrealistically high objectives may increase the budget out of proportion to the value received in achieving the goals. An underload exists when a firm sets its objectives at a level so low that they can be achieved with little or no effort. Unrealistic objectives fail to communicate exactly what is expected from the advertising effort.

Common Effectiveness.   Certain responsibilities relating to effectiveness are common to most units. Such responsibilities as to organize, plan, reach the target market efficiently, be creative, or do the best job for the least amount of money are standards of effectiveness referred to as common effectiveness. They are usually an implicit part of a standard job description. An employer or client expects these standards to be maintained by an employee or an agency. Establishing these standards as objectives is only stating the obvious.

Singularity of Purpose.   For purposes of clarity and ease of evaluation, each objective should be worded so that only one result is associated with each statement. For example, a message strategy may be designed to get prospects to associate "economy of operation" and "high quality" with a particular brand. Is this one objective or two objectives? Having separate objectives prevents the confusion that may occur when only half of a dual objective is achieved. Objectives that are stated in paragraph form or objectives that include three or four desired results in one statement will eventually have to be separated in the evaluation phase of campaign. Otherwise, the researcher ends up having to clarify the results by saying, "We achieved this part of the objective but not that part." It is wiser and more efficient to separate multifaceted goals into distinct goals at the beginning of a campaign rather than at the end.

Measurable.   If an objective is to provide accountability, it must be measurable. Problems with measurement account for much of the reluctance to quantify objectives. Measuring communication criteria is still an imprecise science. Many decision makers undoubtedly feel that there is no sense in quantifying objectives if the measurement techniques are weak. Notwithstanding, even when measurement problems are too difficult to overcome or too costly to resolve, it is still advisable to quantify objectives whenever possible because quantification adds precision to the sense of direction a campaign must follow.

Although it is possible to quantify objectives for the major decision-making areas in advertising, quantifying objectives in the creative area may not make as much sense because of the subjective nature of many message variables (such as image and attitude). Because the specific relationship between these communication criteria and a marketing goal (such as sales) is seldom precisely known, it is no wonder that copywriters and art directors often experience uneasiness when the "quant jocks" evaluate their work. A secondary problem could also occur if the copywriters take measurement too seriously and develop ads that score high on tests but not so well in the marketplace. Similarly, insisting that all media objectives be quantified may place unwanted restraints on creative media planners (see Chapter 7).

An inexperienced decision maker, and in particular students, may regard attempts to quantify objectives as strictly arbitrary and usually just guesstimates. Students may be correct if inexperienced evaluators are doing the work. Talking about things such as establishing new levels of awareness is difficult unless the planner knows what the existing levels are. As one becomes more experienced, quantifying objectives becomes more realistic and meaningful.

Inexperienced decision makers can use the following process to help develop precision in quantifying advertising objectives.

1. Estimate the marketing objectives in terms of either sales or share of market.
2. Determine the specific role advertising should play in the overall marketing mix.
3. Set the appropriate advertising (or communication) objectives. If the budget has not been set, it becomes primarily a matter of determining what it will cost to achieve the objectives (measured by estimating media costs). If the budget has already been set, then the

decision maker compares the cost of achieving the media objectives to the size of the budget. If there is a difference, then some revision of the media objectives would have to take place (or there would have to be an increase or decrease in the size of the budget).

4. Revision of the media objectives should be followed by corresponding revisions of the advertising and marketing objectives. Most beginners and students underestimate how many times objectives need to be revised. In fact, all objectives may need to be in a continuous state of revision until the planning of the advertising campaign is completed. When the planning is completed, the objectives should remain firm, though not necessarily etched in stone.

Specific. Formulating specific objectives helps provide a sense of direction for the unit and establishes benchmarks against which the unit's effectiveness can be evaluated. Using words such as *increase, maximize, satisfy,* or *optimize* without specific quantification is vague and leads to problems in evaluating the campaign. For example, if the advertising objectives are stated as "to maximize (or increase) awareness," what is the standard of success? To make everybody in the market aware of the brand, or only as many people as would be economically practical? Writing specific objectives helps avoid these measurement problems.

Cost-Effective. Objectives should always be planned with the idea in mind that they are worth achieving. Because of the difficulty in relating the achievement of communication criteria to sales, it is easy to overlook the cost of achieving the goal. Unless some type of marginal analysis or return on investment is employed, the planner must remember that the process of setting objectives is still the result of executive judgment. Some objectives may be too expensive to accomplish.

TESTING FOR SOUND OBJECTIVES

During the planning stage or after the objectives have been written, it is helpful to test their soundness by asking the questions listed in Exhibit 4-4 for each objective. Following each question, in parentheses, is the aspect of each objective that is being evaluated.

THE IMPACT OF THE WHOLE VERSUS THE PIECES

The new marketing and promotional environment presents a challenge to complex integrated communication campaigns. In the past, large national campaigns often consisted primarily of mass-media advertising supplemented by smaller amounts of local advertising. Sales promotion, direct marketing, and public relations were frequently separate initiatives. It was fairly straightforward to direct and evaluate each promotional effort. National advertising often would be used to build the brand whereas local advertising was more directed at driving immediate consumer buying action. Sales promotion and direct marketing were often used to stimulate sales with price inducements. In the new marketing environment, companies increasingly

---

EXHIBIT 4-4	QUESTIONS TO ASSESS THE SOUNDNESS OF OBJECTIVES

1. Is this something my _____ (insert marketing, advertising, creative, media, or the like) plan can accomplish by itself without underlap or overlap? (Is this unit oriented?)
2. Is this objective linked to an objective in another unit, area, or department? (Is this unit linked?)
3. Is this sentence a statement of a strategy or tactic, or is it something I want my _____ (insert marketing, advertising, creative, media, or the like) plan to accomplish? (Is this output oriented?)
4. Is there a specific date by which I expect to achieve this goal? (Is this time bounded?)
5. Is this objective realistic and attainable, or is it overambitious or underambitious? (Is this realistic?)
6. Is this objective something I would expect of every _____ (insert marketing, advertising, creative, media, or the like) plan? (Is this common effectiveness?)
7. Is this objective too complex? Can it be separated into a number of simpler objectives? (Does this have singularity of purpose?)
8. Can we measure this objective? (Is this objective measurable?)
9. Is this objective as specific as it can be? (Is it specific?)
10. Is the value of this objective to the _____ (insert marketing, advertising, creative, media, or the like) plan commensurate with the cost of accomplishing it? (Is this cost-effective?)

---

are integrating all their communication so that it leaves a seamless selling message with consumers, albeit with separate objectives for each component. This can make it easier to manage the various activities because all the parties involved focus on the same or related goals using different approaches that communicate a consistent brand identity.

The problem is with evaluation. As companies use an increasing number of traditional and nontraditional approaches to deliver messages or impressions designed to achieve closely related objectives, it becomes increasingly difficult to trace a direct causal relationship between a communication and all of its goals. It can be easy to measure the effectiveness of direct mail or advertising on the Internet by coding an ad and measuring sales with the code. However, if this truly is an integrated campaign, than you would also like to know the effect these media had on enhancing or building the brand. So if the click-thru of a banner ad or the sales generated by a direct mail piece don't meet stated goals, it doesn't mean that these initiatives are a failure. The combined or holistic effect of individual promotions can be greater than the sum of the parts measured separately. The synergy of an integrated campaign can be both indirect, as with creating an identity, and direct, as with sales or a click-thru.

SETTING OBJECTIVES AND MYOPIA

It's usually much easier to measure direct behavioral (i.e., sales) effects than communication effects. However, the goal of integrated marketing is to build long-term brand identity and reputation while also driving short-term sales. To achieve this with consistency, specific nonbehavioral objectives must be set and progress regularly evaluated. The breadth of consideration in setting objectives must be equal to the desired breadth of impact for the whole campaign.

ACCOUNTABILITY AND ROI

Many companies struggle with this problem as they strive to improve the effectiveness of their communication programs by holding outside vendors such as an advertising agency accountable for meeting performance standards. Increasingly, they are tying compensation agreements to the achievement of specific goals. General Motors Corp., for example, ties its compensation agreements with all its ad agencies to performance-based standards.[9] This trend is being driven not by marketing managers, but rather by procurement (purchasing) people who are relentlessly examining costs across the board. The CFOs in particular are especially sensitive to how profitability strongly affects stock prices, especially in the short run. Corporate managements are under pressure from the financial community to improve shareholder value. As a result, companies are scrutinizing their marketing communication investments to better understand how they relate to sales and profits as well as communication goals.

The return on investment (ROI) opportunities help a company prioritize decisions on whom to target, how to reach them, and how much to spend.[10] The measurement problems can be daunting, but marketing science tools are improving, especially in the area of customer relationship management (CRM). The implementation of ROI procedures is beyond the scope of this book. However, setting rigorous objectives that provide for accountability is a critical step in any ROI initiative. Students best learn how to do it because it is a core consideration among the smartest companies.

█ REVIEWING KEY DECISIONS

After the objectives are set, the marketing communication strategy can be developed. Before moving on, it is sometimes helpful to review all key decisions as a final check for clarity and cohesiveness. The most important of these decisions is the definition of the target audience. The target may consist of a single segment of the overall population of consumers, or it may consist of multiple segments, as in primary and secondary targets. These segments should be the prime prospects for the company's products.

The next consideration is the set of decisions surrounding objectives for each of the components. At this stage, the marketing objectives should be firm, but the advertising objectives can still be flexible. Later, after the media strategy and tactics have been decided, the advertising objectives can be firmed up. However, this does not imply that the objectives can't be revised if new information changes the situation. Even in a speculative presentation it's a good idea to acknowledge that if the situation changes so too should the objectives.

Both marketing and advertising objectives should reflect the problems and opportunities that were uncovered in the situation analysis. Of the many problems and opportunities, special attention should be paid to the amount of value, or equity, associated with the company's brand names and what they specifically stand for.

Having done all of the above, the next step is to determine strategic focal points around which the campaign strategy will be focused.

CAMPAIGN PROGRESS CHECKLIST

At this point in the campaign you should generally be aware of the following points:

1. Following the background analysis, the first major conclusion reached is to determine the amount of value, or equity, in the brand.

2. In assessing the company's problems and opportunities, a high priority should be given to developing brand equity (i.e., building the brand).

3. Part of an advertiser's success in building brand equity depends on its ability to solve problems. The best strategists anticipate problems before they occur.

4. Creative thinkers are sometimes able to turn problems into opportunities.

5. The ability to exploit a weakness depends on more than creative thinking; it requires a thorough analysis of the company's internal and external resources.

6. The targeting decision is one of the most important decisions in the campaign and should be deferred until the analysis of all the background information is complete.

7. The target audience (or market) can be delineated in many different ways. A key decision is to figure out which criteria are most likely to influence purchasing decisions.

8. Decisions about which problems to solve or opportunities to exploit will form the basis for the campaign objectives. These, in turn, will provide the direction for the campaign to follow.

9. Marketing or sales goals should be distinguished from communication objectives, which should be set using various communication criteria.

10. Identifying the key communication task that will lead to the achievement of marketing goals requires the identification of the desired effect (such as awareness) and the action taken with respect to the effect (such as reinforcement).

11. Using sound principles for writing objectives helps provide clear direction for people working on the campaign. It also helps managers evaluate the effectiveness of the campaign.

Notes and References

[1] M. Heller, "The Great Cookie War," *Madison Avenue* 27 (January 1985), p. 100.

[2] F. Warner, "Going Private: Keebler Heads into Private Label after Disastrous 1992," *Brandweek*, 1 February 1993, p. 6.

[3] For additional information on opportunity analysis, see Robert J. Hamper and L. Sue Baugh, *Strategic Market Planning* (Chicago: NTC Business Books, 1994), ch. 5.

[4] J.F. Engel, M.R. Warshaw, and T.C. Kinnear, *Promotional Strategy: Managing the Marketing Communication Process, 8th Ed.* (Burr Ridge, IL: Irwin, 1994), p. 162.

[5] G.S. Odiorne, *Management by Objectives: A System of Managerial Leadership* (New York: Pitman, 1965), p. 204.

[6] Some authors, Russell H. Colley in particular, distinguish between an objective and a goal: An objective is general or long term in nature, and a goal is specific or short term in nature. R.H. Colley, *Defining Advertising Goals for Measured Advertising Results* (New York: Association of National Advertisers, 1961), p. 6.

[7] Ibid., pp. 37–38.

[8] R.J. Lavidge and G.A. Steiner, "A Model for Predictive Measurements of Advertising Effectiveness," *Journal of Marketing* 25 (October 1961), pp. 59–62.

[9] Lisa Sanders and Jean Halladay, "GM Overhauls Compensation," *Advertising Age*, 17 March 2003, p. 1.

[10] James D. Lenskold, *Marketing ROI* (New York: McGraw-Hill, 2003), p. 114.

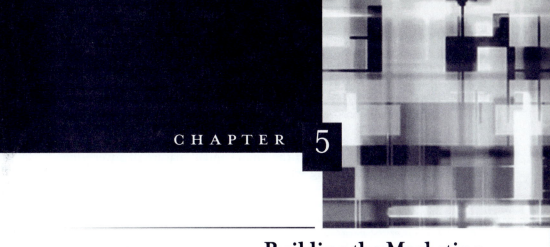

CHAPTER 5

Building the Marketing Communication Strategy

If you are working on a campaign while you are reading this book, you may want to go back periodically and redo your research, rethink your target market, and reset your objectives. You may not want to revisit everything, just some of it. In the business world, revision is simply part of a normal process of fine-tuning your work to produce professional results.

THINKING ABOUT STRATEGY

Advertising or any communication strategy should not be created in a vacuum. Only *after* an analysis of the situation and a systematic delineation of the problems and opportunities is it time to make decisions. These decisions should evolve out of careful analysis. If the problems and opportunities can be determined with insight, decisions about defining the target audience and setting the objectives evolve naturally. The next step is to think about strategy. Strategy is all about identifying the actions that will give the brand a competitive edge. It is general in nature and takes place over time. A good strategy anticipates consumer responses and competitive reactions.

At this point in the campaign process, strategy basically focuses on message content and the ways in which the message gets delivered. However, strategy can consist of more than creative and media decisions or, for that matter, more than decisions involving sales promotion, direct marketing, and public relations. Strategy can also be about funding, managing, and evaluating a campaign. Thinking strategically should permeate all aspects of the campaign.

THE WAY ADVERTISING WORKS BEST

There isn't one way to advertise that will be effective with all consumers. This is no big surprise considering the diversity and unpredictability of consumers. Ad people are generally satisfied if they can say: "most of the time, most of this group of people will respond to our ads . . . (as follows)."

The Classic Approach versus Building the Brand

Salespeople know that selling can be easy if you have something people want. If so, then the best approach is usually to tell prospects what your product has that addresses what they want.

Many years ago, C. H. Sandage, widely regarded as the father of advertising education, discussed the "middleman" nature of advertising. He suggested that advertising serves as an intermediary between business firms with products and services and individuals who might benefit from the purchase of those products or services. Thus, advertising performs the function of *interpreting the want-satisfying qualities of products, services, or ideas in terms of the needs and wants of consumers.*[1]

The classic approach to successful advertising is based on Sandage's understanding of how advertising functions. It begins with a thorough analysis of consumers' needs and wants to determine how a product's qualities match up with these needs and wants. Ads are then created to show how a specific branded product can satisfy the consumers' needs and wants. Viewed this way, advertising functions to inform or educate consumers. If done well, an ad becomes persuasive. What distinguishes one campaign from another is its ability to attract attention, generate interest, instill belief, and remain memorable over time. The classic approach still requires a certain amount of creativity to distinguish itself. In other words, the classic approach is fairly straightforward, but its execution is much more difficult. The challenge is to create an ad that is more attention grabbing, more persuasive, and more memorable—in short, more creative.

Ads can focus on both physical and psychological qualities depending on what consumers find to be important. Procter & Gamble has long focused on softness to promote Charmin, its top-rated brand of bathroom tissue. In a legendary campaign that stretched over two decades, an irritable trade character named Mr. Whipple told customers, "Please don't squeeze the Charmin." For more than 25 years, TV viewers heard Mr. Whipple get across the simple message that Charmin was "squeezably soft." Softness apparently is a highly desirable quality in bathroom tissue.

Consumers often want more out of a product than what it can do for them physically. For a long time, Cadillac produced some of the more comfortable, dependable, and *safe* cars on the road. Yet much of the focus in its advertising has been on the amount of prestige or status one gets from owning a Cadillac.

The classic approach to selling has been to tell potential customers how they will benefit from using a product. If the advantage or gain from using the product is something consumers really want or need, *and* the product can satisfy this need or want, then selling has generally been fairly easy.

Why the Classic Approach Is Not as Effective as It Used to Be

It's very obvious (sometimes painfully) that a lot of advertising does not follow the classic approach. Although there are many reasons for this, some of the more common ones are listed below.

Too Many Product Similarities.   It's hard to get motivated to "interpret the want-satisfying qualities of the product" when you know there isn't much difference among the major brands in the category. VCRs, brownie mixes, computers, laundry detergents, lightbulbs, and aspirin are a small listing of product categories where there aren't significant differences among the major brands.

Too Many Ads.   Consumers are inundated with advertising. Faced with an information overload, consumers both ignore and avoid advertising. The TV remote control is used for more than changing channels. It's often used to mute the sound on commercials. Today, advertising has a much harder task than in earlier days. An ad can feature a great product, but with the overabundance of advertising in the modern mediascape, an ad may simply be overlooked.

Too Many Promises.   Consumers today have been exposed to so many ads that they have become more than media savvy, they're downright hard to convince. It's not surprising consumers are so skeptical, if not cynical, considering all the claims and promises advertisers make. Consumers are promised that a brand is "new and improved," "stronger, yet gentle," or "everywhere you want to be." Not surprisingly, consumers tune out many commercials. If the promise is made in a lighthearted way, consumers may ignore the exaggerated claim.

Do You Believe These Claims?

"Give us a week, we'll take off the weight." (Slim-Fast)
"It keeps going, and going, and going . . ." (Energizer)
"The most exciting thing to happen to your face since your first kiss." (Clairol Facial Care)
"Herbal Essence . . . A totally 'organic' (wink wink) experience." (Clairol Hair Shampoo)
"Ten minutes to beautiful." (Revlon)
"It's everywhere you want to be." (Visa)
"Get a new lease on life." (Acura)
"When you're here, you're family." (Olive Garden)
"Red Bull gives you wings." (Red Bull)
"They melt in your mouth, not in your hand." (M&Ms)

(And if you believe the above lines, you'll also believe us when we say we work for the government, and we're here to help you.)

To reach consumers, many advertisers today use unconventional approaches, featuring highly creative approaches and techniques, often dramatizing a relationship between people and a product. The post-modern approach typically focuses more on associating an intangible value with the brand name and less on a product's want-satisfying qualities. Advertisers often refer to this focus as **building the brand.**

█ BUILDING A FOUNDATION FOR THE DEVELOPMENT OF STRATEGY

At the heart of all strategy are ideas and decisions that form the base upon which strategy is developed. We call this base the **strategic foundation** and it consists of the following five elements:

1. Determining the selling focus
2. Managing brand equity

3. Positioning the message
4. Funding of the marketing communication program
5. Targeting and delivering the message

The strategic foundation provides the core elements of the campaign strategy that will eventually be developed, expanded, and refined by creative and media personnel. At the center of each element should be a **strategic focal point** around which the subsequent strategies revolve. These focal points evolve directly from the research foundation. Once you determine which problems need to be solved or opportunities pursued, you should then translate these perceptions into objectives. Keep in mind the problems you identify must be solvable and the opportunities realistic. The promise you make in an ad must reflect product characteristics, or the advertising is simply not believable and a waste of money. Part of the purpose of setting objectives is to provide direction for the people working on the campaign. The direction objectives provide becomes the strategic focal points for the various strategies (such as message, media, and sales promotion) that get developed in the campaign.

Consider Lee jeans. In the eighties and early nineties, this brand was promoted as "the brand that fits." Its advertising generally consisted of spots focusing on young women having difficulty putting on jeans that were tight and the problems they encountered as a result. Naturally, the ads suggested that these problems wouldn't occur with Lee jeans. Because the Lee brand of jeans is a looser-fitting jean, the advertising promise reflected real product characteristics. The looser-fitting image, promoted at a time when styles tended toward tight jeans, meant a less-than-stylish image. Yet the product sold fairly well because it did satisfy a real need in the marketplace. In the late nineties, jeans in general tended to fit looser and easier, providing more competition for the Lee brand in terms of product characteristics (i.e., a looser fit). Unfortunately for the Lee brand, it continues to carry the less-than-stylish image. The decision to promote product characteristics instead of focusing on more intangible qualities, such as image, often poses a significant problem to planners. When a brand loses its differentiating characteristics, it may have to start over in terms of building the brand. Ideally, the planner would do both, although this is not always easy to accomplish.

Strategy works over time, both during a campaign and from one campaign to another. Separating short-term from long-term effects is a matter of judgment. But it is necessary in order to evaluate comprehensively the effectiveness of a campaign and to plan for future ones. Strategically, each of the above five elements has both short- and long-term ramifications that can influence strategy profoundly. Short-term interests are usually about stimulating sales. Long-term interests are about adding value, or equity, to the brand or company name. This largely intangible value is generally referred to as **brand equity.** This chapter focuses on the decisions involving the management of brand equity. Most of what we have to say about the message and media components of the strategy is discussed in subsequent chapters.

The first strategic element to consider is the **selling focus,** and it evolves out of the situation analysis. If the product's want-satisfying qualities have an advantage over the competition, then this point can be the basis for the promotional effort. If the brand is essentially a parity product, then the emphasis will be more on building the brand. Keep in mind that regardless of the selling focus there should always be some effort to build the brand.

Brand equity considerations, the second element, are easily the most important part of a communication strategy. If a brand loses its equity, it may not survive. Too often campaigns are short term in nature and overly concerned with boosting sales quickly. Often management needs to be educated about the strategic importance of building the brand over the long run. The campaign objectives should reflect the relative importance of building the brand versus merely emphasizing product qualities. Nevertheless, it's usually a good idea to rethink how the value in the brand name will be handled, or managed, during the campaign period.

Until the mid-nineties, McDonald's Corporation did little research to measure the effectiveness of its advertising. Apparently, the company believed it would be too difficult to evaluate its numerous ads by measurement. The bulk of McDonald's advertising is designed to reinforce the brand's core equities: family, good-tasting food, value, fast service, convenience, and cleanliness. These words all reflect ideas and values that are easy to understand but difficult to measure, especially considering the effects a McDonald's commercial has over an extended period. McDonald's is now conducting research in this difficult area, not because it has become easier but because it is even more convinced of the strategic importance of managing the brand's equity.

Positioning, or the way the firm presents the brand in its various forms of communication, is the third element in the strategic foundation. It can be planned to achieve short- or long-term effects. Sometimes it can do both. When McDonald's advertises a promotion tied to Barbie Dolls or action figures, ostensibly it is advertising for the short term. The toys are presented as fun and exciting and only available for a limited time. However, by presenting the toys in a wholesome family environment, McDonald's is also reinforcing one of its core equities and enhancing the value of the brand over a much longer period. A brand's **identity** is, in large part, a reflection of the way a company tries to influence the way consumers think and feel about the brand. Sometimes, as in the case of Lee jeans, it's due to factors beyond the company's control.

Decisions about advertising **expenditures** make up the fourth element in the strategic foundation. Although very important, we decided not to discuss this in detail because these tend to be more corporate decisions than marketing or advertising ones. Their relevance is particularly minor in a typical advertising campaign's class where the size of the advertising/marketing communication budget is frequently predetermined.

Expenditure decisions, however, do have both short- and long-term ramifications. The appropriation decision is of long-term strategic interest. To compete in some categories, a firm must be able to marshal sufficient financial resources. On the other hand, budgetary decisions about how to allocate money are short-term operational decisions only indirectly concerned with long-range strategic planning.

The elements of the strategic foundation that deal with positioning and targeting directly influence the development of message and media strategy. These concepts will be covered in greater detail in Chapter 6 (on message strategy), Chapter 7 (on media strategy), and Chapter 8 (on related marketing communications).

The **targeting** decision, the fifth element in the strategic foundation, can also have both short- and long-range ramifications. On a daily basis, targeting decisions usually devolve to questions about the efficiency with which the media is delivering messages to target audiences. Of more strategic concern, targeting focuses on the extent to which the messages are delivered to the right target. In the 1990s, Oldsmobile began a clever and still memorable 18-month campaign to reposition the brand to appeal to a younger market. It was called "This is not your father's Oldsmobile." The consumers' response was clear: "Oh, yes it is!" The problem wasn't so much the advertising as it was the product. General Motors was trying to distinguish the Oldsmobile from its other brands and models, mostly Buicks, by giving it a more youthful image. Consumers liked the advertising. They just didn't believe it.

Let's look at each of the five elements of the strategic foundation in more detail.

▌DETERMINING THE SELLING FOCUS

Understanding the role advertising and other communication elements play in influencing the consumer's decision-making process is critical to an efficient and effective campaign. Each element often plays a different role. Budweiser uses national advertising to make the brand "cool." The wholesale system drives most of the "heavy lifting" with sales promotions, event marketing, product publicity, and nontraditional media. In analyzing the product's opportunity, the brand steward (the ad director or account executive) should determine the selling focus so that all the elements in the plan complement each other and transmit a consistent selling message. Advertising designed to specifically promote a sale, usually in the short term, is sometimes called **transaction-oriented** advertising. In contrast, building the brand generally takes place over an extended period. This difference can result in very different marketing and advertising strategies. To stimulate demand quickly a company can (in addition to advertising) run sales, offer product samples, or flood the market with coupons. Although these actions can boost sales, they might not be in the long-term interest of the company.

Competing on the basis of price (including samples or coupons) or product superiority works well when the company has an advantage, as is the case with Thrifty Car Rentals, Payless shoes, and Suave personal care products. The marketplace, however, exacts a brutal price on companies that lose their advantages. The marketplace in the future promises to be even more aggressively competitive. The low-price leader today may find it has lost its competitive advantage tomorrow when rivals move their manufacturing offshore to an emerging nation where labor costs are much lower. In 2002, Payless was the industry leader in the $40 billion shoe category with a 4% share-of-market lead over Wal-Mart. By 2005, Wal-Mart had caught up.[2] Which company do you suppose will be first in the next edition of this book? Payless shoes will have to do more than tell consumers to shop with Payless if they want to pay less. Even competing on the basis of product qualities carries a certain amount of risk. In many product categories, there isn't much difference among the top two or three brands. If one company innovates, the other companies quickly adopt the improvement for their own brands. Innovating companies also have to contend with private-label manufacturers. These are companies that manufacture generic equivalents and sell them either under their own label or to retail stores who market them under their house brands.

For example, Perrigo is the nation's largest manufacturer of personal care and over-the-counter pharmaceutical products for the store-brand market. It makes some 1,300 products—everything from pain relievers and deodorants to hair care items and vitamins. It provides private-label merchandise for retailers such as Wal-Mart, CVS, Kroger, Target, and Kmart.

As markets become mature, it becomes increasingly difficult for companies to differentiate themselves from the competition based on physical qualities. Personal computers are fast reaching commodity status. The difference between one box and another is often the software loaded in it, the speed of the microprocessor inside (the chip), and of course, the price.

Smart companies know that it's important to stimulate demand (sales), but it is even more important to manage demand. **Managing the demand** for a product requires the company to gain some measure of control over the thoughts and feelings consumers have with respect to a product. The more control firms have over the associations people connect to their products, the more likely they can influence consumers to become loyal purchasers. The objective of brand-building activities is to generate consumer loyalty to the products a company sells. Generally, it's a lot easier and cheaper to keep a customer than to convince new ones to either switch brands or buy the product for the first time.

The first step toward building loyalty is for the company to put a brand name on its products. A **brand** is a name, term, symbol, design, or some combination that identifies the products of a firm and differentiates them from those of the competition.[3] Branding a product provides something tangible to which consumers can attach associations. For example, when consumers think of Sony, they tend to think quality; Nordstrom, customer service; Federal Express, overnight service. Many of these associations are based on some tangible quality (Federal Express does offer overnight service). However, many associations are based on perceptions and are highly subjective. What's your idea of cool music? U2, Beyoncé, Jimmy Buffet, Eminem, or Britney Spears? (Maybe none of these?)

Perception is often more important than reality. It's not enough for a company to have the best-tasting beer, biscuits, or barbecue. Consumers have to believe they are the best. Sometimes, it's hard to figure how consumers reach the conclusions they do. Pizza seems to be one of those products that even when it's bad, some people seem to like it. Consumers often ignore facts or independent product evaluations such as those in

ier Reports. The idea behind building positive brand associations
*e*nerate loyalty specifically to the brands a company sells rather
*s*mething more general like the company's "products." After all, it
is the company's specific products (brands) that satisfy a consumer's needs
or wants.

Managing the demand for a brand is important because it provides the
company with sufficient time to plan strategy and tactics. By avoiding
price competition, a company can invest in such things as product improvements, line extensions, or new product development. Advertising is
a primary tool firms use to influence brand loyalty. Other factors are also
important, such as the quality and reliability of the product, sales force,
community public relations, company signage, appearance of the product
or store, and the company's ability to deal with consumer complaints.

A major difference between advertising and other factors that influence brand loyalty is that advertising can be changed quickly and dramatically. Unlike changes in a product or a sales force, a new ad campaign
can be altered as the need arises—and changed quickly. Moreover, the
new campaign is typically created by an outside advertising agency.
Change can have a negative effect on company morale. So having an outside agent handle the change can make it easier on everyone involved. In
contrast, changes in the workforce, such as retraining employees or insti-
tuting new policies, sometimes have a dispiriting effect on company
morale.

MANAGING BRAND EQUITY

Brand names have value, or equity, and are an asset every bit as important
as the mortar and brick in a company's building. Like an investment property, brand equity must be managed. Brand equity is all about the value—
implicit and explicit—in the company's names and symbols. A company's
names and its associations can have a significant effect on whether consumers buy the product. Consumers buy brands as much for intangible
qualities as they do for physical ones. Budweiser beer is aged in beech-
wood, but it is doubtful this means as much to the typical consumer of
Budweiser beer as its claim, "the king of beers," or its association with
Clydesdale horses. A company's branding opportunities must be culti-
vated and nurtured, its position in the market reinforced and intensified,
and its problems dealt with by protecting and defending the brand from
any situation that would undermine its status in the marketplace.

David A. Aaker, in his widely influential book *Managing Brand Equity,*
discusses five categories of largely intangible assets and liabilities upon
which brand equity is based:

1. Brand loyalty
2. Name awareness
3. Perceived quality
4. Brand associations
5. Other proprietary assets such as patents, trademarks, characters,
   and channel relationships[4]

BRAND LOYALTY

Establishing, building, reinforcing, and intensifying brand
easily the most important aspects of managing brand equity.
axiom in marketing that suggests it is easier to keep customers than to get
new ones. Consumers fall into routines and will often buy a product simply out of habit, especially if they are satisfied. The cost of acquiring new
customers is typically greater than that expended on maintaining existing
ones. Existing customers also help expand demand by promoting the
product through word of mouth. If a company takes the proper steps to
satisfy its customers, it is amazing how loyal consumers can be to a brand.
Exhibit 5-1 compares the leading brands of various products in 1925 with
the leaders in 1985, 1998, and 2002. With only a few exceptions, the
leaders today are the same as they were in 1925 and 1985.

Simply being a leader, however, is no guarantee of long-term success.
The saying "The bigger they are, the harder they fall" applies to companies as well as to giants. Eastern Airlines and Oldsmobile, category leaders
in the 1970s, are no longer in business. Not all companies can be the leaders in their field. Enlightened companies understand that brand loyalty
doesn't automatically follow brand-share leadership. As Figure 5-1 illustrates, firms seek to gain control over consumers by moving them along a
continuum beginning with brand awareness and ideally ending with brand
insistence.

Brand awareness can range from a point where consumers are barely
familiar with the brand name to a point at which the brand is the first word
that comes to the consumer's mind when the product category is mentioned. Simple brand awareness is only a very mild form of control
whereas top-of-mind awareness can be a distinct advantage, particularly in
a generic category where the differences among products are slight. In
some consumer groups or areas of the country, a brand may have high
top-of-mind awareness because the brand name is used generically.

In Tennessee, a lot of Coca-Cola is sold to people who use the word
coke as a generic equivalent for soft drinks. Several years ago, a young man
asked the author's daughter to pick up a couple cases of "coke" for a pic-
nic. When she arrived at the park with two cases of Coca-Cola, the young
man asked her why she hadn't bought any Pepsi, which was his favorite.
Uncharitably, she laughed. Later, he conceded that from time to time he
was served Coke simply because it was the first word that came to his
mind, and, to him, it really didn't matter very much.

Most consumer brands fall into the classification *brand acceptance.*
Consumers typically find several brands in product categories satisfactory
and appear willing to base their purchase decisions on a sale price or a
coupon. Increasingly, the nationally advertised brands are discovering that
consumers are extending their level of acceptance to include many store
brands and private-label merchandise.

Brand preference is a measure of loyalty that most companies would
like their brands to achieve. A brand can achieve leadership in a category
even when it is only preferred slightly. Budweiser is clearly the number-
one beer in the United States, a position that reflects the preference

EXHIBIT 5-1   THE LEADING BRANDS

Product	1925	Position in 1985	Position in 1998	Position in 2002
Bacon	Swift	Leader	Number 3	Number 3
Breakfast cereal	Kellogg	Leader	Leader	Number 2
Cameras	Kodak	Leader	Leader	Leader
Chewing gum	Wrigley	Leader	Leader	Leader
Chocolates	Hershey	Number 2	Leader	Leader
Mint candies	Life Savers	Leader	Leader	Leader
Razors	Gillette	Leader	Leader	Leader
Shortening	Crisco	Leader	Leader	Leader
Soap	Ivory	Leader	Number 6	Number 6
Soft drinks	Coca-Cola	Leader	Leader	Leader
Soup	Campbell	Leader	Leader	Leader
Tea	Lipton	Leader	Leader	Leader
Tires	Goodyear	Leader	Leader	Leader
Toothpaste	Colgate	Number 2	Leader	Leader

Sources: For 1925 and 1985 data, the source is Thomas S. Wurster, "The Leading Brands: 1925–1985," *Perspectives* (Boston: The Boston Consulting Group, 1987). Quoted in David A. Aaker, *Managing Brand Equity*; 1994 data courtesy of Information Resources, Inc (IRI); 1998 data is derived from information supplied by IRI and Responsive Database Services, Inc. 2002 data supplied by IRI and *Brandweek*.

FIGURE 5-1 BRAND LOYALTY CONTINUUM

| Brand Awareness | Brand Acceptance | Brand Preference | Brand Insistence |

consumers have for the brand. How strong is this preference? Even though many beer drinkers claim to "love" their Bud, it is *highly likely that they would quickly order some other brand* if Budweiser was unavailable.

Budweiser does not have brand insistence that is the ultimate level of brand loyalty. Brand insistence means that consumers will *take no substitutes.* So, if a store is out of Budweiser, it's out of beer. (Beer drinkers generally take substitutes.) Schlitz used a variation of this line in the 1970s: "When you're out of Schlitz, you're out of beer." It's a nice line that speaks of a highly desirable state of brand loyalty, but as legend has it, it was originally spoken by a Budweiser beer salesman. Apparently, after ordering a Budweiser and learning that the bar was out of his brand, he cried, "When you're out of Bud, you're out of beer." A copywriter at Leo Burnett reportedly heard the line and used it in the Schlitz campaign. Unfortunately for Schlitz, nice line that it was, it did not save the brand from declining from the second best-selling beer to a point where it is virtually out of the beer business.

Perhaps the ultimate level of brand insistence has been attained by Harley-Davidson. Not only will potential buyers wait months to purchase the brand, but buyers belong to owners' clubs, attend Harley-Davidson rallies, wear shirts with the company logo, and tattoo their bodies with the brand name. Obviously, it is unrealistic to expect this kind of loyalty for the average product. A key part of the background analysis is to determine what level of brand loyalty is realistic to attain.

Cultivating Brand Loyalty

The key to developing brand loyalty is to get consumers to make an emotional attachment to the company or its brands, or both. Companies that consistently produce better products have a much easier time developing this emotional bond. However, a better product is often a matter of opinion and a function of perspective. In the twenty-first century, many companies cultivate brand loyalty by *extending* the marketing concept—by giving people not only what they want but also "more": more attention, more recognition, more satisfaction—in short, more value.

Estée Lauder is a company that has built its success on the idea that for many women the experience surrounding the purchase of cosmetics is as important as a product's physical attributes. Selling cosmetics is tricky, partly because you're selling a product that people don't really need. (The author freely recognizes there are readers who would dispute this point.) Estée Lauder, the legendary founder of the company, knew that the way to get customers to buy more than they probably needed was to make each customer feel special. In a typical high-end department store, "beauty advisers," "consultants," and "analysts" try to build a relationship with customers by getting physically close to them in a relaxed and non-threatening way. To do this, salespeople lightly place their fingers on a woman's forehead, smooth lotion on her cheeks, or apply gloss to her lips. To reinforce the special feelings it provides to its customers, the company spends almost a billion dollars, or nearly 30% of sales, on advertising and promotions. This approach has been so successful that in 2004, sales of Estée Lauder products reached $5.12 billion. Of the top 10 prestige makeup products (mascara, lipstick, foundation, etc.), 7 belong to Estée Lauder. Of the top 10 prestige skin-care products, 8 are Estée Lauder brands.[5] Some companies attempt to formalize this approach by giving it a special name: **relationship marketing** (or customer relationship marketing).

Relationship Marketing

The key to developing a relationship with consumers is attitude. The firm must be willing to provide extra value to consumers in return for greater brand loyalty. This is a simple paraphrase of the Stuart Smalley pop psychology saying of the 1980s: "If you want to be loved, give love." Many brands maintain substantial amounts of brand equity without resorting to warm and fuzzy marketing, but many companies find that a more caring, consumercentric approach is good for business. As the differences among products appear to be getting smaller each year, companies search long and hard for ways to provide extra value to consumers.

Companies can forge a positive relationship at all three stages of a consumer's experience with a brand: (1) before the purchase, (2) while the consumer is using the product, and (3) after a customer has stopped using or purchasing the brand. Pepsi Cola and Nike are two advertisers that make extensive use of the relationship concept.

For years, Pepsi has invited consumers to join the Pepsi generation using a fun, even funky, approach. Its message is simple: If you're conservative or stodgy, drink Coke. If you're hip, join us. In the 1990s, Nike segmented its approach to selling athletic shoes. To reach men, it used a traditional campaign with famous athletes, like Michael Jordan, often in humorous situations. To appeal to women, it showed the product less than in its advertising for men, if it appeared at all. Instead, the ads used a lot of empathic copy to discuss, if not celebrate, what it is like to be a woman, especially one who works out. The implied message is simple and subtle: "We understand real women. If you're in the market for a pair of shoes, who understands your needs and wants better than Nike?" Lately, Nike has begun using a similar approach with men, in effect telling them Nike understands sports. The trick for Nike is to act like the average sports fan when everyone knows it's a goliath. So far, it seems to be working. Companies that use the relationship marketing approach understand that making the sale is only part of the transaction. Consumer satisfaction can be a transitory thing. What satisfied a consumer yesterday, happened yesterday. Consumers are continually exposed to all kinds of promotions. Phone carriers, such as Sprint, MCI, and AT&T, regularly call their customers to see whether they are satisfied with their service.

Companies are also beginning to understand the importance of pursuing a relationship with customers after they stop buying. Terry Vavra, in his book *After-Marketing,* argues that some of a company's best prospects are consumers who no longer buy the company's products or services. He gives three reasons.[6] First, there is a wealth of information to be learned from previous customers: Were they dissatisfied with the product or service? Did they switch for a lower price? Have they simply moved on to new interests or wants in their lives?

Second, it is often cheaper to get back old customers than to acquire new ones. Many firms have accumulated a considerable database of previous customers. Instead of purging files of inactive customers, it may be less expensive and easier to retarget old customers than to launch a campaign aimed at winning new ones.

Third, with the information obtained from old customers, a firm can often fix the problems that led customers to buy elsewhere. Consumers who purchased from a company more than once probably have residual positive feelings about a company even after they go elsewhere. In developing campaign strategy, consider prospecting for new business with old customers. It may be possible to rekindle the warmth associated with an old relationship.[7]

Staples, an office-supplies store, builds its database of customers by offering them membership cards that entitle them to a special discount. These cards enable the store to track purchase behavior; identify monthly patterns, including responses to various promotions; and detect whether each customer has decreased or stopped purchasing. With this information, Staples is able to mount marketing-oriented countermeasures aimed at regaining business.[8]

Companies increasingly are using e-mail to keep in touch with their customers. When used as a retention tool, e-mail is cheaper, quicker, and more user friendly than the phone or postal mail. Jupiter Communications estimates that by 2005 companies will spend $7.3 billion on e-mail marketing, $6.3 billion on customer retention, and the rest on customer acquisition.[9]

It is becoming increasingly obvious to companies that employing a consumercentric approach can pay big dividends in terms of sales. In developing campaign strategy, it is important to identify the company's consumer-friendly attitudes and policies so these can be publicized and promoted.

NAME AWARENESS

Awareness is an aspect of brand loyalty, but it is important enough as a tactical and strategic concern to merit special attention. Simple awareness by itself does not contribute much to brand loyalty. However, without awareness there can be no loyalty. This premise may be why awareness seems to be the primary objective of so much advertising. In a survey of more than 3,000 directors of advertising designed to look at the way decision makers set objectives, more directors stated "awareness" as an advertising objective than any other criterion.[10]

Awareness and Value

David Aaker suggests that awareness contributes to a brand's equity in at least four ways:

1. A name provides an anchor to which you can attach other associations.
2. A recognizable name provides a sense of familiarity that people usually like.
3. A well-known name signals that there is substance and commitment behind it.
4. A well-known name signals that others have found the brand worth considering.[11]

Exhibit 5-2 presents a list of names with some common associations. If you are familiar with the names, you will probably make similar associations. If you are unfamiliar with a name, you may not have a clue as to where the association is coming from. Of course, familiarity doesn't always generate good feelings; sometimes it breeds contempt, as the saying goes. Even in cases where there are negative associations, however, people may be willing to pay attention to the names because they assume others have. So why has Crest stopped talking about "fighting cavities" and more about whiteness? Probably because it's been talking about "fighting cavities" for years and is concerned that consumers think of it as an old-fashioned brand. Crest used to be the best-selling brand of toothpaste. Today, it's Colgate.

Stages of Awareness

Awareness can vary on a continuum from no awareness to extreme awareness. However, this is not how it tends to be measured. Figure 5-2 presents a continuum of the different stages of awareness. Below the first line is another continuum displaying how these stages of awareness get measured conceptually. The distinction between stages of awareness and measurement can be important for both strategic and operational purposes.

Using a commonsense approach to discussing strategy, you may simply say that you would like consumers to be very aware of the brand name. When copywriters and media buyers devise their plans to achieve this aim, however, they may have differing ideas about what "very aware" means. To avoid confusion, a planner may suggest a more specific goal, such as

---

EXHIBIT 5-2 NAMES AND COMMON ASSOCIATIONS

Crest	fights cavities
JiffyLube	fast service
Wal-Mart	low prices
Jerry Lewis Telethon	Muscular Dystrophy Association
Nashville	country music
Uno's, Due's, and Gino's	deep-dish pizza
Baskin Robbins	31 flavors
Budweiser	king of beers
Hallmark	cards
ESPN	sports

FIGURE 5-2 DIFFERENT STAGES OF AWARENESS

No Awareness — Slight Awareness — Generally Aware — Very Aware — Extreme Awareness

Unaware of Brand — Brand Recognition — Brand Recall — Top-of-mind Awareness

"We would like X% of our target market to be able to recall the brand name." Brand **recognition** is the weakest form of awareness, and it is measured simply by asking respondents, usually by phone, if they recognize any of the names an interviewer mentions. **Recall** is measured by asking respondents to name a brand within a product category without any prompting or aid. Both recognition and recall are memory tests. Many planners do not feel comfortable using memory tests both for methodological reasons and because the evidence is not compelling that high scores on a memory test translate into increased sales.

Top-of-mind awareness is basically measured in one of two ways: (1) Respondents are asked to indicate the first word that comes to mind when prompted by a product category, or (2) top-of-mind status is simply assigned to the first brand mentioned in a recall test.

Top-of-Mind Awareness

Top-of-mind awareness can be a distinct advantage to a brand in certain categories. It usually helps to be the first name considered for impulse items and products in categories where many of the brands are comparable in quality and have achieved brand acceptance. Pizza is often an impulse item. Pizza is also a good example of a product category in which many brands have achieved brand acceptance. Even bad pizza seems to sell, sometimes well. In many markets, when people think about delivered pizza, instead of saying, "Let's order pizza," they simply say, "Let's call Domino's (or Pizza Hut)." Is this because Domino's makes great pizza? Probably not. Over the years, Domino's has invested substantial sums of money in building its equity, so that when consumers think of delivered pizza, they think of Domino's first. Domino's might not hold such a preeminent position in consumers' minds if its products were more expensive, if the quality differences among the national brands were greater, or if consumers had a more discerning palate.

In the campaign process, it is important to determine whether awareness is the problem that is keeping the brand from achieving its marketing objectives.

PERCEIVED QUALITY

An image of quality is an important part of brand equity. Once you have a quality image, it becomes an asset that is an integral part of brand loyalty. Achieving this image can be an elusive goal. Companies with substantial R&D functions learn early in their work that there is more to an image than what one sees. R&D people use the qualities that consumers find desirable in competitive products as a benchmark for their own product. Then they try to produce a product that is better than the one in their specifications (specs). If a company can come up with a comparable or even superior product, it's won only half the battle. The rest of the job is convincing consumers.

Al Ries and Jack Trout, in their book *The 22 Immutable Laws of Marketing,* suggest that "marketing is not a battle of products, it's a battle of perceptions."[12] The best product will not automatically become the market leader. It's not how good a product is; it's how good people believe it is. The magazine *Consumer Reports,* which rates the quality of products, provides ample evidence nearly every issue that the highest-rated products are not necessarily the brands with the largest market share.

What makes a quality desirable can also be a matter of opinion. In California, consumers prefer smaller, crisper-handling cars; whereas in the Midwest, buyers prefer cars that are bigger and more comfortable to drive. What makes a quality desirable can also be a matter of which company has the best chance to get its image registered with consumers. Apparently, once consumers get an impression or image of a person, product, or place, they tend to keep that image and its associations for a long time. Ries and Trout argue that it is "better to be first than it is to be better. It's much easier to get into the mind first than to try and convince someone you have a better product than the one that got there first."[13] As evidence, they cite a number of famous firsts and some not-so-famous seconds. Exhibit 5-3 lists some of their examples along with some of ours.

It is hard to know why the first company to make an impression has such an advantage over other companies. One guess is that when consumers

EXHIBIT 5-3 FAMOUS FIRSTS		
Famous Event or Product	**Famous First**	**Not-So-Famous Second**
First person to fly solo across the Atlantic	Charles Lindbergh	Bert Hinckler
First cellophane adhesive tape	Scotch	3M
First person to walk on the moon	Neil Armstrong	Buzz Aldrin
First sport drink	Gatorade	Unknown
First President of the United States	George Washington	John Adams
First flight	The Wright brothers	Alberto Santos Dumont
First black baseball player	Jackie Robinson	Larry Doby

become satisfied with a brand, they have little motivation, reason, or incentive to pursue further information. For example, Whitehall Labs was the first company to take advantage of the Food and Drug Administration's approval allowing ibuprofen to be sold as an over-the-counter drug. In its early advertising, it introduced Advil® as the same pain reliever that consumers had been buying under the prescriptive name Motrin®. Later, when Upjohn (now Upjohn-Pharmacia) decided to market its own drug as the over-the-counter brand, Motrin IB®, consumers did not flock to the "real thing." Apparently, they were satisfied with Advil. Consumers' perception of Advil's quality is sufficiently high to ward off competition from brands that are equivalent and, in many instances, cheaper. In 2003, Advil was the number-one selling brand of ibuprofen.[14]

Influencing the perceptions consumers have of a product is a challenging task. It is a planner's job to indicate which perceptions should be reinforced or intensified and which should be changed. Obviously, changing consumer perceptions of a brand can be difficult. It is a lot easier to establish a perception for a new brand, or to modify a perception of an established brand, than it is to change the consumer's perception of a brand to something significantly different. The Nissan "Enjoy the Ride" campaign, focusing on excitement, did not reflect the way consumers typically felt. Eventually, Nissan decided to focus on dependability and engineering—the way the car is generally perceived by consumers.

BRAND ASSOCIATIONS

Companies also actively manage the equity in a brand through associations with its proprietary names. Associations can influence perceptions, increase brand awareness, and build brand loyalty. The type of associations companies promote can be almost infinite in scope. In short, the associations consumers make with a brand influence how they think and feel about a product. Some of the more common associations are with celebrities, places, characters, ideas, or words.

The use of celebrities to endorse a product or simply appear in a commercial is widespread. Sales of Gatorade increased significantly when Michael Jordan signed on to appear in the company's ads. The target market, overwhelmingly male, related to the line "Be like Mike."

Other products find positive associations with geographic regions, states, and cities. Jimmy Dean Breakfast Sausage and Bryan sausage both play up their southern heritage whereas Northern Bathroom Tissue associates with the North. Louisiana Hot Sauce and generic products such as California raisins, Idaho potatoes, and Washington State apples associate with states. Cities are also popular associations. There's Old Milwaukee beer, L.A. Gear sportswear, K.C. Masterpiece barbecue sauce, Philadelphia Brand cream cheese, OshKosh clothing, and Raleigh, Winston, and Salem cigarettes. Do these associations have value? Some appear to have more value than others. Apples grown in the state of Washington and potatoes from Idaho do taste better than ones grown in Tennessee. But the association of cream cheese with Philadelphia, or clothing with Oshkosh, Wisconsin, probably does not lend a similar amount of value.

Companies also associate with characters. The characters can be animated, such as the Green Giant and the Keebler elves; or live, such as the Maytag repairman and Mikey, the little boy who said he liked Life cereal.

When the Mikey campaign was first run in the early 1980s, it featured two adolescent boys trying to decide if they should eat a bowl of Life cereal. The boys decided to give it to their younger brother, Mikey, as an acid test because Mikey "doesn't eat anything." When the camera zoomed in on Mikey's cherubic face joyously eating the product, his brothers made advertising history by exclaiming, "He likes it." As soon as the people at Quaker Oats, parent company of Life cereal, saw the commercial, they knew it was magic. They rushed the spot on the air without pretesting it, something they rarely did. Later, Quaker Oats tested the commercial, and it did poorly both in terms of the communication measures the company was using and in its sales impact. Consumers could recall the ad but had difficulty recalling the brand advertised. Someone at Quaker came up with the brilliant idea of putting "Mikey's" picture on the Life cereal package and announcing that this was "Mikey's cereal." During the first 18 months following the start of Mikey advertising, sales increased 25%. Today Mikey is an adult who regularly appears on talk shows.

Simple word associations can be so strong that a single word or two can be indelibly associated with a brand in the minds of consumers. Budweiser is known as the king of beers. It's a powerful association, and it belongs to Budweiser. Even if it weren't trademarked, a company would be foolish to try and use it. There simply wouldn't be any credibility. Consider the following: "Pabst, the king of beers" or "Coors, the beer of kings." Or how about "Miller Genuine Draft: the royalty of bottled beer." In fact, by its association with royalty, Budweiser has preempted the use of all terms that denote royalty. It's unlikely there will ever be a "prince of beers" and certainly not a "queen of bottled beer."

Consider the following associations:

Ivory	floats
Domino's	delivers
Lee's	fit
Michelin	cares
John Deere	runs

How about two words?

Charmin	squeezably soft
Avis	tries harder
Crest	fights cavities
Allstate	good hands
Energizer	still going
Johnson & Johnson's baby shampoo	no tears

The best word associations are probably those that communicate the message in a word or two. Sometimes a word or two will be used less for its literal associations and more for the associations it stimulates. In the late 1990s, a story, perhaps apocryphal, was circulating within the

Chicago advertising community. Four executives from a top 10 ad agency were quitting the business to enter the microbrewed beer business. Their chief asset was an association. Allegedly, they were going to call their beer Naughty Boy. The copy and visuals would be simple: Two attractive women walk up to a bar. The first woman says, "I'll have a Naughty Boy." The second woman leans forward and with emphasis says, "Make that two Naughty Boys." Tacky? A gratuitous use of sex appeal? Probably. But it might be a powerful use of an association (or so the executives thought), even for the beer business. As the beer business shows signs of fragmenting into smaller segments, or niches, this kind of ad could build awareness. (Gratefully, the brand does not exist today.)

As good as some associations are, their value in maintaining brand equity may be limited over the long term. As advancements continue in the field of computer software, other companies may take over Apple's "user friendly" association. An association based on a physical quality may be more difficult for a company to maintain once its product loses its distinctness.

The fact that Ivory soap floats has nowhere near the value today as it did when it was introduced by Procter & Gamble in 1881. At the time, floating soap did not exist. A worker accidentally fed air into a mixture of soap, and the company was unaware of its buoyant properties until customers tried to reorder the "floating soap."[15] Today, other soaps float, and people take more showers. Times change.

A bigger potential problem occurs when a company voluntarily gives up its associations before they have lost their effectiveness. A maxim in the agency business is that clients usually get tired of a strategy or slogan long before it loses its effectiveness. Clients may simply be eager to try new ideas, or may feel the agency is not doing enough to earn their compensation. There is also a temptation to capitalize on the equity in a brand by entering a new category.

In 1993, Miller Lite was the second best-selling brand of beer, Budweiser was easily first, and Coors Light and Bud Light both came in a distant third. In 1991, Miller changed its advertising campaign in an attempt to close up the considerable distance between Budweiser and Miller Lite with a new campaign that used the tagline "It's it and that's that." They were trying to suggest that consumers were drinking Miller Lite for itself and not because it was a beer with fewer calories. The message simply wasn't credible. Taste may be subjective, but do any beer drinkers actually prefer the taste of a thinner (light) beer to a full-bodied (regular) beer? It was a nice idea, but the opportunity simply wasn't there. In 1994, Bud Light overtook Miller Lite as the second best-selling brand of beer.[16] By 2004, Miller Lite's share of market continued to slide. The best-selling brands of beer in rank order were Bud Light, Budweiser, Coors Light, and Miller Lite.[17]

Of course, there may be many reasons why the Miller brand has not done well, but it is clear that the advertising for Miller Lite in the last several years has not generated the kind of sales the company would have liked. An important part of strategy development is determining which brand associations are worth reinforcing or intensifying and which are worth changing or pursuing. In the case of Miller Lite, they may have given up on their "Tastes great, less filling" campaign too soon.

OTHER PROPRIETARY BRAND ASSETS

Another important part of a brand's equity is assets (or liabilities), such as patents, trademarks, characters, and channel relationships.

Patents and Trademarks

Many companies have exclusive ownership of distinctive assets that contribute to a brand's equity. Until late 1993, Monsanto owned the patent rights to aspartame, a sweetener the company branded under the names Equal®, when sold in packages, and NutraSweet®, when used as an ingredient in other products. Many people thought that after the patent ran out other companies would enter the market with a cheaper generic equivalent, which would also be aspartame. These people forgot the lessons learned with Tylenol®.

Many companies can easily duplicate acetaminophen, the generic name for Tylenol, but consumers won't buy very much of it. Tylenol is not only by far the best-selling brand of acetaminophen, but sales of Tylenol are 75% greater than those of the next best-selling brand of over-the-counter pain reliever (Advil).[18] Doctors rarely recommend acetaminophen; they simply say Tylenol.

Similarly, Monsanto shrewdly managed its asset so that even after it no longer owned the patent, the brand was still protected. Monsanto set up a separate company, The NutraSweet Co., to manage the brand and give it corporate identity. It invested heavily in advertising and required the thousands of products that use NutraSweet as an ingredient to list the brand name and its symbol on their labels. The only way a new company could compete would be on price, and even then it is likely that Monsanto would meet any competitor's low price. A competing company would have to overcome both consumer loyalty to the Equal brand and resistance within the production areas of companies reluctant to change their advertising and packaging to reflect the absence of NutraSweet. As a result, no *significant* competition to NutraSweet appears on the horizon.

Characters can also be used to manage the equity in a brand. Putting Mikey's face on the box of Life cereal and Morris' picture on the outside of a can of cat food can stimulate sales in the short term and have lasting effects over an extended period. The effects can also be permanent.

Characters

In 1950, the Minnesota Valley Canning Company changed its name to the Green Giant Company to reflect its use of the Green Giant character in its advertising. The giant first appeared in the company's ads in 1925, hunchbacked and looking like a "fugitive from a Grimm's fairy tale." Later it evolved into an amiable character, somewhat obscure but most of all imaginary. Leo Burnett added the word *Jolly* to a proof of a *Ladies Home Journal* ad, and the company has kept the word in its vocabulary ever since.[19]

Channel Relationships

The relationship within the channel of distribution is another important influence on a brand's equity. This relationship, along with the various messages consumers receive from other marketing communication tools, directly influences the image of the company, which in turn influences brand loyalty, perceptions of quality, and brand associations. For example, salespeople put a high premium on the value of their contacts. Frequently, it's not what you know or what you have to sell as much as whom you know and how much people like working with you. Personal relationships can be very important. Over time, a network of relationships tends to become institutionalized. Companies within a channel of distribution get accustomed to working with certain suppliers. New vendors may require company employees to learn new product specifications, new procedures, and new contacts within their organization. If the company uses any of the supplier's equipment, as often is the case with vending operations, changing suppliers can be a significant inconvenience.

Channel relationships are important, but also the extensiveness of the channel networks can be a positive influence on what consumers and channel members think of a brand. Gatorade is the number-one sport drink with substantial brand equity, but when Coca-Cola entered the market with POWERade® and Pepsi with All Sport®, Gatorade had reason to be nervous. Both Coca-Cola and Pepsi have substantial resources to spend promoting their products and extensive distribution networks that can make their products available in many locations that are not available to Gatorade. These networks add value to the brand's image because consumers and dealers know Coca-Cola and Pepsi are considerable forces to be reckoned with in the marketplace. So instead of marketing warfare, Gatorade joined forces with Pepsi.

A critical part of the strategy-building process is to assess the amount of value there is in the company's proprietary assets, such as its patents, characters, and channel relationships. Although these assets can get old and lose their value to the firm, once a company stops promoting them, it may not be able to get them back should the firm later decide it made a mistake.

■ PROTECTING BRAND EQUITY

Underlying the development of all communication strategy should be an understanding that the protection of the brand name is of paramount importance. Whereas managing brand equity is part of the strategic foundation that is used to build the marketing communication strategy, protecting brand equity is a philosophy that pervades all strategic and tactical thinking.

Brands can be a fragile asset for a company. Consider the current status of once-proud names, such as Eastern Airlines, Plymouth, Pan Am, Schlitz, WordStar, Foster Grant, Oldsmobile, and White Cloud. A brand can be a strong player one year and next to nowhere within a few years. At the local level, businesspeople need to work hard to shore up the erosion of their company names. If all the local hardware or garden supply store has to offer is merchandise and equipment, then it surely will be squeezed out of business by Wal-Mart and other mass-merchandise retailers.

Through all the steps in building the strategic foundation and while pursuing its strategy and tactics, companies need to be sure that their names are protected. Figure 5-3 presents a diagrammatic view of the relationships involved in managing and protecting brand equity.

■ SHORT-TERM THINKING VERSUS LONG-TERM INVESTMENT

Much has been written about the differences between Japanese and American businesses. American firms tend to pay more attention to short-term performance because it influences the company's stock prices. Japanese companies seem more concerned about success over the long haul. In the United States, many brand managers are evaluated on a quarterly basis. If sales haven't reached marketing goals near the end of a quarter, many managers will run price promotions, such as trade discounts, consumer rebates, coupons, and price reductions. These promotions eat into profit margins and send a not-too-subtle message to consumers: Our position is not very strong, they seem to say, so we're lowering prices. (If you can't buy now, wait around; we'll probably lower them again.) Price promotions undermine consumers' confidence in the brand's worth. The value in having a brand with equity is that consumers are generally willing to pay a premium for a strong name.

Investing in advertising to build a brand's equity or keep it from eroding is a lot more difficult to measure than short-term behavioral effects, such as coupon redemptions, price promotions, Internet click-thrus, or

---

FIGURE 5-3 | MANAGING AND PROTECTING THE BRAND

1-800 inquiries. Focusing on brand equity is more long term in nature because the effects of advertising to build a brand tend to accumulate over an extended period. But brand managers working their way up the corporate ladder may not want to wait. It is easier for them to document their accomplishments with sales figures than it is with something that can be as vague and difficult to measure as brand equity. New technology, especially checkout scanners, allows managers to track even minor sales downturns and bump them up with price-oriented promotions. Though this practice may be to the brand's long-term detriment, the availability of technology makes the temptation hard to resist.

WHO PROTECTS THE NAMES?

If brand managers cannot be relied on to protect the brand's long-term interest, whose responsibility is it? The answer should be everyone's, but in most companies that's not the case. Most companies consider it easier to measure short-term effects than long-term effects, and the results make a decision maker's position more defensible and less subject to the demanding scrutiny of a client or supervisor. Much of what is written about setting and writing objectives, including what we have written, works better with short-term effects.

At a minimum, the protection of the brand should be the responsibility of the marketing director and the advertising director. In 1981, McDonald's replaced its advertising agency, Needham, Harper Worldwide, with the Leo Burnett Co. This move stunned the advertising business because Needham had won numerous awards for its creative efforts, and *Advertising Age* had named it the "Advertising Agency of the Year for 1977." Sales were doing fine at McDonald's, but according to insiders, McDonald's had posed a number of marketing questions to Needham, which usually responded with more creative executions. What McDonald's wanted was more insight on strategic planning. In what directions should they take the brand? How might they capitalize on the brand's equity without undermining its value? McDonald's was thinking long term, and Needham was focusing on short term.

The transition from Needham to Burnett appeared to be smoother than it really was. Although Burnett did provide the desired marketing information, the early Burnett ads were not consistent with the way McDonald's had been promoted. McDonald's had to educate Burnett about McDonald's approach to protect the brand equity. As we've mentioned, until 1993, McDonald's had used little to no research to measure the effectiveness of its advertising and acted largely according to its judgment. With a major retail operation like McDonald's, you can often see the effects of an ad or campaign in the marketplace the day after a new campaign begins. Although you may not be able to statistically validate its effects, an experienced manager can make a reasonable judgment. Fortunately for McDonald's, it has had that kind of judgment. In 1997, McDonald's replaced Burnett with DDB Needham (same company, different name). Sales had been flat for a number of years and, in a management shake-up at McDonald's, a decision to replace Burnett as the lead agency on its account (Burnett did retain some business) sent a signal that the company was moving decisively to boost its flagging sales.

On the agency side, the guardianship of a brand's equity should nominally belong to the account executive (AE). However, AEs are a lot like brand managers in that they are so involved in day-to-day details, such as checking copy, approving coupons, and reviewing media schedules, that they too run the risk of sacrificing long-term equity for short-term performance. Account supervisors, who rank higher than an AE, should do a better job of focusing on brand equity because they are likely to be more experienced than an account executive and are less involved with day-to-day details.

Perhaps, in recognition that building brand equity is a long-term strategic concern, many agencies are putting more people into positions where their main responsibility is strategic planning. And in recognition, perhaps, that their agencies are not doing the job, advertisers are hiring outside consultants to help them with brand strategy or hiring a second agency to help them build the brand.

■ SPELLING OUT BRAND PROTECTION

Protecting the equity in a brand can be viewed either as a core element in a strategic plan or as a mindset that should pervade all aspects of any campaign. We prefer to assume that protection of the company's names should be of paramount importance in all activities and need not be spelled out in a firm's marketing plan. Protecting equity is somewhat different from managing brand equity. Protecting equity implies a defensive strategy, whereas managing equity suggests a proactive strategy. A company that is trying to build brand X for Acme Mfg., for example, may recommend an action that could damage the brand or the company name. To manage Acme's equity, someone might interject, "That's not Acme" (meaning, that's not the way we do things around here) or "That's not the brand-X way" (meaning, that's not the way we do things for the brand either). Usually, on a day-to-day basis, the questions that come up deal more with managing than protecting brand equity.

However, when a public relations disaster occurs, companies often adopt a circle-the-wagons approach, in which they try to protect the brand name from all sides. In 1990, traces of benzene, a toxic liquid, were found in Perrier bottled water, forcing a global recall of all supplies of the company's bottled water. At the time, Perrier was the brand leader with more than a 50% market share. There appeared to be little that could be done to protect the brand. Consumers assumed the problem was in the company's product because benzene, a carcinogen, had entered the water in the production process.[20] Nearly three years later, the Perrier brand had sunk to less than a 4% market share, ranking number eight in the bottled-water category, according to Nielsen.[21] By 1994, the best-selling brand of bottled water continued to be a product sold by the Perrier Group of America, only the brand name was Arrowhead instead of the company's best-known name, Perrier.[22] In 1998, the top-selling brand of bottled water was Poland Spring, another Perrier brand.[23] In other words, the only way Perrier could find to manage the crisis was to concentrate on another name and let the Perrier name drop. By 2001, the Perrier Group, including Arrowhead and Poland Spring, continued to hold the dominant share of the bottled-water market, outpacing Pepsi Cola and its Aquafina brand and Coca-Cola's Dasani.[24] By 2004, Aquafina and Dasani were the leading brands of water.[25] (Apparently, not much brand loyalty in the water category.)

DETERMINING THE RIGHT STRATEGIC FOCUS TO BUILD THE BRAND

A brand can't rest on past laurels. If it can be improved, it should strive to do so, or the competition will pass it by. Increasingly, leading marketers are selling off their second-tier brands to concentrate on the top performers in their portfolios.[26] However, some brands are limited in their potential to physically improve. Procter & Gamble may try to persuade consumers that "new improved" Tide® is an improvement over an older version, but the typical "improvement" is very slight, if even noticeable.[27] Part of the challenge to a strategic planner is to figure out how to add value to a brand by reinforcing or building brand equity. Of the five elements that influence brand equity, each generally requires different emphases or focus. An important decision in the development of the campaign strategy is to determine the strategic focus, or focal points, for the rest of the brand team to follow.

Brand awareness is not a problem for Campbell Soup. Perceptions of quality may be a problem, but the company is limited in what it can credibly tell consumers. Campbell Soup is good soup, but great soup it probably is not. As a result, the advertising for Campbell Soup often focuses on brand associations that are designed to reinforce brand loyalty. One common theme involves getting consumers to remember the warm fuzzy feelings they had when Mom gave them warm Campbell Soup on a chilly day. The nostalgia associated with simpler times, the comforting memories of a loving parent, all add value to what is basically a simple, and even bland product.

▌POSITIONING THE MESSAGE

Positioning is the next important element of the strategic foundation. It is highly interrelated with the management of brand equity. In a broad sense, positioning refers to the way advertisers try to get consumers to think or feel about their products in relation to some context, such as an emotion or an experience. It's a way that a company forges an identity for its brands. Calvin Klein, for example, wants consumers to feel an emotional connection to Obsession® perfume. Ray Kroc, one of the cofounders of McDonald's, always reminded his people that "McDonald's sold more than the hamburger, they sold the experience the hamburger was wrapped in."

Consumers seem to have a perceptual map in their minds that places, or positions, one product in relation to something else. In a narrower use of the positioning concept, that something else is the other brands in the market, and consumers compare brands consciously or subconsciously according to their similarities and differences. When a company tries to influence what consumers think of a brand with respect to its competition, this kind of positioning is called **competitive positioning.**

Chevrolet, for example, is usually thought of as a family car; Volvo as a safe, durable car; and Cadillac as a luxury car. Consumers also make fine distinctions within subcategories. Cadillacs are not simply luxury automobiles; they are also cars that have a more traditional image, conveying status and prestige, a car that might be purchased by a banker or a small-business owner. In contrast, a Lexus has a more contemporary luxury image, a car you might expect an investment counselor or a CEO of a midsize company to own.

Positioning reflects the decisions that companies make to intentionally influence the images and associations that consumers have of their products and, sometimes, even those of the competition. For example, Pepsi would like consumers to believe that it is a product for hip, young-minded people. In contrast, it likes to portray Coca-Cola as an older, more conservative, and somewhat stodgy brand. Coca-Cola mostly ignores Pepsi. Even though Coca-Cola outsells Pepsi by over a billion cases with its two top brands (Classic and Diet)—and increased its lead in 2004—this portrayal probably was a source of irritation at Coke.[28] In early 2005, Coca-Cola CEO Neville Isdell, at the launch of the new "Make it Real" campaign, commented that they needed "to integrate the brand back into popular culture."[29]

In Chapters 2 and 3, we discussed some of the procedures and tests you can use to determine consumers' perceptions of a brand. A goal of many of these activities is to determine and understand a brand's image or personality. This information can then be used to change, reinforce, or intensify the image. The brand's image or its personality can be the result of many factors, including advertising, pricing policies, signage, packaging, and of course, the want-satisfying qualities of the product. Positioning is action oriented. It's what companies do to influence what people think or feel. A brand or a company's image takes time to establish, but once it is implanted on the consumers' perceptual map, it remains firmly established—sometimes even when the company would like to see it changed.

Sears has long had the reputation as a seller of quality merchandise, especially for appliances and hardware. However, in the 1980s it was having a difficult time dealing with two major problems. Its merchandise, especially soft goods, was often perceived as slightly too conservative. Sears was also being undercut badly by discount merchandisers such as Wal-Mart. In some stores, nearly half of all revenue was generated by items on sale.

In the spring of 1989, Sears changed its pricing structure to a policy featuring fewer sale items and everyday low(er) prices (EDLP) on most items. Sears achieved some success with this move but, after an initial spurt in business, stores were allowed to run more sale items. Over the years, Sears had trained its customers to expect sale items; that was part of the consumers' perception of how Sears operates. Despite heavy promotion announcing the new plan, Sears relented, and its pricing policy began increasingly to resemble the old structure. Consumers simply did not accept Sears' new position.

Sales continued to be a problem. In 1993, Sears restructured its clothing and apparel lines, updating them with a more contemporary look. It then introduced the lines with the very successful advertising campaign, "Come see the softer side of Sears."[30] Sears has been successful with the repositioning of its image because the restructure was not a complete change, but merely an update, which consumers accepted. In 2004, Sears was again having major problems with its position. Chains such as J.C. Penney, Kohl's, and Goody's have undercut Sears in terms of offering low prices and a more contemporary image. Higher-end department stores such as Dillards, Hects, and Belk often are perceived as having higher-quality or more stylish clothing.

Positioning decisions are strategic in nature and provide the direction for a campaign to follow. Competitive positioning usually implies that the company is willing to sacrifice some component of the overall market to be more effective within a narrower focus. Pepsi positions its brand as a drink for young people, or those who think young. It's willing to sacrifice an appeal to the "older" market. However, Pepsi does quite well with its "limited" appeal. After all there are a lot of people who think they are young.

POSITIONING A PRODUCT

Various authors have noted that there are at least seven different ways to position a product:

1. By product characteristics or customer benefits. (Lee jeans is the "brand that fits.")
2. By a price-quality relationship. (Sears is a "value" store.)
3. By use or application. (Cortaid Cream "relieves itches.")
4. By product user. (Trix "are for kids.")
5. By product class. (Dove is not just a soap, but is a cleansing product for dry skin.)
6. By cultural symbol. (Harley-Davidson, "Born in the U.S.A.")
7. By competitor. (Avis positions itself with Hertz.)[31]

After the basic positioning strategy has been determined, it is up to the copywriters and the art directors to execute a message strategy with creative tactics. The development of the message strategy and tactics will be covered more extensively in Chapter 6.

▮ FUNDING THE MARKETING COMMUNICATION PROGRAM

The decision about how much money to allocate for marketing communications is simple in concept but complicated in practice. This decision is of strategic interest because it has a profound influence on the way a company can compete. Companies compete in terms of both the quality and the quantity of the messages they disseminate. The size of the advertising budget, usually called the **appropriation,** can influence the creativity involved in the message strategy. It may have an even greater impact on media. Although creativity can flourish independently from expenditures, media exposure cannot. One common viewpoint is expressed as follows:

Share of media expenditures
equals
Share of media voice
equals
Share of mind and heart
equals
Share of market.

Of course, this view only works within a certain range of expenditures. Beyond a specific level of expenditures, each additional dollar spent on advertising or promotion is unlikely to generate sufficient sales to cover expenses and still contribute to net profit. It is relatively easy using marginal analysis to understand the relationship between advertising expenditures and sales in retrospect; it is a lot more difficult to predict this relationship in advance.[32] Determining the optimum amount of money to spend for advertising may be one of the most difficult tasks facing advertising and agency planners.[33]

A complete discussion of all the variables that can influence the appropriation and how to determine the optimal level of expenditures is beyond the scope of this book. Such a discussion would include modeling procedures using multiple regression analysis to explain and predict the relationship between advertising and sales over time.

The typical reader of this book does not usually deal with these issues, and the size of the budget is usually a given in advertising campaign classes. Agencies, also, do not usually determine the advertising appropriation but receive it from their clients. It is, however, important that the amount of money allocated to marketing communications be appropriate for the expected tasks: solving problems and exploiting opportunities. To provide a rough idea about how these decisions are made, we'll look at some traditional methods for determining the appropriation and some of the factors that influence their size.

TRADITIONAL APPROACHES TO DETERMINE THE APPROPRIATION

A number of widely used methods appear in advertising textbooks. It is important to understand that a company doesn't necessarily use one method. It is more likely that companies use a combination of methods.

All You Can Afford
The use of this method appears to be on the decline. The chief advantage of this method is that it is simple and, for companies of limited resources, may be the only option. Its main disadvantages are lack of a rational basis for the decision and insufficient resources to generate enough advertising exposure to stimulate an impact in the marketplace. It is likely that many

companies start out using another method and wind up using this one because of budgetary constraints.

Percentage of Sales

This widely used method involves multiplying past or anticipated sales by a certain percentage to determine the amount of money to be appropriated for the marketing communication budget. This percentage can be obtained from a variety of sources: industry contacts, trade associations, trade publications, government data, conferences, and conventions. This method is especially useful if the decision maker's expertise does not lie within the area of marketing or advertising. If the percentage used as the multiplier is typical of successful firms in the field, then this method is likely to be a good one, depending on the degree to which the advertiser is similar to other companies. Its main disadvantage is that sales are usually used to determine the advertising expenditure. When sales are high, the advertising budget will be high. When sales are low, the budget will also be low. Logically, the situation may require the exact opposite, especially when sales are low.

Competitive Parity

This method uses the competition's expenditures as a benchmark against which the company determines its strategy. Companies use this approach for at least two reasons: First, a company may assume that if the competition is successful, it must know what it is doing, including determining how much to spend. Second, a company may feel that it needs to match the competition's expenditures to be competitive.

Limitations of this method vary according to how similar the companies in the category match up. Companies that appear to be similar from afar may have significant differences when scrutinized up close.

Objective and Task

This approach is the most logical method, but it is probably also the most difficult one to use. It is employed by nearly two-thirds of the largest advertisers.[34] To use this method, a planner first defines specific objectives. The next step involves determining the various tasks required to achieve the objectives. The last step, also the easiest, involves estimating the cost of implementing the tasks.

This approach is logical because it links marketing communication expenditures to the achievement of specific goals. If the objectives are defined in terms of behavioral objectives such as sales, then the first step, defining objectives, is relatively easy, but the second step is difficult, determining the marketing communication tasks that will likely achieve the objectives.

In the case of sales goals, many of the marketing communication tools, such as advertising, could influence sales. Determining which variable had which effect often leaves a gap in the linkage between sales goals and a specific communication tool, such as advertising or sales promotion. To solve this problem, some advertisers define their communication objectives (at least their message-oriented ones) in terms of communication criteria, such as top-of-mind awareness or attitude change. This makes the link between the objectives and the communication tasks much clearer. It still leaves difficult questions pertaining to the degree to which the achievement of communications criteria, such as attitude change, will result in the achievement of marketing goals, such as sales. Although the objective and task method is more complicated than many of the other approaches, it attempts to deal with questions the other methods leave unanswered.

It's ironic that the most popular approach to determining the size of a marketing communication budget is likely one that is never included in industry surveys—*historical precedent*. Companies often base their budgets on what they spent the previous year.

■ TARGETING AND DELIVERING THE MESSAGE

Targeting is the last element of the strategic foundation. In its broadest sense, targeting the message involves both the people to whom the message is aimed and the means by which the message gets delivered. At this stage in the development of a campaign, the target market has typically been determined. Nevertheless, during the development of strategy, new opportunities may present themselves that call for either a reexamination or a modification of the target market. This is another example of how the development of a campaign can be an ongoing process.

For example, in 1992, when Coca-Cola hired CAA out of Hollywood to produce television commercials, it was looking for breakthrough advertising. Coca-Cola's strategy was simple: Hire famous, highly creative film directors to produce highly creative television commercials. The spots were often highly creative, very visual, and *mostly unrelated* except for the tagline "Always Coca-Cola." Although the campaign was criticized for not having enough continuity, the company's response was that it used different spots to appeal to different market segments.[35]

Whether this strategy was in place before the spots were produced or they came up with this strategy after they saw the commercials is moot for this discussion. It's easy to argue that the decision to determine the target audience should be made before the strategy and tactics are determined. However, it is also common and strategically sound to modify the positioning and targeting strategies as new opportunities develop.

The targeting decision usually ranges from a point where a company will use one message, or appeal, for all consumers to a point at which it uses separate messages for different market segments. Figure 5-4 presents typical targeting options.

| **FIGURE 5-4** | TYPICAL TARGETING OPTIONS |

One Message   Multiple Appeals

Targeted Market Segment   General Target Market   Multiple Segments

When a company makes a decision to position its message against a specific competitor, it logically follows that it will be segmenting at least part of the market. By influencing consumers to think of a product in a certain way, the company, in effect, is implying not to think of the product in a different way. When Pepsi positions its products as youth oriented, it is targeting its messages to segments of the overall population who are young, who think young, or who would like to be young.

Companies that use one message to appeal to a mass audience tend to have brands that are used across broad demographic categories, such as Wesson oil, Hunt's tomato paste, and Nabisco saltine crackers. To be successful with this approach, the message should be general or diffuse enough to allow a variety of consumer groups to read into it a benefit that appeals to them. Campbell Soup's "Good for the body, good for the soul" campaign was an example of this type of message. This approach usually works best for the market leader in a category. Campbell Soup sells more than 50% of all canned soup. As product categories become increasingly competitive and as the products within the generic class approach parity, companies usually opt for a strategy positioned around a message that appeals primarily to a portion of the overall market.

Companies that use multiple messages to target multiple market segments tend to be large companies. In many cases, these companies are simply applying the marketing concept to an increasingly fragmented market. When Coke first developed its "Always Coca-Cola" campaign, it used a variety of musical formats, such as rock, rap, and country, to send different messages to various segments with the same general low-keyed theme: No matter what's going on, Coca-Cola is always around. To be successful with different messages, a company must be sure to tie each message into the brand's core equities, as Coca-Cola does. This approach probably didn't work very well for Coca-Cola because eventually its spots became much more consistent and less varied and Coke eventually moved on to other campaigns.

DEVELOPING A MARKETING COMMUNICATION MIX

Much has been written in recent years about the importance of integrating the components of marketing communication into a marketing communication mix. Surprisingly, very little has been written about how much of the marketing effort or budget should be devoted to advertising and how much to other types of marketing communication. Companies offer little insight. The same company that will divulge proprietary information off the record will seldom provide any usable information about how it allocates money to different types of promotion. Generally, companies say they use judgment based on experience. Other times they will indicate they use marketing mix or advertising and marketing (A and M) models, but "they are proprietary." These models may be sophisticated, but the usual impression companies give is that the models are rudimentary or even crude.

Media-Oriented Approach
One approach to determining the marketing communication mix is to view each type of communication as a means of delivering messages or

impressions to consumers. Each promotional tool can then be evaluated in terms of its ability to *efficiently* generate exposure for the brand. Values can be assigned to the importance of traditional media criteria, such as cost-efficiency, competitive share of voice, and optimal reach and frequencies, and an allocation model can be constructed. There are a couple of problems with this approach. Some forms of marketing communication, such as public relations or the use of nontraditional media, are difficult to measure. Any type of quantitative analysis would only be as good as the measurements. However, the main problem with this approach is that it is difficult to integrate a value for message content into a quantitative model.

Message-Oriented Approach

Some scholars have argued that it is wrong to evaluate media channels in terms of vehicle exposures. Instead, promotional tools should be evaluated on the basis of the information they communicate. Therefore, each medium, or type of marketing communication, can be looked at in terms of its ability to effectively deliver certain types of information. For example:

Network television	delivers a strong brand identity
Magazines	good way to show product detail
Newspaper	localizes and generates a sense of immediacy
Internet	enables site visitors to interact with ads
Brochures	deliver specific information
Radio	reminds consumers to act
Outdoor	size and location can be powerful reminders of ad message
Yellow Pages	move consumers to specific buying locations
Public relations	provides information that is more highly credible
Infomercials	provide in-depth persuasive information
Store displays	stimulate action at point of sale[36]

Both the media- and the message-oriented approach require substantial amounts of judgment. Although it is possible to do a mathematical model to apportion amounts of money to marketing communication tools, expectations of a rigorous approach probably await further research developments. In-depth coverage of marketing communication strategy and tactics will be covered in Chapter 8.

Advertising Media Strategy

In the development of an integrated marketing communication plan, the strategic decision about the marketing communication mix should ideally precede any decisions about what kind of media to use. However, advertising usually will be the dominant form of marketing communication.

For this reason, media strategy will be covered in depth in Chapter 7. Related types of marketing communication, such as sales promotion, public relations, and direct marketing, which typically supplement traditional media such as radio, television, magazines, and newspapers, are discussed in Chapter 8.

CAMPAIGN PROGRESS CHECKLIST

At this point in the campaign you should generally be aware of the following points:

1. Campaign strategies should be based on a strategic foundation consisting of five elements: determining selling focus; managing brand equity, positioning the messages, funding the marketing communication program, and targeting and delivery of messages.

2. The long-term success of a brand requires that the intangible value, or equity, associated with the brand name be managed to avoid competing on the basis of price or product distinctions (which it may not have).

3. Cultivating brand loyalty is the most important aspect of managing brand equity.

4. For many brands, simple awareness is less important than top-of-mind awareness.

5. Perceptions of a brand's quality can be more important than its actual quality.

6. The associations consumers make with a brand influence how they think and feel about a product.

7. A company's proprietary assets, such as patents, characters, and channel relationships, are an important part of the product itself and should be carefully evaluated and promoted or the brand may lose part of its value.

8. Positioning the product is an important strategic decision because it provides direction for the writers and art directors to follow helping to ensure that the ads will be on target and on strategy.

9. Understanding how the marketing communication appropriation was determined is important because it can have a profound influence on the way a company can compete.

10. There are at least three important targeting decisions: whom to target, how to reach them efficiently, and how to use media and related communication tools effectively to get the message across.

Notes and References

[1] C.H. Sandage and Vernon Fryburger, *Advertising Theory and Practice, 7th Ed.* (Homewood, IL: Irwin, 1967), p. 5.

[2] Alice Z. Cuneo, "Wal-Mart Gains on Payless Turf," *Advertising Age,* 28 July 2004, p. 26.

[3] L.E. Boone and D.L. Kurtz, *Contemporary Marketing* (Fort Worth, TX: Dryden Press, 1999), p. 399.

[4] D.A. Aaker, *Managing Brand Equity* (New York: Free Press, 1991), p. 16.

[5]N. Munk, "Why Women Find Lauder Mesmerizing," *Fortune,* 25 May 1998, pp. 96–106. See also, Stephanie Thompson, "Cosmetic Legend Lauder Dies," *Advertising Age,* 3 May 2004, p. 27.

[6]This article is an excerpt from Terry G. Vavra, "After-Marketing: How to Keep Customers for Life through Relationship Marketing," *Brandweek,* 7 December 1992, p. 20.

[7]T.G. Vavra, "Learning from Your Losses," *Brandweek,* 7 December 1992, p. 21.

[8]Ibid., p. 20.

[9]Amanda Beeler, "Jupiter Projects Email Marketing Will Jump to $7.3 Billion by 2005," *Advertising Age,* 8 May 2000, p. 80.

[10]D.E. Parente, "A Look at the Way Advertisers Write Objectives," Unpublished working paper, p. 9.

[11]Aaker, *Managing Brand Equity,* p. 63.

[12]A. Ries and Jack Trout, *The 22 Immutable Laws of Marketing: Violate Them at Your Own Risk* (New York: HarperBusiness, 1993), p. 18.

[13]Ibid., p. 3.

[14]Christine Bittar, "Purple Pill on Counters No Source of Indigestion," *Brandweek,* 21 June 2004, p. S60.

[15]Aaker, *Managing Brand Equity,* p. 1.

[16]"Beer, Wine, Liquor," *Brandweek,* 9 October 1995, p. 120.

[17]Mike Beirne and Kenneth Hein, "Feisty Feds Weigh In against Low-Carbs—and Tasteless Ads," *Brandweek,* 21 June 2004, p. S27.

[18]Bittar, "Purple Pill," p. S61.

[19]The information on the Green Giant character is abstracted from unpublished, undated, and unnumbered material on "Enduring Campaigns" from the Leo Burnett Company, Inc.

[20]"Newsmakers 1990," *Advertising Age,* 24 December 1990, p. 5.

[21]B. Crumley and E. Bowes, "Perrier Moves to Publicis," *Advertising Age,* 30 November 1992, p. 53.

[22]*SuperBrands* (1989–1994).

[23]K. Benezra and G. Khermouch, "Enough Niche Product, the Cola Giants Strike Back," *SuperBrands,* 15 June 1998, p. S32.

[24]K. Hein, "Look Out Water, Juices B-b-bubbles Are Back," *Brandweek,* 17 June 2002, p. S34.

[25]Kenneth Hein, "Colas Stuck in the Middle, as Alternatives Wring Sales," *Brandweek,* 21 June 2004, p. S30.

[26]J. Pollack and J. Neff, "Marketer Decree: Be a Top Brand or Be Gone," *Brandweek,* 15 September 1997, p. 2.

[27]S. Mehegan, "P&G Makes Tide More Efficient," *Brandweek,* 4 August 1998, p. 9.

[28]Sales statistics reported in Kenneth Hein, "Colas Stuck in the Middle, as Alternatives Wring Sales," *Brandweek,* 21 June 2004, p. S30.

[29]Kenneth Hein, "Coke Evolves 'REAL' with Positive Spin," *Brandweek,* 17 January 2005, p.4.

[30]E. Underwood, "Weathering the Storm," *SuperBrands* (1995), p. 123.

[31]D.A. Aaker et al., *Advertising Management, 5th Ed.* (Englewood Cliffs, NJ: Prentice Hall, 1995), pp. 190–201.

[32]For more information on marginal analysis, see Aaker et al. *Advertising Management,* pp. 548–551.

[33]J.Z. Sissors and L. Bumba, *Advertising Media Planning, 5th Ed.* (Lincolnwood, IL: NTC Business Books, 1995), p. 407.

[34]C.H. Patti and Vincent Blasko, "Budgeting Practices of Big Advertisers," *Journal of Advertising Research* 21 (December 1981), pp. 23–29.

[35]B. Garfield, "Coke Ads Great, but Not Always," *Advertising Age,* 15 February 1993, p. 60.

[36]Adapted from Ron Kaatz, "An Integrated Media Planning System," in Dean M. Krugman et al., *Advertising: Its Role in Modern Marketing, 8th Ed.* (Fort Worth, TX: Dryden Press, 1994), p. 327.

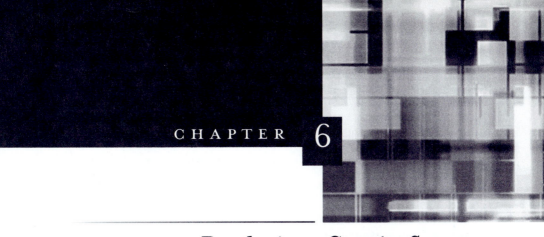

CHAPTER 6

Developing a Creative Strategy
That Moves People

There are few places you can now go without being exposed to some commercial message. Because of a massive message overload, consumers are not only jaded and cynical—they're downright annoyed! To get through a cluttered media landscape, an ad has to have stopping power—something that makes people pause and pay attention. That "something" must engage consumers with the ad enough to trigger brand associations so they will remember the special feeling or information conveyed to them by the brand. It's easy to talk about "something" in the abstract but putting it into practice takes imagination and creativity.

Today, lots of advertising can make you laugh and engage your interest. Whether these ads are persuasive generates debate. An ad that is creative but doesn't sell might be termed "*creativity for technique's sake*." These are ads that appear to have been created to showcase some creative effect, even if the effect is simply to make people laugh. An ad might be a brilliant piece of film (or tape), but not a good commercial. Although it is probably true that some of these ads are created for the wrong reasons, many are the results of well-intentioned efforts to do something special for the brand. Naturally, executives like to present ads that are both "creative" *and* persuasive. Although these qualities are not necessarily inversely related, sometimes to achieve both creative and persuasive ads you might have to take a little away from one or the other.

A copywriter's challenge is to balance an ad's need to be persuasive with a similar need to be creative. It's still very much an art. Our challenge in this chapter is to help the reader make these decisions based on something other than intuition. We divide this chapter into several sections as follows:

- Essential and optional elements found in a creative plan
- Analysis of the opportunity to develop a message strategy
- Examination of the strategic approaches to developing a message strategy
- Modest proposal on how to be creative
- Traditional approaches to creating advertising
- New rules for talking to today's consumer

We are mindful that trying to break down the creative process into discrete components is not without risks. Exactly why something is persuasive often defies analysis. Furthermore, we understand many advertising minds feel you can't really teach someone to be creative. Still, to repeat something we said earlier, we do have some suggestions.

■ ELEMENTS ESSENTIAL TO A CREATIVE PLAN

Following the situation analysis, the campaign should begin to take on a strategic focus. The creative, or message strategy, is often the most important part of this focus. The purpose of a creative strategy is to inspire great "creative." Great strategy, great ideas, and great ads—why settle for less? However, great creative is usually based on more than just an intuitive feeling. There has to be some substance behind creative decisions. Basically, there are four typical elements found in this section: target audience, objectives, strategy, and tactics.

THE CREATIVE TARGET AUDIENCE

This target audience is essentially the same as the campaign target audience, only it may be described somewhat differently. The target audience for a brand of hair shampoo may be females between the age of 16 and 22. However, agency creatives may try to get a better feel for this consumer by describing them as "the hair involved." Naturally, in this situation, profiling the target with demographic characteristics is not enough. The target audience is often delineated more subjectively in the creative area because the writers have to create ads that are interpretational and this generally requires that they address the target in more personal terms. In fact, when account planners and creatives get together to write an informal creative brief, they sometimes refer to the target using the name of someone they know (say, Cathy Lou, the switchboard lady). Although this information isn't put into the campaign report, it is useful in generating ideas. Profiling the target as "hair involved," however, will most likely make it into the campaign document.

CREATIVE OBJECTIVES

An advertising objective consists of a message element and a media element. Creative objectives are the message part of the advertising objective. In the following advertising objective, the first part of the statement refers to a mental effect the ad is supposed to have (i.e., the message), and the second part focuses on the delivery of the message (i.e., the media).

- To establish top-of-mind awareness (the message part) in 60% of the target audience by the end of the first quarter (the media part).

There are a number of ways to take the above advertising objective and use it to write a creative objective. To do this, focus on the message part of the advertising objective, perhaps as follows:

- To get the target audience to associate the brand name with the product category before any other brands.

The objective of the creative strategy is to get across a message that affects the way the target audience thinks or feels about the brand. If planners understand correctly how consumers make decisions, then these thoughts and feelings should transfer to what the advertiser would like the consumer to do—that usually means buy the product. The mental effect that the writer or artist is trying to achieve with the ad is the core element in a creative objective. This effect is often some variation of the communication criteria we discussed in Chapter 4, such as awareness, comprehension, attitude, or image.

Aflac used to be a little-known insurance provider. Name awareness was low and understanding of what the company offered was even lower. Reportedly, Eric David, creative director at the Kaplan Thaler Group ad agency, was stuck for ideas and spent an hour walking around the block. Eventually, he realized he was quacking like a duck and within minutes the first Aflac duck spot was written. Sales soared.

In the beginning, the creative objective was simply to establish brand awareness. Over the life of the campaign, the objective probably changed to intensifying awareness and strengthening the association between the Aflac brand and supplementary life insurance.

CREATIVE STRATEGY

Creative strategy consists of the guidelines for the thoughts, feelings, and impressions that are communicated with advertising and other marketing communications. These guidelines provide direction for the copywriters and artists to develop ads that are on target and within the message strategy. A creative plan is an articulation of the strategy. You might think of it as a map. This map outlines or profiles the important strategic considerations for the campaign's creative thrust, which ultimately drives the message.

There are many formats and structures available for creative plans, and each agency tends to use a different one. In the first edition of this book, we presented eight different versions.[1] In the following editions, we decided to present elements that can go into a creative plan and let the account team custom-tailor the elements that it feels are appropriate for the particular campaign. We call the more important elements the **critical elements** of a creative plan.

Critical Elements of the Creative Strategy

There are at least three elements that ought to be part of every creative strategy:

1. Strategic focal point
2. Positioning statement
3. Big unifying idea

Strategic Focal Points.   To be sure all creatives concentrate on the same strategy, it is helpful to state the creative focus clearly. You can also think of this focus as a statement of the creative strategy. The focal point is that particular aspect of the company's problem or opportunity the campaign is intended to address. We assume you realize that this focus doesn't

| EXHIBIT 6-1 | FAMOUS STRATEGIC FOCAL POINTS |

Brand	Creative Strategy Statement
Energizer	Energizer batteries keep things going (longer) than the other guys.
Mountain Dew	The brand for guys who take it to the extreme.
Lee Jeans	Lee makes jeans for women who have trouble finding pants to fit their body.
Altoids	Really strong mints.
Coca-Cola	Coca-Cola is the real cola (thing).
Charmin	Charmin is so squeezably soft you won't be able to resist squeezing it.
Red Bull	Red Bull gives you the energy to excel.
Subway	Subway offers a healthy alternative to eating fast food.
Gatorade	Gatorade is a drink that quenches the thirst of hardworking athletes.
Wheaties	Wheaties is a cereal eaten by famous athletes.

materialize out of thin air, but evolves out of research. Exhibit 6-1 presents a list of creative strategy statements that appear to have been the focal points of some very memorable campaigns.

Positioning.   Once you determine the focus of the creative plan, your next step is to provide the context, or background, for the advertising messages. Positioning, as suggested earlier, refers to the way one generally gets consumers to think or feel about the product, especially with respect to the competition. Although the focal point of the Coca-Cola strategy in Exhibit 6-1 is to emphasize that Coke is the real thing, these messages are delivered amid a wholesome background where consumers satisfy their taste for something refreshing with a Coke. On the other hand, Pepsi Cola uses a narrower type of positioning called **competitive positioning** by suggesting that consumers drink Pepsi—not Coke. Coke positions itself (as category leaders often do) against a broad range of competitors, whereas Pepsi often specifically mentions Coke. Pepsi extends the comparison by stating (in varying ways) that Pepsi is for young people and that Coke is for the older crowd.

Big Unifying Idea.   It can be helpful to use an attention-getting device to make ads memorable and to tie together the various elements in a creative plan. Many agencies simply call this device a *big idea*. We like to call it a *big* **unifying** *idea* to signify that the idea should be a vehicle that provides

EXHIBIT 6-2	MEMORABLE BIG UNIFYING IDEAS
Energizer	Toy bunny keeps going and going because Energizer batteries last longer.
Maytag	Maytag repairman is bored since he has nothing to repair because Maytag washers don't break down.
Big Red Gum	Makes your breath so fresh you'll want to kiss a little longer.
Michelin Tire	Baby/tire image evokes benefits of using safer tires on your family car.
Target	Stylish use of logo and the color red.
Secret Deodorant	Is strong enough for a man, but pH balanced for a woman.
Frosted Mini Wheats	Has good taste and nutrition for the adult and the kid in you.
Subway	Jared Fogle loses weight by eating at Subway restaurants.
Serta	The counting sheep are out of a job because Serta mattresses make you sleepy.
Chevrolet Truck	"Like a Rock" music.

a common bond to unify all ads within a campaign. The frustrated duck in the Aflac commercials is what makes its commercials interesting and memorable. Exhibit 6-2 presents our nomination of some of the more famous big unifying ideas in recent years.

Note the similarity between a creative strategy statement and a big unifying idea. For Energizer batteries, the strategic focus is placed on the idea that their batteries last longer. The pink bunny gives them a vehicle to say it in many different ways and still stay true to the strategy. The three elements we've discussed so far (strategic focal point, positioning statement, and big unifying idea) provide the bare outline of a creative strategy. To give depth to a creative plan, other elements can be added to supply nuance and richness to the strategy. By using some of these optional elements, you can wind up with a more complex strategy that works on different levels. The desired result is a total effect that is both synergistic and ultimately more persuasive.

OPTIONAL ELEMENTS OF THE CREATIVE STRATEGY

It's the interaction among the various elements in a strategic plan that give a campaign more persuasive power than merely using a series of unrelated ads. The idea is to integrate the elements into a cohesive selling message so that one aspect of the campaign reinforces another. These elements can be something observable (physical) or simply something one thinks about (psychological). The elements weave a thread of continuity throughout the campaign and give it lasting power or "legs" as they sometimes say.

PHYSICAL CONTINUITY

In a campaign, the general plan is to put something in each ad that leaves a similar impression with consumers so that they feel one ad is a continuation of the others. What separates a campaign from a collection of ads is the degree to which each execution is connected. Advertisements that look and sound alike help keep creative work on target. Consumers notice new ads and remember them longer when a common element (or thread) ties together all the ads in a campaign.

Slogans, taglines, and trade characters are devices that add continuity to a company's advertising. A slogan or tagline may be used for a single campaign, or it may endure for many years. The line, "Can you hear me now?" is not a slogan or quite a tagline, but many people think that it is. Because the line is repeated so often in Verizon Wireless ads, it effectively gets across the idea that Verizon Wireless users get better reception.

Like a good slogan or tagline, an effective trade character can last for years. The Leo Burnett agency has been as successful as any in the business of developing trade characters. Some of its animated characters include Tony the Tiger, the Pillsbury Doughboy, and the Keebler Elves; among its live-action characters are Maytag's Lonely Repairman, Charmin's Mr. Whipple, and Morris the Cat. Exhibit 6-3 lists some of the trade characters developed by the Leo Burnett Co.[2]

The simple line, "Can you hear me now?" is used as a continuity device to tie together Verizon Wireless ads. Adding a distinctive sound is another

---

EXHIBIT 6-3 LEO BURNETT TRADE CHARACTERS

Account or Product	Year of Arrival	Character
Green Giant	1935	Jolly Green Giant
	1973	Little Green Sprout
Pillsbury	1965	Pillsbury Doughboy
Frosted Flakes	1952	Tony the Tiger
Marlboro	1955	Marlboro Man
9-Lives	1969	Morris the Cat
Maytag	1967	Lonely Repairman
Starkist	1961	Charlie Tuna
Froot Loops	1963	Toucan Sam
Keebler	1968	Keebler Elves
U.S. Department of		Vince and Larry
Transportation	1985	(the crash test dummies)
7-UP	1988	Spot

way to add a unifying element to a campaign: The sound of a bass drum, followed by the gentle marching of a pink bunny, signals consumers of an arriving Energizer commercial.

PSYCHOLOGICAL CONTINUITY

Advertisements may look and sound alike, but unless they are psychologically similar or consistent, they are not likely to function as a campaign. Advertisers strive to unify the way people think about their advertising by developing a consistent **theme, image, tone,** or **attitude** in their ads. Each of these constructs is similar to the others in that they affect the way people think or feel about an ad. Although a campaign may not have a consistent theme, image, attitude, or tone in every ad, the campaign will present a more cohesive message if they do.

The unifying element in most campaigns is the **theme**—*the overall idea underlying the advertisement.* The theme can be expressed in many different ways. It often is stated most clearly by a **slogan,** which is one reason why slogans are repeated so frequently. Slogans also add physical continuity because they invariably appear in print or as a graphic.

BMW's use of the slogan "Ultimate Driving Machine" also is the theme in many ads that are designed to showcase how the car performs. The slogan "You're in good hands" is designed to communicate a sense of trust—exactly what you would hope to feel from an insurance company. The insurance company also could tell you that it is "Like a good neighbor"—another way to communicate trust. Do you know the two companies associated with each slogan?

Knowledgeable advertisers recognize that a brand's **image** can significantly affect sales. Campaigns can *establish, reinforce,* and *intensify* images or replace them with new ones. Perhaps the most successful image campaign of all time has been that of the Marlboro Man, which exemplifies each of these actions. Before 1955 (when the Marlboro Man was introduced), filter-tip cigarettes were largely smoked by women. In fact, Marlboro cigarettes were originally known as "Mild as May."[3] Male smokers, however, far outnumbered female smokers. Recognizing the greater market potential in appealing to men, Leo Burnett, president of the company that bears his name, decided to replace the earlier, more feminine image with one that would appeal to men, by introducing what he called "The Marlboro Man," a rugged, self-assured individual. This mental picture established the brand as one with which men could feel comfortable.

In 1955, the Leo Burnett Co. reinforced this image by giving the Marlboro Man a tattoo, thereby distinguishing him from any male images used by competitors. In 1967, the company intensified this image by introducing in its television commercials music from *The Magnificent Seven,* a movie about gunslingers that was very popular with men at that time. From this point on, the music influenced the character and quality—or tone—of all subsequent commercials. By 1975, Marlboro had become the number-one cigarette brand in the United States, and the Marlboro Man living in Marlboro Country set the tone and direction for all subsequent advertising. At the turn of the century, Marlboro was easily the best-selling cigarette in the world. For many people, especially those living in emerging nations, the Marlboro brand is a symbol of Western or American culture.

Campaigns with **attitude** tend to be judgmental, whereas image campaigns usually focus on an idea or concept of a product, person, or institution. People from certain schools, some companies, and even various parts of the country often have similar attitudes. We frequently notice that some people simply have an *attitude*. Campaigns, too, can sometimes be described as having an attitude. The question for the marketing strategist becomes: Does the consumer agree/disagree or identify with the situation? The number-one animal in the world with an attitude is the common cat. Unlike dogs, cats assume no guilt for house-training mistakes, they won't try to make you feel better when you're down, and they don't get excited if you throw them a crumb. In fact, if you throw cats good food, they are just as likely to turn up their noses and walk away. They're fussy, finicky eaters. Many cat owners both admire and love their cats for their independent ways.

In 1969, 9Lives®, a division of StarKist Foods, adopted a strategy using a trade character named Morris to show that 9Lives has the cat food even finicky cats can't resist. Eventually, 9Lives got around to putting a picture of Morris on the product's packaging. Within four months of his appearance on the label, the company's share of market in two cat food categories doubled. Such can be the power of a trade character.[4]

CREATIVE TACTICS

Once the strategy has been developed, it must be executed in a detailed way to get the most out of it. It's remarkable how writers and artists can take a simple strategy and turn it into something creative. The goal is not simply to create ads that entertain or appeal to one's aesthetic tastes; the goal is to create ads that help sell the product. Later in this chapter we'll cover some approaches to developing persuasive ads.

▌APPRAISING THE CREATIVE OPPORTUNITY

Once you understand what goes into a creative plan, the next task is to figure out how to execute one. It's not enough to determine what you want to do, it's important to understand what you have a realistic opportunity to do—well. There are numerous approaches to figuring out how to proceed, everything from simple intuition to rigorous analysis. We'll explore only a few approaches. And keep in mind, these are only guidelines.

Probably the easiest and most direct approach is to analyze the product to determine what the product has that addresses what consumers want. If a product's want-satisfying qualities are significantly different from the competition, then the rest is easy. The most effective way to advertise, then, is to simply interpret the want-satisfying qualities of the product in terms of the needs or wants of the consumer.[5] Can there be a more effective way to advertise? To paraphrase Leo Burnett, if a product has something that meets the needs or wants of the consumer, that product is *inherently dramatic to them*. If you are working with a product that is not only significantly different from that of the competition, but better as well, the world will beat a path to your door. Maybe.

There are a few problems with this approach. Even if the product is significantly different, it can be a tough proposition to get the message through a cluttered media landscape and still have impact. Consumers are often skeptical, indifferent, and even cynical. It's not enough to have the better product; consumers have to think or feel that it's better. A creative task that starts off sounding fairly simple and straightforward can quickly become complicated. As a result, many advertising people approach developing creative strategy largely on an intuitive basis. This approach may be appropriate if you are an experienced professional; if you are a student, we have some alternative suggestions.

THE FCB GRID

Copywriters have several broad strategy options from which they can choose. Advertising can focus on product benefits, it can develop or reinforce brand personality, or it can evoke specific feelings and emotions. It can also develop group or brand associations.[6] At the Foote, Cone & Belding (FCB) advertising agency, an analytical approach was developed to help its creative people understand how to focus message strategy. After conducting extensive research—in the United States and Europe—FCB concluded that it could classify products into four distinct categories. These categories are then assigned to one of four cells in a grid. The first classification includes products consumers primarily "think" about, as opposed to products they buy more on the basis of "feelings." The second classification depends on whether consumers feel high involvement with the product or low involvement. The classifications breakdown is as follows:

- Products consumers tend to **think** about and have **high involvement** (life insurance, car batteries, exterior house paint, and stereo components)
- Products consumers have **feelings** about and have **high involvement** (perfume, hair coloring, sports cars, wine for a dinner party)
- Products consumers tend to **think** about and have **low involvement** (liquid bleach, paper towels, insect repellent, regular shampoo)
- Products consumers have **feelings** about and have **low involvement** (peanut butter, barbecue sauce, diet soft drinks, fast-food restaurants)

These product categories are placed on a grid to illustrate the degree to which consumers have high or low "involvement," and the degree to which consumers relate to the product on the basis of "thinking" or "feeling." Exhibit 6-4 is an example of the FCB grid.

Using the FCB Grid

This grid is used to help guide both message strategy and executions. The FCB grid is based on Foote, Cone & Belding's research. The location of a brand or any number of products on a custom grid can be constructed using some of the scales (or questions) we covered in Chapters 2 and 3.

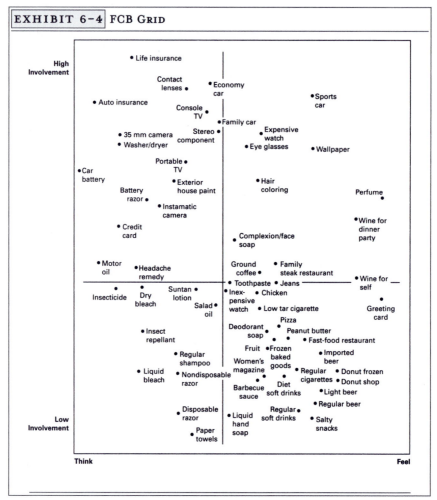

EXHIBIT 6-4 FCB GRID

Source: Slightly altered version from John J. Rossiter et al., "A Better Advertising Planning Grid," *Journal of Advertising Research* (October/November, 1991), p. 12.

In fact, it should be understood that the grid location of the many brands *within a product category* will likely vary. For example, Anheuser-Busch runs what it calls "heritage" advertising on television. In these spots, the commercials talk about the brewing traditions handed down from the founder that make Budweiser the beer it is today. On the FCB grid, "regular beer" is placed in the area of Low Involvement and Feel. Although a sense of tradition is something most people have feelings about, it is also clear that the heritage ads are designed to influence what people think about Budweiser.

The FCB grid is used to predict responses consumers make to advertising. Another grid, the Rossiter-Percy model, offers an improvement over the FCB grid. The Rossiter-Percy model offers two additional classifications of motives consumers have for buying a product or brand. In addition to low/high involvement and think/feel motives, Rossiter-Percy suggest consumers have motives that derive from informational needs, such as the desire to solve or avoid problems, and transformational motives, which stem from the consumer's desire to find some meaning or satisfaction in the experience that surrounds the purchase of a brand. This model is divided into six cells and is an excellent model. We, however, use the FCB model because it keeps things fairly simple. Creatives, especially students, sometimes resist using complex analytical approaches to developing ads for fear of it inhibiting a process they regard as essentially intuitive and nonrational. Nonetheless, we recommend that the student/ reader consult additional sources for more information.[7]

KNOWING YOUR CREATIVE APPROACH

Once you have a good grasp of your strategy and the creative opportunity, you need to decide on the best creative approach to meet your objective. Patti and Frazier cite seven creative approaches that can serve as a guideline for your crafting of ads (see Exhibit 6-5).

The **generic strategy,** which makes no competitive or superiority claims, is best used for products or brands that dominate a category. It is easily identifiable with a market leader and can rely on a combination of attributes and benefits, with little or no comparison to others made. The advertising for Campbell Soup has promoted the product as "Soup is good food." Because Campbell's sells well over 50% of all canned soup, the advertiser realizes that if it can get people to eat more soup, the brand will reap most of the sales.

The **preemptive claim** predicts or upstages the competition by advertising a point of difference for the brand. Competing brands may provide similar benefits or have similar attributes, but not advertise those benefits or attributes. Thus, you can preempt them by being the first to lay claim to the key benefit or salient attributes. Coca-Cola has preempted the claim "It's the real thing." In its earlier days, getting this message out was important as other companies tried to trade on the value of Coca-Cola's name by selling brands such as Cay-Ola, Candy Cola, Coca, Fig-Cola, Cola, Cold Cola, and Koca-Nola. These brands were outlawed by the courts in 1916.[8]

The **unique selling proposition** (USP) is used when a distinct competitive advantage exists; namely, a differentiating factor for your brand. Rosser Reeves made this technique famous with M&M candy's slogan, "Melts in your mouth, not in your hands." This strategy is difficult to employ in today's highly competitive environment, which is defined by explosive product and brand proliferation. Still, as you examine what your brand has or can do in relation to the competition, you should be watchful for positive and useful differentiating factors. Figure 6-1 for the Gillette M3Power is an example of an ad able to take advantage of a strong USP.

The **brand image strategy** relies on factors not inherent to a brand because specific product attributes are relatively meaningless. Rather, the advertising should build, reinforce, or change the target audience's attitude toward the brand, primarily by concentrating on psychological or emotional appeals.

Product positioning is a strategy that calls for carving out a niche for your brand in consumers' minds relative to the competition. It's a means for differentiating your brand from that of the competition and is especially helpful for new brands or those wishing to gain on the competitive leaders in market share. Pepsi says it's hip and Coke is not.

EXHIBIT 6-5 CREATIVE STRATEGY ALTERNATIVES: A SUMMARY

Strategy	Description	Most Suitable Conditions	Competitive Implications
Generic	Straight product or benefit claim with no assertion of superiority	Monopoly or extreme dominance of product category	Serves to make brand synonymous with product category
Preemptive	Generic claim with assertion of superiority	Most useful in growing or awakening market where competitive advertising is generic or nonexistent	May be successful in convincing consumer of superiority of advertiser's product; serves to convince consumers of brand superiority
Unique Selling Proposition	Superiority claim based on unique physical feature or benefit	Most useful when point of difference cannot be matched readily by competitors	Advertiser obtains strong persuasive advantage; forces competitors to imitate or choose more aggressive strategy
Brand Image	Claim based on psychological differentiation; usually symbolic association	Best suited to homogeneous goods where physical differences are difficult to develop or may be quickly matched; requires sufficient understanding of consumers to develop meaningful symbols/ associations	Most often involves prestige claims that rarely challenge competitors directly
Positioning	Attempt to build or occupy mental niche in relation to identified competitor	Best strategy for attacking a market leader; requires relatively long-term commitment to aggressive advertising efforts and understanding consumers	Comparisons limit options for competition; counterattacks seem to offer little chance of success

| EXHIBIT 6-5 | CONTINUED |

Strategy	Description	Most Suitable Conditions	Competitive Implications
Resonance	Attempt to evoke stored experiences of prospects to endow product with relevant meaning or significance	Best suited to socially visible goods; requires considerable consumer understanding to design message patterns	Few direct limitations on competitor's options; likely competitive response; imitation
Affective	Attempt to provoke involvement or emotion through ambiguity, humor, or the like, without strong-selling emphasis	Best suited to discretionary items; effective use depends on conventional approach by competitors to maximize difference; greatest commitment is to aesthetics or intuition rather than research	Competitors may imitate to undermine strategy of difference or pursue other alternatives

The **resonance approach** relies on fond or positive memories or feelings the target audience associates with the brand. Obviously, the lack of differentiating characteristics for your brand would make this approach appropriate. When the "Always Coca-Cola" campaign was first run in 1992, it had a minimal affect on the public (discussed in Chapter 1). The only copy in the early spots were the words "Always Coca-Cola." Over the years, those two words have come to mean something a lot richer than when the campaign first began. The words "real thing" as part of a Coke slogan functions in much the same way. Consumers will often attribute to Coca-Cola whatever positive feeling they have held about that brand over the years. So, to some people, Coca-Cola is a wholesome part of Americana. To others, the brand may simply be a dependable beverage to drink when they want something refreshing. And to others, it may simply be a comforting image. The value of a resonance approach is the very general way images and brand associations bounce back and forth in the mind of the consumer.

An **affective strategy** seeks to form an emotional attachment between the brand and consumers. Highly charged and symbolic images or words, often combined with music, evoke heightened emotional responses from consumers. Such a strategy is useful for brands with little to differentiate them in the marketplace or for those brands whose success depends on the emotional attachment of consumers. FUBU is a popular brand of urban streetwear clothing. The company was founded in 1992 by five African Americans to design and sell clothes to African American consumers. Its

FIGURE 6-1	AD FOR GILLETTE MACH3 RAZOR

Source: The Gillette Company.

name is an acronym for "For Us By Us," a slogan that is an expression of black empowerment.

Although we discuss these seven strategies or approaches as though they exist apart from other approaches, it is important to understand that they often overlap. For example, you may be inclined to use a *brand image strategy* in combination with a *resonance approach,* particularly if your brand lacks distinct differentiation based on attributes and seeks to create emotional ties with the consumer. In recent years, advertising campaigns for Ford Mustang have often referred to the car nostalgically, affectionately, and simply as— "It's a Mustang." As you can imagine, the range of questions for your creative decisions is vast, especially when you begin to consider the relationship of various ads at different times or the dynamic interplay of graphics and copy in one ad or a combination of ads. Should you emphasize the product in use? Use a strong, emotionally charged symbol? Show the price/quality relationship? Dwell on product characteristics or attributes? Preempt your competition? Acknowledge the competition in the hope of positioning yourself effectively against them? Rely solely on a key benefit?

The list of questions could go on, but the key question to remember is this: What is there about your brand that satisfies a salient want or need of the target audience? The satisfaction consumers derive can be physical or psychological. If research tells you that something exists, if you're confident that it's critical to the selling of your product, if it fits with objectives in your strategy, and if you've found an original, creative idea or means to carry the message, then this is probably the most promising route to take. Note, though, how that decision greatly depends on a host of variables, all of which demand careful consideration and thought.

ON BEING CREATIVE

Describing creativity isn't very difficult. We can outline what we look for in a creative ad. We can even explain the stages the great ones go through to produce award-winning ads. But can we tell someone *how* to be creative? Not an easy question to answer. Keep this in mind as we try.

Creativity involves either generating completely new ideas or coming up with new takes on old ideas. Because we concede that we're unable to tell people how to think about things no one else has, our discussion focuses on how to turn common ideas into something different.

What Makes Strategy Creative Is That It Is Both Special and Different

Simply being *different* doesn't make something creative. Sometimes being different is, well, maybe weird. As Leo Burnett was once reported to have said, "If all you want is to be different, you can come down in the morning with a sock in your mouth." To be creative, an ad has to be both different and in some way special. The consumer has to feel that the quality that makes something different is special in order to set a creative ad apart from an average one. Communicating a *special* feeling without that feeling being different won't necessarily make it creative either, especially if the feeling is something that has been expressed countless times, like saying "I love you."

The challenge for someone just starting out, like a student, is to figure out how to be special and different within the context of the strategy. It is, as they say, an art. But by paying attention to the research and by being attentive to details, an aspiring writer or art director can call upon the insights of others to be sure that his or her ideas are at least on target and on strategy.

One approach involves "shaking up" the way people think and over-turning conventional wisdom, both in the way ads are used and in the way ads are created. This approach has been around for a long time and can be found in many creative ads. In recent years, the approach has received a lot of publicity because of the books *Disruption* and *Beyond Disruption* by Jean-Marie Dru.[9]

Disrupting Expectations

As people go through life, their patterns of behavior are shaped by their experiences. They develop a complex bundle of expectations to help them navigate the world efficiently and effectively. We know that when we look both ways before crossing the street, we're likely to make it safely to the other side. When we extend our hand to someone, that person is likely to shake it. We also have expectations about how that person will shake our hand. When the person is of slight stature—especially if that person is a female—and the grip is strong, it makes an impression on most people. It's something unexpected. Adolescent males often try to trick their friends by extending their hand only to withdraw it at the last moment, thumbing their buddy "outta here." (Lots of things are funny only to teenage boys.)

Catching people off guard can be funny and can help people like the ad and, one hopes, the product. Perhaps its most important function, however, is to get people's attention. Jonathan Bond and Richard Kirshenbaum, founders of the award-winning agency Kirshenbaum & Bond, suggest that today's consumers are cynical. Because of a massive overload of media messages, they've developed a filtering mechanism to screen out most of the messages aimed their way. They call this filter their personal "radar." To succeed in reaching today's consumer, Kirshenbaum and Bond suggest crafting ads in such a way as to get in "under the radar" (also the title of a popular book they've written for *Adweek*).[10]

Disrupting people's expectations is one way to make people pause and pay attention. If you can also get them to smile or laugh, so much the better. The key to disrupting consumers' expectations in an ad is contrast.[11] If consumers expect one thing, provide another. There's an old saying, "It's not whether you win or lose, but how you _____" (most readers will add the words *play the game*). If you substitute *place the blame* instead, you may get a few groans, but are likely to get people to pause and think, "Wait a second. What was that?" Of course, you have to use judgment, especially if you substitute a pun for the element people are expecting. As many people have said, puns are the lowest rung on the joke chain. They are nowhere near as funny as some people think.

The creative challenge is not only to attract people's attention, but also to engage their interest. While they are pausing, you want consumers to resolve their momentary confusion within the context of the strategy. Figure 6-2 shows an ad for General Foods International Coffees. Something seems not quite right with the headline "Take the time to stop and smell the chocolate." Most people quickly make the adjustment substituting "smell the roses." But for chocolate lovers, smell the chocolate doesn't

FIGURE 6-2 | AD FOR GENERAL FOODS INTERNATIONAL COFFEES— "SMELL THE CHOCOLATE"

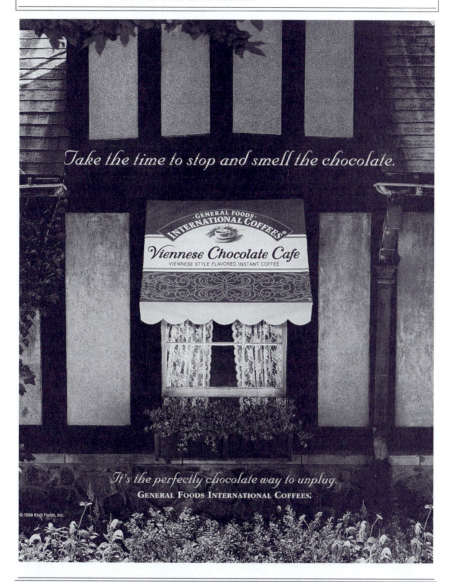

Source: General Foods International Coffees® is a registered trademark of KF Holdings.

seem like such a bad idea either. If that momentary disruption gets people to pay just a little more attention—and perhaps, even read the label—then the ad is doing its job. The ad will work provided the product characteristics reflect the implied promise in the ad. In this ad, the implied message is "if you like chocolate and coffee, this brand is for you." Apparently, many people do.

An alternative to providing contrast is simply to shake up people by making them wonder what an ad means. The key to this kind of ad is to make the target *care*. In the second General Foods ad for coffee (see Figure 6-3), the headline reads, "Fat free? Very hip." This ad was placed in women's magazines and targeted the millions of calorie-conscious

---

FIGURE 6-3 | AD FOR GENERAL FOODS INTERNATIONAL COFFEE FRENCH VANILLA—"VERY HIP"

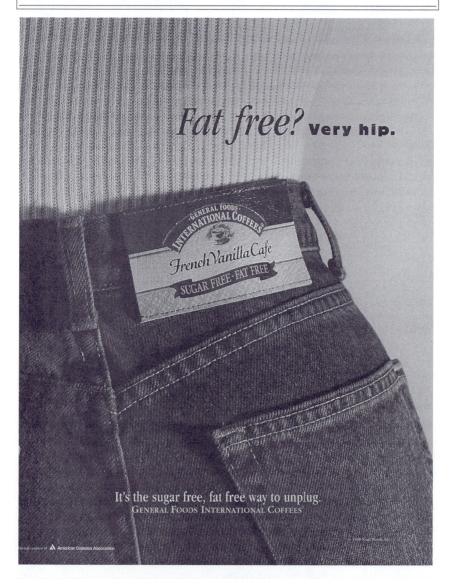

Source: General Foods International Coffees® is a registered trademark of KF Holdings.

women. It flags the target's attention with the words "fat free." Implied here is the promise that the brand is a smart, or hip, way to have hips like the model in the ad. Because this is only implied, it doesn't insult people by promising slim hips—something it can't deliver. But people do like to dream.

So far, the disruption we've discussed has occurred mostly in the headline. Disruption through contrast can also take place within a picture (see Figures 6-4 and 6-5, pages 174 and 175, respectively). Figure 6-4 shows an ad for Defend EXspot insecticide for dogs. The picture shows the incongruous image of a dog underwater with a face mask. Very cute.

Contrast can also take place between or among the various elements in the ad. Contrast is possible with any of the elements in an ad, but it's far more dramatic if the contrast occurs in the major elements, like the headline or picture.

IMPLEMENTING THE CREATIVE STRATEGY

Disrupting expectations may not be appropriate for all situations. Sometimes a direct approach focusing on a product's qualities makes more sense. However, taking a creative strategy and turning it into a creative execution takes practice. It helps to work alongside one who knows how. What often appears as discrete steps or concepts in a textbook, in practice often works better another way. It can inhibit the creative process to adhere to any formula or procedure rigidly.

So far we've considered some ideas on getting creative. The next step is to take these ideas and translate them into **creative tactics.** At this point, professionals often prepare what is called a **creative brief**—simply an outline to help channel their thinking so that it is on target and on strategy. You might even say that the creative brief is an outline of the strategy. Exhibit 6-6 (see page 176) is a copy of a creative brief, slightly modified from one used at the Foote, Cone & Belding advertising agency. Note how simple and straightforward the form is. Although we have been discussing quite a few concepts in this chapter, the goal is to keep these ideas in the back of your mind so as not to inhibit or impede the free flow of ideas. Later, when your ideas are in rough form, you can double back to see how you're doing conceptually. Although there is value in keeping your mind open and receptive to all kinds of ideas, at some point you will have to focus your energy on creating ads that achieve creative and campaign objectives.

The role of the brief is to inspire great creative. The creative brief should be written in conversational style to help inspire creativity. If the creatives don't get excited, the brief is worthless.

We also suggest you develop tactical focal points that you keep uppermost in your mind when storming for ideas to turn into ads. Next, we suggest you consider some of the tried-and-true principles or concepts creatives have used over the years, such as a product's attributes, features, or benefits. You may also want to consider a brand's image, personality, essence, reputation, or position.

FIGURE 6-4 | AD FOR DEFEND EXspot

You Can Dip Your Dog For Fleas And Ticks. Or You Can Use A Squirt Of New Defend.

You know how much dogs hate being dipped. That's why we created Defend™ EXspot® insecticide for dogs. You apply it in seconds, and yet it's as effective as the leading dip. One application of revolutionary new Defend provides your dog with up to four weeks of flea and tick protection. You've never seen a product that's both this easy to use and this effective.

Defend for dogs. Ask your veterinarian about it.

Amazing new Defend applies in seconds, yet works for weeks.

It Works Like Nothing Else.

FIGURE 6-5 | ARMSTRONG FLOORING AD WITH WOODPECKER

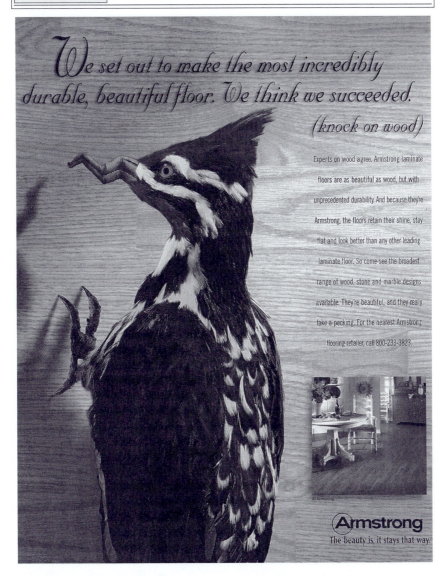

EXHIBIT 6-6 CREATIVE BRIEF FORMAT

---

1. What do we want this advertising to accomplish?
   It is important to keep the focus on the objectives.

2. Who are we talking to, and what insights do we have about them?
   What points can we use to gain leverage? Does the target have
   a "sweet spot" or a "hot button"? Use the insights found in
   research and intuition to guide the way you address the target.

3. How do we want consumers to describe the brand—its essence
   and personality? What do we want the brand to mean to the
   audience? Can we get them to think of the brand in the same way
   they think of a friend?

4. What's the single most important thing we want them to take out of
   this advertising? What's the most important idea, feeling, or
   memory we want our advertising to leave with the consumer?

5. How can we make our promise, claim, or even the ad, believable?
   Are we being honest with the consumer? Can we, and do we
   support the claims we are making in this advertising?

6. Is there anything worth thinking about that might help us achieve
   great advertising? Is there any current trend, fad, or news that we
   might in some way relate to our consumer insight?

7. Is there anything that we must get into our advertising?

Source: Cone, Foote & Belding.

TRADITIONAL APPROACHES TO CREATING ADVERTISING

Although we tend to talk about these approaches conceptually, you will need to translate these ideas using specific details about the brand.

ATTRIBUTES, FEATURES, AND BENEFITS

Whether it's a product or a service that you're advertising, it has qualities or characteristics that help it perform in the marketplace. It helps to think of these qualities in terms of attributes, features, and benefits.

Think of **attributes** as what the product has (what it innately owns). Think of **features** as what the product does (how it performs, what it's used for). And think of **benefits** as what the product promises because of what it has or does. For example, Heinz ketchup has a combination of certain ingredients and a manufacturing process (attributes) that make it slower pouring out of the bottle (feature) than other brands of ketchup. The attributes and feature lead to the benefit, which may be described as richer taste. Ideally, the benefit should be competitive in that it solves consumers' problems better than the competition. A *benefit* may also be termed a consumer consequence because for the consumer it is a result.

Consider, for example, the laddering approach to attributes that was described in Chapter 2. Attributes lead to consumer consequences and ultimately to personal values. Even within the attributes and consequences, you can subdivide categories so that some attributes become physical and some consequences become functional or self-involved. Of course, as you move up the ladder from attributes to personal values, you're moving away from the focus on the product to a tighter focus on consumers and how the product may affect them.

It is important to find a brand's differentiating characteristics. This may be what will give the brand a competitive advantage. In the case of Heinz ketchup, its slow-pouring feature differentiates Heinz from its competition. The idea of slowness and how that benefits the consumer is the tactical focal point in much of the advertising for Heinz.

Not all attributes, features, or the benefits leading from them are equal. Some are more important than others. It all depends on which ones best address consumer needs, wants, and interests. Meanwhile, as you dig and pick at the research, you should be sensitive to finding points of difference between your brand and those of the competition. Eventually, this information will help you identify your brand's **personality, reputation,** and **positioning.**

BRANDING

David Ogilvy has been a vigorous advocate for the importance of brand image. Over the past three decades the concept has evolved considerably. It has been dissected, analyzed, and reconstructed with varying definitions and parts. At its core, however, are a brand's personality, reputation, and positioning. These concepts help make up a brand's identity.

Brand Image

A *brand's* **image** encompasses *all* the associations that consumers have for a brand: the thoughts, feelings, and imagery that are linked to that brand in the consumer's memory, including colors, sounds, and smells. Within the overall brand image are associations with characters, symbols, endorsers, lifestyles, and types of users.[12]

An important part of a brand's image is its **personality and reputation.** From a creative standpoint, it is critical that your big unifying idea and its execution reflect the brand's image. For example, a consumer's perception of a product or service depends on the past advertising and experiences consumers have with a brand and its competition. As a result, a certain brand personality and reputation emerges. To understand brand personality as it leads to image, think of it on a personal level. Your personality has no doubt led to the image you project within your circle of friends and associates. What is that image? How would you like to be known? You may want to answer that question by completing this statement: I would like to be known as a(n) _____.

From a personal point of view, would you fill it in with "good person," "loyal friend," or "understanding partner"? Professionally, would you fill it in with "creative genius," "superb writer," or "good manager"?

Maybe you would like to fill in the blank with most, if not all, of those answers. But that's not what brand image is. With brand image, your answers are limited to other people's perceptions. These perceptions are based on your personality traits, which allow your friends and associates to create an overall meaning of you, your image.

Now, assume you fill in one answer. You would then consciously arrange your actions and behaviors to fit the brand image you want. So, if you wanted to be known as a positive spirit among your colleagues, you would behave in a positive way. In short, your actions would mirror the brand image you claimed as yours, in much the same way that advertising (the visible presentation of a product's personality) mirrors the brand image of that product. This is what David Ogilvy meant when he argued in favor of the long-term importance of brand image in advertising. And if you expanded your self-description, how would you define the personality that led to the image? Friendly? Outgoing? Soothing? Adventurous? Exciting? Such descriptors also apply to products and contribute to the overall perception of a brand's image.

As consumers experience a brand over time they develop expectations about the value they get from a brand. With Sony, it's quality; Nordstrom, service; Victoria's Secret, elegant indulgence; Godiva, just indulgence. Cadillac stands for ultimate luxury and status. (Or does it?) A brand's reputation is a reflection of what consumers think or feel a brand stands for. It can be the result of all the impressions and images consumers receive from the company, or it may simply reflect consumers' changing standards or perceptions—as may be the case with Cadillac.

Typical in brand imaging is the association of feelings or emotions with the brand, sometimes termed **emotional bonding.** With this type of association, the consumers' perceptions play a leading role in aligning the brand with affective or emotional predispositions, usually based on past advertising, promotion, or experience.

Advertising that seeks this kind of bonding is often executionally based: How you say something often is more important than what you say. But emotional bonding can evolve from several creative approaches. For example, your creative may use a functional, symbolic, or experiential approach depending on what your product has and does and what the consumer wants or needs from it. With a functional approach, you concentrate on intrinsic product attributes, such as speed or performance. With a symbolic approach, you concentrate on extrinsic attributes, such as style or prestige. Fashion brands such as Polo or Tommy Hilfiger often use this approach. And with the experiential approach, you concentrate on the pleasure consumers derive from the product, such as relaxation, excitement, or romance. Vacation cruises fit in well here.

You should strive to create this kind of consumer bonding with your brand. Successful brands create emotional attachments with their consumers, whether through relationship marketing or positive and enduring brand associations.

Brand imaging touches on all of these considerations and relies for the most part on the consumers' perceptions, which consumers develop from contact with the products' attributes, features, and benefits. In a sense, the consumer connects, often emotionally, with the brand, thus forming those perceptions. Through that connection, the brand gains equity in the competitive marketplace. If everything works well, consumers become *brand believers.*

Brand Positioning

Positioning describes advertisers' actions in trying to place their brand in one place, or position, in relation to another according to their similarities or differences.

Think of positioning this way: You're in a crowded room and attempting to find a place to stand and be comfortable. The room is analogous to a typical consumer's mind—crowded to the hilt with all sorts of competing products, brands, and messages. How do you find a place that's yours alone—where you feel comfortable? This search for a place is the essence of positioning.

Perhaps you'll have to elbow or wriggle your way to a good place, perhaps preempting someone else who also has an eye on that place (the "best" or leadership position, according to Bruce Bendinger in *The Copy Workshop Workbook*).[13] Perhaps you'll have to wrestle head to head for the place you want (the **"against"** position). Perhaps you'll have to be content with a little room in the bigger space where others want to be simply because it is special or highly desirable (the **"niche"** position). Perhaps you'll have to move to a different place, one not so crowded (the **"new"** position).

Each positioning variation relates to which place you'll occupy in the consumer's mind—the position you'll own. Will you be faster? Crunchier? Shinier? More reliable? Newer? Newest? Of course, the list could go on. The point is that positioning demands you find and occupy in the consumer's mind a certain place that is clear, unmistakable, valued, and yours alone. Positioning provides a direction, or center point, for your campaign around which your creative plan and the creative elements (such as graphics or copy) revolve. You can't simply guess at the position you wish to occupy.

Even traditional approaches may not work with consumers who have been exposed to countless ads. More than ever, writers and artists need to *really* understand consumers. Once again, this demands imaginative, insightful research. Bond and Kirshenbaum have 10 rules they follow for talking to today's cynical, busy, achieving consumer.[14]

▌NEW RULES FOR TALKING TO TODAY'S CONSUMER

DON'T SAY IT. DEMONSTRATE IT

Simply having a talking head tell why a product works isn't enough. Nor will dressing actors in white lab coats build credibility. Consumers literally will not buy it (i.e., the product). If at all possible, show how the product works. Even with something as seemingly difficult to demonstrate as investing with a mutual funds company, an ad could demonstrate how employees rely on the company to invest their money. Fidelity Investments, the giant mutual funds company, was criticized for using a humorous approach in its commercials. One campaign used Lily Tomlin in various comedic situations to indicate the confusion many people face when trying to decide where to invest. In the ads, she encounters Peter Lynch, one of the most respected fund managers of all time. Lynch tells

Tomlin to try Fidelity. The ads were criticized because of the association of slapstick humor with investing—a subject many people take very seriously. Instead, the ads could have talked about how Lynch relies on Fidelity to handle his money—which he does.

DON'T LOOK OR SOUND LIKE AN AD

Consumers are immediately suspicious when they are being sold something—especially if there is something in the ad that strikes them as contrived. A regional phone company ran a spot promoting its Internet access service. In one of its television spots, a thirtysomething man walks over to an open sewer hole where a worker is doing something underground. The man asks a series of questions related to Internet service. The worker responds with utterances that are difficult to understand. Near the end of the spot, the worker climbs out of the sewer hole and takes off her hardhat to reveal a luxurious head of hair. In real life, the probable response would have been—"how about that!" Viewing the ad, a typical consumer's response likely was—"I don't think so."

In years past, Oldsmobile told consumers, "This is not your father's Oldsmobile." The consumers liked the ads but recognized the line as a marketing ploy. Bond and Kirshenbaum emphasize, "Don't let your strategy show" if you want the ad to be accepted and believed. And, write fresh cliché-free copy.

MAKE THE AD THE LOGO

A certain "look" can be so intensely associated with a particular brand that the ad itself becomes an extension of the logo. Over the years, many people have immediately recognized a print ad for Volkswagen just by its use of a distinctive typeface and white space. Ads for Target have at times used the brand's distinctive bull's-eye logo as the main visual element in the ad. This helps make the ad seem less intrusive, something many consumers appreciate.

TREAT BRANDS LIKE PEOPLE

Develop the brand into *someone* consumers feel comfortable with. Comfort is often what motivates consumers to reach for a name brand rather than a private label. McDonald's often goes out of its way to make its commercials seem warm and friendly. The slogans, "McDonald's: We love to see you smile," or "I'm loving it," are examples.

BE HONEST TO A FAULT

One small seed of doubt will send up consumers' red flags, so don't plant any. Many times ads are designed using models who represent what women would like to look like—great figure, stunning hair, or a supersmooth complexion. These ads are said to be aspirational, and generally connect with the target audience. But it is becoming increasingly clear that many consumers do not relate to models in ads, especially with those models who are much thinner than the average woman. As a result, advertisers are beginning to use female models who are older and larger than those they used in the past. However, even when stores create a catalog featuring plus-size models, they usually do not go beyond using size-14 models. Because many women are a size 18 and larger, when they see nothing but 14s in the ads, seeds of distrust are planted.

INVOLVE THE CONSUMER

Letting the consumer help or take part in the ad is one way to build a relationship between the brand and the consumer. Since 1981, the advertising for Absolut® vodka has consisted of more than 500 magazine ads, each of which invites the reader to solve the puzzle and figure out where the bottle is located in the ad. When the campaign began, the brand was selling 20,000 cases a year in the United States. Fifteen years later, the brand was selling more than 3 million cases annually—an increase of almost 15,000%.[15] Can anybody tell the difference between one brand of vodka and another? (Note how we're trying to involve the reader in this paragraph.) Figure 6-6 is an example of involving the reader with the ad.

USE HUMOR TO CREATE CAMARADERIE WITH CONSUMERS

Using humor helps differentiate advertising from the bland competition. It can also help endear the brand to consumers who appreciate the value, however small, they get out of ads that make them laugh or smile. But the humor has to be a part of the selling message or consumers will merely laugh and ignore the point the ad needs to make. The ad for M&Ms introduces its name change along with its usual association of M&M's with fun. Figure 6-7 shows how humor can be used to get across the selling message.

SEX STILL SELLS, BUT BE CAREFUL

Sex remains one of the more powerful motives that influence behavior. However, sex has been so misused throughout the history of advertising that many consumers—especially women—are understandably sensitive. The use of sex appeal to sell products should be relevant to the product used. When in doubt, use sex appeal only to sell sexy products. Even then, it may not be effective. Pioneer Electronics sells automotive electronic products primarily to males ages 16 to 30. In the past, the company used "girls in bathing suits" in its ads. In focus groups, the males told the company they didn't like it, and instead wanted more information to learn about the product. New ads often steer the target to a Web site for product information in greater detail.[16] Figure 6-8 shows how sex appeal can be used in an understated but elegant way.

DON'T CHESTBEAT

If consumers are already cynical about advertising, why would they believe a "We're Number 1" claim? Whether or not the claim is based on objective data, consumers often suspect the claim is subjective. However, when Hertz used to refer to itself as the "Super Star in Rent-a-Cars," it made sense because they were responding to Avis, which was advertising "We're number two, so we try harder." In effect, Hertz was saying, "you're darn right we're the best, and here are some reasons why." Today, in a different advertising climate, they simply make the point, "There's Hertz and not exactly."

FIGURE 6-6 | ABSOLUT VODKA AD—ABSOLUT PERFECTION

Source: Under permission by V&S Vin & Sprit AB. ABSOLUT®VODKA. Absolute Country of Sweden Vodka 7 Logo, Absolut, Absolut Bottle Design and Absolut Calligraphy are trademarks owned by V7S VIN 7 SPRIT AB (PUBI) ©2005 V7S VIN 7 SPRIT AB (PUBL).

FIGURE 6-7 AD FOR M&M's—USING HUMOR

*Whaddya mean this
name change thing has gone to my head?*

Same great chocolate. Much better name.
You know those "M&M's"® you've been calling "Plain" all these years?
Well, now they're called "Milk Chocolate." It's chocolate too good to be called plain.

www.m-ms.com

| FIGURE 6-8 | AD FOR BCBGIRLS—USING SEX APPEAL |

Source: PRNewsFoto/Unilever Cosmetics International.

NOW BREAK RULES

Consumers become immune to advertising approaches. As much as we hate to suggest this to beginners, consider breaking rules and exploring new approaches and techniques.

UNIFYING THE ADS

Because an advertising campaign contains various ads for diverse media, there may be a tendency to treat each ad independently, almost as if it exists in a vacuum. This, of course, should not be the case. Rather, each ad should build on or complement the others regardless of the medium in which it's placed. As you create each ad, be sure to weave some thread of continuity through your executions so that when you are finished you have a campaign and not just a bunch of ads.

CAMPAIGN PROGRESS CHECKLIST

At this point in the campaign you should generally be aware of the following points:

1. Creative ads should be designed to sell the product, not showcase some creative effect or technique.

2. There are four important parts to a creative plan: the target audience, objectives, strategy, and tactics.

3. Creative strategy should contain at least a strategic focal point, a positioning statement, and a big unifying idea.

4. To add depth and complexity to a creative plan, use slogans, taglines, and trade characters for physical continuity and a theme, image, or certain tone or attitude for psychological continuity.

5. A grid like the one developed by FCB can help you evaluate your creative opportunity.

6. There are various strategic approaches around which you can build a message strategy, including a generic strategy, a preemptive claim, product positioning, brand image strategy, a unique selling proposition (USP), a resonance approach, and an affective strategy.

7. To be creative, it's not enough to be different—it has to matter to consumers. One way to be different is to disrupt expectations. If consumers expect one thing, give them another.

8. When you get ready to do your executions, work up a copy brief to help keep the creative ideas on track.

9. For many brands, focusing on attributes, features, and benefits is the appropriate approach to promoting the product.

10. As you approach selling the product, remember the importance of building the brand in terms of an image, a reputation, or a personality.

11. Even though there are rules one can follow to help develop persuasive ads, sometimes it's right to break the rules.

Notes and References

[1]D.E. Parente et al., *Advertising Campaign Strategy: A Guide to Marketing Communication Plans* (New York: Dryden Press, 1996), pp. 150–152.

[2]Information on the trade characters discussed in this section, as well as the information on United Airlines and Virginia Slims is abstracted from unpublished, undated, and unnumbered material on enduring campaigns from Leo Burnett Company, Inc.

[3]University of Virginia American Studies Department Online, "From 'Mild as May' to 'Tough as Shoe Leather,'" 1 April 1997 (accessed 23 October 2002).   http://xroads.Virginia.edu/~CLASS/Marlboro/mman2.html

[4]The information of the trade characters discussed in this section as well as the information on United Airlines and Virginia Slims is abstracted from unpublished, undated, and unnumbered material on enduring campaigns from Leo Burnett Company, Inc.

[5]I first learned this concept in graduate school at the University of Illinois. It is hard to remember the source of the comment. My best guess is Charles H. Sandage.

[6]R. Batra et al., *Advertising Management, 5th Ed.* (Upper Saddle River, NJ: Prentice Hall, 1996), p. 275.

[7]For more information, see John R. Rossiter et al., "A Better Advertising Planning Grid," *Journal of Advertising Research* (October/November 1991), pp. 11–21. This topic is also discussed extensively in Batra et al., *Advertising Management*, pp. 281–285.

[8]K.L. Keller, *Strategic Brand Management* (Upper Saddle River, NJ: Prentice Hall, 1998), p. 23.

[9]Information used from two books by J.M. Dru, *Disruption: Overturning Conventions and Shaking Up the Marketplace* (New York: John Wiley and Sons, 1996) and *Beyond Disruption: Changing the Rules in the Marketplace* (New York: John Wiley and Sons, 2002).

[10]Adapted from Jonathan Bond and Richard Kirshenbaum, *Under the Radar: Talking to Today's Cynical Consumer* (New York: John Wiley and Sons, 1997), pp. 68–92.

[11]I am indebted to Tom Groth who helped me understand the concept of disrupting expectations. It's not surprising that his students have three times won the NSAC sponsored by the AAF.

[12]Batra et al., *Advertising Management*, p. 321.

[13]Bruce Bendiger, *The Copy Workshop Workbook, 3rd Ed.* (Chicago: Copy Workshop, 2002), pp. 52–55.

[14]These rules, first published in 1997, seem as appropriate as ever. Bond and Kirshenbaum, *Under the Radar*, pp. 80–81.

[15]R.W. Lewis, *Absolut Book* (Boston: Journey Editions, 1996), p. xi.

[16]Kris Oser, "Pioneer Targets Tuners by Spurning Sex for Information," *Advertising Age*, 17 May 2004, p. 16.

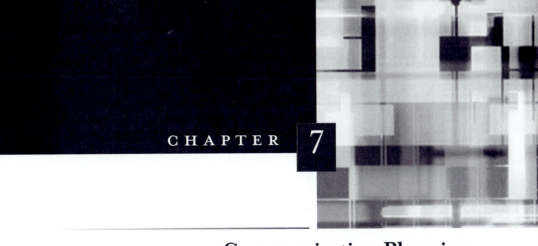

CHAPTER 7

Communication Planning: Media Strategy and Tactics

A sea of change is surging over the traditional field of advertising media planning. The competition to get into the minds of consumers is aggressive, relentless, and increasingly creative. There is a growing dissatisfaction among major advertisers such as Procter & Gamble and McDonald's with mass-media advertising.[1] They wonder if it works—like it used to. They continue to spend large amounts of money on mass media, but aggressively seek new ways to connect with consumers. And it's about a lot more than simple reach and frequency. Today, it's all about contacts and context. Consumers are distracted. The traditional model of a passive consumer watching TV has been replaced by time-starved consumers who jump from TV to computer to PlayStation. When they do watch television, they often multitask (think cell phones). Consumers are exposed to so many messages they have become increasingly selective.

To get an unenthusiastic consumer's attention, advertisers are experimenting with a wide variety of communication platforms, featuring everything from viral marketing, "wild postings," buzz marketing, branded entertainment, and product placement (to be discussed in Chapters 8 and 9). Progressive planners have considerably expanded the ways to deliver messages or impressions about a brand. Media planning has been reconceptualized as **communication planning.** Media planners need more than a calculator or good software. They need good judgment and imagination. The basic purpose of media or any communication is to deliver messages efficiently and effectively. Efficient plans deliver messages to targets at a relatively low cost. They avoid wasting money on media that reach people who aren't likely prospects for the product or service. To deliver messages *effectively,* planners must select media that can both influence and enhance messages.

Media can influence the impact of a message depending on the context in which the audience receives it. The context can vary from a medium's suitability to a creative approach, to the timing of ads, or to reaching targets in situations in which they normally don't expect to receive promotional messages. Smart planners sometimes ignore cost-efficiency and select media because of its ability to deliver messages effectively. Viewed this way, media are more than neutral or passive carriers of a message. They help the message achieve its communication objective.

This type of decision is often based on no more than a gut reaction. The effectiveness of the decision is related to the decision maker's ability and experience. Beginners—especially students—may not have the ability or the experience of a seasoned professional. Recommending a communication plan of mostly nontraditional media may suggest to a client you're creative, but not necessarily that you're knowledgeable enough to base decisions on a rational basis. We usually advise beginners to base decisions primarily on a careful analysis of quantitative factors (such as cost-efficiency), and only after that on other qualitative factors. The purpose of this chapter is to examine some of the basic decisions that media people make and why they make them. Keep in mind: A creative media plan requires imagination. Thinking creatively is an important part of the media process.

MEDIA DECISIONS AND THE CAMPAIGN PROCESS

In a traditional media model, media decisions evolve out of the creative strategy. The basic idea is to figure out what you want to convey in a message and then decide the best way to deliver that message. The best approach, perhaps, is to make these decisions together. In many large national agencies, a brand team consists of both creative and media personnel. This way, when writers are storming for ideas, a media person can lend an in-depth understanding of the way potential messages are likely to be delivered and received. In fact, media people may offer creative ideas based on more specific knowledge of media vehicles. When account planners are included on a brand team, part of their function is to determine what type of advertising communicates best with consumers. As a result, sometimes the media or communication vehicle is critical and the message strategy flows from the way the message is to be delivered.[2]

THE BASIC MEDIA DECISIONS: OBJECTIVES, STRATEGY, AND TACTICS

First and foremost, an effective media plan needs to be comprehensive. The general objective is to deliver messages to as many prospects as is practical and cost-effective—and to deliver these messages with sufficient frequency to achieve the desired effect. As a result, most media objectives are stated in terms of **reach** and **frequency.**

To achieve these goals, planners carefully evaluate an ever-increasing number of media options. In the past decade, this number has increased at a remarkable pace. To be competitive these days, media plans need to be efficient, effective, and *creative.* Using new ways to deliver messages is one mark of creative media planning, but another may simply involve using delivery options that are already available. Keeping track of what's available can be a daunting task. We use the expression **delivery option** because there are infinite ways to get a company's message across. We'll present a large number of these in this chapter, but Chapters 8 and 9 also include message delivery options. To help organize some of the details a planner has to consider, we've structured this chapter to focus on the basic decisions in a media plan: objectives, strategy, and tactics. Note that there is a strong link between the sections dealing with these three decisions.

So if we discuss something that influences media objectives—say, competitive activity or a new product launch, we are also likely to discuss this same influence in the sections on strategy and tactics. The linkage that connects the elements within media is important, as is the linkage between the creative and the media sections. This linkage gives a campaign its synergy. Before we examine in some depth setting objectives, developing strategy, and executing tactics, let's take a brief look at the nature of the basic decisions in media: objectives, strategy, and tactics.

UNDERSTANDING MEDIA OBJECTIVES

At the root of a media objective is the principle: media deliver messages. How, where, when, and to whom the messages get delivered form the basis for setting media objectives. The media you select influence the amount and type of exposure you get with a plan. Media can also have a significant effect on how the message is received. Consider the relative impact of two alternative ways to send the following message:

Jennifer,

I love you. Will you please marry me?

Bradley

The first way is to e-mail the message. The other approach consists of hiring a company to post this message on a billboard across the street from where Jennifer works. Same message, but it will surely have a much different impact.

As a prelude to setting media objectives, planners need to have a clear understanding of the role media are to play in the advertising or marketing campaign. Is the role simply that of generating exposure, or is the role also associated with enhancing the message? Generally, planners focus on exposure. Typically, they set media objectives in terms of reach, frequency, gross rating points, and similar concepts. These are easy concepts to understand and set. They are quantitative in nature and relatively easy to measure.

Setting objectives that refer to the media's ability to enhance a message tends to be more subjective and less precise in nature. Qualitative objectives are usually more difficult to measure. Moreover, in setting qualitative media objectives, planners run the risk of a problem discussed in Chapter 4 (dealing with objectives) called **common effectiveness.** This problem refers to setting as a goal something that would normally be expected of all objectives. For example, if "using media that can enhance the message" is set as a media objective, it then becomes a matter of judgment whether this goal is merely something expected of most plans, or whether this situation is indeed special. In the above example, it is clear that Bradley expects the media placement of his message to have a significant impact on the message content.

Perhaps, because of the vagueness in setting qualitative objectives, many planners only set media objectives that are specific and measurable. We have no simple suggestions and will examine this subject in more detail later.

UNDERSTANDING MEDIA STRATEGY

The strategic component of media planning essentially refers to the *general* plan involving the delivery of advertising messages. The aim of a strategic plan is to give the company a competitive edge, although in some competitive situations a company has all it can do just to survive. Still, even small companies can often find creative ways to get their messages across that give them an edge in part of the market. Media strategy decisions usually focus on the following four elements, each of which we'll discuss later in the chapter:

1. Target audience (or market), including their behavior
2. Media classes
3. Media mix
4. Media timing

Target Audience

Although this is an important decision, frequently the media target is exactly the same as the campaign target. If this is so, then the targeting decision is already predetermined for the media planner. Be sure to determine the target's relevant behavior, including purchase frequency, timing of purchases (weekend, shopping, etc.), and the target's passions (sports, games, music, shopping, etc.).

However, in a marketing communication campaign, media (at least the major media) are merely one way to get out the message. For example, a company could use public relations activities or sales promotion to influence key decision makers and use traditional media to reach a more broadly based target. In this situation, there would be a target audience for the campaign, and a separate and at least slightly different target for the advertising media. One of the targets can be thought of as a primary target audience and the other a secondary target, or they could both be deemed targets of equal importance.

Media Classes

Strategy decisions involve the selection of a media type, such as newspaper, television, or magazine. In contrast, media tactics usually consist of decisions to buy media vehicles, such as *USA Today, SportsCenter,* and *InStyle* magazine. However, for some national advertisers with large ad budgets, the selection of a media type—even television—is more of a tactical than a strategic decision, especially because they often allocate a considerable amount of money to other marketing communication options. It is also somewhat confusing to discuss media vehicle decisions with some media types, such as direct mail or outdoor advertising, because some would argue there are no vehicles within these media classes.[3]

Media Mix

Decisions in this category refer to how much emphasis, sometimes called **advertising pressure** or **weight,** to allocate to various categories, such as target audiences, geographical areas, time periods, brands, and most important, media types. In the campaign process, some of these decisions are often made before a media planner is involved. When this happens, these decisions are usually reflected in the media objectives. Keep in mind that although media objectives are considered before media strategy, it's usually wise to think of both types of decisions at the same time.

The most important weighting decision is the one involving the relative emphasis placed on different media types. Figure 7-1 shows a media mix in the form of a pie chart, a typical way to present this information in a plans book.

Media Timing/Scheduling

Timing is all about scheduling, and there are two basic decisions to consider. Decisions need to be made concerning when the ads appear, and the way these ads are scheduled over time. Timing is an important component of media strategy because *when* someone is exposed can affect that person's receptivity to the advertising message. There are numerous reasons for scheduling advertising at various times. One of the more common reasons has to do with seasonal sales fluctuations.

The sales of many products rise and fall with the seasons of the year. Scheduling media can be tailored to seasonal sales patterns and is referred to as **seasonality.**[4] Another phrase gaining increasing usage among media buyers is called **recency buying.** This idea involves reaching targets as close as possible to the point of sale. This aspect of strategy involves building a lot of frequency into the media schedule. Later in this chapter, we will examine other influences on media scheduling.

The second basic media timing decision focuses on the importance of providing *continuity* from one advertising message to another. For a plan to function effectively as a *campaign* there should be an interconnectedness among the ads in the campaign, each of them trying to achieve the

---

FIGURE 7-1 A BRAND'S MEDIA MIX

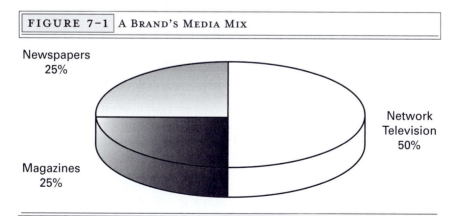

Newspapers
25%

Network
Television
50%

Magazines
25%

same or interrelated objectives. The resulting effect is synergistic—where the whole is greater than the sum of its parts. Although it might seem there are an infinite variety of patterns to follow in scheduling advertising, most are variations of three common types of continuity: flighting, pulsing, and continuous scheduling. We will discuss these on pages 212–214.

UNDERSTANDING MEDIA TACTICS

Media tactics refer to the specific decisions that are made to implement the media strategy. Generally, these decisions involve buying specific advertising units (say, one half-page ad, or a 30-second spot) on specific media vehicles (say, *Sports Illustrated* or *60 Minutes*), and scheduling them within a specific period (say, once a month during the Christmas buying season). Within an agency, these tactical decisions are often referred to as the media schedule.[5]

Scheduling decisions are usually made by a media buyer, someone who selects the media vehicles and places the orders. Buyers need to be good at interpreting the media strategy to produce an effective plan. They also need to be especially good at producing a cost-efficient plan. This, in turn, requires the buyer to have a solid understanding of media audiences and cost analysis. The best buyers possess quantitative skills and an ability to negotiate with the media to secure low prices. The basic quantitative skills usually can be learned in a relatively short time. The ability to negotiate well takes experience. Buyers also negotiate with vehicles to obtain guarantees against audiences falling below expectations, to secure preferred positions within a vehicle, and to obtain merchandising support from the vehicle to support the sales effort.[6] In some agencies, the planners *are* the buyers.

▮ IMPLEMENTING THE MEDIA PLAN

So far, our discussion of media objectives, strategy, and tactics has been designed to give the reader a basic understanding of the kind of decisions that are made in a campaign with respect to media. Let's now examine how media objectives are set and how media strategy and tactics are determined.

SETTING MEDIA OBJECTIVES

A planner's expectations for the media may include both delivering and enhancing messages. The basic unit of measurement used to determine whether a message is delivered is *exposure*. It's far more valuable to know whether an audience saw, heard, or read an ad, but these types of measurements are expensive and difficult to make. Audience measurements capture vehicle exposure and not actual ad exposure. The technical meaning of **exposure** is "open eyes (or listening ears) facing the medium."[7] Exposure indicates that an individual has the opportunity to see, hear, or read an ad. Exposure measurements differ for each medium. We'll examine five measures of exposure: reach, frequency, gross impressions, gross rating points, and targeted rating points. Because these measures can be stated precisely, we refer to measures of exposure as **quantitative** media objectives. The ability of the media to enhance a message is more subjective and does not lend itself to measurement, so we refer to these types of goals as **qualitative media objectives.**

Quantitative Media Objectives

Reach.   Reach can be defined as the number of different people or households exposed to a media schedule within a given period. This number is usually expressed as a percentage of the target audience. The time can vary. It can refer to a four-week period, a four-month period, or the length of the campaign. For example, media objectives can be written as follows:

- To reach 80% of women, ages 18–24, each month of the year. OR . . .
- To reach 80% of women, ages 18–24, by the end of the first quarter. OR . . .
- To reach 80% of men, ages 18–24, by the end of the year (EOY).

We could also substitute for the above demos (short for demographic variables) the words *target audience* or even *primary* and *secondary target audiences.*

Frequency.   Objectives also generally indicate the number of times the demo should be reached. The technical term for this number is frequency. **Frequency** can be defined as the number of times a person or household is exposed to a media schedule within a given period. This number is usually considered an average frequency. For example, an objective can be written as follows:

- To reach 80% of the primary target audience three or more times each week during the first quarter.

Reach and frequency are companion statistics. It's hard to talk about one without considering the other; they are *inversely* related. The more frequency in a schedule, the fewer people it reaches. Planners have to balance the importance of reaching many people a few times or a few people many times. Maximizing both reach and frequency would require a budget of unlimited size.

Reach and frequency objectives need to be linked to campaign objectives. To get prospects to think, feel, or do something, you first have to reach them with a message. If you wanted to establish brand awareness in 80% of the target audience, you would have to reach at least 80% of the target—in all likelihood, more. The number of times, or repetitions, needed to achieve the desired effect would depend on many things, including the effectiveness of the message.

The number of repetitions necessary to achieve a desired effect (e.g., awareness, or sales) is called **effective frequency.** The number or percentage of people who are reached at the frequency level determined to be effective is called **effective reach (i.e., how many people were reached the desired number of times).**

Planners consider effective reach and effective frequency when setting objectives to help them answer two important questions: (1) How *many* people or what percentage of the target audience should they reach?

(2) How *often* should they reach them? Generally, advertisers want to reach as many prospects as they can. However, it may not be cost-effective to do so. A media planner has to weigh the difficulty or expense in reaching each additional percentage of the target audience. At some point, the cost of reaching more prospects is not offset by sufficient sales increases. On a practical level, there are often budgetary constraints. Even though a planner may believe that reaching more prospects (and spending more money) makes sense, if the budget has already been set, a planner may have to work with the funds he or she has been allocated, depending on the flexibility constraints.

Effective frequency levels can be difficult to determine, especially in a classroom. All faculty struggle with questions about how many times they have to repeat themselves to get their messages across and understood. Telling a class it is dismissed usually has to be said only once. Explaining effective reach and effective frequency to a class usually requires more than one explanation.

Similarly, effective frequency in advertising can vary depending on a number of variables—including the product, message, media clutter, competitive environment, and the target to whom the message is directed. Advertisers conduct research on this subject, but their conclusions are likely to be situation specific, applying only to their particular case. The most influential study on effective frequency was published in 1979 (somewhat old, but still followed) by the Association of National Advertisers, authored by Michael Naples. Some of its general conclusions are as follows:

1. One exposure of an advertisement to a target consumer group (within a purchase cycle) has little or no effect.
2. Because one exposure is usually ineffective, the main thrust of media planning should be on emphasizing frequency rather than reach.
3. Most research studies suggest that two exposures within a purchase cycle are an effective threshold level.
4. Three exposures within a purchase cycle, however, are felt to be optimal.
5. After three exposures within a purchasing cycle, advertising becomes more effective as frequency is increased, but at a decreasing rate. If this were drawn on a graph, it would appear as a convex curve rising from a zero point.
6. Wear-out of an advertising campaign is not caused by too much frequency per se. It is caused by copy and content problems.
7. Generally, smaller and lesser-known brands will benefit most by increased frequency. Larger, well-known brands may or may not be helped by increasing frequency, depending on how close they are to advertising saturation levels.
8. Different dayparts on television are affected by different frequency levels. A similar idea applies to thin versus thick magazines, with the thinner ones having better response effects than the thicker ones.
9. Frequency responses are affected by the amount of money an advertiser spends as a percentage of the product category total. Those brands with the greatest proportion of exposures within

their category should also gain greater effects when frequency is increased. The responses due to increased frequency are not affected by different media. What is true for one medium is true for others. Each brand might require a different level of frequency of exposure. One cannot generalize from a given brand's experiences to some other brand. Specialized research is required to find the unique frequency level for a brand.

10. Two brands spending the same amount of money for advertising can have different responses to their frequencies.[8]

The Naples study remains influential, although not everyone agrees with some of its conclusions. One popular conclusion is that a frequency level of three or more within a given week is the ideal level of exposure, but not everyone agrees. Recent thinking, based on John Phillip Jones' book *When Ads Work: New Proof of How Advertising Triggers Sales,* suggests that one exposure is enough to be effective.[9] Some critics point out that the ideal level depends on the product category, something Naples did not find. Others have said that the ideal frequency depends on the quality of the advertising message, something Naples did not consider.[10] Even though people disagree with parts of Naples' study, there is widespread agreement that frequent consumer exposures bring "positive results."[11]

A Time Frame Is an Important Part of the Objectives.   Indicating a time frame in which the goals are expected to be met provides direction regarding when to advertise. It's not enough to say you want to reach 80% of the target audience a minimum of three times. You have to indicate when you want to achieve these goals. Achieving a frequency level of three during a 12-month period is significantly different than accomplishing these goals within a 4-week period. In Chapter 4, we called including a date in the objective **time bounding** the objective. Objectives that are time bounded provide media buyers direction for scheduling the media.

In their book *Advertising Media Planning,* Jack Z. Sissors and Lincoln Bumba suggest six points to consider in decisions about *when* to advertise:

• When sales are greatest or lowest
• According to budget constraints
• When competitors advertise
• According to the specific goals of the brand in question
• According to the availability of the product
• Depending on promotional requirements[12]

Using Sales to Guide Media Scheduling.   An important principle in media scheduling is to advertise when consumers are inclined to buy. To help determine these inclinations, advertisers look at sales trend data. The sales of many products vary considerably over a period of a year, although these variations may be consistent from year to year. The Christmas selling season accounts for over 50% of the sales of many toy and game manufacturers. Linens, tablecloths, and towels sell best during the August and January "white sales." Later in this chapter, we will look at how buyers allocate media dollars on a seasonal basis.

Budget Constraints.   Planners often have tough decisions to make because of budget limitations. On the one hand, they want to *effectively* reach their targets, but because of a limited budget may not be able to build sufficient frequency into their plan. To avoid spreading themselves too thin, they often schedule periods of advertising followed by periods of no advertising (called **flighting**). This type of scheduling allows sufficient frequency to effectively reach the target at least in some of the time periods.

Scheduling When the Competition Advertises.   Many people in business view marketing as a constant battle for the heart and mind of the consumer. Part of the battle involves maintaining a media presence when the competition advertises. Brand leaders often try to match up with the competition. The idea is not to give a rival a potential edge, especially if the leader has superior financial resources. To counter this strategy, a nonleader may advertise in different time periods to gain an advantage, even though the period may be less favorable. Sometimes it's hard to compete directly against the category leader.

Companies may also feel compelled to advertise during the same time periods as the competition. The reason is that consumers expect to see ads for some products during certain times and make a special point of looking for them. January and August is the expected time for "white sale" advertising. In many communities, Wednesday is considered the "best shopping day" in the newspaper and is the day most supermarkets take out major ads. However, in a smaller number of communities, Thursday is considered the "best shopping day" and the day supermarkets schedule most of their advertising. They know shoppers tend to look for grocery ads when there are a lot of food ads in the paper.

Tailoring the Schedule to the Specific Goals of the Brand.   The timing of the media schedule should always reflect advertising goals. But it is also worth mentioning that sometimes an unstated or implied objective of the campaign could also have an effect on scheduling. For example, if the company's marketing strategy suggests reacting aggressively to competitive initiatives, this would suggest adding extra emphasis to counter some new activity, such as a new product introduction. To put extra emphasis and money one place might mean withdrawing media support from some other.

Product Availability.   The availability of the product can result from numerous causes, including unexpected sales increases, labor problems, or material shortages. If the company cannot satisfy the current demand, it is often better to withdraw advertising exposure rather than risk alienating unsatisfied customers.

Promotional Requirements.   Special promotions, especially price deals, require close attention to the timing of the advertising. Sales promotion activities often take place during the brand's regular advertising campaign, so that extra emphasis needs to be added to introduce the promotion.

Setting Objectives in Terms of Reach and Frequency
Reach, frequency, and continuity are core concepts in media planning. The basic purpose of the media is to deliver messages, and reach and frequency

are measures that indicate what's expected in terms of message delivery. The timing or pattern of message deliveries is a result of the type of continuity used. A simple quantitative media objective has four parts:

1. A target audience or market
2. The desired amount of reach
3. The desired amount of frequency
4. The timing or pattern of the message deliveries

The following is an example of a quantitative media objective:

- To reach 60% of women, ages 18–34, three or more times each week during the first quarter of the campaign.

Problems with Using Reach and Frequency in Setting Objectives.   At the conceptual level, it makes sense to set media objectives in terms of reach and frequency. Basically, this is what the media try to do—reach people. However, at the operational level, setting an objective in terms of reach presents problems both in estimating reach and in monitoring whether the objective is accomplished. First, it can get complicated quickly when more than two or three vehicles are used with multiple insertions (frequency) scheduled for each vehicle. The problem becomes more complex when a schedule includes media that are very different from each other, such as newspapers and outdoor, or radio and magazines.

Second, there is mixed value in setting a numerical figure for reach (expressed usually as a percentage) unless you have a good way to measure whether the objective is accomplished. Notwithstanding, students are often advised to set objectives for reach in quantitative terms, even though they have no way of measuring them, because it is a discipline they may use later. It is also a way to communicate more precisely what a planner has in mind when he or she talks about reaching an audience. Professionals, however, are more interested in setting objectives in terms they can monitor or measure, and for many professionals, it is too costly or complicated to measure reach—at least when several vehicles are used with numerous insertions.

Agencies use numerous estimating formulas. These formulas are built into simulation models that use probabilities to estimate reach based on multiple exposures. Most major agencies have their own proprietary models and use them extensively to estimate reach. William J. Donelly, author of *Planning Media: Strategy and Development,* reminds his readers that reach estimators produce radical estimates because they are estimates built upon estimates.[13] As a result, some professionals prefer to set objectives in other types of exposure measures that are easier to measure. The most common measures are **gross impressions, gross rating points (GRPs),** and **targeted rating points (TRPs).**

Setting Objectives in Terms of Gross Impressions, GRPs, and TRPs

Gross Impressions.   An advertising impression (or simply an impression) occurs each time an individual (or household) is exposed to an ad. Gross impressions are the total number of impressions obtained from a media schedule within a given period. This term describes the sum of all vehicle exposures and counts every exposure in a schedule, even multiple exposures to the same person or household. To calculate gross impressions, multiply the reach of each media vehicle times the number of ads on that vehicle as follows:

Program A: 1,000,000 people reached × 4 ads = 4,000,000 impressions
Program B: 2,000,000 people reached × 2 ads = 4,000,000 impressions
Program C: 3,000,000 people reached × 4 ads = 12,000,000 impressions
Program D: 5,000,000 people reached × 1 ad = 5,000,000 impressions

Gross Impressions   25,000,000

Note that the audience of Program A not only was exposed to an ad more than one time, but it is likely that at least some of them were part of the audiences of other programs. This kind of repetition is called **duplication.** Gross impressions are a way to look at the combined weight of a media schedule without regard to duplication of audiences in the schedule. In contrast, reach is expressed as an unduplicated number. In the media models used by some agencies, the weight of a media schedule is as important as the reach. In other words, you can reach many people a few times or a few people many times and the impact of the message may not be significantly different.

Gross Rating Points.   Gross rating points are identical in concept to gross impressions and are another way to talk about exposure. Gross impressions indicate the amount of exposure in a schedule expressed in raw numbers; GRPs are expressed in terms of percentages, although the percent signs are not usually shown.

GRPs are a way to talk about the amount of exposure in a plan. A *rating point* indicates the percentage of a population that is tuned into a broadcast. (Or any medium for that matter. The actual operational definition depends on the medium measured and the company doing the measuring.) For example, a 20 rating in television indicates that 20% of the TV households (TVHH) were tuned into the telecast. This means that 20% of the approximately 100 million TVHH, or 20 million TVHH, were tuned in. To calculate the GRPs in a media schedule, first multiply reach times frequency to come up with the total rating points for each program. A program's rating is used as a measure of reach and the number of times a commercial appears on a program is used as a measure of frequency. Second, add the rating points for all programs together. An example follows:

Rating Points

Program A	20 rating	×	3 ads = 60
Program B	15 rating	×	3 ads = 45
Program C	10 rating	×	2 ads = 20
Program D	13 rating	×	3 ads = 39
Gross Rating Points			164

Like gross impressions, GRPs indicate the magnitude of a media schedule and can be used for various media forms. The amount of exposure a schedule delivers can be described for the population as a whole or for a particular population segment. To make clear the rating points refer to a specific demo, planners sometimes use the expression **targeted rating points.**

Targeted Rating Points. TRPs mean the same as GRPs. It's generally a matter of personal preference as to which term to use. The following examples are basically the same:

- Achieve 50 GRPs per week against women 18–34 (W 18–34).
- Achieve 50 TRPs per week (W 18–34).

Which to Use: Reach? Frequency? Gross Impressions? GRPs? or TRPs?

The above five terms give planners a certain amount of flexibility in the way they can set media objectives. Reach and frequency tend to require more information in both estimating and tracking results. As mentioned, there are computer programs that provide planners with estimates of measures such as reach, frequency, and GRPs. Such computer software is used extensively in the advertising media industry. A software package that is used by many schools and is especially useful for student advertising campaigns is Media Flight Plan—IM (4th edition) by Dennis Martin of Brigham Young University, and Dale Coons, vice president of media research for the Lintas: Campbell-Ewald advertising agency.

Setting objectives in terms of reach and frequency can be especially helpful for new product launches and for campaigns that undergo major strategic changes. For introductory campaigns, it's important to know what percentage of the target is getting the messages. If a product has an advantage, the window of opportunity to exploit that edge is often limited. It's an important strategic concern to know who is and isn't getting the campaign messages. In addition, it's helpful to know how often they get a message.

Setting objectives in terms of gross impressions and GRPs or TRPs tends to be more relevant when planners are interested in the weight of a plan, as they often are for products in the mature stage of their life cycle. As a brand matures, much of the advertising is of a reminding or reinforcing nature because the target audience is generally well aware of a brand. Therefore, planners accept more frequency in their schedules because it is usually more cost-efficient than trying to maximize reach, which can be more costly. Generally, some people in any market segment are more difficult to reach—this translates as more expensive. In the introductory phase of a product life cycle, where a premium is placed on reaching targets at least once, planners are usually willing to tolerate less cost-efficiency.

Planners tend to use rating points instead of impressions because they are easier to use. Because GRPs are based on percentages and impressions are based on actual head counts, the numbers for GRPs are usually reported in the hundreds and thousands, whereas the numbers for impressions are often stated in millions and billions. The smaller GRP numbers also make it easier to compare alternative media schedules (e.g., saying Schedule A delivers 90 GRPs a week and Schedule B delivers 120 GRPs is easier to grasp than saying Schedule A delivers 234 million gross impressions and Schedule B delivers 312 million gross impressions even though it's basically the same information).

Expressing the size of the medium's audience in terms of impressions is used for various purposes. As Jim Surmanek has noted, advertisers like to impress retailers with the breadth and scope of the advertising that is planned to support a product line. Gross impression numbers in the millions sounds more impressive than a GRP number in the hundreds. In addition, impressions can be calculated for any media form (as can GRPs), and are a handy way to compare the audience delivery of different media plans.[14]

Qualitative Media Objectives

Setting objectives in terms of reach, impressions, and rating points gives some indication of the size of the audience a planner wants to expose to advertising. Of increasing interest to many planners is the ability of the media to enhance the messages that get delivered. Traditionally, academicians have shied away from recommending setting media objectives in terms of this ability because of the subjective nature of these kinds of objectives. In their widely used textbook on advertising media, Sissors and Bumba note, "although messages seem to have more impact on consumers in one medium than they do in another, [impact is still a] hazy concept."[15] Hazy or not, it is clear that many agencies expect the media to do more than merely deliver the message. In fact, it is this expectation that drives much of product placement.

Increasingly, many major advertisers are using nontraditional means to create excitement (buzz), and surprise to get in under the consumer's radar. Moreover, traditional media, especially vehicles within a media class, can influence the impact a message is likely to have with the target. An ad for an investment broker in *Forbes* is likely to come off with more authority than one in *Playboy*. The advertising claims of an ad placed in *Parents* or *Good Housekeeping* are backed up by the magazines and are likely to be perceived with more credibility than an identical ad in the *National Enquirer*. On page 202, we present a chart on qualitative media values. Consider the importance these values could have in affecting the way the target receives an advertising message for the brand you are working with. If it is especially important, then set the value up as a qualitative media objective. You might consider specifying that it is a *qualitative* media objective because people usually expect to see media objectives written in specific and measurable terms.

Determining the Media Strategy

The challenge to a media planner is to come up with a plan that gives the advertiser a competitive edge. A better plan can mean one that is more efficient as well as more effective. Although it is easier said than done, it is important to have a competitive attitude. Let's look at the four major elements in a media strategy: target audience, media classes, media mix or weight, and media timing.

Identifying Target Audiences.   Identifying the target audience is a critical decision that is at the very heart of an advertising campaign. The first step in identifying a target audience is to select prospect groups and target markets.[16] Prospect groups include individuals who have some likelihood of purchasing a particular product. Planners want to identify anyone who might be a prospect for purchasing a brand within a product category. Because this group is so diverse, nonspecific, and generally large, tighter criteria for targeting are often used.

   Target markets is the term sometimes used to identify the geographic locations of customers and prospects (target audience is also acceptable). The geographic locations might include a region of the country (say, the Southeast), a specific state (Georgia), or city (Atlanta), or various other geographic boundaries (e.g., a metropolitan area or a specific ZIP code).

Variables for Profiling Target Audiences
Profiling target audiences within a media plan typically is done in terms of several types of variables: (1) demographic, (2) psychographic, (3) lifestyle, (4) product or brand usage, and (5) geodemographic. These variables can be used by themselves or in assorted combinations.

Demographics.   Identifying a target audience by demography is one of the most common methods used in media planning, primarily because there is extensive information available on media audiences. The major syndicated media research firms, such as MRI and Simmons, provide a large number of demographic characteristics such as age, gender, income, education, and occupation. Thus, we might find a targeting strategy that states:

   The primary targeted audience is women between the ages of 25 and 34. This primary target is weighted 75% (so that this segment receives 75% of the budget allocation).
   A secondary target is women between the ages of 18 and 24, which is weighted 25% (and this segment receives 25% of the budget).

   Such a targeting profile shows precisely to whom the planner wants the media effort directed. In this example, there are actually two targets— women ages 25–34, and women ages 18–24. Weights are assigned (75% and 25%) to each target. Such a targeting definition permits the media buyer to execute the plan as efficiently as possible. If the plan consisted solely of magazines, for example, the buyer would search mainly for magazines that deliver audiences of women in these age groups effectively. (Keep in mind that most media vehicles—even direct mail—cannot deliver an audience with absolutely no waste coverage; therefore, the idea is to make buys that are as efficient as possible—given other constraints such as the creative strategy.) We have included a copy of a typical page from *MRI* in Figure 7-2, which reports on the readership of specific magazines by men and women according to audience, readers per copy, median age, and household income.

FIGURE 7-2 | MEDIAMARK RESEARCH, INC. (MRI) PROVIDES MAGAZINE READERSHIP ACCORDING TO DEMOGRAPHIC CHARACTERISTICS

Fall 2004		Audience (000)			Readers Per Copy			Median Age			Household Income		
Magazine	Circulation (000)	Adults	Men	Women	Adults	Men	Women	Adults	Men	Women	Adults	Men	Women
4 Wheel & Off Road	392	3,325	2,788	536	8.48	7.11	1.37	34.8	33.1	39.3	52,096.0	52,263.0	49,982.0
Architectural Digest	790	4,683	2,150	2,533	5.93	2.72	3.21	45.7	43.1	48.3	93,123.0	90,682.0	95,776.0
Barron's	312	1,147	899	248	3.68	2.88	0.80	50.8	50.5	52.3	92,010.0	90,816.0	94,933.0
Bassmaster	558	3,987	3,241	746	7.15	5.81	1.34	40.1	41.1	37.1	50,507.0	51,367.0	48,039.0
Better Homes & Garde	7,678	38,192	8,631	29,561	4.97	1.12	3.85	46.9	45.7	47.2	58,850.0	65,988.0	57,085.0
Black Enterprise	504	3,792	1,618	2,174	7.52	3.21	4.31	40.6	40.3	40.8	50,081.0	55,890.0	46,248.0
Boating	196	2,836	2,214	622	14.47	11.30	3.17	45.0	45.7	42.9	70,614.0	71,847.0	59,021.0
Bon Appetit	1,276	6,187	1,499	4,688	4.85	1.17	3.67	47.0	44.4	48.0	83,871.0	94,276.0	78,750.0
Business Week	992	4,678	3,244	1,434	4.72	3.27	1.45	43.9	43.8	44.1	78,927.0	78,043.0	81,270.0
Car and Driver	1,328	9,757	8,562	1,195	7.35	6.45	0.90	34.2	33.7	38.2	64,978.0	65,954.0	56,259.0
Conde Nast Traveler	773	3,440	1,389	2,051	4.45	1.80	2.65	47.3	48.3	46.7	95,634.0	95,005.0	96,096.0
Cooking Light	1,665	11,378	1,698	9,680	6.83	1.02	5.81	46.9	46.3	47.0	66,212.0	62,673.0	66,942.0
Cosmopolitan	2,665	16,517	2,434	14,083	6.20	0.91	5.28	32.0	34.7	31.4	58,484.0	60,792.0	58,015.0
Country Living	1,700	11,387	2,290	9,096	6.70	1.35	5.35	48.6	48.5	48.6	54,724.0	56,606.0	54,017.0
Delta's SKY Magazine	419	3,412	1,691	1,721	8.14	4.04	4.11	43.6	43.0	44.3	96,997.0	98,101.0	95,569.0
Discover	847	5,459	3,007	2,452	6.44	3.55	2.89	42.4	41.7	43.1	54,647.0	60,686.0	48,515.0
Ebony	1,702	10,512	3,614	6,898	6.18	2.12	4.05	39.6	40.4	39.2	38,580.0	50,926.0	33,116.0
Elle	1,011	4,503	405	4,097	4.45	0.40	4.05	34.8	37.6	34.3	66,130.0	56,996.0	67,180.0
Entertainment Weekly	1,956	9,947	4,092	5,855	5.09	2.09	2.99	34.3	33.7	34.7	59,458.0	62,057.0	57,462.0
ESPN The Magazine	1,820	11,371	9,017	2,353	6.25	4.95	1.29	31.6	31.6	31.7	64,143.0	65,548.0	58,072.0
Esquire	702	2,919	1,833	1,086	4.16	2.61	1.55	42.9	42.7	43.0	65,004.0	73,244.0	45,255.0
Essence	1,129	7,173	1,699	5,475	6.35	1.50	4.85	37.0	38.9	36.3	42,076.0	58,417.0	36,420.0
Family Circle	4,482	21,441	2,034	19,408	4.78	0.45	4.33	49.7	49.8	49.6	52,478.0	53,170.0	52,400.0
Family Handyman	1,162	4,852	3,095	1,758	4.18	2.66	1.51	48.3	48.4	48.3	55,169.0	57,890.0	51,097.0
Field & Stream	1,550	10,621	8,785	1,836	6.85	5.67	1.18	42.6	42.6	42.8	54,921.0	55,438.0	50,382.0
Food & Wine	1,008	5,948	2,188	3,759	5.90	2.17	3.73	43.9	44.8	43.3	69,899.0	72,455.0	67,938.0
Forbes	935	4,591	3,329	1,262	4.91	3.56	1.35	45.1	44.9	45.5	81,370.0	84,336.0	69,437.0
Fortune	920	3,782	2,611	1,171	4.11	2.84	1.27	42.4	42.2	43.0	92,117.0	93,650.0	88,440.0
Glamour	2,285	11,784	1,100	10,685	5.16	0.48	4.68	33.5	33.0	33.6	58,832.0	57,862.0	58,895.0
Golf Digest	1,511	5,584	4,519	1,065	3.70	2.99	0.70	47.3	46.2	49.1	82,671.0	82,165.0	84,992.0
Good Housekeeping	4,590	24,182	2,862	21,320	5.27	0.62	4.64	49.7	51.3	49.3	56,168.0	60,199.0	55,540.0
GQ (Gentlemen's Quarterly)	803	4,743	3,346	1,397	5.91	4.17	1.74	33.5	33.1	34.6	65,450.0	66,561.0	62,344.0
Harper's Bazaar	695	2,873	295	2,579	4.13	0.42	3.71	42.3	39.6	42.5	66,517.0	60,456.0	66,970.0
House & Garden	912	13,887	3,459	10,428	15.23	3.79	11.43	49.5	48.0	50.0	56,307.0	67,851.0	53,616.0
Hunting	350	2,958	2,519	439	8.45	7.20	1.25	41.3	41.2	42.0	44,386.0	45,294.0	33,893.0
In Style	1,620	8,154	862	7,292	5.03	0.53	4.50	34.2	33.1	34.4	76,384.0	65,111.0	77,689.0
Inc.	686	1,259	824	435	1.83	1.20	0.63	43.4	43.2	43.8	98,838.0	91,076.0	109,929.0
Jet	892	8,082	3,307	4,775	9.06	3.71	5.35	41.3	42.4	40.4	35,609.0	45,954.0	30,485.0
Kiplinger's Personal Finance	1,040	2,707	1,731	977	2.60	1.66	0.94	52.5	51.6	53.5	83,647.0	86,326.0	79,743.0
Ladies' Home Journal	4,136	13,959	764	13,194	3.37	0.18	3.19	51.3	53.2	51.1	54,815.0	57,353.0	54,614.0
Martha Stewart Living	2,062	12,078	1,472	10,607	5.86	0.71	5.14	44.1	44.3	44.0	66,620.0	73,710.0	66,059.0
Men's Health	1,647	8,480	6,866	1,614	5.15	4.17	0.98	37.0	36.8	38.0	70,291.0	69,862.0	73,022.0
Modern Bride	397	5,170	582	4,588	13.02	1.47	11.56	29.3	29.4	29.3	54,944.0	50,667.0	55,797.0
Money	2,029	7,428	4,681	2,747	3.66	2.31	1.35	47.5	47.3	48.0	83,105.0	86,265.0	77,382.0
Motor Trend	1,175	6,783	6,029	754	5.77	5.13	0.64	37.6	37.1	40.5	65,969.0	65,865.0	68,133.0
National Enquirer	1,336	11,392	3,754	7,638	8.53	2.81	5.72	42.1	40.7	42.7	41,578.0	44,898.0	39,204.0
National Geographic	5,094	31,241	17,222	14,019	6.13	3.38	2.75	45.5	45.1	45.9	61,200.0	64,126.0	57,720.0
Newsweek	3,202	19,526	10,628	8,898	6.10	3.32	2.78	46.3	45.1	47.6	67,488.0	70,122.0	62,808.0
Parents' Magazine	2,189	14,726	2,489	12,238	6.73	1.14	5.59	33.5	35.9	32.9	57,471.0	66,096.0	55,945.0
People	3,592	37,215	11,743	25,472	10.36	3.27	7.09	41.1	40.7	41.3	62,731.0	66,319.0	60,929.0
Popular Mechanics	1,209	8,182	7,122	1,060	6.77	5.89	0.88	43.4	43.3	44.2	54,164.0	56,844.0	40,275.0
Popular Photography & Imaging	444	2,035	1,264	771	4.58	2.85	1.74	45.3	48.1	41.1	61,764.0	66,222.0	52,029.0
Popular Science	1,424	6,398	5,129	1,268	4.49	3.60	0.89	44.6	44.7	44.3	65,063.0	65,886.0	60,521.0
Prevention	3,241	10,427	1,709	8,718	3.22	0.53	2.69	52.9	55.2	52.5	54,802.0	60,654.0	53,265.0
Reader's Digest	10,731	40,187	15,221	24,966	3.74	1.42	2.33	50.3	50.6	50.2	52,220.0	58,090.0	48,076.0
Redbook	2,356	9,601	803	8,799	4.08	0.34	3.73	43.6	43.0	43.7	55,260.0	61,149.0	56,986.0
Rolling Stone	1,266	10,341	6,080	4,260	8.17	4.80	3.37	29.1	29.6	28.3	59,678.0	63,094.0	55,013.0
Runner's World	543	2,519	1,345	1,174	4.64	2.48	2.16	38.7	37.4	40.3	81,059.0	78,682.0	84,620.0
Soap Opera Digest	551	5,246	510	4,736	9.52	0.93	8.60	39.3	38.6	39.4	42,263.0	37,963.0	42,669.0
Sports Illustrated	3,329	20,055	16,016	4,038	6.02	4.81	1.21	38.8	37.7	42.4	62,845.0	62,476.0	64,800.0
The Source	424	6,440	3,626	2,814	15.19	8.55	6.64	24.2	24.2	24.2	41,138.0	48,919.0	32,029.0
This Old House	1,046	5,996	3,327	2,669	5.73	3.18	2.55	46.3	44.6	48.5	64,282.0	66,419.0	61,061.0
Time	4,174	21,132	11,222	9,910	5.06	2.69	2.37	46.3	45.2	47.5	65,558.0	69,148.0	60,299.0
Travel & Leisure	1,058	4,690	1,813	2,876	4.43	1.71	2.72	46.4	48.9	44.9	80,552.0	87,368.0	76,296.0
TV Guide	9,100	25,579	10,507	15,072	2.81	1.15	1.66	44.1	43.1	45.0	48,516.0	53,336.0	44,040.0
Vanity Fair	1,113	4,757	1,092	3,665	4.27	0.98	3.29	39.7	38.1	40.3	68,236.0	71,773.0	67,392.0
Vibe	872	6,801	3,155	3,646	7.80	3.62	4.18	26.4	26.5	26.3	38,494.0	47,780.0	30,160.0
Vogue	1,186	9,480	1,112	8,368	7.99	0.94	7.06	34.5	37.1	34.3	61,145.0	66,647.0	59,714.0
Woman's Day	4,145	20,504	991	19,513	4.95	0.24	4.71	49.1	49.1	49.1	50,721.0	58,011.0	50,117.0

Source: From 2004 Fall *MRI*.

Psychographics.   Another approach to targeting media audiences involves identification of prospects according to psychological characteristics, commonly called *psychographics.* In measuring the psychographic profile of consumer groups, the researcher attempts to classify people according to such things as their common beliefs, opinions, interests, personalities, and behaviors. For example, some people might be classified (in their shopping behavior) as "economy minded," others as "impulsive," and yet others as "experimenters."

The idea behind such groupings is that a person's shopping behavior is more influenced by sociopsychological factors than by their demographic characteristics. Some limitations in using psychographics in media decisions are (1) the research used to detect psychographic traits is questionable in terms of its reliability (psychological constructs are often difficult to measure), and (2) a lot of data about media usage are not currently available. Nevertheless, advertisers and advertising agencies today are experimenting with behavioral and psychographic approaches to improve their media-planning processes.

Lifestyles. According to Jugenheimer, Barban, and Turk, "Lifestyle profiles are intended to reflect the consumer's priorities—that is, they measure commitment of time, money, and energy to activities, interests, and viewpoints. To gain perspective, lifestyle surveys cover all sorts of things we do and care about."[17] Some examples of lifestyle profiling are:

- Activities (such as sports, recreation, and entertainment)
- Preferences (such as social causes and political perspective)
- Interests (such as music, books, and hobbies)

Identifying target audiences according to lifestyle characteristics is similar to using psychographics, and the two approaches often are treated as one. By the same token, lifestyle research has the same limitations when used for media purposes.

Product or Brand Usage. Profiling target audiences according to the usage level of a product category or specific brand is widely used in developing media strategy. The method is as popular as defining by demography, and the two variables typically are used together. *MRI* usually reports product usage in three categories: "heavy," "medium," and "light."

In Figure 7-3, note that some demographic characteristics, such as the education, age, and census region of bottled-water users, are shown according to product usage levels (*MRI* also includes other demographic characteristics, but only a sample of these appear in the figure). We can use such data to provide an estimate of the size of a target audience and how its usage compares to average usage. *MRI* provides index numbers for population segments. Remember, an index number is a way of looking at the usage rate of a population segment compared to average usage. Think of the number 100 as indicating average usage and a number above or below 100 as above or below average usage. For example, an index number of 125 indicates a population segment has a usage rate of 25% above average usage.

Thus, referring to Figure 7-3, if we considered targeting our media to adults between the ages of 18 and 24, who are heavy users of bottled water and seltzer, *MRI* estimates that such a target consists of 4,869,000 adults (see column A under "heavy users"). Note also that 17.7% of all adults ages 18–24 are heavy users (see column B) and 12.9% of all heavy users are between the ages of 18 and 24 (see Column C). This figure is exactly average based on an index number of 100 (see column D).

Observing all of this information in itself does not tell us to whom to direct our media effort. Deciding the actual target audience is a decision

FIGURE 7-3 | BOTTLED WATER & SELTZER

Base: All Adults
2004 Spring Mediamark Research Inc. weighted Pop. (000)
Bottled Water & Seltzer: Drink in Last 6 Months

	Total Population 18-Plus A (000)	B Horz %	C Vert %	D Index	All (Drank in Last 6 Months) A (000)	B Across	C Down	D Index	Heavy (8+) A (000)	B Across	C Down	D Index	Medium (2–7) A (000)	B Across	C Down	D Index	Light (0–1) A (000)	B Across	C Down	D Index
All	211845	100.00	100.00	100	113334	53.50	100.00	100	37707	17.80	100.00	100	46124	21.77	100.00	100	29503	13.93	100.00	100
Men	101655	100.00	47.99	100	48503	47.71	42.80	89	15757	15.50	41.79	87	20043	19.72	43.45	91	12703	12.50	43.06	90
Women	110190	100.00	52.01	100	64831	58.84	57.20	110	21950	19.92	58.21	112	26081	23.67	56.55	109	11285	15.36	38.25	110
Parents	73494	100.00	34.69	100	43659	59.40	38.52	111	14132	19.23	37.48	108	18241	24.82	39.55	114	11285	15.36	38.25	110
HH status: head of household	130137	100.00	61.43	100	65820	50.58	58.08	95	21677	16.66	57.49	94	26894	20.67	58.31	95	17249	13.25	58.47	95
HH status: homemakers	130274	100.00	61.50	100	70762	54.32	62.44	102	23557	18.08	62.47	102	28709	22.04	62.24	101	18496	14.20	62.69	102
HH status: prof/mgr	42793	100.00	20.20	100	27587	64.47	24.34	121	8803	20.57	23.34	116	11953	27.93	25.91	128	6832	15.96	23.16	115
HH status: sole parent	11993	100.00	5.66	100	6890	57.45	6.08	107	2464	20.54	6.53	115	2718	22.66	5.89	104	1709	14.25	5.79	102
Educ: graduated college plus	51950	100.00	24.52	100	32495	62.55	28.67	117	10162	19.56	26.95	110	13810	26.58	29.94	122	8522	16.40	28.89	118
Educ: attended college	57213	100.00	27.01	100	32435	56.69	28.62	106	11401	19.93	30.24	112	13050	22.81	28.29	105	7984	13.95	27.06	100
Educ: graduated high school	67355	100.00	31.79	100	33563	49.83	29.61	93	11105	16.49	29.45	93	13727	20.38	29.76	94	8731	12.96	29.60	93
Educ: did not graduate HS	35327	100.00	16.68	100	14840	42.01	13.09	79	5039	14.26	13.3	80	5536	15.67	12.00	72	4265	12.07	14.46	87
Educ: post graduate	17196	100.00	8.12	100	10390	60.42	9.17	113	3153	18.33	68.36	103	4372	25.42	9.48	117	2866	16.67	9.71	120
Educ: no college	102682	100.00	48.47	100	48404	47.14	42.71	88	16144	15.72	42.81	88	19263	18.76	41.76	86	12997	12.66	44.05	91
Age 18-24	27492	100.00	12.98	100	16009	58.23	14.13	109	4869	17.71	12.91	100	6443	23.43	13.97	108	4697	17.08	15.92	123
Age 25-34	39096	100.00	18.45	100	22920	58.63	20.22	110	7185	18.38	19.05	103	9622	24.61	20.86	113	6113	15.64	20.72	112
Age 35-44	44333	100.00	20.93	100	25915	58.46	22.87	109	8501	19.18	22.55	108	11248	25.37	24.39	117	6166	13.91	20.90	100
Age 45-54	40026	100.00	18.89	100	23084	57.67	20.37	108	8454	21.12	22.42	119	9000	22.49	19.51	103	5629	14.06	19.08	101
Age 55-64	26743	100.00	12.62	100	13873	51.88	12.24	97	4966	18.57	13.17	104	5572	20.83	12.08	96	3335	12.47	11.30	90
Age 65+	34155	100.00	16.12	100	11532	33.76	10.18	63	3731	10.92	9.89	61	4239	12.41	9.19	57	3562	10.43	12.07	75
Employment: working full time	112161	100.00	52.94	100	64520	57.52	56.93	108	21649	19.30	57.41	108	27230	24.28	59.04	112	15642	13.95	53.02	100
Employment: working part time	23062	100.00	10.89	100	14041	60.88	12.39	114	4481	19.43	11.88	109	5847	25.35	12.68	116	3713	16.10	12.59	116
Employment: not working	76622	100.00	36.17	100	34773	45.38	30.68	85	11578	15.11	30.70	85	13047	17.03	28.29	78	10148	13.24	34.40	95
Occupation: professional	22111	100.00	10.44	100	14334	64.83	12.65	121	4453	20.14	11.81	113	6220	28.18	13.51	129	3652	16.52	12.38	119
Occupation: executive/admin/mgr	20682	100.00	9.76	100	13253	64.08	11.69	120	4350	21.03	11.54	118	5723	27.67	12.41	127	3180	15.38	10.78	110
Occupation: clerical/sales/tech	38455	100.00	18.15	100	23450	60.98	20.69	114	7893	20.53	20.93	115	9633	25.05	20.89	115	5923	15.40	20.08	111
Occupation: precision/crafts/repair	14379	100.00	6.79	100	7067	49.15	6.241	92	2401	16.70	6.37	94	2866	19.93	6.21	92	1800	12.52	6.10	90
Occupation: other	39596	100.00	18.69	100	20457	51.66	8.05	97	7033	17.76	18.65	100	8625	21.78	18.70	100	4799	12.12	16.27	87
HHI $150,000+	14089	100.00	6.65	100	9879	70.12	8.72	131	3575	25.37	9.48	143	3852	27.34	8.35	126	2452	17.40	8.31	125
HHI $75-149,999	51008	100.00	24.08	100	32535	63.78	28.71	119	11409	22.37	30.26	126	13332	26.14	28.90	120	7794	15.28	26.42	110
HHI $60-74,999	24052	100.00	11.35	100	13226	54.99	11.67	103	4001	16.63	10.61	93	5546	23.06	12.03	106	3679	15.30	12.47	110
HHI $50-59,999	18915	100.00	8.93	100	10507	55.55	9.27	104	3039	16.07	8.06	90	4899	25.90	10.62	119	2569	13.58	8.71	98
HHI $40-49,999	21142	100.00	9.98	100	10840	51.27	9.56	96	3252	15.38	8.62	86	4399	20.81	9.54	96	3189	15.08	10.81	108
HHI $30-39,999	23479	100.00	11.08	100	11002	46.86	9.71	88	3525	15.01	9.35	84	4739	20.18	10.27	93	2738	11.66	9.28	84
HHI $20-29,999	24114	100.00	11.38	100	10671	44.25	9.421	83	3845	15.94	10.20	90	4123	17.10	8.94	79	2703	11.21	9.16	80
HHI <$20,000	35046	100.00	16.54	100	14673	41.87	2.95	78	5062	14.44	13.43	81	5232	14.93	11.34	69	4379	12.49	14.84	90
Census Region: Northeast	40543	100.00	19.14	100	23527	58.03	20.76	108	8755	21.59	23.22	121	9466	23.35	20.52	107	5307	13.09	17.99	94
Census Region: South	76644	100.00	36.18	100	39460	51.49	34.82	96	13291	17.34	35.25	97	15476	20.19	33.55	93	10693	13.95	36.24	100
Census Region: North Central	47979	100.00	22.65	100	23622	49.23	20.84	92	6536	13.62	17.33	77	10149	21.15	22.00	97	6937	14.46	23.51	104
Census Region: West	46680	100.00	22.04	100	26724	57.25	23.58	107	9125	19.55	24.20	110	11032	23.63	23.92	109	6567	14.07	22.26	101
County size A	86941	100.00	41.04	100	51225	58.92	45.20	110	18545	21.33	49.18	120	20887	24.02	45.28	110	11793	13.56	39.97	97
County size B	63405	100.00	29.93	100	33507	52.85	29.56	99	10337	16.30	27.41	92	14376	22.67	31.17	104	8794	13.87	29.81	100
County size C	30730	100.00	14.51	100	15173	49.37	13.39	92	4719	15.36	12.51	86	6054	19.70	13.13	90	4400	14.32	14.91	103
County size D	30770	100.00	14.52	100	13429	43.64	11.85	82	4106	13.35	10.89	75	4807	15.62	10.42	72	4516	14.68	15.31	105
Marital status: single	51782	100.00	24.44	100	29039	56.08	25.62	105	9226	17.82	24.47	100	11903	22.99	25.81	106	7910	15.28	26.81	110
Marital status: married	119963	100.00	56.63	100	65675	54.75	57.95	102	21701	18.09	57.55	102	27115	22.60	58.79	104	16859	14.05	57.15	101
Marital status: all others	40100	100.00	18.9	100	18619	46.43	16.43	87	6780	16.91	17.98	95	7106	17.72	15.41	81	4734	11.80	16.04	85
Marital status: engaged	9865	100.00	4.66	100	6084	61.68	5.371	115	1894	19.19	5.02	108	2602	26.38	5.64	121	1588	16.10	5.38	116
HH size: 1	29319	100.00	13.84	100	12911	44.04	1.39	82	4426	15.10	11.74	85	4996	17.04	10.83	78	3489	11.90	11.83	85
HH size: 2	69030	100.00	32.59	100	34434	49.88	30.38	93	11407	16.52	30.25	93	13850	20.06	30.03	92	9178	13.30	31.11	95
HH size: 3-4	80800	100.00	38.14	100	47115	58.31	41.57	109	15544	19.24	41.22	108	19314	23.90	41.87	110	12257	15.17	41.54	109
HH size: 5+	32696	100.00	15.43	100	18874	57.73	16.65	108	6330	19.36	16.79	109	7964	24.36	17.27	112	4579	14.01	15.52	101
Children: any	89093	100.00	42.06	100	52125	58.51	45.99	109	17267	19.38	45.79	109	21594	24.24	46.82	111	13264	14.89	44.96	107
Race: White	165206	100.00	77.98	100	86282	52.23	76.13	98	27163	16.44	72.04	92	35715	21.62	77.43	99	23404	14.17	79.33	102
Race: Black/African American	24003	100.00	11.33	100	14226	59.27	12.55	111	5833	24.30	15.47	137	5144	21.43	11.15	98	3249	13.53	11.01	97
Race: American Indian or Alaska Native	2770	100.00	1.31	100	1567	56.57	1.38	106	449	16.21	1.19	91	786	28.37	1.70	130	332	11.99	1.13	86
Race: Asian	4534	100.00	2.14	100	2873	63.38	2.54	118	1176	25.93	3.12	146	1078	23.78	2.34	109	619	13.66	2.10	98
Race: Other	16480	100.00	7.78	100	9001	54.62	7.94	102	3309	20.08	8.78	113	3678	22.32	7.97	103	2014	12.22	6.83	88
Spanish speaking (in an english language capable HH)	27987	100.00	13.21	100	15059	53.81	13.29	101	5289	18.90	14.03	106	6229	22.26	13.50	102	3541	12.65	12.00	91
Spanish or Hispanic Origin or Descent	25608	100.00	12.09	100	13855	54.11	12.23	101	4907	19.16	13.01	108	5702	22.27	12.36	102	3245	12.67	11.00	91

Source: From 2004 Fall *MRI*.

the media planner must ultimately make. He or she will ask a host of questions about a possible target before making the final decision, including some of the following:

- Is the size of the target sufficient to meet marketing sales goals and advertising/communication objectives?
- Can a large enough portion of the target audience be reached efficiently, with an adequate level of frequency?
- Does our media budget permit adequate delivery of messages to the possible target?

Geodemographics.   With media vehicles becoming more and more local-ized according to geography, it is logical that planners would attempt to combine geographical patterns with demographic characteristics. For example, many of today's consumer magazines offer an advertiser wide choices for geographical pinpointing of target markets. You can buy an advertisement that will appear only in a particular region of the country (say, the Southwest), or a state (Texas). Some magazines even permit a metropolitan area split (Dallas). Other media types have long been struc-tured to permit localized buys—spot television and cable, spot radio, newspapers, and out-of-home media, to name a few.

As we pointed out in Chapter 3, a number of research services such as PRIZM and ACORN have been developed to meet the desire of planners to use geodemographics in profiling target audiences. Such services report a variety of profile characteristics, such as income, education, occupation, ethnic affiliation, population density, and type of housing. Information for such characteristics can be presented for every ZIP code in the United States.

Matching Target Audiences with Media Choices

Regardless of the variable or variables used to profile target audiences, the media planner ultimately must choose the target audience and then match it with available media. The difficulty in doing this is that information that permits a direct match often is not available. For example, if you target "economy-minded" women between ages 20 and 55 and decide to use outdoor posters in the 50 largest cities of the United States, you likely will not have much usable information on how well that target is delivered by outdoor advertising. Your rationale for such a strategy may have to be based on intuition and creative logic or through using informal surveys of possible prospects.

Planners use syndicated research services, such as MRI and Simmons, to match up demographic and product-usage data with target audiences. Thus, if you use a syndicated source to define your target in demographic terms, you will select media vehicles that show heavy usage of the vehicles in the demos in which you are interested.

When a target audience is defined in product-usage terms, the direct approach is to match the target audience with media vehicles according to the exposure level of users (i.e., heavy, medium, or light). A less direct ap-proach involves determining the demographic profiles of heavy, medium, and light users and matching them up with the demographic profiles of the audiences of various media vehicles.

Choosing Media Classes

The second component of media strategy involves the selection of the media classes. This is a planning function. After the media classes are decided, and an appropriate mix of media types is determined, typically this information is turned over to media buyers to execute, or implement, the plan.

The rationale for choosing media classes is widely available in advertising media textbooks. We suggest you consult one to get an in-depth discussion of the advantages and disadvantages of choosing the various media. Figure 7-4 presents a simple listing of the characteristics of the major media and some suggestions as to when it might be appropriate to use them. A more compre-hensive listing of minor media, including nontraditional media, is available in

Chapter 9. At DDB Needham Worldwide, they have expanded on some of the more traditional reasons for choosing media and have developed a grid (not shown) to show how various message delivery options can enhance an advertising message. Figure 7-5 is a modification of that grid and suggests how various media deliver messages well. *The challenge to the media planner is holding the brand position or identity across many pieces of the plan (i.e., media and vehicles) while being true to what the various media do well.*

FIGURE 7-4   MEDIA CHARACTERISTICS AND RECOMMENDATIONS

Major Media	Attributes	When to Use
Newspaper	• Mass audience • Excellent at reaching local market • Short lead time • Very current • Short life span • Poor reproduction quality • Allows comparison shopping • Provide "extra" services (such as ad designing) • Segmented sections used for consultation (travel, business)	• Local retailer • Targeting specific geographic market • Temporary offering (such as a sale) • Specific/special interest offering (such as current air fares) • Brand appearance not important • Need information to be distributed quickly (such as response to negative publicity)
Magazines	• Segmented audience • Long life span • Pass-along readership • Excellent reproduction • Not frequent • Long lead times • Not immediate	• Information intensive product • Rely on a "look" to create an image • Want long lasting image • Want image of editorial content to transfer to product
Television	• Combination of sight and sound allows for more complex messages to be delivered and remembered • Short-lived duration of messages (5–30 seconds) • High reach in general segments • High frequency in specific audiences • Accessible to everyone • Ads seen as intrusive and often ignored • Most cost efficient to reach large audience, although high absolute cost	• Want to build awareness for product (such as product introduction) • Require product demonstration • Want to use peripheral cues for low-involvement product (using popular music or celebrity to attract attention to brand) • Have financial resources to trade high absolute cost for more cost efficient medium • National brand

FIGURE 7-4	CONTINUED

Major Media	Attributes	When to Use
	• Market coverage flexibility (local or national buys)	
Radio	• Immediate delivery • Fleeting duration of message • Good for reaching local market • Low absolute cost • Stimulates imagination • No visuals eliminate using complicated messages or demonstrations • Mobile—able to reach consumers nearly anywhere, including when they are already out and about	• Want to stimulate impulse buying • Reminder advertising • Local retailer • Want to advertise offerings that change frequently (such as weekly grocery specials) • Consumer behavior motivated by time of day (such as eating out) • Product is simple to understand • Low advertising budget
Outdoor	• Excellent reach potential • Offers exposure near/ at point of purchase • Geographically selective • Fleeting message delivery • Limited reproduction quality	• Local business • Want to create traffic for local business • Segmenting audience according to geography • Want to build awareness within community • Want to reach mass community audience

Establishing the Media Mix

The third component or aspect of media strategy involves the amount of emphasis, or weight, put on the various media types and their relative importance.

The balance of the media types for a plan logically flows from the situation analysis, the target audiences to whom the plan is directed, and the media goals. Even if only a single media class is chosen—say, network television—there will typically be a mix. The mix might consist of a balance among television dayparts—that is, available segments in a 24-hour schedule. For example, a planner may spend 35% of the budget on daytime programs, 50% on evening programs, and 15% for late evening television. Or, even if the planner chooses only one daypart (say, evening programs), there might be a mix among different programming formats: situation comedies, action, drama, and news magazines.

Factors to Consider for Media Weighting

There are several factors a planner likely will consider in determining the weighting of a particular set of media.

FIGURE 7–5   VARIOUS MEDIA AND MESSAGES THEY DELIVER WELL

Newspaper
- Influence
- Credibility
- News
- Immediacy
- Value

Radio
- Intrusiveness
- Humor
- Flexibility
- Immediacy
- Imagination

Television
- Demonstration
- Influence
- Emotion
- Enthusiasm
- Humor

Magazines
- Information
- Sensuality
- Style
- Attractiveness
- Elegance

Direct Mail
- Information
- Education
- Immediacy
- Innovation
- Value

Target Audience.   A media planner typically will have to decide on different media based on the size and composition of the target audience or audiences to whom the media effort is directed. A narrow target might be reached effectively by a single media type, but an assortment of different media may be required to reach a diverse population. The planner and media buyer will usually look to audience data to see how different media vehicles deliver specific targeted audiences. For example, *Redbook* magazine may be quite efficient in reaching your target and thus would be a part of your mix. Yet, the number *Redbook* delivers may be only a small proportion of the total audience sought, and you will have to bring in several other magazine vehicles, say, *Ladies Home Journal* and *Better Homes and Gardens.*

Target Market/Geographic Region.   As mentioned earlier, a target market relates to the geographic location of customers and prospects. In developing a media mix, with appropriate weights among media types, the planner must look to the size and potential product or brand use of differing geographic areas. Some media types deliver audiences directly on a national scale, for example, network broadcast media (television, cable, and radio) and many magazines. However, other media types can be bought in a variety of geographical ways. Thus, daily newspapers are available in more than 1,500 local cities; television can be purchased on more than 1,300 individual stations in around 210 markets in the United States.

A planner must take into account the various potentials of certain geographic areas in arriving at media weights. Consider the following hypothetical example about product usage arranged by major marketing regions:

Region	Number of Users of the Product Category (in millions)	Index of Product Users
Northeast	22	89
East Central	13	83
West Central	22	119
South	37	111
Pacific	17	89

The South is the largest region in terms of product users, 37 million. Note that the relative use of this product in the South is above average (the index of 111 indicates an 11% above-average use). This information might lead a planner to add extra media effort to southern markets. However, all five regions have sizable numbers of users (the East Central is the lowest but has 13 million product users), and none are dramatically above or below average (index ranges from 83 to 119). So a planner has to be careful not to spread the advertising effort too thin across these other markets. In the final analysis, interpreting such data is subjective, and a planner's decision must be justified based on logical analysis and intuition.

Linking the Media Mix with Other Strategies

Although there are countless ways to compose a media mix, two varied approaches delineate the situation. Media mix strategies can be viewed as being either *concentrated* or *assorted*.

A **concentrated mix** is one in which you typically use a single media type, say, network television. You can also think of a concentrated mix as including one or a very limited number of vehicles within a media type (say, only *Sports Illustrated* as your magazine choice).

Concentration provides some of the following benefits:

- **Effect on Competitors**—by focusing your media effort in a very limited way, there is a strong chance of dominating that medium relative to competition. Thus, your advertising likely will have greater impact in the minds of consumers exposed to that medium or vehicle.
- **Effect on Dealers**—by limiting media buys, dealers may readily note your advertising and be impressed by its concentrated effort. Perhaps you have chosen to put most of your money into a single vehicle (say, an important miniseries on television or a blockbuster event such as a Super Bowl game). This may have a desirable effect on the retailers and wholesalers in the channel of distribution.
- **Effect on Media**—by concentrating your media money in a single type and a few vehicles, you will often gain a negotiating advantage with the media. They may be more inclined to offer better prices or merchandising help because you are spending the bulk of your media dollars with them.
- **Effect on Production Costs**—there will likely be certain economies of scale associated with a concentrated media buy. If you use both television and magazines, for example, the cost to produce commercials and advertisements will be greater than if you used a single media type. The same may be true if you spread your vehicle buys over a large base.

An **assorted mix** uses several media types in the mix by spreading dollars across a large base of media opportunities. Certain situations may more logically warrant this approach over a concentrated one. For example, if a target audience is subdivided into several segments, you will be more likely to use an assortment of media. A primary target of working mothers and a secondary target of working mothers' children, for example, may logically break down into magazines for the primary target and Saturday morning television for the secondary target.

Assorted mixes can result in some of the following advantages:

- **Effect on Target Audiences**—an assortment of media facilitates delivering different messages to different people. Today planners use many media types, including nontraditional media and unconventional communication approaches, to reach increasingly smaller audience segments. The more targeted audiences are split, the more likely an assortment of media will be used.
- **Effect on Message Content**—if you would like to communicate with the same prospects but in different psychological contexts, assortment makes sense. This approach might be used where there is a lengthy period through which messages take a prospect through the communication cycle, from initial awareness of a brand to getting a prospect to intend to make a brand purchase. Each of these stages may best be presented in different media.

- **Effect on Reach and Frequency Goals**—whereas a concentrated mix often results in frequency being more easily attainable than reach, an assorted approach can affect both. Most typically, however, assortment translates into reach being extended beyond that which a concentrated mix provides. Because there are heavy and light users for each medium, adding a second (or third or fourth) medium will usually extend the reach of a single medium. For example, you may get a reach of 75% against the target with a network television buy. By shifting some of the money spent in television to magazines, the television reach may go down somewhat, but the combined television-magazine delivery may increase to, say, 80%.

The effect of an assortment on frequency comes about through a balancing of exposure opportunities. In some concentrated media schedules, frequency exposures are particularly high at the low and high ends of the distribution. In other words, the number of target audiences exposed is relatively large for those who receive only one and two exposures, as well as by those receiving the largest possible number of exposures. If additional media are included into the assortment, the extremes of the exposure distribution usually are reduced, with a corresponding increase in the midrange exposures. This process smooths out the overall frequency distribution and may result in a more effective achievement of media objectives.

Media Timing

When to Advertise. The last component of the media strategy involves the timing, or scheduling of the advertising. As we discussed earlier in the chapter, there are two basic decisions related to timing: when to advertise and what kind of continuity, or pattern, to use. The timing of the advertising can be based on many factors including a number of considerations internal to a firm. For example, a company may schedule advertising depending on product availability or when new products are introduced. The following are some of the more common considerations planners address:[18]

1. **Budget Constraints**—This factor influences scheduling in many ways. Is there sufficient money available to initiate a campaign at reach and frequency levels the planner deems necessary and still have enough left to sustain the campaign over an extended period? If not—an all too common reality—a planner will have to make some tough decisions about when to advertise, and the type of continuity used when the brand is advertised. Budget constraints influence each of the following considerations.
2. **Seasonality**—The sales of many products vary with the time of year. Men's casual slacks sell best during spring and fall, as do many types of clothing. A media schedule will need to support sales efforts during these periods.
3. **Purchase-Repurchase Cycle**—Ideally, advertisers want to advertise before consumers make each purchase decision. "Recency buying" underscores this desire by striving to schedule advertising as close as possible to the time the consumer makes a purchase. Depending on the length of the purchase-repurchase cycle, it can get expensive—especially when you realize that it is generally not enough to simply

reach consumers during this cycle. They also need to be reached with sufficient frequency to achieve the desired effect, usually sales.

4. **Stage of the Product Life Cycle**—Products in the introductory phase of the product life cycle generally require more advertising—more defined in terms of both exposure and dollars expended. New brands generally require more exposure than mature ones do to get a message across and accepted. Moreover, during an introductory period, it's important to reach prospects quickly. If a brand has a differentiating feature, it may only have a small window of opportunity to capitalize on its advantage before the competition catches up and copies its edge. Some prospects are expensive to reach, but in an introductory period it's important to reach them. As a product matures, you can often reach them in different ways that are frequently more cost-efficient.

5. **Competitive Advertising Patterns**—Because strategy is competitive in nature, it's important to know when the competition is advertising in order to plan how to match their promotional efforts. There really are no simple, safe generalizations about whether it is better to confront or avoid the competition. For example, the media expenditures for Burger King and the Miller brands are proportionately higher than those for McDonald's and Budweiser, respectively. In the case of Burger King, the higher expenditures may be because the company feels it can increase its share of the fast-food business at the expense of McDonald's—which it has done in recent years. In the case of the top two Miller brands, the company continues to lose share of market. Although there are similarities between the two brands, there are enough differences to underscore the importance for media planners to have a firm grasp of the company's marketing strategy and corporate culture—how ambitious is the company? How much risk is it willing to tolerate? In the case of the Miller brands, the company spent nearly as much—$237 million compared to $242 million for the top two Budweiser brands (2004)—yet only generated less than a third as much in sales: 21 million barrels versus 69 million barrels of beer.[19]

6. **Media Dominance**—This consideration is related to the previous one on competitive activity not only in its concern about whether to confront or avoid the competition, but also in how to match them. Many companies, especially category leaders, want to dominate a medium or a vehicle to demonstrate to consumers that they are the brand leaders.

Continuity.   Media practitioners use the term **continuity** in a variety of ways. We refer to continuity as the way media messages are scheduled over time. Although we present three specific types, or patterns, of continuity—continuous, flighting, and pulsing—planners commonly use variations of these types, adapting them to meet the requirements of the situation. The continuity used for a particular media plan depends on many of the same factors that influence media timing. Figures 7-6A, 7-6B, and 7-6C show graphs (media schedule) of the three patterns.

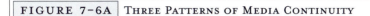

FIGURE 7-6A THREE PATTERNS OF MEDIA CONTINUITY

Continuous Media Schedule

FIGURE 7-6B THREE PATTERNS OF MEDIA CONTINUITY

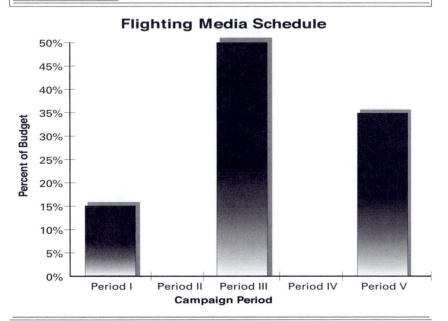

Flighting Media Schedule

FIGURE 7-6C	THREE PATTERNS OF MEDIA CONTINUITY

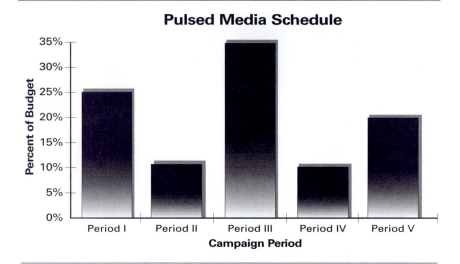

A **continuous** continuity pattern (Figure 7-6A) is one in which approximately the same amount of money is spent in each period of the campaign. Such a strategy might be related to a brand with a relatively fixed share of market, with sales fairly equal across each month or period. This pattern is sometimes called *straight-through advertising.*

In a **flighting** strategy (Figure 7-6B), advertising varies from period to period. During certain times of the campaign, there is no advertising at all. This approach is often considered for a brand with a limited budget relative to competitors and a varying sales pattern throughout the year. A brand like FTD Florists schedules its advertising in flights to time its advertising before major flower-giving holidays such as Valentine's Day, Easter, Mother's Day, and Secretary's Day.

A **pulsed** schedule (Figure 7-6C), or pulsing, is similar to flighting—advertising varies from period to period—but there is at least some advertising media scheduled in each period. For example, a heavy media effort may be placed just before a peak sales period, yet at other times media messages would continue in order to maintain top-of-mind brand awareness.

It is important to realize that continuity means more than simply scheduling impressions over a period of time. The impressions contain information, ideas, or images designed to achieve communication goals. In the end, it is the messages that should have the strongest influence on the particular continuity schedule selected. An example of campaign continuity is as follows:

EXAMPLE The brand's new advertising theme will be introduced to the target audience during the first two months of the campaign (January and February), followed by a three-month period of focusing on brand attributes (March, April, May). There will be no advertising scheduled during the low sales months of summer (June, July, August), followed by a big back-to-school push in September because of peak sales. The campaign will finish the year using a message strategy designed to build the brand during the last three-month period (October, November, and December).

DETERMINING THE MEDIA TACTICS

Once the strategy is determined, the next step is to implement the plan by making the media buys. In the business world, the actual buys will depend on a number of factors that are difficult to fully consider in a textbook, including the availability of advertising space or time, the negotiating skill of the buyers, and special media opportunities (some of which present themselves on a nonrecurring basis). For example, there is a finite amount of broadcast time and billboard space available to purchase. Unlike newspapers and magazines that can add pages to an issue, a TV station can't schedule additional time, and an outdoor advertising company can't add additional billboards (at least not in the short run) to meet new demand.

Historically, the rates media set for advertising space or time have been subject to varying amounts of negotiation. Broadcast media rates have been heavily negotiated, print media much less so. Some buyers maintain that all media rates are negotiable. Basically, the rates that can be charged for a media vehicle are a function of supply and demand.

Buyers also consider **special opportunities** on both a regular and a nonrecurring basis. Magazines offer special demographic breakouts from their regular editions geared toward special segments, such as a students' edition. Newspapers periodically offer special features centered on a theme such as gardening or automobiles.

Making the Media Buys

Because the media buy is an execution of the media strategy, all the factors that influence the strategy will also affect the tactics. Among the most important considerations are those associated with the target audience, costs, seasonality, and geography.

Target Audience. Selecting media vehicles that reach the target audience makes obvious sense. It is also important to reach targets while minimizing *waste*—media talk for reaching nonprospects. Another relevant consideration in matching the right vehicle with the target audience involves the circumstances surrounding the conditions under which the target will be exposed to the vehicle. At DDB Needham Worldwide they've developed a proprietary system called Aperture to evaluate people's receptivity to an advertising message. This system looks at when and where the target is exposed to an ad because these considerations can influence how the audience feels about the messages in the advertising. A radio spot on Saturday night will typically reach people in a different frame of mind than the same spot on Sunday morning. The circumstances surrounding the conditions under which the audience is exposed to an ad influence the impact of a message.[20]

Considering how a vehicle will impact a message is always important when matching specific vehicles with a target audience. Yet all too frequently, media buyers purchase a vehicle on no more than its ability to deliver reach at a cost-efficient price. We hope this discussion emphasizes the importance of using judgment in making media purchases. It also underscores the importance of understanding the target beyond demographic considerations.

Costs.   Purchasing media at cost-efficient prices is a critical part of media buying. The greater the savings, the more money that can be committed to increasing the advertising weight of the media plan. To help evaluate the relative cost-efficiency of various media vehicles, a planner can use three related measures: cost per thousand (CPM), cost per thousand prospects (CPMP), and cost per point (CPP).

Cost per Thousand.   This is the basic measure used to compare media vehicles or media schedules. It can be used for intermedia comparisons (between media) or intramedia comparisons (within a media class). It refers to the cost of reaching every 1,000 individuals or homes with a particular media vehicle or schedule, and can be calculated as follows:

$$\frac{\text{Cost of the unit} \times 1,000}{\text{audience base}} = \text{CPM (audience base)}$$

The unit can refer to a unit of time or space, such as 30-second spots or full-page ads. The audience base can be households, circulation, demographic or product usage segments.

Consider the following example from *Ladies Home Journal*:

$$\frac{\$127{,}000 \text{ (4-C Page)} \times 1{,}000}{4{,}915{,}000 \text{ circulation}} = \$25.84 \text{ CPM circulated copies}$$

Analyzing media vehicles on the basis of circulation or total audience provides a media buyer with the relative value a vehicle has in delivering all the people that are exposed to the vehicle. However, the real value of a vehicle is in delivering prospects (i.e., people who may be predisposed to buy the product). In the above example, a buyer will want to know how efficiently *Ladies Home Journal* delivers people who are in the target audience. So instead of calculating the CPM for circulated copies, or the total audience in the case of television, a CPM is calculated for the target audience. To find information on the exposure of various demographic segments to media vehicles look in *MRI* or *Simmons* (the demographic volumes—not the product usage ones).

Cost per Thousand Prospects.   CPMP is a measure that is sometimes used to focus on the efficiency with which a vehicle delivers the target audience. Let's say in the above example, the target audience is women between ages 25 and 54. To calculate a CPMP, first determine the number of women ages 25–54 who are in the audience of *Ladies Home Journal*. This figure can be obtained from *MRI* or *Simmons*. Next, calculate the CPMP as follows:

$$\frac{\$127{,}000 \times 1{,}000}{9{,}560{,}000 \text{ (W 25–54)}} = \$13.29 \text{ CPMP (or CPM W 25–54)}$$

Note that in the above example, the denominator for cost-per-thousand prospects (9,560,000) is larger than the denominator for CPM circulation (4,915,000). This is because the audience figure, women between ages 25 and 54, is arrived at by multiplying the circulation figure by the readers per copy (RPC).

Comparing the cost-efficiency of vehicles based on circulation or total audience rather than prospects can obviously lead to differing conclusions. For example, comparing *Ladies Home Journal* to a similar magazine such as *Good Housekeeping* led to the following comparison (the calculations are derived from Optimum Media Research based on data obtained from *SRDS* and *MRI*):

	CPM Circulation	**CPMP (W 25–54)**
Ladies Home Journal	$12.29	$25.84
Good Housekeeping	$11.59	$33.14

In the above example, *Ladies Home Journal* is the more cost-efficient purchase based on circulation, but *Good Housekeeping* is more efficient based on cost-per-thousand prospects. Media buyers nearly always want to know the cost-efficiency of a vehicle in delivering the target audience, but this information isn't always available (especially to students). Sometimes the relevant information is contained in psychographic data and is not easily (or inexpensively) obtainable. Sometimes you end up comparing what you can, especially if you are with a small organization.

Cost per Point.   Cost per point, also called cost per rating point, is another measure used to compare media alternatives. It is used mostly for broadcast media and is arrived at by dividing the cost of the commercial by a program's rating as follows (although this example uses TV, CPPs can be calculated for other media as well):

$$\frac{\text{Cost of a commercial}}{\text{Program rating}} = \text{Cost per point}$$

EXAMPLE

The first dollar amount ($595,000) is the cost of a hypothetical top-rated situation comedy.

$$\frac{\$595,000}{20 \text{ rating}} = \$29,750 \text{ CPP}$$

CPPs can be used to compare alternative broadcast vehicles or alternative media schedules. They are also often used to indicate the amount of exposure that can be obtained from a defined budget in a local market. For example, if you have a budget of $1,000 and an estimated CPP of $10, you can purchase 100 rating points of exposure.[21] Although CPPs are used primarily with television and radio, they can also be used with print media. Analysts use the concept of coverage as a substitute for a rating because coverage can be expressed as a percentage of a demographic or product usage segment.[22]

Note of Caution.   Cost-efficiency analysis is an important part of media buying. Nonetheless, it is important to remember that these analyses are based on exposure—they really tell nothing about the likely effectiveness of the media selected. In other words, buying the most efficient media won't necessarily give you the most effective plan.

Seasonality. The seasonal allocation of media dollars is one way media buyers schedule advertising over the campaign period. The idea here is to coordinate media expenditures with the varying sales pattern of the brand.

By scheduling advertising in line with existing sales trends, the advertising attempts to channel the needs or wants of the consumer into demand for the brand. Naturally, there may be some corporate strategic reasons to even out sales patterns, perhaps to better manage the labor force. Usually, however, it's a lot easier to "go with the flow" than to try to change existing patterns of consumer behavior.

Exhibit 7-1 is a simplistic example of how a packaged goods advertiser allocates its media budget based on bimonthly sales.

Usually advertising is scheduled during a period prior to when sales are anticipated. Jim Avery, in his book *Advertising Campaign Planning*, points out that to do otherwise assumes "that the advertising works instantly." He uses a statistical approach called "smoothing" to allocate media dollars over a period of a couple of months so that there is an advertising "lead-in" to when sales are expected to take place.[23] The timing of the advertising schedule is also often influenced by the purchase-repurchase cycle (discussed on page 211). A buyer needs to know the strategic importance of scheduling advertising as close to the time consumers make a purchase, or whether he or she should give substantial lead time preceding when the consumer is likely to make a purchase.

Geography. The geographical allocation of media dollars is based on the same idea we considered with seasonality—advertise where (or when) there

EXHIBIT 7-1 SEASONAL ALLOCATION OF MEDIA DOLLARS				
Months	**Sales**	**Percent of Total Sales**	**Media Budget***	**Budget Allocation****
Jan./Feb.	$54,233,600	9.7%	$57,088,000	$5,537,536
March/April	$97,620,480	17.1%	$57,088,000	$9,762,048
May/June	$117,601,280	20.6%	$57,088,000	$11,760,128
July/Aug.	$128,448,000	22.5%	$57,088,000	$12,844,800
Sept./Oct.	$105,041,900	18.4%	$57,088,000	$10,504,192
Nov./Dec.	$67,934,700	11.9%	$57,088,000	$6,793,472
Total	$570,879,960	100%	$57,088,000	$57,202,196

*Media budget is approximately 10% of sales
** Budget allocation is determined by multiplying percent of total sales by the Media Budget ($57,088,000)

is a history of sales doing well. Naturally, there may be strategic reasons why you may want to put extra emphasis in areas where sales are low, but the general rule is to advertise in line with existing trends of consumer behavior.

There are two basic geographical considerations: (1) Advertise only in those areas where there is sufficient market opportunity, and (2) advertise everywhere (i.e., nationally) and add extra emphasis, or weight, in selected areas where the brand sells especially well. For example, in Exhibit 7-2 half of the brand's budget of $57 million is allocated to national advertising (say, network television), and half of the budget is earmarked toward adding extra advertising pressure (say, spot television) in the four geographic regions where sales are proportionally higher.

Contingencies and Alternative Plans

As you develop the strategy and tactics, it is wise to consider alternative courses of action should unexpected conditions occur during the life of the campaign. This is called **contingency planning.** Some of the problems that can influence a decision to move the campaign in a different direction include the following:

- **Changing Economic Conditions**—For certain products, the general economic condition affects sales. If the economy turns downward (or upward), then it may be smart to adjust the plan. If economic changes affect different parts of the country in varying ways, then a national plan may have to switch to a more localized one.
- **Changing Sales Results**—Regardless of how economic conditions affect a product class, individual brands can go through sales changes that were not expected when the media plan was finalized. Sales expectations could decrease or increase. The key is to know how best to change a media plan if this occurs.
- **Changing Competitive Activity**—It usually is difficult to predict how competitors will behave in the future. Thus, the media activity of competitors may be a contingency area. For example, you might have planned a four-month introduction of a new candy bar on the premise that major competitors do not have similar brands. But, if Hershey Foods introduced a similar brand a month before your introduction, your timing pattern, among other things, would likely be affected. In turn, media objectives would need revision.

The logical follow-through to the consideration of contingencies is to formulate alternative plans. If a particular contingency occurs, there will be a specific alternative plan ready to go. The whole process of formulating contingencies and alternative plans is like a "what if" game. What if predicted economic conditions—estimated at a modest 2% growth next year—turn downward? What would our alternative plan be?

Taking into account contingencies and alternatives, of course, complicates the entire planning process. If it is difficult to develop a single plan, what about having three or four alternatives? Yet, many media people

EXHIBIT 7–2 BUDGET ALLOCATION OF SELECT GEOGRAPHIC MARKETS

Geographical Distribution of Brand X Users

Marketing Region	Users (000)	Percent of Users	Index Number	Adjusted Percentage**	Budget Allocation***
New England****	3,659	6.6%	126*	10%	$2,854,440
Middle Atlantic****	11,379	20.6	121*	32	$9,134,080
East Central	5,681	10.3	77		
West Central	7,353	13.3	88		
South East	6,475	11.7	61		
South West****	6,133	11.1	98*	17	$4,852,480
Pacific****	14,509	26.3	140*	41	$11,703,040
Total	35,680	100%		100%	$28,544,040

*Markets selected for heavy-up emphasis for highest index numbers
**Adjusted Percent determined by dividing 64.6 (that is, the sum of the top four markets Percent of Users) by each market's percent of users
***Budget Allocation is determined by multiplying the Adjusted Percent of the top four markets by $28,545,040 (the budget)
****Top four markets

believe that having other options available if something unforeseen occurs is worth the added effort. Companies often build a dedicated amount into their budget to handle contingencies. This part of the budget is sometimes called a **contingency fund,** or simply a **reserve.**

Finishing the Media Effort

At this point in the campaign, the media section is unlikely to be finished. Still ahead is the task of determining media prices and putting together a budget. In addition, a **media calendar** (also called a **continuity schedule**) needs to be prepared. These documents provide information so that planners and buyers can reevaluate the situation should conditions change. We'll cover these documents in Chapter 11 on putting the plans book together.

A modern marketing communication campaign consists of more than advertising media. It includes other tools such as sales promotion and direct marketing. Increasingly, the distinction between one of these tools and the media is blurred. We cover these tools in Chapter 8.

Finally, agencies increasingly are marketing their media services apart from the rest of what they offer a client. Creative media planning is a label they often attach to their ability to do more than just the quantitative or negotiating aspects of planning and buying. In short, creative media plans should be different or unusual. Part of what makes a plan different is its use of nontraditional media outlets. In Chapter 9, we'll take a look at some of the extra things creative media planners can do to enhance the marketing communication effort.

CAMPAIGN PROGRESS CHECKLIST

At this point in the campaign you should generally be aware of the following points:

1. The best media plans are communication plans that deliver messages and impressions that enhance the message strategy.

2. Media objectives are generally set in terms of exposure (reach, frequency, gross impressions, GRPs, and TRPs), but also consider setting qualitative objectives that are designed to enhance the creative strategy.

3. Media strategy generally includes decisions about target audience, media classes, media mix, and media timing.

4. Each quantitative objective should normally include the desired target, the desired amount of reach and frequency, and the timing or pattern with which the messages are expected to be delivered.

5. In defining the target audience, it is often helpful to go beyond demographic and product usage variables and delineate the target in terms of psychographic, lifestyle, and geodemographic variables.

6. In selecting media classes it is often a good idea to look at more than the traditional characteristics of the media and look at how media add something to the message.
7. The strategic decision about when to advertise not only influences the cost-effectiveness of a plan, but can also influence the target's receptivity to a message.
8. The cost-efficiency of a plan is best measured by the cost of reaching prospects who are most likely to buy a product.
9. The seasonal and geographical allocation of media dollars is a way to efficiently get the messages to the target audience where and when they are most likely to buy the product.
10. Contingency planning and the dedication of a portion of the budget as a contingency fund is one way to plan for unexpected changing conditions in the marketplace.

Notes and References

[1] Jack Neff and Lisa Sanders, "It's Broken," *Advertising Age,* 16 February 2004, p. 1.

[2] For a good discussion of the evolution of media planning, see Joe Mandese, "A Brief History of Planning Time & Space," *Media,* December 2004, pp. 29–34.

[3] Donald W. Jugenheimer et al., *Advertising Media: Strategy and Tactics* (Dubuque, IA: WCB Brown & Benchmark, 1992), p. 12.

[4] J. Avery, *Advertising Campaign Planning: Developing an Advertising-Based Marketing Plan* (Chicago: Copy Workshop, 1993), pp. 143–144.

[5] For an expanded discussion on media tactics, see Jugenheimer et al., *Advertising Media,* pp. 264–283.

[6] W. Wells et al., *Advertising Principles & Practice,* 4th Ed. (Upper Saddle River, NJ: Prentice Hall, 1998), pp. 361–363.

[7] Jack Z. Sissors and Lincoln Bumba, *Advertising Media Planning,* 5th Ed. (Lincolnwood, IL: NTC Business Books, 1996), p. 69.

[8] M. Naples, *Effective Frequency* (New York: Association of National Advertisers, 1979), pp. 63–82.

[9] J.P. Jones, *When Ads Work: New Proof that Advertising Triggers Sales* (New York: Lexington Books, 1995).

[10] Sissors and Bumba, *Advertising Media Planning,* pp. 141–145.

[11] William J. Donnelly, *Planning Media: Strategy and Imagination* (Upper Saddle River, NJ: Prentice Hall, 1996), p. 151.

[12] Sissors and Bumba, *Advertising Media Planning,* pp. 222–225.

[13] Donnelly, *Planning Media,* p. 157.

[14] Jim Surmanek, *Introduction to Advertising Media: Research, Planning, and Buying* (Lincolnwood, IL: NTC Business Books, 1993), p. 82.

[15] Sissors and Bumba, *Advertising Media Planning,* p. 159.

[16] The discussion of these terms is based on Jugenheimer et al., *Advertising Media,* pp. 186–187.

[17]Jugenheimer et al., *Advertising Media,* p. 193.

[18]Arnold M. Barban et al., *Essentials of Media Planning, 3rd Ed.* (Lincolnwood, IL: NTC Business Books, 1993), p. 72.

[19]According to Competitive Media Reporting data, the top two Budweiser brands had media expenditures of $154.1 million and top two Miller brands spent $170.5 million. Reported in Mike Beirne and Kenneth Hein, "Feisty Feds Weigh in against Low-Carbs—and Tasteless Ads," *Brandweek,* 21 June 2004, p. S26.

[20]For more information, see Bruce G. Vanden Bergh and Helen Katz, *Advertising Principles: Choice, Challenge, Change* (Lincolnwood, IL: NTC Business Books, 1999), p. 286.

[21]For an expanded discussion on cost per rating points, see Surmanek, *Introduction to Advertising Media,* pp. 95–104.

[22]For an expanded discussion of coverage in print media, see Sissors and Bumba, *Advertising Media Planning,* pp. 88–91.

[23]For an expanded discussion of smoothing, see Avery, *Advertising Campaign Planning,* p. 167.

CHAPTER 8

Integrated Communications

After the creative and traditional or mass-media plans are developed, it's time to consider other marketing communication elements. The most important of these elements are sales promotion, public relations, and direct marketing.

▌DEVELOPING INTEGRATED MARKETING COMMUNICATIONS

You should continue to think strategically. It's important to integrate the marketing communication recommendations with the advertising plan so that the target audience gets a consistent message and "feel" from every contact it has with promotional activities. Consistency does not necessarily mean that all campaign materials must look alike. It does mean that the target audience members should receive messages and promotions that are consistent and carefully developed to reflect their past and present experiences with your client's product or service.

The relative emphasis to put on each element in the communication mix is a key decision. Although this is primarily a budget allocation and payout problem, there should be good strategic rationale behind this spending decision. Start analyzing consumers in terms of where they are in the sales process or purchase cycle, what types of responses you are looking for from them, and how selective (i.e., targeted) you want your strategy to be.

If the consumers are prospects who have yet to purchase the product, then you may have to improve their product knowledge through awareness-building communication such as advertising. You might also consider using sales promotion to induce consumers to try the product. Past users of the product or brand can be further analyzed according to how much and how often they buy. Sales promotion can be used with past users to stimulate more frequent or larger purchases. Direct marketing and personal selling are other options, but can be more costly. Nonetheless, they might be cost-efficient in terms of the likely sales response of your prospects. For loyal customers, consider reinforcing types of promotion, such as public relations, to maintain an ongoing relationship with them. Figure 8-1 provides a

---

FIGURE 8-1 | RESPONSE, COST, TARGET MIX

Where Consumers Are in Purchase Cycle

Nonuser   Prospect   Infrequent User   Loyal User

Cost of Targeting/Marketing Communication Elements

High Cost/Targeted

Personal Selling

Direct Marketing → *Marketing Communication Mix Strategy*

Sales Promotion

Advertising

Public Relations

Low Cost/Not Targeted

Awareness/   Trial   Increase Purchase   Repeat Purchase/
Knowledge   Amount/Frequency   Retention

Response Desired to Marketing Communication Element

---

three-axis matrix against which you can compare your marketing situation to determine the relative strategic weight to give to the marketing communication elements.

As a general rule, the more targeted your media and closer to actual sales you want the customers' responses to be, the more costly your per-customer marketing communications plan will be. The less targeted and further from sales (awareness, for example) the responses are likely to be, the less expensive per customer your plan will be. However, the more expensive plan could be more cost-efficient overall if the targeted consumers are better prospects. The approach you take may depend on the quantity and quality of information you have about your target audience.

If you build a consumer database of demographic, psychographic, geographic, and geodemographic characteristics and add to it information on purchase behavior and media usage, you should be able to subdivide your market into consumer segments, such as the best customers, those who buy less frequently, those who buy competitive brands, and nonpurchasers.

Next, your task is to determine how to use available communications elements to meet your objectives against the targeted consumer segments. To increase sales and gain market share you may have to work hard to retain current customers while influencing the less frequent purchasers and competitors' customers to buy your brand. This strategic decision leaves you with three consumer segments, each with a different profile and purchase behavior pattern. Your potential target groups might be labeled as follows:

- **Brand Loyals**—These are your best customers who purchase large quantities of the brand on a fairly regular basis. When the brand is not available, they will wait or go to another store.
- **Brand Switchers**—This is a group of less frequent purchasers of the brand who also buy the competitors' brands. They might switch brands for a change of pace or because of a promotional incentive, such as a coupon, sweepstakes, or premium. They move from brand to brand and are not loyal to any particular brand in the product category.
- **Competitors' Brand Loyals**—These brand-loyal consumers are loyal to competitors' brands. They purchase competitive brands on a fairly regular basis, and will shop around for those brands when they are not available in the stores where they typically shop.

This market situation can be reduced to (1) retaining brand loyals, (2) building volume among brand switchers, and (3) initiating trial and gaining some conversion among your competitors' loyals. This task requires strategic differences in how you approach each consumer segment.

What might you do? There are a number of marketing communications options best suited to meet the objectives for each segment. Sales promotion incentives delivered through direct marketing channels can be used to build volume among switchers and initiate trials among the competition's loyals. These same incentives, supported by image-oriented advertising, can increase volume among loyals while rewarding them for being your best customers. Special events and carefully placed public relations items might also impress your loyals and convey the message that you really value their business.

This marketing situation demonstrates how communications should be approached from a strategic and tactical perspective by considering the client's relationship with potential consumer segments. Integrated marketing is accomplished by managing all of the elements so that they complement each other while allowing each to achieve its separate objectives. The following sections focus on the use of sales promotions, public relations, and direct marketing to achieve marketing and advertising campaign objectives. Exhibit 8-1 will give you some feel for the scope of the promotional activities available as you plan to extend the impact of the campaign.

▋SALES PROMOTIONS

The rise in importance of sales promotions to marketing programs over the past 20 years highlights significant changes in the marketplace and the way marketers allocate their promotional dollars. Two decades ago it was not unusual for the typical consumer products advertiser to spend almost 70% of its promotion budget on advertising. By 1981, the percentage of the promotion budget spent on advertising was down to 43%, and by

---

EXHIBIT 8-1	PROMOTIONAL OPTIONS FOR EXTENDING YOUR CAMPAIGN

Sales Promotion

Consumer Promotions
Sampling, couponing, premiums, rebates and refunds, contests and sweepstakes, bonus packs, price-offs, and event sponsorships

Trade Promotions
Slotting allowances, off-invoice allowances, dating, free goods, price reductions, display and merchandising allowances, advertising allowances, count/recount allowances, point-of-purchase displays, cooperative advertising, sales contests, trade shows, and sales meetings

Public Relations

Product Publicity
News stories (new product introductions, dispelling misinformation, and the like), press kits, newsletters, pamphlets, brochures, press conferences, staged events such as celebrity appearances, event sponsorship and trade show support, annual reports, and information hotlines

Direct/Database Marketing
Direct mail, direct response advertising (delivered through all traditional advertising media), catalogs, infomercials, TV home shopping, telemarketing, and interactive computer services

---

1992, it was down to 27%. In the same period, various types of sales promotions had grown from less than 30% to more than 70% of most consumer marketers' promotion budgets.[1] As an example, Leo Burnett USA and H. J. Heinz ended a 36-year relationship in 1994 because of Heinz's decision to reduce its advertising spending from more than $130 million to close to $40 million and put more of its marketing budget into couponing, trade promotions, and price deals.[2] In 2002, Heinz and Leo Burnett were again working together as Heinz felt it needed to put more of its promotional effort into consumer advertising.

Advertising started to regain some of its lost ground in the mid-1990s because of an improving economy, and the industry began to place increased faith in advertising. Still, whether confidence in advertising can be restored to previous levels remains to be seen. The 1980s will always be the decade that saw a complete turnaround in emphasis away from advertising and toward sales promotions.

The main controversy surrounding the use of sales promotions has been the question of its long-term impact on brand equity. Marketers who would like to see a return to the day when advertising was king argue that promotions are simply a bribe to steal sales and market share at the expense of brand equity. The more you induce purchase through "deals," the argument goes, the less likely consumers can be persuaded of a preference for one brand over another based on tangible or intangible qualities promoted through advertising. Sales promotions experts counter that in a cluttered marketplace, other aspects of the marketing program—such as shelf placement and in-store display—are important contributors to a brand's image, an important part of brand equity. Busy consumers, they add, have less time than ever to ponder and absorb the clutter of messages from typical national brand advertising.

The key argument for a primary role for sales promotions in marketing programs is that sales promotions, when done very well, provide companies the ability to combine short-term sales results with long-term equity building. Manufacturers are no longer in a situation where they can make a choice between the long-term equity-building strengths of advertising and the short-term sales-generating advantage of sales promotions. They simply have to be able to achieve both. Think of McDonald's as a prime example of this tug-of-war where hamburgers have to be sold systemwide day in and day out. And at the same time, McDonald's has to maintain its wholesome all-American family image so that the decision to eat there becomes routine for its target audience (mostly parents and their kids). One executive at McDonald's put it succinctly when he said that the company has to *think like a retailer and act like a brand*. This is a key strategy for anyone who wants to be successful in the changing marketplace. And the way to do this is through the successful integration of all aspects of your marketing and advertising programs.

SALES PROMOTIONS DEFINED

Sales promotions offer an incentive to buy a product that takes the form of either a price reduction or value-added offer.[3] Sales promotions activities can be divided into consumer-oriented and trade-oriented promotions.

Consumer-oriented promotions are targeted to the final consumers in the channel of distribution to induce them to buy a brand. Consumer-oriented promotions include product samples, coupons, premiums, rebates, contests and sweepstakes, bonus packs, price-offs, and event sponsorship. The goal of these promotions is to stimulate demand at the retail level.[4]

Trade-oriented promotions (usually shortened to trade promotions) are aimed at distributors and retailers to influence them to carry a product and promote it. Trade promotions account for over two-thirds of all sales promotions and half the dollars spent on promotions and advertising combined.[5] The dollars taken away from advertising over the past 20 years have gone primarily into trade promotions. There is some evidence that trade promotions' share of marketing budgets is declining slightly in favor of consumer promotions and advertising. However, it is not clear if this is a trend or a temporary blip in the cycle.

Manufacturers can choose from a number of trade promotion alternatives to induce distributors and retailers to push their products. Typically, they employ some combination of trade allowances, dealer contests, point-of-purchase displays, cooperative advertising, trade shows, and other incentive programs. A **trade allowance** is a reduced wholesale price charged to distributors and retailers in return for preferential treatment. It has been the most widely used promotion and the most controversial. It is perceived by some as a payoff or bribe to the distributor for special consideration. And because the allowance is often subtracted from the advertising budget, this special treatment is sometimes used at the expense of equity-building consumer messages. The goal of a balanced campaign should be to incorporate the advantages of both trade promotions and advertising in gaining trade acceptance and stimulating consumer purchases. Exhibit 8-2 presents some of the more common types of trade spending.

To successfully incorporate promotions into a marketing communications campaign plan, it is important to know which type of objectives can reasonably be set for the sales promotion program.

EXHIBIT 8-2 A GLOSSARY OF WIDELY USED TRADE
PROMOTION TERMS

A trade-speak-to-English glossary of some of the most common types of trade spending, translated by A.T. Kearney consultant Burt Flickinger III.

Off-invoice allowance: A per-case rebate paid to retailers when order is placed.
Billback: Additional money paid for retailers' display, ad or price cut.
Market development funds (MDFs): Money spent via a retailer to expand category sales; used to develop share in markets where category growth is high and a brand's share is embarrassingly low.
Brand development funds (BDFs): Similar to MDFs, this money pinpoints problems by brand rather than geography.
Category development funds (CDFs): Specifically drives a given category, supporting all brands at once.
Street money: Cash spent in the field, i.e., "at street level," to get more display.
Spiff money: Rewards brokers and buyers with everything from thermoses to TVs to Hawaiian vacations for "assist" in hitting case sales objectives.
Cooperative merchandising agreement (CMA): Annual incentive contract to get retailer to commit to ad, display or price feature for a brand for a time period.
Corporate sales program (CSP): An umbrella promotion across a marketer's total brand portfolio. Products often are shipped directly from the factory in ready-to-display pallets.
Producing plant allowance (PPAs): An incentive to retailers to buy full or half-truckloads direct from the factory. Saves manufacturers distribution costs.
Back haul allowances (BHAs): Money manufacturers pay retailers who'll send trucks to pick up shipments at manufacturer's own plant or distribution center.
Drop ship allowances (DSAs): Money to retailers who bypass the grocer's distribution center for preplanned orders or customized pallets.
Cross-dock or pedal runs: Cash incentives for placing full-pallet orders for four or five stores, distributed by a single truck. Marketer saves distribution costs.
Display-ready cases and pallets: Marketers pay retailers for using these cost-efficient shipments ready for immediate display.

SALES PROMOTION OBJECTIVES

Sales promotion objectives should be set with the bigger picture of the marketing plan in mind. Good sales promotion objectives are targeted and measurable. However, sales promotion objectives have the added characteristic of being directed specifically toward increasing the speed or frequency (sometimes referred to as **sales velocity**) with which consumers buy your brand. Typically, they focus on achieving a sales response. Some types of sales promotions are as follows:

- Induce new customers to try the brand. Samples, coupons, or refund offers can help move consumers toward consideration and eventual trial of the brand.
- Retain current loyal customers and perhaps influence them to buy more. Premiums such as recipes and calendars that provide ideas for new product uses can help reinforce and increase brand usage.
- Increase the overall sales of the brand. Special sizes, multiunit packaging, and premiums can be used as incentives to induce consumers to buy and use more of the product.
- Reinforce advertising efforts by incorporating sales promotions into the campaign. Contests and sweepstakes, for example, can generate consumer and trade involvement and excitement in a campaign.
- Build trade support. The goal is to demonstrate to the trade your effort to stimulate sales, which is the retailers' primary motivation for considering carrying your brand.
- Generate excitement in the sales force at all levels of the distribution channel. Contests, special displays, premiums, and price-off incentives can all provide a salesperson with an extra edge.

Sales promotions not only add an action-oriented component to the campaign, but also provide a vehicle for reaching the trade and sales force. Trade objectives for sales promotions often include obtaining or improving shelf space and position, building inventories for the brand, gaining trade support through display and advertising help, and generating enthusiasm for a new product introduction. A distributor's salespeople can be influenced to give the brand a higher selling priority and put more effort and enthusiasm behind selling it when they know that it is supported by a good promotional program.

Sales promotion objectives should be stated in the same concise terms as all the objectives. The results you expect in terms of sales, product trial, multiple purchases, or improving product display should be stated clearly and specifically. Sales promotion results, like all marketing communications elements, are expected to occur within a specific time frame that should be included in the objective. Do not expect too much from your sales promotions effort. It is unusual for one program to accomplish multiple objectives against differing target audiences.

SALES PROMOTION TECHNIQUES

After setting sales promotion objectives, think about specific techniques to use in implementing the plan. The simplest way to think of the options available is to divide them into consumer and trade promotions. Consumer promotions can then be grouped into the major types used by marketers, including:

sampling
couponing
premiums
contests and sweepstakes
refunds
bonus packs
price-off deals
event sponsorship

Trade promotions take the form of different purchase and performance incentives and allowances that encourage the members of the distribution channel to carry, store, and promote your brand. Together, trade and consumer promotions become part of a **push-pull strategy** to move your brand through its channel of distribution to the final consumer. Trade promotions *push* the product through the distribution channel to the retail outlet and consumer promotions *pull* the ultimate consumer into the store to buy the brand.

Consumer Promotions
Sampling is a highly effective but relatively expensive way to achieve a trial of a product. The expense comes from having to manufacture, inventory, and distribute special trial sizes of the product. However, it is a sound way to get a product into the consumers' hands. Sampling has gained favor with marketers because the amount of time in which a product has to succeed has dwindled, in some instances, from a year down to three months. Product trial, therefore, has become a more urgent objective to new product introductions than ever before. If you cannot get people to try your product, you can never achieve repeat purchase behavior, the lifeblood of business success.

Sampling can be accomplished through a number of different delivery systems. The most common distribution systems are placement in the store, delivery by mail or door-to-door placement, and inclusion with the package. In-store sampling can be done by placing the trial-size products in special point-of-purchase bins or displays. Sometimes a demonstrator is hired who can help customers sample products such as new food items, cosmetics, or home appliances. This demonstrator can also provide additional product information and help deliver other promotional items, such as coupons.

Samples can be delivered to customers' homes by mail. Mail delivery can be an effective way to combine sampling with direct marketing to target consumers who are most likely to use the product.

Samples may be attached to or included along with another of a company's products. This is a good method when the market for original purchase is also the market for the new product being sampled. Other distribution possibilities include magazine and newspaper distribution for small products and sample packs, such as those given out to college students at the beginning of a new school year. Organizations such as Welcome Wagon that greet newcomers to a neighborhood, town, or city are also potential distributors for a sampling program.

Sampling is not without problems. In-store sampling (the most desired form of sampling because it is so close to the point of purchase) requires the support of the trade that can result in additional fees and allowances to keep them happy and behind your program. The method you select to deliver the sample has to be measured against the expense of doing so. Be sure that the payoff is worth the expense.

Couponing is a promotional practice dating back to the late 1800s. Coupons have a number of advantages that make them worth considering. First, coupons allow you to offer a reduced price on a product to those in your market who are price sensitive without having to offer the discount to everybody. Second, unlike trade allowances that a retailer does not have to pass along to customers, a coupon assures the manufacturer that the savings are going to consumers. Third, coupons offer a temporary price reduction that is seen as a special offer and not perceived as a permanent reduction in price. When the offer is over, the brand can return to its normal price. Fourth, retailers can use coupons for their own promotional programs, by offering double or triple the face value of the coupon to consumers. This way, retailers can use the coupons as a traffic-building promotional device.[6]

Couponing has disadvantages. Because of the popularity of couponing, increased clutter has led to a decline in redemption rates. Often, it is the already-established consumer who uses coupons, whereas the marketer had issued the coupons to tempt new users to try the product. *Coupon fraud* can also be a problem. Successful coupon programs are a good example of the adage that things are seldom as easy as they seem. Exhibit 8-3 presents some of the basic types of coupon deals upon which other variations can be built.

Most coupons (upwards of 80%) are delivered to consumers in *free-standing inserts* (FSIs) in newspapers. This type of distribution system takes advantage of consumers' newspaper reading habits, which include searching for coupons in the inserts that typically arrive with the Sunday paper. However, the clutter of the FSIs has cut into the redemption rates for coupons.

Coupons can also be delivered through the mail, in stores, on and in product packaging, in newspapers as part of the *run-of-the-paper* (ROP) *advertising,* and through other media such as magazines. Manufacturers and retailers are constantly searching for new ways to deliver coupons. Many stores use coupon dispensers attached to shelves near products, coupons on the back of receipts, and coupons handed out by product demonstrators. Many marketers predict eventual widespread use of systems that deliver coupons to customers at home via e-mail or fax machines connected to home computers and entertainment systems. Consumers are also aggressively searching for coupons by visiting Web sites to "click and clip."

EXHIBIT 8-3	BASIC TYPES OF COUPON DEALS

Coupon Deal	Description
Cents-off	Most common form of couponing. Deal is a certain amount off the regular price for a specified period of time.
Free	Free product offered to those redeeming coupon. Efficient method of sampling because you only give a free sample to consumers who are interested in it.
Buy one, get one free (BOGO)	Get a free product with purchase of product at regular price. Stimulates multiple purchases. Can be used to reward regular customers. Can require customers to buy more than one unit to get the free one.
Time release	Several cents-off coupons are offered at same time but with different expiration dates to encourage repeat purchase.
Multiple purchase	Coupon offer only good when more than one unit of product is bought. Can be used to increase sales and consumption in short term or to take consumers out of the market by loading them up with the product.
Self-destruct	Two or more coupons are printed to overlap each other so that when one is redeemed the other is destroyed. Can be used to create different deals for different consumers without having to print multiple coupons. Can also be used with the time-release deal to encourage customer to redeem earlier to get a better deal.
Personalized	Coupon is personalized by location or store so that it can only be redeemed at that location. Can be used to get trade support from retail outlets.
Cross-ruff	Purchaser gets a coupon for another unrelated product with the purchase of a product. Can work when users of one product overlap with those of another.
Related sale	Coupon received from the purchase of one product is for a related product. Food manufacturers that sell related products, such as condiments that might go with cold cuts or hot dogs, could place coupons for one of their related products in the package of the other product.
Sweepstakes entry	The coupon also becomes the entry form for a sweepstakes promotion. Consumer information for databases can be collected this way.

Source: Tamara Brezen Block, "Couponing," in *Sales Promotion Handbook, 8th Ed.*, ed. Tamara Brezen Block and William A. Robinson (Chicago, Ill.: Dartnell Press, 1994), 103–104.

Stimulating consumers to redeem coupons is the objective of any couponing program. By following these simple design guidelines when you create your coupon, you can help achieve that goal:

1. Make the coupon instantly recognizable as a coupon.
2. Be sure that the face value and expiration date are easy to see and read on the coupon.
3. Include the UPC and manufacturer's coupon code.
4. Put a picture of the package on the coupon to help the consumer redeem the coupon for the right product.
5. Do not bury the coupon in complicated graphics in an ad or wherever it is being displayed.[7]

Sampling and couponing are among the most frequently used consumer promotions. Premiums, rebates, contests and sweepstakes, bonus packs, price-offs, and event sponsorship tend to be more problematic but can also be effective devices.

Premiums, or merchandise incentives, are offers of merchandise or services (such as travel) for free or at a reduced price as tangible rewards or incentives for the purchase of a product. Consumer premiums can be offered free of charge, or they can be self-liquidating. Free premiums are often small items included in, on, or near the product in the store. Cracker Jacks uses in-pack premiums in the form of small toys, as does McDonald's with its Happy Meal®. Cereal companies make similar use of in-pack incentives. Consumers like in-pack or on-pack premiums because they get an immediate reward for buying the product. Mail-in premiums, on the other hand, require that consumers respond to an offer by mailing in their request. A typical premium tries to stimulate repeat purchases by having consumers mail in proof of having made more than one purchase of a product. Response to mail-in premiums is much lower than to in- or on-pack premiums.

A self-liquidating premium is an offer for which the consumer pays all or part of the cost of the premium before receiving it. Self-liquidating premiums are often merchandise of some value to the consumer that the manufacturer can offer at greatly reduced prices. The goal is to offer something of real value that enhances the brand's image and creates goodwill among consumers and the trade. The manufacturer's goal is only to recoup the costs of offering the premium and not to make a profit.

Premiums can also be used as part of *continuity* plans to encourage consumers to use the brand on a continuous basis by saving coupons, proof of purchase, stamps, or some item that is then turned in for the premium. The purpose of a continuity plan is to bring your customers back time and time again. Airline frequent-flyer programs are among the most popular continuity programs. These programs encourage travelers to fly one airline in order to accumulate enough miles to earn free tickets and other perks. Retailers employ this type of premium-driven program when they ask customers to save their receipts (usually requiring that a minimum amount be spent over time). The key to a successful continuity program is a premium or reward of enough value to keep the customer interested and involved in the program.

Rebates and **refunds** are offers by product manufacturers to reimburse some portion of the purchase price of a product upon receipt of consumer proof of purchase. To obtain a refund or rebate, consumers are typically required to send in proof of purchase to the manufacturer. The refund-and-rebate program has the advantage to the marketer of being easy to set up on short notice to combat competitive activity. The program requires no merchandise inventories or elaborate coupon-redemption procedures. Computer technology allows companies to keep track of who has already received a refund so as not to get caught by consumers trying to take advantage of the offer.

Rebates and refunds are used by a wide variety of companies. Refunds are used to stimulate product trial, move large inventories, and boost sluggish sales of durables. The delay between purchasing and receiving a refund is the main deterrent to consumers' responses to the offer. Automotive manufacturers overcame this problem by allowing consumers to use the rebate as part of their down payment on a car. This gives them an immediate reward for their purchase. Marketers have to be careful not to rely too heavily on refunds and rebates because consumers become sensitive to the practice and only buy during the refund-and-rebate program.

Contests and **sweepstakes** have become increasingly popular. A *contest* is a promotion that awards prizes based on a test of skill or talent. It can require the submission of recipes, photographs, slogans, an essay, or other evidence of an ability. Judges select winners among entrants based on their skills or talents. A *sweepstakes* is a promotion in which prizes are awarded based on chance. Sweepstakes are closely regulated by federal and state lottery laws. One common lottery law requirement is that consumers not be obligated to purchase a product to enter a sweepstakes. Most sweepstakes do not require a purchase but do ask that an entrant do something such as write the brand name on a card.[8] A game is a type of sweepstakes where winning is based on chance but involves collecting game pieces or removing ink from a scratch-off card to win. A game can be extended over time to encourage repeat purchases, such as McDonald's popular Monopoly game.

Consumers prefer sweepstakes and games to contests because they are easier to enter or participate in. There are some basic types of sweepstakes, games, and contests. Sweepstakes can take the form of a simple entry blank mailed to the target audience, included in an ad, or made available at the point of purchase. Consumers enter by mailing a form or dropping it into a box at the point of purchase. The drawing takes place at a specified date. Another version of the sweepstakes requires consumers to submit multiple entries to become eligible for winning different prizes. Each prize then becomes equivalent to a separate sweepstakes, which can increase consumer involvement in the game. In yet another form of sweepstakes, entrants read an ad and write down the key copy points to be eligible to enter. Finally, some marketers have been using coupons as entry forms. This sweepstakes requires entrants to fill out their name and address on the redeemed coupon.

Games are typically used to build store traffic. They come in three varieties. The matching-instant-winner game requires customers to match something from an ad to something at the store to win. There are games in which the consumer has to collect parts to a puzzle or game pieces to be able to win. And then there are the instant-winner games often requiring consumers to peel off or scratch off the surface of a card to see if they have won.

Contests and sweepstakes can add obvious excitement to an advertising campaign, but they should be planned very carefully to avoid detracting from the brand image and becoming the entire focus of the campaign.

Bonus packs add value to a purchase by giving customers an added quantity of the product for the regular price. Compared to coupons, refunds, and rebates, bonus packs provide consumers with more immediate value. However, if the bonus pack increases the size of the product, shelf space could become a problem with the trade because retailers will have to provide this extra space. Bonus packs can also be a good competitive maneuver to counter promotional activity by other brands because they load up consumers with your product.

Price-off promotions are reduced-price deals that are indicated on the package. The consumer knows immediately that this is a deal and may use the price reduction to save money or buy more of the product. The price-off promotion can be popular with both consumers and the trade when the manufacturer allows the retailer to maintain margins. The marketer incurs the reduction as a promotional cost and passes along the savings directly to the customer.

Event sponsorship has become one of the more popular types of promotions over the past several years. Some estimates put event-marketing expenditures above the $5 billion mark. The idea behind event sponsorship is that a marketer associates its product or company with entertainers, athletic events, or other notable people or occasions for the purpose of trading off on their popularity to achieve its marketing objectives. Sponsorship of an event can be an important focal point to an integrated marketing communications campaign. First, the event can support and be supported by advertising and public relations. Second, the event can involve all important targets of a campaign from consumers to the trade to the sales force. The event not only builds enthusiasm, it also invites participation by members of the trade and sales force.

Marketers' logic behind event sponsorship is that some of the enthusiasm the highly involved and loyal audience members or fans feel for the event will rub off on the brand. Also, the assumption is that fans of an entertainer or sporting event have something in common that has brought them to the event. The event transcends differences and allows the sponsor to associate its brand with this commonality. Most important is that event sponsors believe that the association with the event translates into sales for their brands.[9]

Sporting events receive most of the event sponsorship money (more than two-thirds). Although beer, cigarette, and car companies have been the big sponsors in the past, the appeal of these events is broadening to other marketers (like energy drink SoBe in extreme sports and Federal Express with the Super Bowl).

Trade Promotions

One of the important goals of any sales promotion program is to gain the support of the retail trade and distributors as well as to elicit a consumer response. Certain techniques are geared specifically toward the trade.[10]

Almost 45% of all marketing expenditures go toward trade promotions. The purpose of trade promotions is to obtain distribution and support for new products, maintain support for established products, and gain a priority for certain brands in terms of display support, shelf position, and advertising and other promotional support. Trade promotions can be divided into those that are primarily *purchase incentives* and those that are *performance allowances*. Additional trade support is often provided through sales contests, point-of-purchase display items, cooperative advertising money to support local promotions, and participation in industry trade shows and sales meetings to get distributors and retailers behind an advertising campaign.

Purchase incentives are payments made primarily in the packaged goods business to distributors and retailers to encourage them to purchase a brand if they have not done so before, restock it if they do carry it, or increase their inventory. Purchase incentives can be offered in four basic ways: (1) as a slotting allowance, (2) as an off-invoice purchase allowance, (3) as dating, or the extension of payment terms, and (4) in the form of free goods.

A *slotting allowance* is a payment to distributors and retailers to gain distribution, warehouse space, computer space, and shelf space. It is typically 5% to 15% of the nonpromotional cost of the product being sold and comes directly out of the marketing budget. Although slotting fees help to gain distribution, they are problematic for new products because they take away significant amounts of money from introductory advertising efforts.

Off-invoice purchase allowances are reductions in the price of the product to the trade, usually in the range of 5% to 25% of the regular invoice price. These allowances are limited to a certain period and number of orders. The objective of using this type of trade promotion is to obtain higher-than-normal inventories.

Dating, or the *extension of payment terms,* is a trade promotion that gives the distributor a discount if payment is made within a specific period, such as 10 days, but allows a longer period, such as 60 days, before full payment is required. This incentive lets the trade buy inventory early or use the savings to purchase more of the product.

Marketers can also use purchase incentives to offer *free goods.* Free goods are provided to the distributor based on a predetermined ratio to cases or amount of product purchased (e.g., 10% to be added to amount purchased). Free goods are an effective way to build inventories of your product and tend to be more effective than invoice allowances.

Marketers offer performance allowances to distributors and retailers as incentives to get them to increase their products' rate of sale to the consumer. The marketers' aim is for distributors and retailers to push the product through the channel of distribution by (1) price reductions to consumers, (2) advertising the brand in store advertising, (3) point-of-purchase and other display support, (4) expanded shelf space, and (5) in-store demonstrations.

Distributors and retailers are not going to participate in these activities of their own volition. Performance allowances in the form of price reductions to the trade, display allowances, and advertising allowances can be effective in obtaining trade support for a product.

Price reductions to retailers so that they can reduce the price of a brand to the consumer have become the largest category of marketing and promotional spending for many brands. It is an effective technique for gaining retailer support for brands because it has a direct effect on sales. However, price reductions have also become the primary reason for declining support for brand advertising.

Display and *merchandising allowances* are paid to retailers to obtain extra in-store effort to make a product more visible to consumers. Allowances may also be used to encourage other forms of merchandising, such as product sampling, in-store demonstrations, and support for special celebrity appearances. The difficulty for marketers is in monitoring retailer compliance with this type of deal, but in-store support from the retailer can have a significant effect on the sale of your product.

Price reductions and in-store merchandising support work best when backed up by store advertising that includes the brand. Thus, *advertising allowances* are normally part of a marketer's performance-based trade promotions package. This allowance is paid to the retailer in return for advertising the product in the retailer's store ads. Normally, the marketer provides an illustration of the product for the retailer to use in the ad. Some allowances carry stricter creative requirements, but most give the retailer a fair amount of leeway in developing the advertising.

Point-of-purchase display items that manufacturers provide to retailers can add to a brand's visibility in stores. These items can vary from something as simple as a shelf-talker (a small sign on the front edge of the shelf) or poster to elaborate bins that add shelf space to a retailer's store. The primary disadvantage of point-of-purchase materials is that retailers do not use a lot of the items manufacturers provide. To prevent this type of waste and ensure retailer support, it is important for manufacturers to support these activities with other forms of trade promotion.

Cooperative advertising is an agreement between the manufacturer and retailer to share the cost of promoting the brand at the local level. The agreements can vary, but a 50-50 split of the cost is common. Most cooperative advertising is placed in newspapers but radio, television, and other media can also be used. Although advertising allowances can be provided for the inclusion of a brand in a store's advertising, most cooperative advertising is designed to feature the manufacturer's brand and provide a smaller space for listing a retailer's name and location.

Trade shows and *sales meetings* are two promotional channels that are often an important part of a brand's marketing communications campaign. Trade shows exist in almost any industry and provide an important opportunity to showcase and demonstrate new products to members of the trade. Distributors as well as retailers attend key trade shows to identify new products to stock and sell. The trade show is also an important social occasion for manufacturers to meet with and entertain their best trade customers.

Sales meetings are promotional opportunities for kicking off an advertising campaign or introducing a new product to distributors' sales forces. Automotive manufacturers, for example, conduct annual sales meetings for dealers to introduce new models. Sales meetings can be simple or very elaborate. A big sales meeting in an enticing travel destination can be an added incentive to the trade to get behind a manufacturer's brand.

Trade promotion has become an important part of the promotional program for the typical consumer-goods marketer and should be carefully considered as part of an integrated marketing communications campaign.

▌PUBLIC RELATIONS

There is an increasing need for better public relations. Many consumers lack trust and confidence in corporations, in part because of scandals associated with companies like Enron and WorldCom, but also because of the communication overload many consumers are experiencing that is aimed at promoting products with not many differentiating characteristics.

The traditional role of public relations, to bring about public understanding and acceptance of an organization's relevant policies and procedures, will continue.[11] In some businesses, such as health care providers (HMOs), companies often have to deal with negative publicity about their businesses. Managing and influencing public perceptions will always be important. However, an increasingly important role for public relations is for a brand to engage consumers in more dialogue, participate with them in events, champion their causes, and espouse their values—all to forge a stronger relationship between the company or its brands and the consumer.

The role of marketing public relations will likely increase. It differs from corporate public relations in terms of the activities that are involved as well as its function in a firm. **Corporate public relations** activities are focused on a company's nonmarketing communication goals, which might fall broadly under the corporate umbrella image. A long-term mission of any company is to maintain open lines of communication with its various constituencies or publics to ensure that they understand and accept its policies, procedures, and activities. Public relations to support the firm's promotional activities and build strong relationships between the company and consumers will likely take on added importance in the foreseeable future.

MARKETING PUBLIC RELATIONS

Marketing public relations (PR) brings advantages to an integrated communications program. Consumers understand that the intent of advertising, sales promotions, and direct marketing is to sell them something. Thus they approach these types of promotion with a fair degree of skepticism. Public relations in the form of news stories prepared by a company can be more credible because it is not overtly identified with the company but with the medium (such as a newspaper, magazine, or TV station) that carries it. Because the media tend to have more credibility with consumers, awards and recommendations from them (such as *Good Housekeeping*'s seal of approval or *Motor Trend*'s car of the year) can be used to add believability and trust to the campaign. The downside of this advantage is lack of control over message content and timing—and control is the main advantage of advertising.

Public relations activities in general are less expensive than other kinds of promotion. Refer to Figure 8-1 to see that cost is a major consideration in deciding how to integrate the marketing communication elements of a campaign. Public relations efforts often require more sweat and tears than money. The trade-off, once again, is that the precision and control you pay for in advertising, sales promotions, and direct marketing has to be achieved through hard work and the powers of personal persuasion with the media (contacts) when you add public relations to a plan.

Public relations can easily be integrated into a campaign to support other marketing efforts. For example, event sponsorships and trade shows can be used to publicize the company or its brands. News stories in key media vehicles can provide information about the events or shows to generate awareness, interest, excitement, or "buzz" among consumers and the trade. Interviews, press conferences, social events, and press releases can all be used to achieve this type of exposure. Likewise, new product introductions can be supported with public relations activities to extend the exposure generated by advertising. Public relations' use with new product introduction is unusually effective when the product is a technological advance that creates natural interest in the media.

Hard-to-reach audiences can make public relations a welcome option for your campaign. Some audiences might be too hard or expensive to reach using traditional promotional devices. Suppose your campaign requires the support of your employees, government officials, stockholders, or the local community. Public relations professionals call these people *publics* or *stakeholders* in your business. Activities such as meetings, workshops, annual reports, company newsletters, executive speeches, and information hot lines can reach these groups when advertising cannot.

Marketing public relations offers a great deal of flexibility, but it usually takes more coordination ability than other forms of promotion. One of the most important marketing public relations activities is the generation of positive publicity for the brand and company.

PRODUCT PUBLICITY

The effective use of public relations in marketing often comes down to getting good publicity for a brand. To get positive publicity, it is necessary to provide interesting and newsworthy information to the media. Positive publicity can contribute to your ability to achieve the marketing objectives by . . .

- informing your customers how to select, buy, and use the product. Informational brochures and product literature can be useful in helping consumers learn to use complex or risky products. News stories and pamphlets might inform people about the broader issue of knowing how to select a car, computer, insurance carrier, or legal service.
- persuading the target audience to purchase your brand. Well-placed and well-timed stories can carry more persuasive power than advertising and might be the extra nudge consumers need to buy the brand.
- dispelling negative opinions or information about your brand. Consider what you might do if someone found a syringe in a can of your product, or you had to recall several hundred thousand cars or trucks. Publicity can help to counteract misunderstandings that people have formed about your brand. The next time you watch the evening news, consider how much of a story about a company might have been generated by well-placed publicity.
- building store traffic. The appearance of celebrities in a store, for example, can get customers to come out when they otherwise would not. These types of events are more successful when supported by publicity.

- supporting event sponsorships, trade shows, and other promotional activities. Good publicity can persuade key publics or audiences to turn out for company-sponsored activities. Advertising can only go so far in building awareness. Sometimes good publicity and associated word-of-mouth communication can be the missing ingredient to the achievement of your objectives. Something as simple as a news story on the business page of a local newspaper can result in hundreds of people attending the opening of a new McDonald's restaurant or Barnes & Noble bookstore.

Publicity and public relations can play supportive roles for a large marketer with the resources to spend on advertising, sales promotion, and direct marketing. However, public relations can be an important promotional element for the smaller companies. With small clients, public relations are an important strategic and practical consideration.

▌DIRECT MARKETING

Direct marketing allows a firm to combine the typical image-oriented qualities of advertising with the opportunity for consumers to respond directly to the company's offer. With this approach, the company can build the brand and still achieve short-term sales goals.

Basically, **direct marketing** is any activity a company uses to communicate directly to prospects that allows them to respond back to the company. This definition takes into account the tremendous changes in direct marketing technology to include the growing importance of **database marketing.** Database marketing has made any channel of communication a potential vehicle for direct marketing. One simply has to watch the infomercials, television commercials with toll-free numbers, and home-shopping channels to see that direct marketing has grown beyond the U.S. mail as its only distribution channel.

Direct marketing has grown in importance for a number of reasons, which together have changed the marketplace and greatly influenced campaign planning. The changes most closely associated with the new and growing importance of direct marketing are as follows:

- **The Credit Card**—The convenience and widespread use of credit cards make it easy for consumers to purchase products through direct response channels. Credit cards also reduce the financial risk for the direct marketer because payment is immediate and automatic.
- **The Toll-Free Number**—The toll-free number adds to credit cards' practicality and convenience. Purchase and payment are easy, quick, and practical. Together with credit cards, the toll-free number allows direct marketers to sell both low-cost and high-cost merchandise to consumers who purchase easily by picking up the telephone.
- **Computer Technology**—Advances in computer technology make it possible for direct marketers to gather, store, and analyze vast amounts of consumer information. This information is used to segment and target audiences and to customize offerings. Marketers

can develop their own databases, or buy them from direct marketing and commercial cluster-segmentation firms, such as Claritas (PRIZM), that offer large databases of consumer information.

- **Accountability**—Advertising has one major weakness that also happens to be the key strength of direct marketing—accountability. When you use direct marketing, you know right away whether it is working. You can gauge the response and tell how effective your offer has been.

Direct marketers have become increasingly sophisticated in their ability to identify and reach target audiences with a minimum of waste. This ability is mostly because direct marketing has become database driven. In fact, some marketers have suggested changing the name *direct marketing* to database marketing.

DATABASE MARKETING

Database marketing starts with either the existence or development of a database of customers' and prospective customers' information stored in a computer. Most databases are built around the names, addresses, and purchase histories of customers. The more purchase-relevant information that can be added to this basic data, the better an advertiser or marketer will be able to establish an ongoing relationship with customers.

Databases vary widely by product categories and company needs. However, the following basic customer information is a typical starting place for company-created databases:

1. Accurate names and addresses of individuals or organizations, including ZIP codes
2. Telephone number
3. Source of inquiry or order
4. Date and purchase details of first inquiry or order
5. Recency/frequency/monetary purchase history by date, dollar amounts of purchases, and product or product lines purchased
6. Credit history and rating
7. Demographic data for individual consumers, such as age, gender, marital status, family data, education, income, and occupation
8. Organizational data for industrial buyers, such as Standard Industrial Classification (SIC) code, size of firm, revenue, and number of employees[12]

The effectiveness of database marketing depends on keeping the database up to date, qualifying customers, segmenting the market, and being able to predict the best prospects. Database information can quickly become dated. Because most of your strategic and tactical decision making will use database information, the currency and accuracy of the data are crucial. Keeping the database current should become part of a firm's normal direct marketing activities. Exhibit 8-4 illustrates how some companies have collected their data as part of promotional programs.

EXHIBIT 8-4	DATABASE USERS AND HOW THEY COLLECT THEIR DATA

Company	Brands	Data-Collection Program
Procter & Gamble	Cheer Free, Cascade Liqui-Gel, NyQuil LiquiCaps	Collects data through reply cards in freestanding inserts offering free product samples by mail. P&G can recontact consumers about future line extensions or related new products.
MCI Communications	Long-distance service	Friends & Family program offers 20 percent discount to customers who identify people called regularly. MCI then targets those names with mail and phone solicitations.
AT&T/Walt Disney World		Callers enter joint sweepstakes using interactive phone program and are asked about Disney product and resort usage for future contacts by company.
Kimberly-Clark	Huggies diapers	Buys lists of new mothers and sends coupons, brochures, and new-product information during babies' diaper-wearing stage.
Pepsi-Cola	Pepsi	"Summer Chill Out" promotion developed mailing list with discount offer to kids.
Hallmark Cards	Greeting cards	Envelope glued to magazine so when filled out with buyer demographics and where buyer shops can be redeemed for free greeting card.
Coca-Cola	Coke Classic	"Pop Music" promotion provides CD buyers' names to partner, SONY.
Philip Morris	Merit cigarettes	"Blind" freestanding insert mail-in coupon offered unidentified product sample as part of contest promotion.

Source: "Data Collection Activity by Major Marketers," *Advertising Age* (October 21, 1991): 22.

Various strategic and tactical programs can be tested using a database because you will know exactly how your customers are responding to different approaches and appeals. The measure of the effectiveness of the direct marketing efforts is built into your direct marketing items because you are always asking for some type of response. The response to different creative executions, for example, can be tracked using database marketing.

A database is a powerful tool for profiling customers and organizing them into meaningful consumer segments from which you can select target markets and audiences. After target prospects are identified, you can turn to strategic decisions involving the positioning of the product or service offering. Databases can help you combine demographic, geographic, lifestyle, purchase, and ZIP code information to locate the most appropriate target audience. Most advertisers and marketers do not have access to this much information on their customers, but syndicated cluster-segmentation services based on geodemographic data exist for the marketer who can afford them.

Database marketing offers marketers the potential to more precisely identify their target prospect and that prospect's likely response to the message—but this should, of course, be the goal of *all* advertising and marketing planning. Database marketing provides the technology to achieve greater precision. However, even if database marketing is not affordable, a smart marketer can still use its strategic principles to improve the sophistication of the campaign.

DIRECT MARKETING OBJECTIVES AND STRATEGY

The direct marketing objectives and strategy should be developed with the overall advertising and marketing communications' objectives and strategies in mind. The direct marketing plan should evolve from the total plan and identify those direct marketing actions and activities that must be accomplished for the overall plan to be successful. To be a vital component of the overall marketing communications effort, the direct marketing portion of the plan should have its own objectives and strategies.

Direct marketing objectives are statements that accurately describe what is to be accomplished over a specified period. Direct marketing strategies are the methods, activities, and events that will be employed to achieve the objectives. The objectives for direct marketing should flow from the problems and opportunities that have been identified during the early stages of campaign planning. Some of the problems and opportunities will suggest the use of direct marketing if it is to become part of the overall campaign. For example, IBM decided to enter the direct marketing business by publishing its own personal and small-business computer catalogs. Dell, Gateway 2000, and others were pioneers in this kind of direct marketing.

Direct marketing objectives (along with sales promotions) are among the most action oriented of the marketing communications objectives you will set for the campaign. Typical objectives include consumer responses such as:

generating inquiries about a product or service
purchasing the product or service
gaining trial
increasing usage
enhancing a product's image among a well-defined target audience
gathering information
building an ongoing relationship with customers

The ultimate reason for including direct marketing in a plan is to stimulate action on the part of the consumer and build a relationship that leads to repeat purchases. Direct marketing is a long-term commitment to information gathering, storage, and its effective use. It should not be a one-shot tactic in one campaign.

Direct marketing strategies will be influenced by your ability to develop a well-defined target audience who can be reached with direct marketing channels. The strategy must be built around a well-conceived offer that will encourage consumers to respond. Ten factors to consider when creating your offer are as follows:

1. **Price.** The product's offering price should be both competitive and enticing and allow you to make a profit. Over time, you should test this element of your direct marketing strategy.
2. **Shipping and handling.** The cost of shipping and handling might have to be incorporated in the price. Most direct marketers do not charge more than 10% of the base price for shipping and handling.
3. **Unit of sale.** Your direct marketing objectives will help guide you in the selection of how to offer your product. If you want to gather information, you will get more responses by offering smaller units (one or two). If you want to increase the number of units sold, then multiple units such as sets might make better sense.
4. **Optional features.** Some products lend themselves to the addition of optional features. Colors, sizes, personalization, and unusual options that cannot be found in stores can add value to the offer.
5. **Future obligation.** One common way of keeping a customer over the long term is to make the initial offer unbelievably good (10 records for $5) in return for membership that requires buying future products at higher prices. Record and book clubs offer these "continuity" programs. However, both the initial and future offer must be of value to customers.
6. **Credit options.** Credit cards have been a primary reason for the growth in direct marketing. When customers can charge their purchases, sales increase.
7. **Incentives.** Including incentives in direct marketing offerings carries certain risks. You want customers to buy the product for its value—not because of the incentive. Incentives should be tested whenever possible. Free gifts and coupons are among the more common incentives.
8. **Time limits.** All direct marketing programs should prod the customer to take action as soon as possible. One way to create this sense of urgency is to add a time limit to the offer.
9. **Quantity limits.** A limited supply of an item can add value to the product in the customers' minds. Watch the home-shopping channels on cable TV and note that quantity limits are displayed on the screen for some items, especially for collectibles. The notion of a limited supply makes the item more enticing.
10. **Guarantees.** Guarantees are essential to direct marketing because it reduces risks associated with buying items consumers can't inspect firsthand. You must guarantee customers' satisfaction up front by allowing them to cancel and receive a refund or a replacement. This assurance gives customers confidence in what they are going to buy.[13]

After you have considered these factors in building your direct marketing offer, you can then engage the creative process to make the offer as enticing as possible. Additionally, the offer must fit (be integrated) with the rest of your marketing communications plan.

Because the main task of direct marketing is to elicit an immediate response, all copy and design work must work together toward that end. The wide range of media channels available will alter the actual execution of a direct marketing item. To illustrate this, we'll use the classic direct mail piece, and outline the use of copy and design that come into play when creating effective direct marketing programs.

Copy Guidelines

The first and perhaps most important thing a copywriter can bring to a direct marketing task is the attitude that the job at hand is to sell the product or service, and not to write prose. Direct marketing expert Don Kanter says that writing is to copywriting what talking is to a salesperson. In both cases, the job is not to write or talk but to sell persuasively.[14]

Direct marketing differs from other forms of selling in that the consumer can't inspect the product—he or she does not get to handle the item physically. Therefore, the customer must rely on the content of the copy. The most important things to sell are (1) the value of the benefit to be derived from the product or service and (2) confidence in the company. All copy should be benefit oriented. Confidence in the company can be enhanced through the use of testimonials from satisfied customers, experts, or celebrities. Guarantees, free trial offers, right of cancellation, and the company's reputation can all help to reduce the risk of purchasing through direct marketing.[15]

Effective advertising and marketing communications writing relies on appealing to basic human nature in a way that is relevant to the product or service benefit being offered. Products or services can either help one gain something or do it better, or avoid some pain or loss. Most people like to make money, save time, avoid extra effort, and be praised and popular. Likewise, they would like to avoid the opposite of these situations.

Chapter 6 has covered the key principles of good copy. Here, we provide only a checklist of pitfalls for the copywriter to avoid when creating good direct marketing items—from ads to brochures and beyond. The following advice has been suggested by Carol Nelson in her book, *The New Road to Successful Advertising: How to Integrate Image and Response:*[16]

On Headlines

1. Avoid headlines that fail to involve your readers (appeal to their basic human nature and self-interest).
2. Never assume your reader knows as much as you do (provide information).
3. Stifle the urge to be subtle or obscure (the appeal and offer should be obvious).

On Visuals

1. Get rid of visuals that do not reinforce the written message.
2. Eliminate visuals that overpower the message and therefore create confusion.
3. Do not use clever visuals as an excuse for not being able to create a genuine message.

On Consumer Motivation

1. Do not confuse your enthusiasm and knowledge of your product with the fact that others will not know how good it is unless you tell and show them.
2. Do not assume that simply showing your product will make people run out to buy or order it from you. Sometimes they need an extra incentive, time limit, or promise of exclusivity to get them moving.

On the Offer

1. Fine print, tiny type, asterisks in your copy, and minisupers on TV put your customers on guard and work against their confidence in your offer.
2. Offers with strings attached or hidden disclaimers will hurt your image and future sales.

On Your Ego

1. The reader does not care about you but about what you can do for him or her. This is a business transaction.
2. Make the reader feel special even when you are claiming that he or she is one of a large group of people who have bought the product or service.

Media Alternatives

One of direct marketing's main advantages is the flexibility it offers because of the variety of media that can be used to deliver a message. Direct marketing media offer greater selectivity than the major media. In addition, the goal of most direct marketing campaigns is to emphasize frequency of exposure over reach. Using direct marketing to narrow in on people who have potential to buy the product helps a company establish an ongoing relationship with them. This type of strategy requires frequent contacts with the target audience. In addition, some of the individual direct marketing media vehicles offer flexibility in terms of timing and ability to personalize the message.

For years, most consumers thought of direct marketing as "junk mail" that accumulated in their mailboxes. Although direct marketing has grown beyond its emphasis on the mail, direct mail is still among the top advertising media categories in terms of advertising expenditures. Only newspapers garner a larger share of the total advertising expenditure pie.

The **mailing list** is the most important element in a direct marketing effort that uses the U.S. Postal Service. Acquiring and building a good list is the foundation for a successful direct mail program. There are two basic types of lists: internal and external. The internal list of past customers that many companies maintain is a place to start. This internal database can save you a lot of money because external lists purchased from a list service or another company can be expensive. Start with the company's internal customer list, assess its value as a mailing list, and then decide what type of external list to buy.[17]

If you are building a mailing list for the first time, you have to consider its cost in relation to your long-term commitment to direct marketing and the value of your customers as repeat purchasers. Seldom is the commitment to direct mail a one-shot proposition. Direct mail has been the primary medium of the catalog business.

Catalogs have become the primary medium (along with the Internet) used to sell merchandise to highly segmented audiences on a national scale. Major reasons for the growth and success of the catalog business include the decline in the quality of service at the retail level, and the shrinking leisure time for many consumers. The catalog business has expanded at the same time other time-saving devices have appeared, including automatic teller machines, toll-free numbers, credit cards, overnight mail delivery, computer online inventory confirmation, and improved service from the catalog companies themselves. All these developments allow us to control "when we do things, where we do things, how fast we do things, and how much hassle we're willing to put up with."[18]

Some companies (such as Sears) have decided to exit the catalog business in favor of focusing on in-store retail business. Successful catalogers have done just the opposite—they have expanded into the retail store business. Eddie Bauer, Banana Republic, and Victoria's Secret are among the catalog business group that now has stores in many shopping malls nationwide. Direct marketing has made some of its most dramatic inroads into electronic media, where the applications run from direct response TV spots to infomercials from home-shopping networks to direct marketing over the Internet. Once the domain of companies selling books, audiotapes, CDs, and magazines, direct response advertisers on TV have expanded to include American Express, Time-Life, Soloflex, and other formidable marketers.

Part of the attraction of direct response TV advertising has come from the growth of cable TV. Viewers/subscribers of cable TV are more clearly defined, so advertisers and marketers can reach audiences with specialized interests such as sports, news, business and finance, movies, music, and even legal cases.

The relatively low cost of buying time on **cable TV** and the availability of nonprogrammed time has spawned a long-form direct response spot called the **infomercial.** The decision whether to use infomercials is different from buying traditional TV advertising time. Infomercials are judged by the amount of business or sales they generate, not by the TV rating for the time purchased. Thus, infomercials are created, used, and evaluated in the same manner as any other direct marketing effort.

An interesting phenomenon of the past decade or so has been the success of **home-shopping networks** on TV. Home-shopping shows such as QVC broadcast 24 hours a day, seven days a week. They provide prescheduled programs often based around specific product categories, such as jewelry, clothing, or electronics. QVC takes viewers' testimonial calls on the air to increase their involvement with the programming. It also uses traditional direct marketing techniques, such as limiting quantities and time to order. The toll-free phone number flashing on the screen and credit card payment options make shopping on QVC easy.

The **Internet** is increasingly an important medium for direct mail (and will be covered in Chapter 9). Catalogs are available on the World Wide Web. Consumers use computer technology to shop the catalogs by specifying price ranges, subject interests, age groups, and gift occasions, for example. The interactive nature of the experience and power to use computer technology to make shopping easy and efficient are likely to make shopping in cyberspace a major competitor in the media landscape. In 2002, 20% of all e-commerce retail sales came from the mail-order house industry.[19]

Print media provide traditional delivery systems for direct marketing in the form of direct response advertising. Magazines provide both mass audiences and highly selective vehicles to choose from. The added high production quality can help increase the response rates to an offer. Newspapers have the value of natural timeliness and immediacy so important to achieving consumer response. Direct marketers can consider run-of-the-paper placement, freestanding inserts, or Sunday-paper magazine sections as possible outlets.

Radio is a little more difficult than other media to use in a direct marketing program because of its lack of a visual component and the fleeting nature of radio spots. This difficulty can be offset by high levels of repetition of product information and telephone numbers announced during the spot. The use of radio also requires that you run your spot frequently to get listeners to remember it. Local radio is very selective, which increases its ability to reach narrowly targeted audiences and is relatively inexpensive compared to other media.

Telemarketing (selling via the telephone) is a rapidly growing form of direct marketing. There is considerable consumer resistance to telemarketing as an intrusion on privacy resulting in rather low response rates. Yet, the use of 900 and 1(800) number has created the voice information-service phenomenon through which a company can provide information and market its products. Also, consumer advocates have managed to accomplish the enactment of laws that limit the time of day when telemarketers can call. Additional restrictions are likely to come from do-not-call registries, which prohibit marketers from contacting a specific consumer in the future, as soon as the legalities are sorted out.

The future for direct marketing looks bright because it relies heavily on the improving media and computer technology. The options for its use appear to be limited only by marketers' imaginations. It is likely that many student projects will involve small companies without the resources and knowledge to become serious users of direct marketing. However, the targeting-and-response emphasis of direct marketing should be carried forth into your campaign in principle as you develop your other promotional areas.

FINISHING THE MARKETING COMMUNICATION PLAN

The integration of the marketing communications elements of advertising, sales promotions, public relations, and direct marketing is a process of evaluating each element's strengths and weaknesses in being able to (1) reach the target audience with a minimum of waste and (2) elicit the responses that will result in the accomplishment of the marketing objectives. You will not always have the luxury of unlimited resources with which to make these decisions. Therefore, you have to learn to live with trade-offs and still meet the requirements of your marketing communications program.

As this chapter has illustrated, the four major marketing communication elements have tremendous complementary value. Sales promotions and direct marketing push the hardest for an immediate response, often in terms of product sales. Advertising and public relations are aimed more at communications objectives, such as awareness and acceptance. However, it is when you bring the four qualities together that you realize a strong campaign can strive for both communication and sales objectives.

You should always be aware of where your target consumers are in the purchase-and-response cycle in relation to your brand. You want to reach customers with the right combination of promotional messages that will take them to the next desired step in the purchase process. This level can be awareness and trial for an introductory campaign or a higher velocity of purchase for established products.

Stay on top of emerging technology. An interest in sales promotion and direct marketing will assure that you will be where the latest technology is being applied to marketing. Computer technology is changing the way we deliver messages and offers to consumers in their homes. The technological advances in interactive media demand full integration of image-oriented promotions with response-based promotions. Remember, you have to strive for both short- and long-term results in today's marketplace. You have to be able to think like the trade and push for sales while striving to maintain valuable equity in your brand. Marketing and advertising have become more competitive and more results oriented. The campaign that wins the day is the one that reflects this reality and takes advantage of the new opportunities to create the many brand contacts that form the consumers' reality of an integrated marketing communications campaign.

CAMPAIGN PROGRESS CHECKLIST

At this point in the campaign you should generally be aware of the following points:

1. Marketing tools such as sales promotion, public relations, and direct marketing are a way to extend and integrate the marketing communication strategy.

2. These communication tools each have their own objectives, strategy, and tactics and, in return, should be linked to the creative and media plans so that they put forward an interrelated complementary message.

3. The use of sales promotion tools to supplement advertising can be a point of differentiation between brands.

4. Care needs to be exercised in using sales promotions to avoid training consumers to respond to inducements rather than other intangible aspects associated with the brand, such as a favorable image.

5. Public relations can include corporate public relations designed to help consumers understand the company's policies and activities.

6. Marketing public relations can be thought of as working similar to advertising, especially product publicity.

7. Marketing public relations should do more than generate publicity; it should increase the bond consumers feel with the company or its brands.

8. Direct marketing is increasing in importance to advertisers because of companies' increased ability to reach highly selective groups of consumers through database marketing.

9. Some marketing communication activities such as sales promotion and direct marketing can be an effective way to stimulate sales in the short run. Companies, however, should continue to employ strategies to build over a long term.

10. Even though the short-term goal of sales promotion, public relations, and direct marketing often differs from that of advertising, the long-term goal of building the brand by communicating a consistent brand identity is of paramount importance.

Notes and References

[1] *Media Trends 1994* (New York: DDB Needham Worldwide, 1994), p. 9.

[2] "Burnett, Heinz Split Up," *Advertising Age* daily fax, 23 November 1994, p. 1.

[3] K. Smith, "Introduction and Overview," in *Sales Promotion Handbook, 8th Ed.*, eds. T. Brezen Block and W.A. Robinson (Chicago: Dartnell Press, 1994), p. 5.

[4]G.E. Belch and M.A. Belch, *Introduction to Advertising and Promotion: An Integrated Marketing Communications Perspective, 4th Ed.* (Chicago: Irwin, 1995), pp. 470–471.

[5]Ibid., p. 472.

[6]T.B. Block, "Couponing," in *Sales Promotion Handbook,* pp. 99–100.

[7]Ibid., p. 111.

[8]D. Jagoda, "Sweepstakes, Games, Contests," in *Sales Promotion Handbook,* p. 129.

[9]K. Wulff, "How to Compete at Sports Marketing," *The Advertiser* (Spring, 1992), pp. 73–76.

[10]This section is based in part on James Kunz, "Trade Promotion," in *Sales Promotion Handbook,* pp. 320–334.

[11]Belch and Belch, *Introduction to Advertising and Promotion,* p. 514.

[12]B. Stone, *Successful Direct Marketing Methods, 5th Ed.* (Lincolnwood, IL: NTC Business Books, 1994), p. 38.

[13]Ibid., pp. 79–81.

[14]Ibid., pp. 376–377.

[15]Ibid., p. 377.

[16]C. Nelson, *The New Road to Successful Advertising: How to Integrate Image and Response* (Chicago: Bonus Books, 1991), p. 195.

[17]Stone, pp. 212–215.

[18]J. Walker, "Catalogers, There May Be a Fax in Your Future," *DM News,* 31 December 1990, p. 23.

[19]"E-Commerce Sales," *Chainstore Age Executive Fax,* 22 February 2002, p. 2.

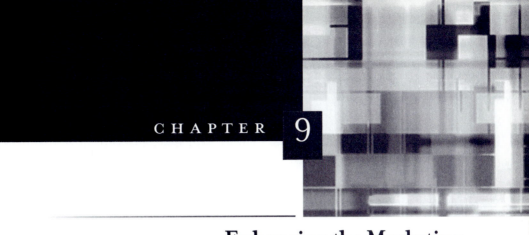

CHAPTER 9

Enhancing the Marketing Communication Mix

Competition can be brutal. Oftentimes it's not enough to be satisfied with the status quo. Things can change dramatically overnight. In the age of information, consumers know more and change faster than ever before. Consider what has happened to Michelob. How did such a popular beer lose favor to where today the brand is a faint image of what it once was? Times, styles, and tastes change. Companies need to make the most out of their opportunities. If they don't, a rival will. Allow a company a small part of your market share, and you run the risk of the competitor using its new position as leverage to acquire an even greater share of the market. Agencies also hate losing even a small part of an account to another agency.

Consider McDonald's. In 1977, DDB Needham was named Agency of the Year by *Advertising Age*. Three years later the agency was fired and replaced by Leo Burnett. After several years, McDonald's gave DDB Needham some assignments and the agency gradually got back a small part of the business. In 1997, McDonald's gave DDB Needham the lead role for its account. Leo Burnett? It got to keep a smaller part of the account (the advertising to kids and "tweens"). Why didn't McDonald's give all its business to one agency and integrate its marketing communication effort by consolidating it in one source? The answer may be complex, but one bet is that it keeps both agencies hustling.

Although this chapter sounds as if it consists of the extra things companies do to maximize their opportunities, many of the things we will discuss are today considered *essential*. We've divided this chapter conceptually into thirds. In the first section, we discuss the special audience segments advertisers covet in addition to the target audience they set for the campaign. The second section examines some of the less common strategies advertisers employ that are not typically associated with traditional message strategy. The last section focuses on special media strategies, including the use of nontraditional media.

SPECIAL MARKETS

To fully exploit a company's sales potential, marketers increasingly look both beyond and within their traditional markets for additional sources of opportunities. Within an overall market, there are other and usually smaller markets that don't quite identify with more mainstream advertising. We've identified some of the more important markets: (1) global, (2) African American, (3) Hispanic, (4) Asian, and (5) gay/lesbian/bisexual/transgender (GLBT).

GLOBALIZATION

It's only because we're sensitive about the length of this book that we don't devote an entire chapter or more to this very important market. For many advertisers, sales outside the United States are higher than their domestic sales. There are numerous reasons why firms must consider the entire world when considering their opportunities, including:

- There are obviously more consumers outside than inside the United States. According to the *Statistical Abstract of the United States,*[1] in 2001, the gross domestic product (GDP) of the European Union alone was $9.969 billion. The GDP of the United States was $8.978 billion.
- Many overseas markets are less developed than those in the United States. Competing in some markets can be easier than competing at home.
- Brands from Western countries in general—and those from the United States in particular—are in high demand in many parts of the world.
- The information age is here. Marketing to locations around the world is only a click away in cyberspace.
- Multinational companies headquartered overseas are flocking to the United States in increasing numbers. Allowing them to come here without you going there could mean these firms eventually would get bigger in size than your company. Sometimes size matters.
- The United States does not have a monopoly on ideas. There is much we can learn from other countries. London, in particular, has been a vibrant source of advertising ideas. The account planning revolution began there.
- Selling overseas helps ease the trade deficit.

Understanding Global Marketing Communications.   Most people realize intuitively that advertising is different in other parts of the world. Because the United States has been such a dominant economic and military power, there may be a tendency on the part of some to assume that we understand how advertising works better than "they" do. That is a mistake. Advertising is different in other parts of the world often because it needs to be different. It would be the height of American arrogance to assume that what works here ought to work in other places that have older and probably much richer cultures than ours.

There are numerous ways in which other countries differ from the United States—far too numerous to categorize and adequately explain here. The more obvious differences—which, unfortunately, are not always so obvious to American tourists—involve language and culture.

Understanding Language Problems.   It's not enough to study language out of a book. It helps to have lived in the country to understand the subtleties that words can convey in any language. Even within a country, not everyone understands the connotative meaning that words pick up through usage. A simple word like *bad* clearly is perceived as something negative among most Americans. But it can also mean something cool! However, it may also mean you are using a word that is "so, like, 1980s." Every country has language peculiarities (semantics) that are not easy for foreigners to pick up. Some words have neither literal translations nor pronunciations. Take the pronunciation of the author's name, Parente. Americans tend to pronounce it Paren-tee or Paren-tay. The actual pronunciation in the Italian language is somewhere in between. Exhibit 9-1

EXHIBIT 9-1 | INTERNATIONAL ADVERTISING MISTAKES

When Vicks first introduced its cough drops on the German market, they were chagrined to learn that the German pronunciation of "v" is "f" which in German is the guttural equivalent of "sexual penetration."

Not to be outdone, Puffs tissues tried later to introduce its product, only to learn that "Puff" in German is a colloquial term for a whorehouse. The English weren't too fond of the name either, as it's a highly derogatory term for a non heterosexual.

When Pepsi started marketing its products in China a few years back, they translated their slogan, "Pepsi Brings You Back to Life" pretty literally. The slogan in Chinese really meant, "Pepsi Brings Your Ancestors Back from the Grave."

When Coca-Cola first shipped to China, they named the product something that when pronounced sounded like "Coca-Cola." The only problem was that the characters used meant, "Bite the wax tadpole." They later changed to a set of characters that mean "Happiness in the mouth."

A hair products company, Clairol, introduced the "Mist Stick", a curling iron, into Germany only to find out that mist is slang for manure. Not too many people had use for the manure stick.

When Gerber first started selling baby food in Africa, they used the same packaging as here in the USA with the cute baby on the label. Later they found out that in Africa companies routinely put pictures on the label of what's inside since most people can't read.[2]

When Nokia adapted its "freedom of expression" slogan promoting its differently colored mobile phones for the German market they inadvertently substituted the German equivalent of the Latin saying "to each his own" which had been posted above the entrance to the notorious Buchanwald concentration camp during World War II. Around 3,000 billboards were quickly covered over when Jewish groups voiced their outrage.[3]

shows what can happen if the translator does not have a good grasp of the local language.

Understanding the Importance of Cultural Differences.   Difficulties with language problems often exist on the surface. Once they are pointed out, it's easy to see them and make appropriate modifications. However, cultural differences are not always so easy for outsiders to see or understand. For example, it's easy for Americans to see that European advertising differs from their own. The advertising is usually more entertaining, contains less hard sell, and takes a more liberal approach to the use of nudity. There is a definite difference in the visual style. What we often see are the differences in the way advertising is executed. We may not fully appreciate that the differences are more strategic and stem from the differing cultural values in various countries.

It's been observed that in France, less than 10% of the commercials feature someone who addresses the camera; whereas in the United States, better than 70% of the commercials have this feature. In the United States, salespeople are often advised to look the customer in the eyes. It can be a mark of sincerity. In contrast, the French are more reserved and consider it a lack of modesty to be so straightforward with a sales pitch.[4] Similarly, Japanese people place a high premium on social harmony. The Burger King campaign that suggested, "Sometimes you just gotta break the rules" goes against Japanese values. Yet the campaign worked fine in the United States and Australia where individualism is valued.

Coordinating Global Marketing Communications.   Increasingly, companies are restructuring, reengineering, and refining their operations to compete in the global marketplace. Companies plan ahead comprehensively, controlling an array of functions in every detail. They analyze situations, specify policies and procedures in meticulous detail, then spell out for their workers what can and cannot be done in particular circumstances.[5] They analyze risks, set objectives, establish strategy, and anticipate contingencies. Like a socialist or communist economy, this type of centralized control has limitations.

Its major limitation is that it inhibits initiative. If managers at the local level do not have the opportunity to experiment or adapt their ideas to the local market, the company may not be taking advantage of the people who best know the consumer. Not surprisingly, companies have come to understand the merits of the saying, "Think globally, but act like a retailer." Yet, there can be advantages to making decisions centrally. Companies with strong brands have considerable equity tied up in specific brand associations. Companies such as Coca-Cola are reluctant to let local offices tinker with their core equities. Coca-Cola has literally spent billions of dollars getting the world to think of Coke in a certain way. The world is figuratively getting smaller every day. It does not want to compete with itself to maintain its image or identity.

There are at least three models a company can use to coordinate its global marketing communications:

1. **A centrally directed campaign with minimal local options.** We hesitate to mention this one because we don't think very highly

of it. It works fairly well for brands like Coca-Cola and Marlboro cigarettes where the companies largely use appeals and imagery much like they do in the United States. Except for India, Coca-Cola makes very few changes to its advertising worldwide. It works for Marlboro in many places precisely because the local population does identify it as an American brand. In many countries, especially in Asia, people identify Western culture as modern, hip, and ambitious. Unfortunately, smoking Western cigarettes is a relatively inexpensive way many consumers "improve" their self-image by adopting Western products and habits. The primary limitation of this approach is that other countries differ from the United States—in major and minor ways.

2. **A regionally directed campaign with local flexibility.** This approach is used by companies for a variety of reasons. It permits a company, such as Procter & Gamble, to exercise some control over the way its products are marketed, yet still allows a local office the flexibility to adapt a local campaign to what is likely to work in its area. It works for Procter & Gamble because it promotes its products based on the functional value of the products. Telling consumers that Tide gets clothes clean is similar in all countries. However, P&G found that when it tried to standardize the names of some of its global brands it encountered problems. Escuda, a Spanish name for Safeguard, is a strong brand in Mexico. When the company changed the name to Safeguard, sales fell precipitously, only to return when P&G changed the name back to Escuda.[6]

3. **A locally directed campaign with regional direction.** This approach works far better for companies that operate in countries at different stages of development. What works in Germany may not have the same effect in India. Moreover, McDonald's sells its products on the basis of an emotional reward. It not only sells hamburgers, it also sells the experience it's wrapped in. McDonald's gives its local operators direction, but it's more along the lines of telling them how to start up the business and how to anticipate where the business is going to be in 10 years. McDonald's allows its stores outside the United States far more latitude than it allows domestic stores because of the considerable differences in cultures. As a result, McDonald's restaurants can look considerably different, even in the same country. Switzerland is a small country, but it has three very different cultures that tend to cluster in different regions: Italian, German, and French. The stores in each of these regions are often very different in terms of style and appearance. McDonald's calls this approach brand journalism because it tells different stories different ways in the 119 countries in which it operates.[7]

AFRICAN AMERICANS

It has only been since the mid-1960s that African Americans have been represented in advertising appearing in the mass media. Before this period, advertisers used specialized media such as *Ebony, Jet,* and "ethnic" radio stations to reach this segment of the population. Despite the widespread use of African American models in mass-media advertising, companies still understand the value of developing advertising with this specific segment in mind. African Americans are not simply consumers with dark skin. They have different values, lifestyles, interests, and tastes. In short, they are different and special.

African Americans tend to be identified by skin color and genetic heritage. African Americans don't mind being referred to as "black," although "African American" seems to be the preferred term to use in more formal situations.

Demographic Information

Information on African Americans can be found in many sources, including *Simmons* and *MRI*. The most comprehensive data come from the U.S. Census Bureau:

Population: 38,300,000
Percentage of Population: 13.3%
Average Household Income: $29,177
Education: 79% are high school graduates or more; 17% are college graduates or more.[8]

Many U.S. metropolitan areas such as Memphis, New York, Atlanta, Norfolk, New Orleans, and Washington, DC have populations of over one-quarter African American. The African American population is growing faster than the general population rate, but slower than both Hispanics and Asians.

Values. As a result of their historical experiences, African Americans value togetherness and take pride in their heritage. African Americans like to define their own style rather than follow what the establishment dictates.[9] Family, religion, and church are very important to them, with 80% considering themselves "avid church-goers." African Americans value particular holidays and events because of their family or ethnic significance—including Easter, Kwanzaa, Martin Luther King Day, and Black History Month.[10]

To understand what distinguishes African Americans from other market segments, you have to remember that, unlike other immigrants, they were brought to this country against their will. As a result, African Americans often seek products that give them a sense of empowerment and that show that they are important members of society, according to Ken Smikle, publisher of *Target Market News*.[11]

Consumption Habits. This quest for empowerment may also explain why many African Americans buy expensive liquor and clothing. Various studies concerning African American consumers show the following:

- Blacks are the most fashion conscious of all racial and ethnic groups.
- Blacks find shopping very enjoyable. They are the most willing to travel an hour or more to reach a favorite store.
- The principal black shopper is likely to be single, divorced, or widowed.
- Blacks spend more on telephone services; shoes; children's, girls', and women's apparel; TVs, radio and sound equipment; personal products and services; and major appliances.[12]

Best Way to Reach This Segment
In the late 1960s, advertisers struggled with how best to reach this market. They questioned whether it would be best to use specialized media or to simply use black models in their advertising and appeal to African Americans at the same time they appealed to the rest of the market. Today, advertisers do both. In fact, a long list of advertisers such as Kmart Corp., McDonald's, L'eggs Corporation, Kraft General Foods, Quaker Oats Co., and Polaroid Corp. have all hired agencies that specialize in advertising to the African American market, such as Burrell Communications Group Inc.

An influential study done by the Yankelovich Partners for the Burrell Group found that 60% of black consumers feel that the majority of television and print ads "are designed only for white people." Reflecting this point, there are approximately 800 media outlets catering to the African American market. The Black Entertainment Television Network (BET) reaches 98% of black households. *Essence* magazine reaches four million readers. More than 70% of African Americans read community-based publications.[13] Network television also does a good job of reaching crossover audiences of black and white viewers ages 12–17 and age 50 and over.[14]

When developing a campaign or part of a campaign to reach the African American market, consider the following points:

- Think of the African American market as a subculture of the overall market with values, lifestyles, consumption, and media habits that differ from the overall population.
- Use people or agencies who are familiar with this subculture. (Procter & Gamble Co. makes hiring minorities to work in its marketing area a high priority.[15])
- Design a campaign apart from the mainstream strategy that reflects what is special about this market.
- Be sensitive to appealing to African Americans on the basis of what makes them special without using negative stereotypes.
- Recognize that African Americans have many things in common with each other, but diversity exists in this segment just as it does in the overall population.
- Consider cause-related marketing to show this segment the company thinks of them as more than merely consumers.
- Use media that specifically target African Americans.

It is important to remember that as times change, so do the methods of advertising to African American individuals. According to J. Robert Harris, president of JRH Marketing Services in New York, "African Americans and other minorities are much more visible in the media and can be depicted in all types of situations and circumstances. While advertisers must still be aware of being insensitive, the target audience is now much more open to what they see and read." Additionally, Harris mentions that a campaign should reflect the lifestyle of the target market of the campaign, and not be generalized as all "African Americans," because special nuances exist among different groups of African Americans.[16]

Hispanics

Increasingly, advertisers are aware of the growing importance of the Hispanic market. Currently, it is the largest minority group with a population growth rate nearly four times that of the general population. Because of both a high birth rate and immigration, its percentage of the U.S. population is projected to increase from a current 13.7% to 15.5% by 2010. Hispanic buying power is expected to grow from $686 billion to $992 billion by 2009.[17] There are more Hispanics living in the United States than there are people living in all of Canada.

Demographic Information

Population: 39,899,000 (Hispanic origin, of any race)
Percentage of Population: 13.7%
Average Household Income: $32,997
Education: 57% are high school graduates or more; 11% are college graduates or more.[18]

Hispanics are younger, have larger families, and are more likely to have young children in their households than the American average. Although household income is less than average for Hispanics as a whole, the growth of this market makes them attractive to companies. Mexicans make up nearly 60% of the U.S. Hispanic population followed by Puerto Ricans and Cubans.

Identifying Who Is Hispanic.   There is no consensus on the identifying characteristics of exactly what makes someone Hispanic. In the 1970 U.S. Census, the choices included "Mexican," "Mexican American," "Chicano," "Puerto Rican," "Cuban," and "other." Advertisers sometimes use the terms "Latino" or "Latin," as in the "Latin market" to refer to Hispanics in Los Angeles, New York, and Miami. Presumably, however, *Latin* does not refer to someone of Italian, French, or Romanian heritage, or other cultures that also have Latin roots. In the U.S. Census now, respondents are simply asked if they are Hispanic or Latino or *not* Hispanic or Latino. The identity issue is an important one because the cultural value orientations of the different subcultures within the Hispanic market can have a fundamental role in consumer behavior. In other words, one has to be careful not to assume all Hispanic subgroups are the same. There is even some question as to whether the Spanish media isn't overselling the importance of using specialized media to reach the Hispanic market.[19] The argument is based on the idea that many Hispanics have integrated into the overall culture to the point that a specialized approach isn't necessary. Still, it is clear advertisers such as J.C. Penney, Procter & Gamble, Kraft Foods, Avon, Nike, Allstate, and all the major brewers have made strong efforts to target the Hispanic market. The U.S. Census Bureau does not break down Hispanics by race, allowing them to be of any race or races. Consequently, Hispanics can be a mixture of several races, white, brown, or black. The major unifying factors are the Spanish language and Catholicism.

Values.   Hispanics care greatly about preserving their culture, traditions, and language; they have persistently resisted assimilation into the American mainstream. The majority of Spanish-speaking Americans continue to use their native tongue at home and socially. They appreciate music and the arts and are enthusiastic fans of sports such as soccer, baseball, and boxing. They place a great deal of importance on family and children. They take a strong interest in personal appearance and aesthetics. The quality of their lives is very important. As a group, they can be outgoing, and their emotions are often visible.

Consumption Habits.   Hispanics can be very conscious of brand names, and loyally reward companies that advertise in Spanish. Although the average household income is less than that for the general public, it can vary significantly even within the same Hispanic subgroups. For example, Cubans who have lived in Miami since the 1960s are often wealthy landowners; whereas Cubans who have recently immigrated to the United States are often of a much lower socioeconomic status. According to various consumer studies of Hispanic consumers:

- Hispanics prefer to shop at national chains, especially discount stores.
- Hispanics are loyal to clothing brands.
- Hispanics prefer shopping as a family and don't mind bringing their children along.
- A larger percentage of Hispanic disposable income goes to goods and services such as groceries, shoes, clothing, gas and motor oil, and household textiles.[20]

According to Standard Rate and Data Service, there are approximately 42 major Spanish-language magazines, 31 English or bilingual Hispanic-oriented magazines, 103 Spanish-language newspapers, and more than 300 radio stations with Spanish programming. Univision and Telemundo broadcast networks are most popular among Hispanic audiences. Univision controls 80% of the Hispanic audience and Telemundo holds about 20%.[21]

Best Way to Reach This Group
A key decision early on is whether to use "Hispanic marketing," including Hispanic media and ad agencies, or to connect with Hispanics as part of the regular marketing program. Hispanics may not be as brand loyal as some people think. Their loyalty may simply reflect a lack of information on available alternatives. Currently, only 3.2% of total annual U.S. leading advertiser's expenditures goes toward Spanish-language advertising.[22] A joint survey conducted by Yankelovich Partners and Market Development indicates that 86% of Hispanics watch Spanish TV during the week and appreciate Spanish-language advertising.[23] Stuart Livingston of Galavision recommends reaching this group through grassroots community efforts such as funding literacy and scholarship programs, sponsoring athletic teams, and promoting special events such as festivals and fairs. Regional companies also enjoy an advantage by targeting only one specific group.[24]

It's also important to understand that Hispanics tend to congregate in major cities. Los Angeles, San Francisco, and Chicago are primarily

Mexican; New York City has a large Puerto Rican population; and Miami has large numbers of Cubans.

What Not to Do.   It's important to tap into the characteristics that make Hispanics special without fostering negative stereotypes. If at all possible, use someone who is familiar with the specific subculture. If advertising in Spanish, keep in mind that approximately 20 Spanish-speaking nationalities reside in the United States and that individual words can vary in meaning from group to group. Do not assume that English-language campaigns can translate literally into Spanish. Exhibit 9-2 is an example of what can happen when you do.

ASIAN AMERICANS

Asian Americans are affluent, highly educated, and experiencing rapid population growth. The Asian American market is an important one, but unlike the Hispanic market, it does not share a common language or culture. There are six distinct Asian markets and at least several smaller ones such as Thais, Laotians, and Malays (Indonesians). The six major Asian markets are as follows.

1. **Chinese.** Members of this group usually speak Mandarin or Cantonese and identify themselves as American-born Chinese (ABC) or fresh-off-the-boat (FOB). Not surprisingly, the Chinese who have been here the longest are more upscale, and the more newly arrived Chinese tend to be more blue collar, conservative, and patriarchal (population—2,734,841).

2. **Filipinos.** This is the most "assimilated" group of Asian Americans. Most Filipinos still speak Tagalog, the native language of the Philippines. However, many also speak Spanish or English (population—2,364,815).

3. **Asian Indians.** This group is not as geographically clustered as other groups. Asian Indians have a significant presence in the hospitality industry. There are many highly educated professionals in this group (population—1,899,599).

4. **Koreans.** This group tends to cluster in large metropolitan areas. Many Koreans are small-business owners (population—1,228,427).

EXHIBIT 9-2 SPANISH TRANSLATION MISTAKES[25]		
Company	**English Slogan/Product**	**Spanish Translation**
General Motors	Chevrolet Nova	Chevrolet Doesn't Go
Braniff	Fly in Leather	Fly Naked
Eastern Airlines	We Earn Our Wings Daily	Final Destination Heaven
Coors	Turn It Loose	Suffer from Diarrhea
Budweiser	King of Beers	Queen of Beers

5. **Vietnamese.** This is the fastest-growing Asian group. They tend to be lower on the socioeconomic scale than other Asian American groups, given their relatively recent arrival in the United States. Approximately one-third of all Vietnamese living in the United States reside in California (population—1,223,736).

6. **Japanese.** Members of this group often speak English very well, are upscale, and tend to live in the California or the New York City region. (population—1,148,932).[26]

Demographic Information

Population: 13,100,000
Percentage of Population: 5%
Average Household Income: $52,018
Education: 47% are college graduates or more[27]

Values. Asians place a very high priority on group harmony and family togetherness. They are much more likely to use the pronoun *we* than *I*. Asians identify with other Asians, if only because non-Asians are unaware of the often significant differences among Asian subgroups. Even the geographic region Asians come from is much more spread out than non-Asians generally realize. The Asian region is approximately twice as wide east to west and twice as long north to south as the United States. Asians tend to place a high value on education, often sacrificing household extras to educate the children.

Historically, Chinese, Japanese, Korean, and Vietnamese families differ somewhat from one another, but many derive their basic norms and values from Confucianism. These include obedience to and responsibility for parents, patrilinearity, patriarchy, a preference for sons, respect for education, the use of shame and guilt to control behavior, and considerable personal interdependence. Much of the same has been true for Asian Indians.[28]

Consumption Habits. Although Asian Americans have a lower average income than whites, their median household income is significantly higher because of having more people in the household and workforce. As a result, some Asian subgroups, such as the Japanese, Chinese, and Indians, have significantly more disposable income than whites.

A study by Simmons Market Research discovered the following facts about Asian American consumers:

- Asians are the most frequent shoppers.
- Asians are the most brand conscious, but least brand loyal.
- Asians are the most concerned with keeping up appearances.
- Asians the most likely to buy from traditional department stores.
- Asians are the least likely to shop alone.
- Asians rarely go shopping without a plan.[29]

Best Way to Reach This Segment

Advertising targeting Asian Americans should contain messages promoting the family and traditional values. Ads currently in use highlight cooperation, support traditional sex roles, portray actors or models as successful professionals, and frequently feature elderly family members who are highly esteemed in Asian society. Advertisers can effectively target the six main subgroups using native-language media in their tightly concentrated communities located in major metropolitan areas in California, New York, Hawaii, and Texas. It is important to recognize differences as well as similarities in the Asian market and to portray Asians in a positive way.[30]

What Not to Do. Do not try to challenge the status quo in advertisements targeting Asian Americans. Advertisements with sexual themes or stressing individualism are not well received.[31]

GAY/LESBIAN/BISEXUAL/TRANSGENDER

This market received increasing emphasis in the 1990s. Today, society is somewhat more accepting of gays and lesbians, and marketers have become increasingly aware of this group's considerable disposable income. This market is largely white and male.

Demographic Information
Obtaining accurate information for this population segment is difficult. The 2000 census was designed to measure only the number of same-sex households, not individuals. Some gays and lesbians are reluctant to identify themselves or respond to a survey. The estimated information that follows is based on several sources including the 2000 census.

> Population: Speculated at anywhere from 11 to 27 million, although most sources suggest 13 to 16 million
> Same-sex Couples in the United States: 594,391
> Average Income $61,300[32]
> Annual Spending: $485 billion
> Education: 41% have graduated from college[33]

Values. The GLBT community places a high priority on the value of friendships. Among heterosexuals, the patterns of social behavior often take place with members of one's family or coworkers. In contrast, the gay community interacts more with friends, usually those who share the same sexual orientation. Delozier and Rodriguez found that gays and lesbians are very aware of current social issues and are often politically active. Gays and lesbians most often reside within a city in major metropolitan areas and are highly interested in career building. Homosexuals living in suburban areas tend to be interested in traditional focuses such as home ownership, gardening, and community activities.[34]

Consumption Habits. There is widespread consensus that gays spend freely on a wide variety of goods and services. Reports suggest that gays' spending at least equals and probably exceeds that which heterosexuals spend, especially on entertainment, dining out, travel, exercising at private clubs, and material goods such as consumer electronics, liquor, clothing, fragrances, books, greeting cards, and compact discs. They also tend to be trendsetters, likely to seek out and adopt new technologies, but remaining brand loyal.

Best Way to Reach This Group

Gays appear to be especially receptive to companies that are accepting of their lifestyle even if they aren't totally satisfied with their goods and services, according to Steven M. Kates, author of *Twenty Million New Customers.* On the other hand, they will avoid and even boycott companies they feel are "homophobic."[35] In the late 1970s, Coors allegedly performed polygraph tests on employees. Among the questions they asked were ones about sexual orientation. Even though Coors now includes sexual orientation in its antidiscrimination policy, many gays harbor negative feelings about the brand.[36] To convince this segment that a company is at least tolerant of their lifestyle, some experts suggest a company needs to be proactive and do something significant, such as sponsor socially responsible events. This involvement can range from supporting the arts or AIDS research to sponsoring community specific events, such as the Gay Games and Gay/Lesbian Parades. Additionally, advertisers cannot treat this group as part of the "general public." They have special needs and are therefore a special market. This group is especially favorable toward companies that support causes important to the gay community, are gay friendly, or show a serious commitment to diversity.[37]

There are a growing number of media vehicles to reach this group, including the following:

- Local and regional gay/lesbian newspapers, such as the *New York Blade News*
- Cable and public broadcasting service television programs, such as *Will & Grace, Queer as Folk, Queer Eye for the Straight Guy*
- Radio shows, such as Sirius Satellite Radio's *OUTQ* (GLBT content 24/7)
- National magazines, such as *The Advocate, Out, Curve,* and *Passport*
- Internet, such as gay.com (advertisers include Scion, British Airways, Travelocity, and Diesel)

There are also a small number of firms that specialize in offering advertising and marketing services to companies interested in reaching the gay and lesbian market.

▌SPECIAL MESSAGE STRATEGIES

The first section of this chapter described how advertisers target special population segments to get the most out of their market opportunities. Here, we examine some of the special strategies companies use to influence the way consumers think or feel about the brand or the company. These special strategies can be part of the mainstream campaign, but are usually in addition to what the company might do normally.

MULTI-TIERED ADVERTISING

Companies have long used a multitiered approach to pricing their products. Anheuser-Busch Inc., for example, sells a popular-priced beer, Busch; a premium-priced beer, Budweiser; and a super-premium beer, Michelob (although in some markets, Michelob is barely priced higher than

Budweiser). Similarly, Gap Inc. sells upscale clothes at Banana Republic, moderately priced clothes at its Gap stores, and uses its Old Navy division to sell budget-priced clothing.

Companies, however, do not generally like to run more than one message strategy at a time. The feeling is the messages diffuse the effectiveness of the strategy by competing with each other, even if only slightly. Advertisers do, however, occasionally use differing message strategies. Although advertisers seldom use more than two strategies, theoretically, the number could be unlimited. The idea behind the multi-tiered approach is to communicate different layers of meaning to the audience. This is not unlike the approach used to promote Saturn automobiles. The national campaign has been heavily image oriented, promoting the idea that Saturn is a different kind of a car made by a different kind of company. In a separate campaign funded by the Saturn dealer associations, the emphasis is on product advertising, which is a trade expression meaning they promote the car, not the image. Similarly, advertising by the big tire brands, such as Michelin and Goodyear, often feature image advertising on the national level to "build the brand." On the local level, the ads are more product oriented. To extend the reach of local advertising, companies provide substantial co-op funds to dealers for advertising placed locally.

The above examples are typical of an advertiser that wants to build the brand and at the same time push product sales. What's more unusual is for an advertiser to run separate image campaigns that all target basically the same audience. There is substantial risk involved in this approach. The more firmly you establish one image with the audience, the more difficult it is to establish another. But this is exactly what Anheuser-Busch has tried to do periodically with its Budweiser brand.

Before the turn of the century, sales were somewhat flat for Budweiser. Although Budweiser was the top-selling beer in the United States, worried executives were concerned that stagnant sales could be a portent of future problems. Everyone in the beer industry is mindful that in the 1970s, Schlitz was the number-two brand of beer in the United States.

Part of Budweiser's problem could be traced to the increased popularity of imported and craft-brewed beers, such as Samuel Adams. Another part of the problem, however, could be traced to the brand's weakness in attracting young consumers, many of whom have been attracted to beer brands that have been in existence less than 10 years.

To counter this problem, Anheuser-Busch has employed humor and a variety of youthful images (remember the frogs and lizards?). These approaches freshened up what had previously been a fairly conservative image. The danger with these approaches is that they can erode the substantial brand equity that built up in the Budweiser name over the years. To counter this potential problem, the company periodically runs variations of its Budweiser heritage campaign. In one campaign, August Busch III, a descendant of the founder, talks about Budweiser's adherence to traditional standards, thus assuring confirmed Budweiser consumers that the brand is still the same. This two-tiered approach works for Budweiser because it has the financial muscle to run two separate campaigns at the same time. In 2004, the company's estimated media expenditures were over $250 million for Budweiser and Bud Light.[38]

Not many companies can afford to run separate campaigns. McDonald's, however, runs at least four major campaigns and likely several minor campaigns simultaneously. McDonald's, however, is not targeting the same audience. Instead, one agency handles its national campaign, another agency develops the marketing communication program aimed at "kids and tweens," and separate agencies are used to advertise to the African American and Hispanic markets. As markets become increasingly fragmented, the explosion of consumer contact points will likely result in different words for different folks. Ten years ago, it was common to hear the expression "surround the consumer with myriad points of brand contacts." Today, agencies stress their creativity by pointing out how they reach consumers "all kinds of ways" with creative and increasingly *different* messages.

CAUSE-RELATED MARKETING

Companies understand that in the new marketing environment, it is not enough to gain sales. A company also has to capture customers. Companies are now rethinking how they address consumers' needs and wants. They are shifting away from transaction-based marketing designed primarily to stimulate sales to relationship-based marketing designed to build the brand over the long haul. However, it's not enough to tell consumers that the company understands them. A company needs to prove it. Convincing skeptical consumers that the company understands them better than do the other firms can be difficult. Today, consumers buy products for psychological as well as physical reasons. **Cause-related marketing** refers to the activities a company undertakes to support causes that are in the public's interest, such as AIDS awareness and research, environmental concerns, animal rights programs, homeless shelters, and diseases, such as sickle-cell anemia, cystic fibrosis, and muscular dystrophy.

In **transaction-based marketing,** the relationship between a seller and a buyer is of short duration. Once a sale takes place, the buyer and the seller may not connect again until the next buying opportunity presents itself. In the meantime, another company may win the attention if not the hearts of consumers. The idea behind relationship marketing is to let customers know that the company thinks consumers are important before, during, and after the sale. Cause-related marketing is a way for a company to demonstrate to skeptical consumers that it shares some of the same core values as the customer.

An important dimension to a relationship-marketing program is the bond that ties together the seller and the buyer. The minorities profiled earlier tend to be strongly brand loyal. Perhaps because they are not part of the majority, they appreciate the recognition companies pay to their core values and interests. A company that sponsors or contributes money to a cause helps reaffirm to people that their values and interests are important.

The *IEG Sponsorship Report* projected that together companies would spend $991 million on cause marketing in 2004. In 2003 Nike Inc.'s "WEARYELLOW LIVESTRONG" yellow bracelet campaign benefiting cancer research through the Lance Armstrong Foundation raised millions of dollars benefiting both Nike and the cause.[39]

Ben & Jerry's Homemade Inc. contributes a percentage of all profits to help social and environmental concerns. The founders, Ben Cohen and Jerry Greenfield, espouse a corporate philosophy of "caring capitalism." Consumers generally like the quirky names the company gives to its flavors like Cherry Garcia and Rainforest Crunch. The company is perceived by consumers as different, both in the way it names its products and in its corporate philosophy. At least in part because of their cause-related marketing philosophy, consumers of the brand are thought to be extraordinarily brand loyal.

The 2004 Cone Corporate Citizenship Study, which measured changes in public opinion, found that "90% of Americans were likely to switch brands, with price and quality being equal, to help support a cause." Additionally, the survey found that 8 in 10 Americans indicate that corporate support of causes wins their trust in the company.[40] This study suggests that a firm can improve its image by participating in cause-related activities, but it also concluded that its efforts have to be in some way related to the company's image. Arizona, the iced tea and juice brand, played on its so-called western heritage to fund a campaign to save mustangs and burros. (Actually, the company was founded in Brooklyn, NY.) It offered consumers signed lithographs and museum-quality posters of "western impressionist" art. All proceeds were to go to the International Society for the Protection of Mustangs and Burros.[41]

Cause-related marketing works best when both the community and the company benefit. Calphalon, a maker of gourmet cookware, has aligned with the antihunger organization Share Our Strength (SOS). Twice a year the company sells a cooking pan with the SOS logo on the packaging, promising that the company will donate five dollars for every pan sold. Sales of the pan with the special label were said to have increased tenfold over what they were without the special designation.[42]

Consumers can suspect the motives of a company's charitable activities, particularly if the recipient is a member of the fine arts. If the charity is not something an average consumer can identify with, he or she may feel that the top executives are merely supporting activities that they attend personally—selfish rather than altruistic motives. Although conventional wisdom suggests that consumer skepticism can be reduced if a company's altruistic activities are related to what the company sells, a study published in the *Journal of Public Policy and Marketing* suggests it may not matter. Consumer responses to a cause-related marketing campaign were found to be more strongly affected by the amount of money or the help they expect the cause to receive than by the motives attributed to the firm for participating.[43]

Target Stores has a policy of giving back to the community and contributes $2 million per week to various causes including the Take Charge of Education program, which donates a percentage of Target charge card purchases to schools. Along similar lines, Tom's of Maine, a company specializing in all-natural products, contributes 10% of all profits to charity. Both companies are said to enjoy strong brand loyalty to their products.

GREEN MARKETING

Green marketing is a variation of cause-related marketing. It refers to the activities a company takes to protect and enhance the environment and make this information known to the public. Increasingly, companies are aware of the public's concern about environmental problems. A 2002 study reported that over half of all Americans say they have purchased a product because the label or the advertising indicated that it was environmentally safe.[44] Companies' activities can range from producing toxic-waste-free products to recycling waste material and using recycled materials. Companies understand that they have a social responsibility to be good corporate citizens, but they also know that it can be good for business.

Pressure to be green can come from consumers or can result from the actions of a competitor. McDonald's replaced its polystyrene packaging with waxed paper in response to consumer concern over the CDCs produced in making polystyrene. StarKist announced it was going "dolphin free" in making its tuna. Its competitors quickly followed suit rather than risk losing market share. Anti-SUV advocacy and the support of celebrities such as Leonardo DiCaprio have increased the popularity of hybrid automobiles such as the Toyota Prius® and the Honda Insight® even though they cost more.

However, when a company makes green claims it needs to be cautious because there is considerable consumer skepticism about environmental claims. Consumers are also generally confused over what claims really mean. The Federal Trade Commission, for its part, has tried to reduce confusion by issuing guidelines to prevent the misleading use of environmental terms in both advertising and packaging. One expert advises that it is not enough to talk green, a company must *be* green. "Green hype" can backfire if the company doesn't have a solid record of environmental accomplishments; consumers will be skeptical at best or resentful at worst.[45]

CROSS PROMOTIONS

Increasingly, companies are teaming up with each other to get more mileage out of their promotional campaigns. Cross promotion is a strategy whereby marketing partners share the cost of a promotion that meets mutual needs.[46] These cooperative arrangements can be fairly simple, such as when Oscar Mayer hot dogs and French's mustard are included in the same ad. This arrangement makes sense because the demand for each product is somewhat derived from the use of the other. The brand equity in each brand can help leverage the demand for both products, and the cost of the advertising can be shared equally or can vary depending on how much focus is on each product.

Arrangements can be informal and consist of no more than a brand like Nabisco advertising that its cookies contain Hershey chocolate chips. Or the partnership can be more complex, such as the 10-year deal McDonald's and Disney have formed whereby each company agrees to promote the other company's products. Basically, McDonald's agrees to spend millions of dollars promoting Disney movies and, in return, McDonald's gets to use Disney movie characters, such as Mulan and Flubber, to attract consumers to stores where they can buy toy replicas. Disney promotes McDonald's at its Epcot Center theme park. There are several different forms of cross promotions, including co-branding, co-marketing, and coalition marketing. There are at least two benefits common to each of these substrategies.

First, there is a potential synergistic effect whereby each brand gains some increment of value in associating with the other. If this does not occur, then the partnership is destined to fail. Many credit card companies have teamed up with national advertisers to jointly offer a credit card. However, some companies, like Ford, have learned that consumers do not always have pleasant thoughts about their credit cards. As a result, Ford dropped its association with Citibank, concerned that those negative feelings might rub off on its products.

The second benefit from cross promotions occurs through the potential for increasing the number of brand contacts by being included in another brand's marketing communication. Sun Maid® raisins was once featured on the boxes of all Post® Raisin Bran cereal, thus giving it far more exposure than it could get on its own promotional budget. The Taco Bell logo appeared on the package of Doritos® tortilla chips. Both Doritos and Taco Bell have been divisions of PepsiCo.

Co-branding.   This type of strategy exists when two or more companies closely link their brand names together for a separate product. This approach has been very popular in the credit card field as numerous companies, such as State Farm, Met Life, Hartford, General Motors, Ford, and True Value Hardware Stores, have all sought to extend their equity by combining forces with a financial institution. There are also several types of co-branding, including **ingredient branding** as with a microprocessor (such as Intel) included in a personal computer (such as Compaq). There's also **cooperative branding** where two brands receive equal promotion borrowing on each other's equity, such as with credit card partners American Airlines and Citibank or American Express and Sheraton Hotels. A third type of co-branding is called **complementary branding (also known as endorsement branding)** where products are advertised together to suggest joint usage, such as when Seagram's whiskey is paired up with a mixer like 7-UP. Part of the value of co-branding is that it gives a company an opportunity to move into a new area to sell its products. When Fannie May Candies paired up with Hallmark Stores and placed the Hallmark's gold crown logo on its celebrated collection chocolates, part of the benefit was that it gained entry into over 1,000 Hallmark stores.[47]

Co-marketing.   This strategy involves a pairing up of two or more companies to jointly market each other's products. The emphasis with this strategy is on marketing. Brands such as Frito Lay and Pepsi-Cola can combine promotions and together approach a retail chain, such as Wal-Mart to secure in-store deals on pricing, end-aisle displays, and chainwide ads. As big as each brand is, the combined marketing muscle of both is considerably larger.

Manufacturers often contact retailers with suggested promotions built around a theme. For example, Procter & Gamble might develop a special spring-cleaning promotion for retailers like Wal-Mart centered on the use of its cleaning products. Procter & Gamble provides marketing expertise, and the retailer furnishes in-store resources in the form of personnel, additional space, and promotional funds.[48]

Coalition Marketing. This strategy resembles but differs from the frequent-flyer programs offered by many airlines (sometimes called **loyalty marketing**). In coalition marketing, a third party coordinates the awards that consumers earn by trading at a wide variety of places including airlines, hotels, rental companies, and even purveyors of packaged goods. A company such as Loyalty Management Group's Air Miles allows members to redeem their points for many of the same kind of purchases for which they received points. This includes airlines such as United, American, and Northwest, and companies such as Hertz, Hyatt, Citibank, and LensCrafters. The idea behind this approach is that it gives consumers flexibility where and when they make their selection. Businesses can benefit because much of the administrative arrangements are handled by a third party. However, much of the success of these programs depends on participating businesses to keep restrictions to a minimum.

MARKETING IN THE DVR ENVIRONMENT

In the new communication revolution, companies face a paradigm shift in the way marketing communications are created, distributed, and consumed. Digital video recorders (DVRs), like TiVo and Replay TV, are spawning much of this shift. DVRs, also called personal digital recorders, allow a viewer to record television programs directly to a hard disc. Among the features of a DVR is the ability to zip through commercials with unprecedented ease. And early reports suggest that this is exactly what is happening. At the end of 2004, DVRs were in 6% of U.S. households, according to one estimate. By 2009, that figure is expected to reach 32.2% and by 2014 to close in on the reach of cable at 49.2% of TV households. Advertisers are clearly concerned.[49]

The traditional model of somewhat captive viewers sitting in front of TV sets has been replaced by one where viewers have easier access and greater control over what they watch. New communication strategies are likely to be less intrusive and more inviting to consumers. To meet the challenges of a new media environment, advertisers are responding with new types of product promotion that don't neatly fit into a message or media strategy category. These involve the integration of branded marketing and entertainment and are covered under the broad heading of "branded entertainment."

The value of branded entertainment programs is multifaceted. First, the sheer exposure of the brand in use has value. But more important, the involvement of a brand in the right content environment and in the right way confers a "social validity" on the brand. Indirectly, these efforts say to consumers "this brand is cool, this brand is part of how people live today"—in short, "this brand is relevant in society—it is worthy of consideration."

THE WORKING STRUCTURE OF BRANDED ENTERTAINMENT

In this emerging discipline, the type of involvement between a marketer and an entertainment property can vary greatly, based on a number of factors. At the most basic level are product placements and at the most involved level are branded content concepts.

"Traditional" Product Placement

In its most basic form, product placement has been around Hollywood and the television industry for decades. These placements involve providing products as props for sets and background scenes. Much of this activity is driven by the relationship with prop masters and is handled for marketers by product placement agencies.

Branded Entertainment—Higher Levels of Involvement

In this level of association between products and properties, the product moves from "background" to "foreground" and becomes more integral to the program concept. Beyond this come opportunities for promotional programs and other extensions. In the early days of television, it was common for a single brand to sponsor an entire television show. Hallmark Cards, Chevrolet, Gillette, and Kraft sponsored hour-long programs. Often the programs were created for an advertiser by its agency. What is new about this "marketing space" are two factors. First is the level of conscious consideration given to this area by program developers, networks, and marketers. Second is the financial component—"integration" fees, free merchandise, and usually a commitment to purchase commercial spots are seen as a source of revenue by content providers and as a marketing expense by advertisers. With entertainment properties that have the highest level of profile and visibility, these costs can often be substantial.

The impetus for the collaboration between commerce and content (entertainment) can come from the advertiser or the entertainment provider. The place where they meet has colorfully been called **"Madison + Vine."** NMA Entertainment & Marketing, which started out as a product placement agency, is an industry leader in connecting advertisers with entertainment properties. NMA has worked with Interstate bakeries to link the introduction of the Shrek2 DVD with a special Twinkies product featuring green filling.

For branded entertainment to work well, the association between the property and the brand must seem natural, not contrived. So when Sears sponsored the *Extreme Makeover: Home Edition* TV program, the fit seemed natural because Sears sells home-improvement items. Naturally, many were visible throughout the show. Another key to a successful partnership is to integrate the association throughout multiple forms of marketing communication. Coca-Cola is one of six sponsors of *American Idol* and it promotes its involvement in network, retail, broader print, and online promotions as well as with outreach to consumers via viewing parties and campus activities.[50]

Branded content is a special form of branded entertainment and is created specifically for a brand. Sears, American Express, and BMW are among the major advertisers using this type of promotion. ESPN created a concept called "ESPN Shorts" featuring short films with the sponsor's brand integrated. These ran periodically during commercial breaks on *SportsCenter.* Among early advertisers signing up for this concept were Sears, Miller Brewing, and Toyota. For example, ESPN and Sears created a multichapter story about a baseball scout who discovers a 12-year-old groundskeeper "phenom." Sears Craftman brands are integrated throughout the story. Another dimension of this is exemplified by the BMW films known under the title of "The Hire." This effort used top Hollywood talent to create eight action-packed, visually stunning short films for its BMW films Web site, each showcasing the car.

The challenge to advertisers is to develop compelling content that viewers go out of their way to see. With high-performance cars like BMW and exciting chase scenes, the creative opportunities are unlimited. However, American Express used Jerry Seinfeld and an animated Superman in a five-minute spot for its Web site that was well received creatively. Though an estimated 500,000 people downloaded the spot, there was some question about its effectiveness given the likely cost of producing the spot.[51] In another example, the American Express card was integrated into the storyline for the cable program *The Restaurant,* produced by reality program provider Mark Burnett. The proprietor's use of the card appeared contrived and a too-obvious attempt to push the product.

SPECIAL MEDIA STRATEGIES

All of the following strategies fall into the category of what might be called nontraditional media. Although we have relegated these strategies to a place in the book following other marketing communication tools, we recognize that in the twenty-first century many of these strategies will occupy a position of importance comparable to the "major" media.

ADVERTISING AND THE INTERNET

The Internet is an important and integral part of many people's lives. Investors realize this importance by placing a market value of around $30 billion on Google, the leading search engine—far above the $23 billion value placed on General Motors, the leading national advertiser.[52] The Internet is no longer simply an option in a company's communication strategy. It is an essential element. Millions of consumers are now regularly logging in online. They are still, however, in the process of forming what they want to do when they get there. Like someone moving to a new city, consumers will be reevaluating with whom they will do business.

Companies that ignore the Internet, or ones that wait to see how it develops, run the risk of giving rival firms an advantage that they might not overcome. Barnes & Noble refers to itself as the world's largest bookseller, yet its sales are less than half of online bookseller Amazon.com. Amazon saw an opportunity early and moved fast; Barnes & Noble waited and now is struggling to catch up.

In her book *The Internet Strategy Handbook,* Mary Cronin suggests that it's not enough for companies to get involved with the Internet, they have to do it right. If it's not working for them, then they need to figure out what's missing. Planners need to link any Internet strategy to corporate and marketing goals. Selling, and even advertising, on the Web, can have a profound effect on the way the company does business. What they sell online can affect the way people do their jobs. Price sales, inventory control, and customer service all need to be coordinated with the information going out on the Web.[53] In addition, companies need to communicate the thrust of their online advertising to employees or run the risk that the image and information consumers get from the Internet differs from what they get elsewhere.

There are at least three ways in which the Internet can be of value to a company:

1. **Internet as a Direct Marketing Tool.** There is enormous potential to sell directly to consumers, via e-mail or through the World Wide Web. Visitors who "opt-in" to a Web site (i.e., give permission) can later be targeted with an e-mail message based on the information they provide. But companies may not have much choice to sell this way if their competitors are already actively doing so. In many product categories, this is exactly what the competition is doing or will be doing in the near future. And there are advantages to getting there first, as Barnes & Noble discovered.

2. **Internet as an Advertising Medium.** Advertising expenditures on the Internet are 4% of what businesses spend on advertising.[54] By 2006, Internet advertising expenditures will surpass those of radio and magazines.[55] It would be a mistake, however, to think of the Internet as simply another medium. Consumers interact with this medium unlike other media. Moreover, the Internet of today will be profoundly different tomorrow.

3. **Internet as a Tool for Various Communication Purposes.** Companies can establish Web sites to connect with consumers in a variety of ways. Web sites can deepen a relationship between a company and the consumer on a one-to-one basis. The Web site can also be a source of public relations–oriented information; it can provide electronic coupons, shopping opportunities, or simply entertainment.

E-commerce

This category can be broadly defined as *any transaction that stimulates a sale or purchase order over the Internet.* It includes financial transactions, business-to-business (B2B), and business-to-consumer (B2C) sales. According to Department of Commerce figures, about 94% of e-commerce is B2B. E-commerce continues to grow much faster than overall retail sales.[56] Although the focus of this book is mainly on B2C, or e-tailing, B2B considerations are an important part of a company's marketing plan.

Shopping online has become a reality. According to ComScore Networks, online spending in 2004 grew by 26% to over $117 billion.[57] Stock market investors were so bullish on Amazon.com, the online bookseller, that at one point they bid up the market value of the company to $29.2 billion.

Many traditional bricks-and-mortar retailers are turning into bricks-and-clicks companies, often reluctantly. In late 1998, Levi Strauss & Co. finally got around to selling online after resisting the opportunity for more than three years. The company had a Web site as early as 1995. It was a cool site with lots of things to look at including graffiti "art." It had lots of interesting stuff, except what consumers wanted most—a way to purchase jeans online. The company was wary about incurring resentment from its big retail customers, which at the time generated nearly all of the $7 billion in sales. However, the company had been steadily losing market share and competitors, such as Eddie Bauer and The Gap, which do sell online, were gaining share of market. In the end, the company may have felt it had no other choice.[58]

For companies that understand online shopping, the rewards seem considerable. The key to successful online marketing is to understand why consumers shop and what they are looking for when they get online. Gary Hamel, chairman of Strategos, an international firm specializing in strategy, believes online shoppers want freedom, choice, and control. Shopping online lets consumers avoid pesky salespeople and allows them to shop at their own pace. They buy what they want, when they want, without any distracting interruptions from salespeople anxious to earn a commission.[59]

Online marketers are likely to find the competition in cyberspace even more competitive than at the local mall. Companies have to provide real value to customers. Online shoppers generally want what all shoppers want, but their priorities may differ. The following points are worth considering in evaluating what consumers want when they shop online:

- **Convenience**—The hectic lives of many consumers make it difficult to find the time to travel to stores. This is undoubtedly the reason why catalog sales are so popular. Companies need to reinforce the convenience of shopping online by making sure consumers have easy access to whatever information they desire.
- **Variety**—It is difficult for many stores to stock the many sizes wanted by consumers. With an online operation there are economies in distribution and a company should be able to stock unusual sizes.
- **Information**—For a variety of reasons, consumers sometimes do not get the information they need. Consumers may be in a hurry, or the salespeople aren't knowledgeable. Consumers also simply may not feel they can trust the salespeople to tell them what they want to know. Many car buyers shop online for information before they go to a dealership. They learn about a car's options, but mostly they find out information about dealer costs.
- **Service**—Consumers do want service, but they want it on their terms—they want to be in control. Without adequate arrangements to service inquiries, an operation can get into trouble quickly. Charles Schwab is the number-one Internet brokerage firm. Its share of the daily trading of stocks and bonds exceed the next three online competitors combined. Schwab's online commissions are higher than other discount brokers. What Schwab offers its customers, according to company CEO David Pottruck, "is the ability to deliver personalized information to the customer in real time, at virtually no cost."[60]

Schwab, the discount broker, may compete based on price, but service is the key to its success.

- **Price**—Yes, consumers want low prices, but it may not be the overriding factor in influencing buyer behavior. Even if it were, companies need to be as wary of competing on the basis of price online as they do off line. Many consumers visit popular price-comparison sites such as BizRate.com, Shopzilla.com, and Shopping.com. Unless companies provide additional value to consumers, their attraction to consumers can be tenuous at best.
- **Security/Privacy**—Consumers don't quite trust giving credit card information online. They are nervous about credit card fraud. Even though consumers would lose no more than $50 under the terms of their card, they still feel uneasy. Companies can provide an 800 number for those people who are still concerned about security.

One futurist predicts that shopping malls in the future will move toward offering goods that are best seen in person, such as fashion and home furnishings. Other malls will move toward lifestyle centers offering entertainment and dining as well as shopping.[61]

Companies also need to understand there are risks involved when selling online. If the company isn't offering consumers real value, it's much easier for consumers to comparison shop. But there are also risks in *not* selling online. Consumers are increasingly aware that they do not have to accept high-priced inferior quality merchandise simply because there aren't any nearby alternatives. Today, consumers can shop all over the world in minutes.

ADVERTISING ON THE INTERNET

Internet advertising expenditures are increasing much faster than off-line advertising and are projected to go over $10 billion in 2005, increasing more than 20%. However, there are profound differences between traditional media and the Internet, both in the way consumers are exposed to the media and in the Internet's potential to involve the consumer in a selling message.

Despite earlier disappointment with lackluster results, today advertisers are flocking to the Internet for three reasons:

- **Interactivity.** The Internet is better able to engage consumers with advertising or editorial content because it allows site visitors to control how much they want to see, hear, or read. This freedom allows consumers who are exposed to an ad (or a Web site) to pursue more information or entertainment if their interest is stimulated. Potentially, if the advertising is done right, consumers make an emotional connection with the brand.
- **Selectivity.** On the Internet there are thousands of sites, including blogs, that sell advertising. These sites cater to very specific or narrow consumer interests. In addition, several companies have developed software to track a consumer's past Web site surfing behavior called **behavioral targeting.** Snapple wanted to reach women who were

concerned about health, diet, and fitness. Rather than simply putting an ad on the diet and fitness channel of iVillage, a site popular with women, behavioral targeting allows the company to advertise only to women who meet defined criteria—those who visit the diet and fitness channel on iVillage three times in 30 days. A Snapple ad then follows her around wherever she visits on the iVillage site.[62] Consumers leave tracks when they visit a site, including how much time they spend in one location. Publishers are collecting this information and selling it to advertisers. Behavioral targeted revenues are expected to reach nearly $1 billion in 2005.[63]

- **Accountability.** The ability to trace the effectiveness of online ads to a variety of metrics including sales, click-thrus, cost per search, and time spent on a site, is giving online advertising a reputation for accountability rivaled only by direct mail. ROI models adapt easily to online metrics far better than for those of television or magazine advertising.

The variety of ads is growing exponentially in a way that resembles what is going on offline. Among the most popular type of ads are the following: banner ads, pop-ups, video, search ads, and site sponsorships.

Banner Ads. By far the most popular ads on the Web, banners can be nonenhanced or enhanced. With nonenhanced banners, when the user clicks on a banner, another screen appears. With enhanced banners, all of the information appears on the banner and the user never leaves it. Enhanced banners promote consumer involvement by allowing them to type in information. On some sites they can e-mail a friend.

First-generation banners were static—nothing moved. Today's banners can be animated with GIFs to increase the likelihood of attracting attention. Most of these ads are fairly easy to construct and are relatively inexpensive. However, a banner on a prime site such as Yahoo can run $300,000 per day. There are mixed reports regarding their effectiveness.

Pop-Up Windows. The idea behind a pop-up is that it doesn't get in the way of the content on the page. Double exposure pop-ups are another kind of pop-up that reappear after five seconds. The disadvantage to an advertiser is that site visitors can close the pop-up—which they often do. Another disadvantage of pop-ups and double exposure pop-ups is that they can be irritating (often very irritating) to have to close if you don't want to see or use it. It is increasingly likely that consumers will install programs on their computer to kill pop-ups, some of which may come loaded on their computer when they buy it. Moreover, service providers such as AOL, Earthlink, and others feature pop-up prevention software as part of the basic subscription service.

Content or Site Sponsorships. This arrangement exists usually when an advertiser is identified as the sponsor of some content on a site. For example, Kraft's Maxwell House sponsors an online "coffee break" that utilizes the *New York Times'* crossword puzzles and book reviews. This approach has the advantage of taking on the credibility of the site. Detractors say it blurs the lines between advertising and editorial matter, something they find undesirable.

Search Ads.   The market for search ads has exploded, going from less than $1 billion in 2003 to well over $4 billion in 2005. Advertisers pay to have their names and ads appear next to an Internet search result. For example, every time somebody clicks on the phrase "car insurance," Progressive Insurance pays $8.08. The prices are set through an auction-style bidding for top position on popular search engines like Yahoo and Google. The rates for certain terms like "VIOXX®" and "mesothelioma," a cancer caused by asbestos exposure, have been run up by class-action lawyers. Perhaps out of jealousy, competitive pressures, or corporate vandalism, it's estimated that a significant number of all clicks on search ads are bogus.[64]

Video.   One of the newest forms of advertising is provided mainly by a company called Unicast. A video ad is loaded in the background and it plays when a site visitor moves to a new page. The ad is intrusive, but because it's "more interesting" than other ads, consumers aren't supposed to mind. Ford and Colgate-Palmolive were among the earlier users of this format.[65]

What is also clear is that advertisers are still sorting out the most effective formats to use. In some ways, as one form becomes more popular (say, search ads), it becomes less attractive to advertisers. Pop-ups and banner ads, so maligned in recent years, are expected to show 20% to 25% increases (in 2005), according to some analysts.[66]

The Future of Advertising on the Internet
It is difficult to predict what advertising will be like even in the near future. What is clear is that it will be different. The government and industry continue to extend the Web page descriptive language, HTML (hypertext mark-up language), in a variety of ways to make it more interactive and interesting, especially through greater use of JavaScript and XML (extensible mark-up language).

These changes will make it easier to manipulate and share documents across the Web. Along with these developments has come the widespread availability of greater bandwidth via television cables, phone lines, and wireless technology. This increased bandwidth allows access across the Web to be significantly faster than 56K modems. In addition, new technological breakthroughs promise to deliver even more technical surprises.

Marketers are also intrigued by wireless devices, mainly PDAs (personal digital assistants) like the Palm Pilot and cell phones. Emerging Wi-Fi networks will allow consumers easier access to the Internet. Under one scenario, advertisers would be able to deliver messages to consumers virtually anywhere, especially when shopping. Skeptics point out that the intrusiveness of these messages would likely outweigh their benefit.

In the future, the distinction between a television set and a computer screen will be somewhat blurred. At some point, the images on the respective screens will begin to resemble each other. However, until television goes interactive universally, there will remain some profound differences. Early promoters of Internet advertising talked about the ability of the Internet to deliver thousands of eyes. But people who use the Internet are not passive viewers and will actively tune out content that does not interest them. Unlike television, where you must sit through a commercial (unless you use a remote to switch channels), on the Internet consumers can control exposure by clicking past an ad—especially as more bandwidth delivers faster speeds.

What is also clear is that, in the future, advertising on the Internet will be every bit as important to an advertiser as television. However, the distinction between television and the Internet will not be that clear to the typical consumer, especially as television too becomes an interactive medium on a widespread basis. It's also likely that at least some television programs will begin running banner ads, probably along the bottom of the screen. This scenario is still off in the future, but the future may not be as distant as most people believe.

The key to advertising effectiveness on the Internet is to involve consumers so that they interact with the advertising. The best way to do that is to offer consumers value, either in the form of entertainment, more information, or the opportunity to make a satisfying purchase.

Web Site Communication

A Web site offers a company numerous opportunities to enhance its marketing communication program. Web site communication combines the ability to drive awareness, develop interest, and move consumers to action, including getting people to buy products. Many companies understand what a Web site can do, if only intuitively. An important key is to figure out how to do it better.

Web sites must be even more consumer centered than traditional media. To visit a site, Web surfers must go out of their way. To attract them, a site must be sufficiently entertaining and interesting. But interesting can be interpreted in different ways. A site can look interesting because of "cool" graphics or it can be interesting because consumers perceive they will receive something of value from the site. Companies that had sites in the early days of the Web had an advantage over a company that waited. Something is usually better than nothing. In the new marketing environment, having a Web site is no longer distinctive, it is the norm. Therefore, companies must strive to construct superior sites for the same reasons they try to make better television commercials or new product innovations. The Web is another channel to deliver a company's message. But unlike most media advertising, the messages can be multiple, and are delivered in a low-key style over an extended length of time.

To understand how to build better sites, consider the basic building blocks of a Web site:

- **First, there is the Web site's infrastructure.** This refers to the wire or fiber optics that connect a site to the switchers and routers that connect the Web surfer to the site somewhere in cyberspace. Because companies all get their service from the same providers, there isn't any point of differentiation here.

- **Second, sites consist of content.** To provide information, the full range of marketing communication tools can be employed. In the advertising area, companies provide all kinds of promotional information in depth. Search virtually any automobile Web site and you'll find more information than you probably want to know. Companies also use their Web sites to communicate their public relations efforts. Most sites have news releases to read and, if not, they are likely to describe in detail their community-oriented activities. If they are involved in cause-related marketing, you're also likely to read about that in their site. In the sales promotions area, many companies give away free samples, provide coupons, and invite visitors to enter contests or sweepstakes. (If you haven't received a free sample of jelly beans from Mr. Jelly Belly, be sure to go to the site early in the morning because the company only gives away 500 samples a day, and they go fast.) In the direct marketing area, companies not only sell products, but numerous product paraphernalia as well, such as hats, T-shirts, jackets, umbrellas, and tote bags all imprinted with the company or brand logo.

  If the above sounds typical, that's because content is not really a point of differentiation for most sites. Sites have many of the same kinds of problems that parity products face. It's not easy to differentiate themselves from the competition. Neither is spending large sums of money any more likely to produce effective sites than it is to produce strategic advertising that works. For most Web sites, the critical task is to build a better site.

- **Context is the third building block of a Web site.** It is this element that offers the best opportunity to exploit. Context refers to the environment or distinctive atmosphere that exists within a site. For example, if you enter some sites, say the Tommy Hilfiger site, there are vivid colors and interesting graphics. It is, as some might say, a cool site. Whether this is important or merely nice depends on how the site's context meets consumer expectations. Levi Strauss had a "cool" site for three years before it conceded that what its visitors really wanted was to buy jeans. Can you have both? Perhaps, but there are trade-offs site builders need to consider. The more graphic details you put into a site, the longer it takes to load. Although delays are no longer the problem they used to be, it is still worth considering. The site planner needs to understand what consumers want and expect when they visit a site.[67]

Understanding Web Site Visitors.   Earlier in this book, we emphasized the importance of understanding how and why consumers buy certain products or brands. It is equally important to understand why someone might visit a Web site. Are they curious? Do they want to be entertained? Play games? Do they want information? Are they simply interested in making a transaction quickly and easily? For many, online shopping will never replace shopping in a mall or in a brick-and-mortar store because they enjoy the whole experience surrounding a shopping expedition. Getting out, meeting and seeing new people, window-shopping, trying things on—all can add value to what a consumer actually buys.

Consider why Web surfers visit Google, a popular search engine. It's not because the site is interesting. The plain white background and minimal use of graphics does not make for a very interesting site. Web surfers who use Google want information, they want it quickly, and then they want to leave. Site interest is not a priority. In this case, less can be more. In contrast, when you visit the Nike site the appearance of the site is visually attractive. Inside the site, there is a lot of information on training for various sports. It appears to be a site that people want to visit and stay a while. In the past, accessing the site from a home computer with a slow modem was a problem. Today, more than half of Americans who go online connect through a broadband connection.[68]

Visitors to the Charles Schwab discount broker site want information and the ability to execute trades quickly and easily. The investors who trade at the E*Trade and Ameritrade brokerages are there because they charge lower commission fees. These visitors expect less advice and are primarily interested in making trades quickly. Waits are unacceptable.

To learn about the target audience's Web usage and their expectations, some companies get information from a syndicated research service such as Forrester Research or Jupiter Media Matrix. However, many of the techniques we discussed in Chapters 2 and 3 can easily be adapted to this area.

Building the Brand and Web Sites

Along with many people in advertising, we stress the importance of building the brand. A Web site provides a company a unique opportunity to reinforce and expand upon the brand associations and other intangible qualities consumers attach to both the company and its brands. A Web site can help build the brand because visitors are usually willing to spend time when visiting a site. Although visitors may visit a site merely out of curiosity, once they are there, a company has an opportunity to build a relationship between the visitor and the company and its brands. The key is to give the visitor value. But it has to be value on the consumer's terms, not the company's. The persuasive appeals that work on television have the luxury of at least a semicaptive audience. Site visitors will quickly click through the site unless interest is developed quickly. The Internet is a content-oriented medium driven by consumer interest.

Web sites are now an integral part of a company's promotional mix. Automotive Internet ad spending is estimated at $350 million in 2005, and Jupiter Media projects it will reach $1.7 billion by 2008. Companies such as Ford and Mitsubishi use network advertising to build or reinforce brand identity and to drive viewers to their Web sites for information and videos of the car performance capabilities.[69]

A Web site is not just a marketing communications medium, it is a *communications* medium capable of delivering what consumers get from the media in general: news, entertainment, information, education, shopping opportunities, and more. A Web site can provide the above delivered with a full multimedia experience: sight, sound, motion, and interactivity. Some of the media experiences, such as motion and picture resolution, are not as good as they can get elsewhere, but they will be tomorrow.

Using a Web site to sell to consumers on the basis of convenience or price can move a lot of products, but the bigger opportunity is to get consumers to connect with the brand and deepen the relationship between the company and consumers. At the Robert Mondavi Winery Web site, you can't buy any wine. Mondavi wines sell in the premium, super premium, and ultra premium price categories. The Mondavi Winery has long been a producer of high-quality wines. The prime prospect for Mondavi wines has an above-average income, and generally knows more about quality wine than the average consumer. The site is filled with information on wine, gourmet recipes, and the winery. The winery is a tourist destination and visiting this site is designed to increase interest in both the wine and the winery. Like many companies, Robert Mondavi participates in numerous charitable activities. Many of its cause-related activities involve contributions of special wines to raise funds for charitable organizations. To wine aficionados, this information can be interesting because even if they do not attend these functions, they often imagine what it might be like to be a purchaser of special wines. There are no coupons, no rebates, and no sales offers on this site, and that helps reinforce the image that Mondavi wines are special.

It's no mystery that Web sites offer great potential. Companies now understand that what might have been an experiment a few years ago is now a necessity. Three things will increasingly become apparent: First, companies that do not have a Web site will be operating at a competitive disadvantage. Second, companies that do have sites will face increasing competition for a decreasing amount of time consumers can spend at their sites. And third, companies need to do a better job with their sites than they are now doing.

▎NONTRADITIONAL AND TRADITIONAL MEDIA OPTIONS*

The mass media are dead. Not really, but you do hear people talk as though traditional media are dying—even though prices continue to increase. But as consumers grow numb (and eventually immune) to the ads that inundate them through traditional media channels, advertisers seek new formats to distribute their messages. It is almost literally true that today every message platform is for sale (or could be tomorrow). If you can put a message on something, it's mostly a matter of price. People even rent out their bodies. Boxers and surfers wear logos on their skin. An enterprising Web designer in Nebraska auctioned the space on his forehead ($37,375 for 30 days) on eBay. It's doubtful that the CPM (cost per thousand) was very efficient, but the publicity was enormous. CNN and numerous other media outlets picked up the story—even the BBC. A pregnant woman agreed to wear a temporary tattoo on her belly for $4,000 to generate publicity for the Golden Palace Casino.

Today, smart companies think in terms of communication planning. Marketers are looking for new, unexplored ways to reach their target audience. Call it **creative media planning, guerilla marketing,** or even **mischief marketing.** The idea is to reach the target audience in a different

---

*These media options were obtained from a variety of sources, including George E. Belch and Michael Belch, *Introduction to Advertising and Promotion: An Integrated Marketing Communications Perspective* (Chicago: Richard D. Irwin, 1995); Donald W. Jugenheimer et al., *Advertising Media: Strategy and Tactics* (Dubuque, IA: William C. Brown, 1992); and Optimum Media, *Media 98: Upping the Ante to Stay in the Game* (Chicago: DDB Needham, 1998).

way. Reach and frequency are important, but getting consumers to engage with the message because of the way it is delivered often has a higher value. The makers of the film *The Blair Witch Project* led people to believe that the events depicted in the film were real. With virtually no budget, the film received enormous publicity, much of it over the Internet. This film helped spawn the term **viral marketing** because the idea is to have the receiver of an e-mail message send it to someone else, with the number of contacts increasing like a virus infection. When Sony Pictures launched the movie *Crouching Tiger, Hidden Dragon,* it held numerous screenings in martial arts schools. Doing things differently can be better, but is perhaps harder.

Many of the greatest successes in nontraditional marketing have been the result of inspired intuition—and some luck. The key to understanding successful approaches is to understand *why* they worked. Usually, successful nontraditional marketing grows from an insightful understanding of the product, and the target's passions, lifestyles, and habits combined with an understanding of human nature in general (say, people's curiosity about a mysterious disappearance). Combining this knowledge with creative ways to deliver a marketing idea can result in a message getting across with high impact relative to the expense. Done badly, these efforts disappear into the "white noise" of marketing.

Some 50 years ago, Katz and Lazarsfeld in a landmark study concluded that personal influence was significantly more successful than mass communication in converting people from one point of view to another.[70] Though there never really has been much disagreement with that finding, it's amazing how this principle is applied in today's marketing environment.

THE POWER OF BUZZ

There are a number of explanations or definitions of "buzz," even a book written on buzz marketing. At its core, creating buzz is all about getting people to talk. However, if you try too hard, consumers may identify the pitch as just another marketing ploy and ignore it. In contrast to mass-media advertising, most of the promotion of the brand comes from consumers who talk about the product. Companies hire young people to visit chat rooms to talk up brands—all unobtrusively. Beer marketers hire young women to visit bars and clubs to buy drinks—without disclosing that they are being paid to do so.

When the Hard Rock Hotel opened in Chicago, a guerilla marketing team hired fashion models to walk down selected streets near the hotel in their bathrobes. The idea behind **guerilla marketing** is to catch people by surprise, promoting something in a place or a way that's unexpected. The models stopped numerous people on the street asking for directions *back* to the hotel. They explained, it seems, that there had been a huge party the night before and they went outside the hotel for some fresh air and got lost. The models created lots of buzz for the hotel—one can only imagine what people said after the models moved on. Guerilla campaigns are street campaigns. Think subversive, or at least humorous. Ortho-McNeil pharmaceuticals used port-a-potties as a platform to publicize its antidiarrhea brand, Imodium AD®.

Great buzz does more than generate publicity, it influences people. Durango Boots, a small boot company located in Franklin, Tennessee, discovered much to its surprise that its boots were being purchased in a few urban markets as far away as Brooklyn. Its agency used street teams to "seed" numerous markets, often going to clubs and identifying the coolest dudes and offering them samples. Durango Boots is a traditional southern company and most of the prospects it was trying to win over were card-carrying members of the hip-hop culture. Durango Boots used these opinion influencers to gain street credibility in a way it could never achieve directly.

Sometimes it also makes sense to capitalize on existing nontraditional approaches not previously considered. Below is a partial list of media options that have found some acceptance. This list was longer in previous editions, but we've shortened to send the message that it is only a partial list—otherwise the list would be seemingly endless.

Transit
Including car cards, ads on outside of public, transportation, train/subway, and commuter-station posters.

In-Store Media
Including point-of-purchase, banners, racks, cash-register units, floor stands, signs, overheads and mobiles, shelf talkers, shopping carts, and bags.

Sports and Theatrical Events
Including programs, stadium scoreboards, poster type ads, stadium signs, and revolving banners.

Nontraditional Out of Home
Including audience segment, "hangouts," ski resorts, golf course signage, displays on military bases, college campuses concerts, painted walls, "wild postings," kiosks (malls, airports), restroom advertising, shopping mall displays, bus stop benches, inside taxicabs, skywriting, blimps, hot air balloons, freestanding inflatables, moving billboards, and in-flight advertising (airlines).

Directories
Including Yellow Pages, universities, churches, professional associations.

Electronic Advertising
Including Internet, e-mail, DVDs (games), video, pop-up windows and search engine ads, text messaging.

Motion Picture Advertising
Including product placement, videocassette, DVD, and "Channel One."

Miscellaneous
Including game show sponsorship, hotel movie channel preview, and infomercials.

Specialty Advertising
Including calendars, business gifts, writing instruments, desk accessories, trade shows, and airline ticket envelopes.

Imprinted Specialties
Including money clips, golf ball markers/tees, drinking glasses, calculator cases, tape measures, balloons, tote bags, beverage coasters, key

rings, mug insulators, bumper stickers, pocket planners, maps/travel guides, coffee mugs, trash bags, auto sun protectors, luggage tags, magnets, buttons, notepads, litter bags, letter openers, mousepads, ice scrapers, and hats.

Telemarketing
Including opt-in calls and blind calls.

The most important other media strategy is not in this paragraph, but in the readers' imaginations. In a dynamic and competitive media environment, it's hard to stay ahead of the competition. It takes imagination, but it also takes initiative and courage to do something unique. As examples, we'll examine two strategies that have been used occasionally: ambush marketing and fresh TV.

Ambush Marketing.   Ambush marketing is a promotional strategy aimed at creating the false impression that a company is an official sponsor of an event when it is not. The best examples occur around major events such as the Olympics. Event managers offer varying degrees of corporate sponsorship. Companies sign on for the prestige of associating the brand with the event. There are numerous ways to give what many people call a misleading impression. One way is to buy commercial time on the broadcast rather than pay the event committee a sponsorship fee. During the 2004 Athens Olympics, Mary Lou Retton, the famous Olympic gymnast, appeared in commercials for Sprint without any mention of the trademarked word *Olympics* or use of the Olympic rings.[71] Sprint was not an official Olympic sponsor. In the 1996 Olympics held in Atlanta, Visa paid $40 million to be an exclusive sponsor in the credit card category. Yet, when a survey conducted a month after the Olympics asked consumers to name official sponsors of the Olympic games, 72% named Visa, but 54% also named American Express, which was not a sponsor. Significantly, American Express was referred to as an "ambush marketer."[72]

During the Winter Olympics in Salt Lake City, Nike had its "swoosh" mark on almost all of the ice hockey teams, but Nike was not an official sponsor. Additionally, Nike spent more on ambush marketing at a London Marathon than it would have cost to gain official sponsorship rights by buying billboard space along the entire marathon route.[73]

Depending on one's perspective, ambush marketing can be referred to as "parasitic" marketing, "stealth" advertising, "guerrilla" marketing, or simply clever marketing. Our point in discussing this strategy is to use it as an example of a creative approach to getting a message across, not to pass judgment on whether it is ethical.

Fresh TV.   This strategy is an example of how the creative use of media can enhance a message. Fresh TV is really more of a technique than a strategy. It refers to producing and airing a commercial within a matter of a few days, if not hours. As an example, the day after the Super Bowl, viewers often see the game's top performers promoting some product or their impending trip to Disney World.

In actuality, the term "Fresh TV" dates back at least to 1992. To illustrate that Chevy's Mexican Restaurants was dedicated to serving fresh food, the advertising agency Goodby, Berlin, and Silverstein filmed a series of commercials very early in the morning and aired them later that night. The spots used a man-in-the-street interview format to help establish credibility. In one spot, the day's newspaper was shown to prove the spot had been shot that day. As a result of its innovative approach, the company got significant publicity in the media and sales were said to have increased significantly. The timing of the commercials helped reinforce the company's "fresh" positioning in consumer's minds.[74]

CAMPAIGN PROGRESS CHECKLIST

At this point in the campaign you should generally be aware of the following points:

1. The extra things that companies do to enhance their campaigns are increasingly likely to be essential in the new marketing environment.

2. Companies can no longer ignore global markets. To compete overseas, companies need to tailor their campaigns to local markets, being sensitive to language and culture differences.

3. Specialized markets such as African American, Hispanic, Asian American, and gay/lesbian respond favorably to targeted appeals. However, companies need to understand how these markets differ from mainstream markets in terms of values, consumption habits, and the way these markets respond to promotions.

4. Occasionally, it can make sense to use more than one message strategy in the same campaign. This, however, should be an exception rather than the rule.

5. Companies that are involved in charitable and other altruistic activities often find that communicating their efforts to the public in a sensitive and appropriate way makes good business sense.

6. Cross promotions are an effective way to leverage the equity in another brand and synergistically improve the image and the sales of all parties involved.

7. The Internet is no longer an optional element in a company's communication program. Involvement is essential.

8. Although online shopping seems to offer a company the quickest return, it is likely that advertising will begin to catch up and eventually pass e-commerce in importance.

9. Web site communication is an excellent tool to deepen the relationship between a company and the consumer on a one-to-one basis.

10. Creative media planning often consists of using non-traditional media options, but can also include many of the special options associated with traditional media that have been underutilized.

Notes and References

[1]U.S. Census Bureau, "Gross Domestic Product (GDP) by Country: 1995–2001," *Statistical Abstract of the United States* (2003), p. 852.

[2]Excerpted from Louisa Ha, "Classical Examples of International Advertising Mistakes," from *American Demographics*. International Advertising Resource Center, accessed 7 February 2003 (28 January 1999). http://bears.ece.ucsb.edu/personnel/astornet/humor/humor91.html

[3]"Nokia Hastily Pulls Ad Using Nazi Slogan," *Advertising Age International,* June 1998, p. 5.

[4]J.M. Dru, *Disruption: Overturning Conventions and Shaking Up the Marketplace* (New York: John Wiley and Sons, 1996), p. 3.

[5]K. Ohmae, *The Mind of the Strategist: The Art of Japanese Business* (New York: McGraw-Hill, 1982), p. 3.

[6]Jack Neff, "P&G Flexes Muscle for Global Branding," *Advertising Age,* 3 June 2002, p. 53.

[7]Mercedes M. Cordona, "Mass Marketing Meets Its Maker," *Advertising Age,* 21 June 2004, p. 1.

[8]U.S. Census Bureau, Facts for Features: African American History Month: February 2004. Accessed 17 January 2005, from http://www.census.gov/Press-Release/www/releases/archives/facts_for_features_special_editions/001667.html

[9]K.L. Keller, *Strategic Brand Management: Building, Measuring, and Managing Brand Equity* (Upper Saddle River, NJ: Prentice Hall, 1998), p. 585.

[10]Julie Clark, "Is Retail Getting a Bad Rap?" *Display and Design Ideas* (2001), p. 28.

[11]A.J. Jewler and B.L. Drewniany, *Creative Strategy in Advertising, 6th Ed.* (Belmont, CA: Wadsworth, 1998), p. 48.

[12]Rebecca Gardyn and John Fetto, "Race, Ethnicity and the Way We Shop," *American Demographics* 25 (February 2003), p. 31; and Jeffrey M. Humphreys, "The Multicultural Economy 2004: American's Minority Buying Power," *Georgia Business and Economic Conditions* 64 (2004), p. 3.

[13]M.L. Rossman, *Multicultural Marketing: Selling to a Diverse America* (New York: AMA-COM, 1994), pp. 129–130.

[14]C. Fisher, "Black, Hip, and Primed (to Shop)," *American Demographics* (September 1996), p. 5.

[15]Jack Neff, "Diversity," *Advertising Age,* 16 February 1998, p. S1.

[16]Robert J. Harris, "Black Power; Old Tricks Won't Lure Af-Am Consumers," *Marketing News* (2002), p. 21.

[17]Humphreys, "The Multicultural Economy," p. 6.

[18]U.S. Census Bureau, Facts for Features: Hispanic Heritage Month 2004: Sept. 15–Oct. 15. Accessed 17 January 2005, from http://www.census.gov/Press-Release/www/releases/archives/population/001720.html

[19]"No Habla Espanol," *Forbes,* 23 December 1992, p. 140.

[20]Gardyn and Fetto, "Race, Ethnicity and the Way We Shop," p. 31; and Humphreys, "The Multicultural Economy," p. 7.

[21]Allison Romano, "Hispanic-American TV Booms: Expanding Demographic Fuels Univision, Telemundo Growth," *Broadcasting & Cable,* 20 May 2002, p. 29.

[22]Association of Hispanic Advertising Agencies, Missed Opportunities: Vast Corporate Underspending in the U.S. Market. Accessed 22 January 2005, from http://www.ahaa.org/research/Missedopportunities.pdf

[23]K. Van Hoof, "Surveys Point to Group Differences (Ethnic Differences)," *Brandweek,* 18 July 1994, p. 32.

[24]Stuart Livingston, "Marketing to the Hispanic-American Community," *Journal of Business Strategy* (March/April 1992), pp. 56–57.

[25]D. White, "When Slogans Go Wrong," *American Demographics* 14, p. 14.

[26]Rossman, pp. 86–87; Anonymous, "Diversity in America: Asians," *American Demographics,* November 2002, p. S14.

[27]U.S. Census Bureau, Facts for Features: Asian Pacific American Heritage Month: May 2004. Accessed 17 January 2005, from http://www.census.gov/Press-Release/www/releases/archives/facts_for_features_special_editions/001808.html

[28]J.X. Fan, "Expenditure Patterns of Asian Americans: Evidence from the U.S. Consumer Expenditure Survey, 1980–1992," *Family and Consumer Sciences Research Journal* 25 (June 1997), p. 341.

[29]Gardyn and Fetto, "Race, Ethnicity and the Way We Shop," p. 31.

[30]V. Seitz, "Acculturation and Direct Purchasing Behavior Among Ethnic Groups in the U.S.: Implications for Business Practitioners," *Journal of Consumer Marketing* 15 (Winter 1998), p. 27.

[31]J. Burton, "Advertising: Targeting Asians," *Far Eastern Economic Review,* 21 January 1993, p. 43.

[32]Jed Kolko, Michael E. Gazala, and Charles Q. Strohm, Consumer Technographics Brief. "Gays are the Technology Early Adopters You Want." Accessed 17 January 2005, from http://www.forrester.com/ER/Research/Brief/0,1317,17004,00.html

[33]Statistics obtained from the following: U.S. Census Bureau, PCT14. Unmarried-Partner Households by Sex of Partners, Census 2000 Summary File 1. Accessed 17 January 2005, from http://factfinder.census.gov; Christie Schweinsberg, "Perfectly Queer" *Ward's Dealer Business* 38 (May 2004), p. 14; *ABI/Inform Complete.* ProQuest. Middle Tennessee State University Library, January 26, 2005. http://proquest.umi.com; Kolko et al., "Gays are the Technology Early Adopters You Want."

[34]M.W. Delozier and J. Rodriguez, "Marketing to the Homosexual (Gay) Market: A Profile and Strategy Implication," in *Gays, Lesbians & Consumer Behavior: Theory, Practice & Research Issues in Marketing,* ed. Daniel J. Wardrop (New York: Haworth Press, 1996), p. 205. According to the U.S. Census, same-sex households exist in 99% of U.S. counties.

[35]Daniel B. Baker et al., *Cracking the Corporate Closet* (New York: Harper Business, 1995).

[36]Delozier and Rodriguez, "Marketing to the Homosexual (Gay) Market," p. 210; and L. Penaloza, "We're Here, We're Queer and We're Going Shopping!: A Critical Perspective on the Accommodation of Gays and

Lesbians in the U.S. Marketplace." In *Gays, Lesbians, and Consumer Behavior: Theory, Practice & Research Issues in Marketing,* ed. Daniel J. Wardrop (New York: Haworth Press, 1996), p. 27.

[37]Sandra Yin, "Coming Out in Print," *American Demographics* 25 (February 2003), p. 20.

[38]M. Beirne and K. Hein, "Feisty Feds Weigh In against Low Carbs—and Tasteless Ads," *Brandweek,* 21 June 2004, p. S26.

[39]Lauren Gard, "We're Good Guys, Buy from Us," *BusinessWeek,* 22 November 2004, p. 72.

[40]Cause Marketing Forum, "2004 Cone Corporate Citizenship Study Results." Accessed 17 January 2005, from http://www. causemarketingforum.com

[41]G. Khermouch, "Arizona Gets on High Horse with First Cause-Marketing Program," *Brandweek,* 21 October 1996, p. 16.

[42]S. Lodge, "Is Cause-Related Marketing Worth It?" *Sales and Marketing Management* (June 1982), p. 72.

[43]D.J. Webb and L.A. Mohr, "A Typology of Consumer Responses to Cause-Related Marketing from Skeptics to Socially Concerned," *Journal of Public Policy and Marketing* (Fall 1998), p. 234.

[44]Joan Treistman, "It's Not Easy Being Green," *Point of Purchase* 8 (June 2002), p. 46.

[45]J.A. Ottman, "Back Up Green Program with Corporate Credibility," *Marketing News Chicago,* 26 October 1998, p. 9.

[46]Adapted from Louis E. Boone and David L. Kurtz, *Contemporary Marketing* (Fort Worth, TX: Dryden Press, 1999), p. 633.

[47]Stephanie Thompson, "Co-Branding," *Brandweek,* 23 February 1998, p. 26.

[48]J. Burnett and S. Moriarity, *Introduction to Marketing Communications* (Upper Saddle River, NJ: Prentice Hall, 1998), p. 325.

[49]Ann M. Mack, "Adjustment," *Brandweek,* 20 September 2004, p. 25.

[50]T.L. Stanley, "Idol Sponsors Plan to Sing Along Loudly," *Advertising Age,* 5 January 2004, p. 19.

[51]Bob Garfield, "AmEx Superman Spot: Heroic Effort for Minimal Audience," *Advertising Age,* 19 April 2004, p. 61.

[52]"Web Worth More Than Mere 3.4%." *Advertising Age,* 16 August 2004, p. 13.

[53]Excerpted from Mary Cronin (Interview), "Getting Your Company's Internet Strategy Right," *Fortune,* 18 March 1996, pp. 72–78.

[54]Jon Swartz, "Growth of Online Ads Hits High Speed," *USA Today,* 17 January 2005, p. B1.

[55]Stephen Baker, "Where the Real Internet Money Is Made," *BusinessWeek,* 27 December 2004, p. 98.

[56]"E-Commerce Sales," *Chainstore Age Executive Fax,* 22 February 2002, p. 2.

[57]comScore Networks, Press Release. Accessed 17 January 2005 from http://www.comscore.com/press/release.asp?press=546

[58]G. Hamel, "The E-Corporation," *Fortune,* 7 December 1998, p. 82.

[59]Ibid., p. 82.

[60]E. Schonfeld, "Schwab Puts It All Online," *Fortune*, 7 December 1998, pp. 92–100.

[61]Christian Peralta, "The Shape of Digital Things to Come," *Planning* 68 (September 2002), p. 24.

[62]Kris Oser, "Snapple Effort Finds Women as They Browse," *Advertising Age*, 3 May 2004, p. 22.

[63]Anita Jain, "Web Ad Firms Go through Behavior Modification," *Crain's New York Business*, 8 November 2004, p. 4.

[64]Rob Kaiser, "Internet Word Search Results Trigger Intense Price Bidding," *Knight Ridder/Tribune Business News*, 24 January 2005.

[65]Mark Gibbs, "Ads Infinitum," *New York World*, 26 January 2004, p. 68.

[66]Susan Kuchinskas, "Forecast 2005: Interactive Media," *Mediaweek*, 3 January 2005, p. 18.

[67]J. Gehman, "E-Commerce: Size Doesn't Matter, Context is Everything," *Marketing News*, 1 February 1999, p. 2.

[68]Pew Research Center, Trends 2005. "Internet: The Mainstreaming of Online Life," p. 60. Accessed 25 January 2005, from http://pewtrusts.com/pdf/trends2005-internet.pdf

[69]Karl Greenberg, "Automakers Drive Sales with Internet Advances," *Brandweek*, 2 February 2004, p. 16.

[70]Elihu Katz and Paul F. Lazarsfeld, *Personal Influence; The Part Played by People in the Flow of Mass Communications* (Glencoe, IL: Free Press, 1955).

[71]Kevin G. DeMarrais, "Ambush Marketers Avoid Using the "O" Word in Ads," *Knight Ridder Tribune Business News*, 26 July 2004, p. 1.

[72]D. Shani and D. Sandler, "Counter Attack: Heading Off Ambush Marketers," *Marketing News*, 18 January 1999, p. 10.

[73]Patrick Elliot, "The Loveable Rogues Who Devalue Sporting Events: Brands That Do Not Want to Fork Out on Expensive Sports Sponsorship Often Turn to Ambush Marketing," *Marketing Week*, 27 June 2002, p. 14.

[74]B. Carlino, "Creative Marketing Fuels Customer Recognition," *Nations Restaurant News*, 12 October 1992, p. 52; and Gold, "Fast Food & Family Restaurants: Chevys," *Brandweek*, 15 June 1992, p. S12.

CHAPTER 10

Evaluating the Effectiveness
of the Campaign*

Searching for a measure of advertising effectiveness is like searching for the Holy Grail—it goes on and on and on—for two basic reasons. First, the evaluation of advertising is often a critical factor in marketing success. A slight change in an advertising campaign brought about through some form of evaluation can lead to significant increases in sales and profits. In an aggressively competitive market, an insightful evaluation can provide a company with an edge over its rivals. When other types of marketing communications tools (such as sales promotions, direct marketing, and public relations) are included in the promotional mix, it further underscores the importance of a good measure of effectiveness.

Evaluation also gives businesses some means of control over the tremendous sums of money spent on marketing communications. Increasingly, many companies, including General Motors Corp., RJR Nabisco, Campbell Soup Company, Hershey Foods, and Nestlé Enterprises, tie their advertising agency compensation to performance evaluations.[1] Thorough and accurate evaluations not only enhance the success of the marketing communications program, they also strengthen the morale of the internal and external people working on the campaign.

Second, the search continues because it remains difficult to isolate all the effects of a communications campaign on sales. The measurement task is not impossible, but the large number of controllable and uncontrollable variables can turn even a simple market test into a meaningless exercise producing useless data. A simple market test can easily become complicated. In the pizza delivery business, companies often use a direct mail firm like Advo Inc., the largest direct mail services company in the United States, to deliver coupons to households in their market areas.

Normally, the effects are fairly easy to measure. Sales typically rise dramatically the day coupons are delivered, and continue to be high for the

---

*This chapter has been developed and written in part by Michael P. Kalasunas, senior vice president and director of planning at J. Walter Thompson in Chicago. Mike has been at JWT for more than 20 years and directs all advertising research for the agency. Increasingly, he spends a good measure of his time on strategic planning.

remainder of the week. If it rains, sales spike upward even higher. But if the competition is also running coupons the same day—a common situation—it is nearly impossible to determine the effect of each variable on sales. The situation is complicated even further if you consider that there are variations in the intensity of rain and differences in the degree to which a rival company is a direct competitor of the product being evaluated. Traditional researchers might describe this situation as confounding the effects of the variable you are interested in (i.e., direct mail–delivered coupons) with extraneous variables (i.e., rain and competitive promotions) so that their effect on the variable you are measuring is all mixed up. A typical manager is likely to ponder these questions and simply conclude that measuring these relationships is scarcely better than using personal judgment.

▌EVALUATION AS A STRATEGIC CONCERN

Managers, of course, realize that evaluation is vital to all aspects of the campaign. In today's intensely competitive marketplace, enlightened management understands that the older style of marketing practices that were often based on experience and even hunches are not likely to be as effective in the future as they were in the past. As Phillip Kotler of Northwestern University observed, "Companies find themselves competing in a race where the road signs and rules keep changing, where there is no finish line, no permanent 'win.'"[2] Smart companies integrate evaluative procedures into all areas of their decision making, including marketing communications. These procedures are often part of a system rather than project or task oriented.

Evaluation has been an important part of each chapter in this book. Chapters 2 and 3 examined many of the tests, techniques, procedures, and sources of information that are part of the research used to develop the strategic foundation of the campaign. This aspect of research is sometimes referred to as **developmental research.** Chapters 4 through 8 integrated the concept of evaluation as part of the method to develop the objectives, strategy, and tactics of the campaign.

The focus of this chapter is primarily on measuring the effectiveness of advertising and secondarily on evaluating related marketing communications. This focus is less a comment on the relative importance of advertising and more a function of the scantiness of methodologies known for measuring the effectiveness of other types of marketing communications. The measurement for advertising and related marketing communications is sometimes referred to as **evaluative research.**

Planners tend to ask three basic questions before measuring the effectiveness of a campaign:

1. Whether to measure?
2. When to measure?
3. What to measure?

Each of these questions is fundamentally connected to the other, so much so that a reasonable argument could be made that each of the above questions should be considered first. The second question, **when to measure,** is probably the most logical place to start, but usually the decision to use or not use measurement is decided first. The first two questions—**whether to measure** and **when to measure**—have an obvious effect on what to measure, but in many ways, the last question is the most important of the three. Because of the problems associated with measurement, **what to measure** frequently gets translated to what you *can* measure, either because of the cost of a measurement or because planners do not feel they can measure what they would really like to evaluate (sales), as we will later discuss. These feelings no doubt cause some planners to question whether it is worth measuring anything.

▮WHETHER TO MEASURE EFFECTIVENESS

In their book *Advertising and Promotion,* George and Michael Belch point out that to ensure success in a marketing communications program, it is important to determine how well the program is working by measuring its performance against some predetermined standards. They offer the following reasons why companies do or do not use measurement.[3]

REASONS FOR MEASURING EFFECTIVENESS

1. *Avoiding Costly Mistakes.* In 2002, according to *Ad Age,* more than $231 billion was spent on advertising in measured media in the United States. This amount probably constitutes less than half of all the money spent on marketing communications. If measurement could potentially increase a campaign's efficiency or effectiveness as little as 1%, then it would amount to savings of more than $13.1 million for Sony Corp. (based on total advertising expenditures of $1.31 billion), and more than $9 million for Coca-Cola Co. (based on total advertising expenditures of $903.5 million).[4]

2. *Evaluating Alternative Strategies.* Human behavior can rarely be predicted to any degree of certainty. Advertising is still very much an art. Companies often have more than one strategy under consideration, each of which seems promising and may have its own supporters within a company. The right kind of test can reduce the uncertainty in decision making. For example, Coors is a heavy buyer of spot television. Frequently, Coors tests alternate versions of its advertising to determine which strategy or execution is the most effective.[5]

3. *Increasing the Efficiency of Advertising in General.* The advertising business is replete with many highly competent and creative individuals. These people often have so much of their spirit and individuality invested in an assignment that it is difficult for them to be completely objective when evaluating their own work. The instincts of even the most successful and talented people can sometimes be wrong. When millions or tens of millions of dollars are on the line, measuring effectiveness as an aid to judgment often helps decision makers discern a near miss from a big success.

NOT MEASURING EFFECTIVENESS

1. *Cost.* Research can be expensive. As companies strive to keep costs down, research is one of the first expenses cut or significantly decreased. Measures to evaluate advertising after it is run are particularly vulnerable. In the 1970s, when many agencies were able to retain a full 15% commission on advertising they placed for their clients, advertisers often requested their agencies to conduct special studies as part of the compensation agreement. In the 1980s, when companies began to negotiate reductions in the commissions agencies were allowed to keep, agencies increasingly returned the task of measuring the effectiveness of advertising back to the companies. Many companies found it difficult to fit the cost of testing into their budgets. Companies, and especially advertising agencies, often rationalize that if they put more effort and expense into the developmental phase of the campaign, it will be less important to measure its effectiveness later.

2. *Research Problems.* Advertising people are uncertain about the methodologies that research organizations use and the criteria they test for. For example, many researchers agree that a good test for copy should measure multiple criteria. However, they are still not satisfied with the ones that do. There is frequent disappointment with the limitations of research. Planners are often disenchanted with tests that only measure communications effects, such as awareness and recall. They want tests that isolate and reveal a direct causal relationship between advertising and sales. Few tests achieve these ends.

3. *Disagreement over What to Test.* Along with the debate over the value of measuring communications effects may be a disagreement over which aspect of the campaign to test. A sales manager may want to assess the impact of promotions on sales, whereas the corporate hierarchy may be more concerned about the company's image or the identities of its brands. Disputes over what to test can sometimes lead to no testing.

4. *Creativity Objections.* Many creative people do not like copy testing. They say it inhibits their creativity. Because many tests are inexact and measure only one aspect of communication, such as awareness, copywriters sometimes protest that they do not measure the full impact of an ad, especially television commercials. Moreover, pretesting finished advertising limits creativity. Television commercials, in particular, are expensive to produce. If they do not score well on a test, a lot of money has been wasted. Wasting money is especially irksome if there has been no general agreement about the value of the test in the first place. Advertising can be tested in rough form with storyboards, "animatics," or "photomatics," but because these are not the actual commercial, some may argue that it limits the ability of the researcher to generalize the results from the test situation to the real world.

5. *Time.* Copy testing and other effectiveness measures take time; executive judgment and creative decisions must sometimes be made quickly. Many planners are concerned that with the passage of time they may lose a window of opportunity.

RESOLVING THE DEBATE OVER MEASUREMENT

Measurement is used to add greater precision to marketing decisions. Despite the problems associated with measurement and the need to make decisions in the face of insufficient information, it does not mean there is a good argument for intuitive decision making. Rather, as Kotler says, "it is an argument for improved marketing theory and tools of analysis."[6] Progressive companies should strive to be on the cutting edge of how they evaluate campaigns in the same way that they compete to produce better products.

DEVELOPING A RESEARCH SYSTEM

To foster a corporate environment that encourages innovation, it is important to view evaluative measures as part of a system. This approach tends to offer a firm some of the following advantages over evaluating a campaign on an ad hoc basis.[7]

- *Systems Tend to Evolve.* Once a system is built, it can be fine-tuned and refined to improve its efficiency and effectiveness. Ad hoc studies tend to be viewed as more discrete projects. They start, are executed, and end.
- *Systems Provide Benchmarks for Learning over Time.* After a system is established, it is easier to measure performance against results because the data tend to be collected and analyzed using common terms, standards, and databases. In a world where we rarely measure absolutes, measuring relative change is important.
- *Systems Promote a Holistic Approach Rather Than a Functional Approach to Solving Marketing Communications Problems.* Ad hoc studies often begin with a single aspect, or part, of the campaign (such as specific ads), which an analyst then strives to understand by piecing together all the parts in an attempt to understand the complete impact of a campaign. In contrast, systems foster a mindset that encourages planners to begin with a concept (such as integrated marketing communications), and follow through with measures or procedures that are designed to evaluate both the effects of various aspects of the campaign and the way in which they interact. In other words, systems help predispose the planner to evaluate the impact of the entire campaign.
- *Research Systems Reside in the Company (or Its Agency).* Many ad hoc studies are produced by outside suppliers. Often data that are used to create a report exist outside the company in the supplier's database. Storing data with the supplier makes it difficult for companies to access the data should a need arise. Having a system does not preclude the use of outside suppliers, but a company with a system usually integrates data collected by others into its own database—or at least makes provisions to access the information online.

EVALUATION IS NOT GETTING EASIER

Even as the systems and techniques to evaluate campaigns get more sophisticated, and presumably better, the task itself appears to get more difficult. The very companies that are likely to use the most advanced systems—the large consumer-goods companies—are the same companies that often employ the strategy of surrounding the consumer with myriad points of brand contact. Not surprisingly, many of these points of contact include nontraditional media that often do not lend themselves to measurement. Advertising, along with other communications tools (such as sales promotions, product placement, and public relations), is only one of a number of factors that can influence sales.

Companies such as Procter & Gamble, Quaker Oats, and Kraft General Foods have fairly sophisticated and proprietary systems to evaluate their campaigns. However, it is doubtful that even these companies have obtained the Holy Grail of campaign measurement—a true measure tracing a direct causal relationship between the campaign and sales.

TOWARD A SYSTEM FOR EVALUATING A CAMPAIGN'S EFFECTIVENESS

A comprehensive, detailed system to evaluate the effectiveness of a campaign is beyond the scope of this book, but we can outline some of the fundamental elements involved. Assuming a decision is made to proceed with the development of a system, one can be organized along the lines of the questions when and what to measure. We suspect many, if not most, companies organize their systems based on what they want to measure. These systems focus directly on what the research is supposed to accomplish and are objective oriented. Although this is a sensible approach, many companies, and especially students working on class projects, may find a task-oriented approach to be more practical. *This approach organizes evaluative measures chronologically, according to when the need typically arises to evaluate some aspect of the campaign.* We will now look at the various stages in a marketing communications campaign and examine some of the more common evaluative measures companies use, including what typically gets measured.

WHEN AND WHAT TO MEASURE

There are at least four stages of a campaign during which it is common to use some type of evaluative testing:

- At the beginning of the creative process (concept testing)
- In the middle and at the end of the creative process (copy testing)
- While the advertising is appearing in the media (concurrent testing)
- After the advertising has appeared in the media (posttesting)

Concept Testing

Following the situation analysis and until just before the actual ads are completed, planners often use some type of evaluative testing to get a feel for whether their ideas and strategies are likely to be on target and on strategy. The purpose of this type of testing is to get feedback from the consumers before a lot of time, money, and effort are spent on producing expensive ads.

What to Test. Concept testing is as much a check on the strategic development of the campaign as it is on specific executions. The testing tends to be somewhat exploratory in nature, although tentative ideas and concepts have been developed. Among the concepts typically evaluated are product names, slogans, campaign themes, advertising claims or promises, and the basic product positioning (sometimes referred to as the product concept definition). Later, during the copy-testing phase, specific variables that affect the execution of an ad can be tested (such as the selection of music, choice of words, use of art or humor, and the arrangement of these elements). This is also a good stage to evaluate campaign spokespeople. Celebrity endorsers usually command substantial fees; it is imperative to get some feedback on them before contracts are signed.

How to Test. Because concept testing tends to be exploratory in nature, the research techniques tend to be more qualitative than other types of testing. Among the more common ways of gathering information are the following:

- Focus groups
- Mall intercepts
- One-on-one interviews

One of the keys to obtaining information that is meaningful is be sure that the subjects in the test groups are representative of the target audience. Although widely used, focus groups are not generally satisfactory for checking communications or getting evaluative feedback. The interaction that takes place among respondents in developmental research (see Chapters 2 and 3) is desirable. In evaluative research, it is better to measure the effects of an ad on an individual consumer without the potential biases that sometimes result from one member of a group influencing another. Because of potential problems with interaction effects, mall intercepts and one-on-one interviews are generally more appropriate for concept testing.

Within the various testing situations there are a wide variety of techniques and tests to elicit information. Some tests and techniques, such as projective tests and laddering techniques, are more commonly used in developmental research, although they are occasionally used for concept testing. Some of the more common tests and techniques are:

- Projective tests
- Laddering techniques
- Structured and semistructured questionnaires
- Attitude and opinion scales
- Paired comparison tests

The information obtained from concept testing is generally used to firm up message strategy as well as to evaluate key elements within the strategy. The next step in the campaign is to execute the strategy by developing individual ads or promotional pieces.

Copy Testing

Most of the evaluative testing conducted by companies and their agencies falls into the category of copy testing. It can range from consumer feedback to rough ads obtained from informal interviews to the quantitative measurement of consumer responses to finished commercials. Because the testing takes place before the ads are run in the media, it is often referred to as **pretesting.**

Purpose.   Copy testing is used primarily to predict the effectiveness of an ad or a campaign. A secondary objective is to help understand the ad so it can be developed further. Over the years, many people have questioned the efficacy of copy testing, challenging either specific tests or the concept in general. To assess the value of these tests, the American Research Foundation sponsored a massive project in which it conducted between 12,000 and 15,000 interviews. Called the ARF Copy Research Validity Project, it was completed in 1990, after nearly eight years of struggling with the formidable problems associated with such an ambitious project. Although the study is getting somewhat old, no other has replaced it in terms of scope or influence. Although the project limited itself to television commercials, the general conclusion was that copy testing works. The study confirmed what many copy researchers had theorized: Copy testing is efficacious in identifying television commercials that generate sales.[8] Although this is helpful information to know, the typical copy test is not able to establish a causal link between an ad and sales.

Value.   The value of most copy tests is derived from the ability of the test to evaluate the effectiveness of an ad defined in terms of some criterion such as awareness, persuasion, or likeability (also referred to as liking). After a system is used repeatedly, average scores, or norms, are quickly developed by product type. Frequently, the research company supplying the service provides these norms. Each ad is tested against a norm to assess its effectiveness. As planners become familiar and comfortable with a technique, the results may be used to help make decisions. However, smart managers know that a copy test should only be used as a guide to decision making and not as a substitute for executive and creative judgment.

What to Test.   There are two types of copy tests: diagnostics, to help planners understand the strengths and weaknesses of an ad, and evaluative tests, which commonly focus on one of three criteria: communication playback, likeability, and persuasion.

Although many copy tests have diagnostic value, there is a particular type of copy test that is referred to as diagnostics. We'll look at an example of a general diagnostic test and then consider two more specialized tests: frame-by-frame diagnostics and picture sort techniques.

Diagnostics is a type of testing designed to improve ads. It is rare, however, that a diagnostic test tells a creative person how to improve a commercial. Diagnostics may suggest what is wrong with an ad, but it is highly unlikely to suggest what to do to correct it. These tests are frequently used to pretest television commercials at the rough stage. In a typical 30-second commercial there are numerous scenes, and within each scene there is a variety of elements that can be manipulated. Tests that are designed to improve specific elements within a commercial are sometimes referred to as **executional diagnostics.** In a general diagnostics test, viewers are exposed to a television commercial and then given a series of open-ended questions about reactions to specific elements as well as structural statements to which they indicate their agreement or disagreement.

EXAMPLE

Please answer the following questions.

1. What were your overall feelings as you were watching the commercial?
2. Can you describe what happened in the commercial from beginning to end?
3. What things did you learn or find out?
4. What did you like or dislike about the commercial?
5. How do you feel about specific elements in the commercial?

Using the following scale Agree Completely (1), Agree Somewhat (2), Disagree Somewhat (3), Disagree Completely (4), please indicate how each statement describes the way you feel.[9]

1. This ad told me something new about the product that I didn't know before. _____
2. This ad helps me find the product that I want. _____
3. This ad is funny or clever. _____
4. I learned a lot from this advertising. _____
5. I find this advertising artistic. _____

Although companies generally use diagnostics to help them understand and improve ads, the ARF Copy Research Validity Project found that the responses to some of the statements in a diagnostics test helped companies to predict fairly well which commercials would be most successful in generating sales. The most useful questions were those that dealt with the information content of the ads, such as questions 1, 2, and 4.

Frame-by-frame diagnostics are frequently used to help marketers understand why a television commercial has not tested very well on some other type of test, such as one dealing with recall or persuasion. Even simple commercials are often compilations of separate elements. These tests can provide clues as to which parts of a commercial are connecting with viewers and which parts of a commercial have "dead spots." Before rejecting a commercial, managers will sometimes see if there are any parts worth salvaging. Frame-by-frame tests evaluate consumers' reactions to the individual scenes in a television commercial. In a typical test, a copy-testing organization, such as VIEWFACTS, invites consumers to a minitheater to view a series of commercials. The respondents are instructed to depress buttons indicating how much they like or dislike what they are seeing. Later, an interviewer queries audience members about the reasons for their reactions to specific scenes. Frame-by-frame tests provide the researcher with clues as to the parts within a commercial that work well and those that do not. These clues can be used to provide guidance to creative personnel for further copy development.[10]

Picture sort techniques is another diagnostic tool that can be used to understand the inner workings of a television commercial. One of the most widely known techniques uses a deck of still photographs taken from the television commercial being tested. Respondents are recruited and screened for target audience membership at mall intercept locations.

Respondents are given a randomized deck of photographs and are asked to sort them into two piles—the pictures they remember seeing and the pictures they do not. Researchers then assign a value to each scene in the commercial according to the extent to which respondents indicate they saw it in the ad. A high score indicates that a high percentage of respondents remember seeing the particular scene. An analyst can then plot these scores from the beginning of a commercial to its end to provide insight about the attention value of each scene as the commercial unfolds.[11]

An effective commercial is one in which each scene has a consistently high level of recognition. It yields a line on a graph that is smooth rather than choppy or disjointed. The smooth transition from one image to another is called "visual connectedness." The validity of this approach was verified by establishing a positive relationship between visually connected ads and ads that were independently judged to be persuasive by American Research System (ARS), one of the most respected copy-testing services in the United States.[12]

Communication playback is a type of test that can be used for both diagnostic and evaluative purposes. The intent of this test is to evaluate whether the essential points within an ad have been communicated. The ability of respondents to recall specific information about an ad is an important measure of effectiveness. Communication playback tests can also be used as a diagnostic tool. Viewers are often asked to re-create visual and verbal elements of an ad in their own words.[13] Researchers usually pay special attention to the consumers' recall of the brand name, specific attributes or qualities of the product, the main selling message, and reactions to music, special effects, main characters, key phrases, and story lines. In the ARF Copy Research Validity Project, the researchers asked the following question on a paper-and-pencil test: "Of course, the purpose of the commercial was to get you to buy the product. Other than that, what was the main selling point of the commercial?"[14]

Communication playback information can be obtained using a variety of methods, including focus group discussion (although, as previously stated, it is a misuse of focus groups), one-on-one interviews, mall intercepts, and dummy advertising vehicles. In the latter method, a dummy vehicle can be made to look like an actual magazine, complete with editorial matter and ads. Subjects are asked to read the vehicle as they would normally read a magazine. The interviewer then questions the respondent on a number of criteria, including recall, main selling message, and general opinions and attitudes. Dummy vehicles are used widely because they present a fairly realistic situation to subjects.

A related type of measure can also be obtained via physiological methods. A mechanical device known as a tachistoscope, or *t*-scope, measures respondents' perceptions of various elements in print ads. This instrument is like a slide projector with a shutter attached to it that is able to vary the amount of time a picture is shown on a screen. In the beginning of the test, the image of the ad will flash on the screen so briefly that it will be below a respondent's threshold of awareness (i.e., subliminal). Gradually, as the researcher lengthens the amount of time the image is on the screen, viewers are increasingly able to perceive various elements or messages in the ad, including the brand name, product attributes, and the main selling message. Interviewers then question respondents, as they do with dummy vehicles. The *t*-scope does not appear to be used as much today as it has been in the past.

An eye-movement camera is another mechanical device that can provide an analyst with some insight into how consumers perceive elements within a print ad. There are a couple of variations on the basic methodology. Usually, viewers are seated in front of a desk with a large mechanical device placed on top. While they are viewing test ads, a sensor directs an almost invisible beam of infrared light at one of the viewer's eyes. The beam then follows the viewer's eye and superimposes the path the eyes follow onto a layout of the ad. An analyst is then able to determine which element in the ad first received the viewer's attention (i.e., the dominant point of entry), which path the viewer followed next within the ad and, finally, how much time each element was viewed.

If an analyst wanted to know whether a sexy-looking model attracted attention to the product (rather than detracted from it), an eye-movement camera could provide an objective measurement that might differ from a viewer's verbal reconstruction of viewing patterns. The chief objection to the use of the camera is that viewers are tested under highly artificial conditions rather than as they would normally react. Recent technological developments enable the camera to be concealed within a reading lamp so that unobtrusive measurements can be taken. It remains to be seen if this technological development will overcome researchers' resistance to its use.

Likeability measures appear to be increasing in usage. If this is really occurring, it is unclear whether it is because of a trend toward more entertainment-oriented ads or because of evidence that suggests that likeability measures do a good job of measuring advertising effectiveness. In the ARF Copy Research Validity Project, "the most surprising finding in the study was the strong relationship found to exist between the likeability of the copy and its effects on sales." As the researchers pointed out, it was generally believed that the function of copy was to sell, and whether the copy was likable was unimportant. The "ARF study strongly suggests that ads that are liked outsell those that are not."[15]

Likeability measures are very similar to attitudinal measures in that both types of measurement probe the evaluative dimension of what an ad means to a consumer. There are many direct and indirect questions that can be asked to probe likeability. In the ARF study, the question that was successful at predicting sales was fairly straightforward and is as follows:[16]

Thinking about the commercial you just saw, please tell me which of the statements on this card best describes your feelings about the commercial.

I liked it very much. _____
I liked it. _____
I neither liked it nor disliked it. _____
I disliked it. _____
I disliked it very much. _____

Of all the pretest measures, **persuasion measures** are probably the ones most respected by people in the advertising business. To be persuaded is to be won over to another point of view. The viewpoint of interest to people in advertising is consumers' interest in obtaining or purchasing a particular brand. Although there are numerous variations of a persuasion test, the basic design is used typically to evaluate television commercials and is fairly simple.

Subjects are asked to indicate their brand preference or usage before exposure to a series of television commercials. After exposure, they are retested and asked to indicate their brand preferences should they win a drawing giving them a market basket full of various products, including brands appearing in the tested commercials. Any shift in brand preference is assumed to be a function of exposure to the viewed ads. There are at least several companies that offer this service: Mapes and Ross, which offers a parallel system for evaluating magazine ads; ASI Market Research Inc., which conducts tests with viewers in their own homes via cable channels; McCollum/Spielman, which also offers a parallel system for testing magazines; and American Research Systems (ARS), the successor to Schwerin Research, the company that pioneered the basic system now widely in use.

Television Tests

Testing television commercials can be very expensive, so researchers test them in a wide range of forms. The closer a commercial looks to its finished form, the more realistic the test is likely to be. However, relatively unfinished commercials do a surprisingly good job of serving as a surrogate for the final ad, especially in view of the amount of money spent in producing them. The following are among the most common stages of unfinished television commercials used in tests:[17]

- **Storyboards**—a series of visual frames and script of key audio used to represent a proposed commercial
- **Animatic**—film or videotape of a series of drawings with audio used to represent a proposed commercial
- **Photomatic**—film or videotape of a series of photographs with audio used to represent a proposed commercial
- **Ripamatic**—footage taken from other existing commercials and spliced together (also called stealamatics)
- **Liveamatic**—rough film or videotape of live talent photographed for a proposed commercial; can be close to a finished commercial but does not necessarily use actual sets or talent who will be used in the finished commercial

■METHODOLOGY AND PRACTICES

Providing copy-testing services to advertisers and their agencies has become a highly competitive business. Not surprisingly, there are disputes and controversy over techniques, methodology, and standards—in effect, over which supplier has the better service. In an effort to resolve some common concerns about copy testing, a coalition of 21 major advertising agencies got together and reached "a high degree of consensus" on nine fundamental principles underlying a good copy-testing system. The coalition was called PACT, an acronym for Positioning Advertising Copy Testing.[18] The PACT principles appear in boldface:

1. **A good copy-testing system provides measurements that are relevant to the objectives of the advertising.** This principle underscores the importance of evaluating a test based on its ability to assess an ad's potential to achieve stated objectives.

2. **A good copy-testing system is one that requires agreement about how the results will be used in advance of each specific test.** This principle emphasizes the importance of specifying how the test will be used in advance of the results.

3. **A good copy-testing system provides multiple measurements because single measurements are generally inadequate to assess the performance of an ad.** This principle calls attention to the difficulty of separating out the effects of advertising from the many other factors influencing sales. Because there is no universally accepted single measurement that can serve as a surrogate for sales, multiple measures are necessary.

4. **A good copy-testing system is based on a model of human response to communication—the reception of a stimulus, the comprehension of a stimulus, and the response to the stimulus.** This principle recognizes that ads usually function on several levels:

   - On the "eyes" and "ears"—it must be received (reception)
   - On the "mind"—it must be understood (comprehension)
   - On the "heart"—it must make an impression (response)

   Therefore, a testing system should strive to answer questions on more than one level.

5. **A good copy-testing system allows for consideration of whether the advertising stimulus should be exposed more than once.** This principle endorses the idea that in some test situations the learning of test material is much higher after two exposures than it is for one, indicating that there are situations where a single exposure test could be inadequate.

6. **A good copy-testing system recognizes that the more finished a piece of copy is, the more soundly it can be evaluated and requires, as a minimum, that alternative executions be tested in the same degree of finish.** This principle is concerned with the biases that can creep into a test when alternative executions are tested in different stages of finish.

7. **A good copy-testing system provides controls to avoid the biasing effects of the exposure context.** This principle points out the potential biasing effects of the context in which a program is viewed, such as an off-air test versus an on-air test, a clutter reel of commercials versus a program context, and one specific program context versus another specific program context.

8. **A good copy-testing system is one that takes into account basic considerations of sample definition.** This principle emphasizes the importance of proper sampling procedures, especially ones dealing with the size and representativeness of the sample.

9. **A good copy-testing system demonstrates reliability and validity empirically.** This principle underscores the importance of testing systems that yield the same results each time the advertising is tested (i.e., reliability). For validity, this principle encourages users to provide results or evidence about validity, "which are relevant to marketplace performance." The PACT agencies were concerned that there were many systems in use for which no evidence of validity was provided.

CONCURRENT TESTING

This type of testing refers to research that takes place while the campaign is running in the marketplace. There are two basic types: tracking studies and coincidental studies. Of the two, tracking studies are far more important.

Tracking Studies

Tracking studies are often a major part of the management of a marketing communication campaign. Although the most important tracking a company can do is to monitor sales, a tracking study usually refers to some type of consumer survey. Tracking studies are a way to monitor the pulse of a campaign. If there is some aspect of the plan or some area within the marketplace that is doing particularly well, an alert, well-informed company can often increase its marketing advantage. On the other hand, the marketplace can be brutal to companies that fail to respond quickly to their problems.

Tracking studies work best when they are part of an ongoing information-gathering system. The basic idea behind tracking is to keep in close contact with what consumers are thinking, feeling, and doing. Companies are interested in information like the following.

Awareness.   Companies want to know about brand awareness and top-of-mind awareness as well as consumers' awareness of new information on the product, such as new features or a change in the positioning of a brand.

Attitude.   Companies like to know a consumer's attitude toward the product because of the widespread belief that attitudes strongly affect the consumer's predisposition to buy a product. The nature of the relationship between an attitude and purchase behavior can vary considerably.

Communication Playback.   Basically, companies want to know if they are getting the right message across. As companies employ new and different strategies, tracking studies enable them to closely monitor whether they are achieving their objectives. Traditionally, very simple recall measures were used, but in recent years there has been diminished interest in recall.

Reported Product Usage.   Companies regularly monitor sales on a daily, weekly, monthly, and yearly basis. Some of this information comes from within the organization. Large consumer-goods companies also supplement their databases with information from syndicated research services. Tracking studies are used to understand the nature of the sales taking place. For new products, consumers are asked whether their purchases are new (or trial) or repeat. For existing products, consumers are asked about their frequency of use.

Product Satisfaction. With the increased emphasis on relationship marketing, many companies are sensitive about satisfying consumers and want to know if consumers like their products and their advertising. Among the important measures of consumer satisfactions are questions focusing on consumers' intentions to repurchase a product.

To obtain the above information, companies either conduct in-house testing or use outside suppliers. Agencies do not typically provide this type of research. A company usually sets up a system to gather information on a regular and periodic basis. The system can function on an ongoing basis (weekly, even daily), or it can gather data in large blocs of interviews at a time, called **waves.**

Companies either set up their own panels or use ones set up by research firms. A problem with panels occurs when consumers become overly sensitized to participating in the study, or have reactive effects, and respond in ways that differ from the consumers they are supposed to represent. Some of the more popular tracking methods companies use to gather the information include:

- **Telephone Interviews**—This method is probably the most popular because it is quick, easy, and inexpensive. Consumers can be asked a full range of questions, from those dealing with awareness to questions on product satisfaction.
- **E-mail Interviews**—This method has been rapidly increasing in popularity because like the telephone it is quick, easy, and inexpensive. Moreover, e-mail messages lend themselves to replies more so than phone messages. One major disadvantage is that there are still a large number of people that cannot be reached by e-mail.
- **Diaries**—Consumers are asked to keep a record of various activities such as brands purchased, brand switches, use of coupons, and exposure to competitive promotions.
- **Pantry Checks**—This method provides much the same kind of brand usage information as diaries. Although this method is more expensive to use, the information obtained is more reliable.
- **Mall Intercepts**—Although this method is used widely for other types of consumer research, it is used only occasionally for tracking studies. Its chief advantage is that it is one of the easiest and quickest ways to obtain large quantities of information.
- **Product Audits and Scanner Data**—Traditionally, companies had supplemented internally generated sales data with marketplace product-movement data from research firms such as ACNielsen. These firms were able to estimate product movement by monitoring the flow of goods in and out of retail locations and area warehouses. Estimates were based on location visits as well as store and warehouse records. Today, the information is based largely on scanner data.

The two dominant firms in the business of gathering product and scanner data are ACNielsen and Information Resources, Inc. (IRI). Both firms offer much of the same type of information. In the interest of brevity, we will look at Nielsen, the larger of the two companies.

ACNielsen is the world's largest marketing research company. Although most people are familiar with the Nielsen name from its media research unit, it earns most of its revenue from marketing research services. Nielsen is a true information conglomerate in that it offers services too numerous to explain in one chapter (let alone in a small section). The major users of its syndicated measurements are large companies (such as food manufacturers and those producing health and beauty aids). Nielsen monitors retail activity at the store level through the electronic capture of all UPC bar-coded transactions recorded via scanning technology. Some stores are also measured with physical audits. The basic system is called SCANTRACK, and a related system is called PROCISION. Generally speaking, SCANTRACK is the service that provides information for food, grocery, and general-merchandise manufacturers; and PROCISION is the service for health- and beauty-aids manufacturers. Companies buy information on the United States as a whole or any of 50 major markets. The heart of the SCANTRACK system is a sample of 3,000 supermarkets with more than $2 million in all-commodity volume (ACV, or the total amount of sales in a given category).

Nielsen strives to be a full-service market research company providing information on all the major elements in the marketing mix. Some of the information Nielsen provides can be summarized as follows:

- **Product**—Provides sales figures for specific categories for the total U.S. market, each of the 50 major markets, and customized geographic trading areas. Sales figures include those for all significant brands in the ACV.
- **Pricing**—Provides information on the prices retailers charge for the brands in an ACV. This information can be broken down into types of retailers, such as supermarkets, mass merchandisers, drugstores, warehouse clubs, convenience stores, and independent drug or grocery stores.
- **Distribution**—Provides information on how a category is performing within a specific retail account or type of store versus the market. Also provides information on which key items are handled in the market but not in certain retail accounts. ACV is generally expressed as a percentage of the sales volume in a product category that can be accounted for by stores that distribute the product. If a particular store or chain has an ACV of 50% in a market, that means it sells 50% of all the products in its category in that particular market. ACV indicates the extent to which one's product is available to consumers.
- **Promotion**—Provides information on the amount of merchandising support (e.g., features and displays) to brands and categories. The media research unit provides information on ratings, and Nielsen Monitor Plus provides information on media occurrence (also called incidence), expenditures, and ad descriptions for network television. Nielsen Monitor Plus also provides occurrence data for national and local newspapers (top 50), outdoor, freestanding inserts, and magazines (national, Sunday, and top 50 local).

Coincidental Studies

Coincidental studies, another form of concurrent testing, are designed primarily to evaluate or measure advertising and media usage while consumers are exposed to the media. The telephone interview is the principal means by which information is obtained. This method used to be called the telephone coincidental method. Interviewers usually ask respondents questions pertaining to what they were doing just before they answered the phone. Its chief advantage is the reduction in measurement error due to memory loss. The use of this technique in recent years has diminished considerably.

POSTTESTING

The distinction between posttesting and concurrent testing is mostly semantic, but it is also traditional. Essentially, both types refer to testing for the effects of an ad after it has appeared in the media. Posttesting usually refers to testing at the end of a campaign, whereas concurrent testing generally refers to testing that takes place in an ongoing campaign. Posttesting is done for two basic reasons: (1) measuring the effects of a campaign provides a rigorous, objective way to assess the performance of the individuals, including agencies, who have worked on the campaign and (2) a well-conceived testing program can provide benchmarks against which future campaigns can be developed.

From an operational point of view, it is important for management to have a thorough understanding of which aspects of the campaign have gone well, which should be replaced or improved, and which should be avoided in the future. This understanding extends to the people working on the campaign, including those at the advertising agency. By establishing benchmarks based on past performances, management can use the information to fine-tune day-to-day operations as well as to integrate the information into the strategic foundation for the planning of the next campaign.

Posttesting can be divided into two types: tests measuring communication effects and those measuring behavioral effects. The following are among the most popular criteria used for posttesting:

- **Recognition** (a communication effect)
- **Recall** (a communication effect)
- **Attitudes** and **awareness** (communications effects)
- **Sales** (behavioral effects)
- **Inquiries** (behavioral effects)

Recognition tests are some of the most widely used forms of posttesting, especially for print ads. The *Starch Readership Report,* offered by Starch INRA Hooper, is a popular test of this type. The basic technique involves sending out a battery of interviewers the day after an issue of a magazine has hit the newsstands. A minimum of 100 readers of each sex who indicate that they have read the publication are interviewed. The interviewer goes through the issue page by page and asks the interviewee to respond to certain questions about each ad as a whole and various elements within the ad such as the headline, illustration, copy blocks, and logo. The test produces the following scores for each ad in the issue:

- **Noted**—The percentage of issue readers who remembered having seen the ad previously.
- **Seen Associated**—The percentage of readers who remembered seeing some part of the ad that clearly indicated the brand name or advertiser.
- **Read Most**—The percentage who read 50% or more of the copy in the ad.
- **Signature**—The percentage of readers who remembered seeing the brand name or logo.

A recognition test is a memory test. As we previously pointed out, it is based on the assumption that an ad cannot affect a purchase decision if consumers cannot remember the advertising. However, even though consumers may not remember a specific ad, they may have internalized its message. So an ad with a low recognition score does not necessarily mean the ad has failed. Another limitation of the Starch service is that its study is not conducted on targeted consumers; companies generally want information on their target audience. Unless the readership of the magazine closely approximates the company's target audience, the information may not be usable.

For all its limitations, the Starch service is still used, partly because it is relatively inexpensive and partly because Starch is the grandfather of all advertising research companies and many people are familiar with it.

Recall tests are a form of posttesting that appears to be on the decline. There are two basic types: unaided recall, which is similar to fill-in-the-blank tests, and aided recall, in which a respondent is asked to recall an ad as an interviewer provides subtle cues to aid the respondent's memory.

Gallup and Robinson is a company that offers posttesting services for both magazines and television. Its InTeleTest service is a test based in part on recall that is designed to provide at least four measures of the impact of a television commercial:

- **Intrusiveness**—This measure is an indicator of the commercial's ability to get the viewer's attention. It is defined as the percentage of respondents who can describe the commercial accurately the day after exposure.
- **Idea Communication**—This measure is defined as the percentage of respondents who can recall the commercial, including specific sales points.
- **Persuasion**—This is determined by a pretest and posttest measurement of respondents' "favorable buying attitude." The pretest questions about attitude and awareness are administered to respondents during a telephone call inviting them to be in the test. The following day, each respondent is given the same set of questions, and any change in attitude represents a measure of persuasion.
- **Commercial Reaction**—This measure looks at the degree to which consumers like a commercial (as measured on a 5-point scale) and the degree to which consumers agree or disagree on the excellence of a commercial (also measured on a 5-point scale).[19]

The Gallup and Robinson Rapid Ad Measurement (RAM) is one of the best known of the magazine-aided recall tests. The test produces measurement scores similar to those obtained for the company's InTeleTest television service: proven name registration, idea communication, favorable buying attitude, and net effectiveness.[20]

Over the years, recall tests have been one of the most widely used forms of posttesting. There are indications that recall will not be as popular in the future. One of the more widely used recall measures of the 1980s, the DAR (day after recall) measure, offered by Burke Marketing Research, is no longer in use. Burke sold its commercial evaluation business to ASI, which incorporated it into its Apex system, which measures persuasion. The separate services are now called Recall Plus and Persuasion Plus.

There have been numerous articles questioning the value of recall testing, especially as compared to persuasion measures. One of the strongest articles was by Gibson, who summed up his analysis and review of the literature on the recall/persuasion controversy as follows:

> Our summary can be brief because the record on recall is so clear. We know that recall data are inherently weak. We know that the theory on which recall data are based is empirically shaky. We know that the evidence for the validity of recall is—to be charitable— "checkered." This "checkered" validity of recall is in striking contrast to the evidence for the validity of persuasion.
>
> We may not know the answer to the longest playing controversy in all of marketing research, but we do know what the answer is not—and it's not recall.[21]

Recall measures, though still widely used, appear to be on the decline. Perhaps because some of the negative publicity directed at the measure focused on the word *recall,* some systems use the term *communication playback* instead. The decline in the use of recall measures may also be in part because of the overall decline in posttesting. Still, there is a long tradition of using recall measures. Researchers are familiar with the term and have developed norms for its usage. Although its use may decline in popularity, it will likely remain in use for some time.

Attitude, awareness, and likeability tests appear to be used more at the pretesting and tracking stages than as posttest measurements. This timing is due—at least in part—to the widespread availability of syndicated services that measure other posttesting criteria, such as recall and persuasion. Syndicated studies are usually cheaper than customized testing, although the latter can be conducted with a minimum of ease and expense, depending on the extensiveness of the sample. Syndicated sources usually provide ad norms as part of the service so that advertisers can compare the relative effectiveness of their advertising against their competition's.

Attitude testing is conducted because many advertisers believe that favorable attitudes are a necessary precondition to purchasing. Although this point is widely questioned, many companies try to affect attitude change as part of their marketing communications strategy, and testing for this effect can be viewed as part of their evaluative program. Companies can use a wide variety of tests to measure for attitudes, awareness, and likeability, including the ones discussed earlier in this chapter and in Chapter 3.

Many advertisers believe that measuring communications' effects is not a valid indicator of advertising effectiveness. They may believe, as does Josh

McQueen (former director of research of Leo Burnett U.S.A.), that testing recall and persuasion is not relevant to what advertisers want to accomplish. McQueen argues for measuring clear behavioral objectives.[22] For most advertisers, this means drawing a causal relationship between advertising and sales or inquiries, the two most common behavioral measures. For many companies, the task is not as difficult to accomplish as one might assume, judging from what is written about this problem in textbooks and journals.

One reason so little is written about successful measurement systems is that they are proprietary, and are likely to work only in very specific situations. Thus, even if they were published, the applicability of the techniques employed would be limited. Moreover, a test's usefulness or value to a company may be more as a partial indicator of a campaign's success rather than as the one indicator of an ad's or a campaign's ability to stimulate sales. Commercial testing organizations face a near impossible task of developing systems that can be of value to a wide variety of companies and still be without some methodological flaw. Almost every technique or test that has been described in the literature about testing has some limitation.

Using sales as a criterion for the posttest measurement of an ad or a campaign's effectiveness is done widely. Most of this evaluation, however, is informal. For example, McDonald's is able to monitor the sales of its stores on a daily basis. The day after a new ad or campaign breaks in the media, the company can "feel" and measure the impact in the marketplace. From a methodological point of view, all kinds of factors could be responsible for the ad's success or lack thereof, but from McDonald's perspective, its experience enables the company to feel confident about separating the winning ads from the also-rans.

Companies do use more sophisticated techniques. Typically, these are quantitative models that include gross rating points and persuasion measures as key variables influencing sales. The companies may develop these advertising/sales models internally, or may rely on an outside supplier such as ACNielsen, especially because Nielsen collects most of the data needed as input for these models. Nielsen has a special unit that offers customized models to clients. This unit largely replaced one of the most talked-about testing procedures in recent years: single-source data measurement.

Single-source measurement used scanner technology and media exposure data to monitor product movement (i.e., sales), sales promotions, and advertising exposure from the same panel of respondents. Because all of the information was obtained from the same set of respondents, an analyst could evaluate which ads and promotions appeared to have the strongest effect on sales. In the late 1980s and early 1990s, single-source data analysis was widely lauded as the closest technique yet to a Holy Grail of advertising measurement. By 1993, interest had diminished considerably, and the largest of the systems, based on Nielsen's SCANTRACK data, was officially discontinued.

What happened? Within a span of about seven years, there were three systems from which companies could choose: InfoScan by Information Resources, Inc., a variation of Behavior Scan, the first service offered by IRI or any company; SCANTRACK by ACNielsen; and SAMSCAN, which was the last system in and the first system out of the marketplace, offered by an alliance between the SAMI Corporation and Arbitron.[23]

These systems were able to do a sophisticated job of isolating the effects of advertising and other promotional tools on sales. Because of these systems, many large companies, such as Procter & Gamble, Helene Curtis, and Campbell Soup, were able to evaluate their promotional campaigns in terms of behavioral criteria, such as sales and market share. However, the single-source research systems that were able to produce these results did not offer bulletproof evaluations.

Although these systems did a fine job of tracing the short-term effect on sales of a particular ad, promotion, or campaign, they were unable to assess the longer-term effects on brand equity. Moreover, for many companies, the quality of the information was less important than the cost and time it took to complete a market test.

Along with a number of concerns about methodology, there were some practical concerns that probably led to the downfall of single-source systems. In the 1990s, companies were desperately trying to cut costs because of a sluggish economy. Nielsen's system was not only expensive to buy, it also was apparently prohibitive to maintain. The expense of installing and maintaining people meters in particular was too costly in view of declining sales. Moreover, some of the clients that were using the SCANTRACK system contracted with Nielsen for other services from their Advanced Analytics unit, such as customized modeling systems. Media buyers also failed to embrace Nielsen's system because the SCANTRACK system provided target audience information on a household level, and buyers preferred the information on a person or individual level. Finally, even though a company might receive usable information about what had occurred, there was no guarantee that what was successful in the past would operate the same way in the future. In the end, the Nielsen system that had shown so much promise ended without any fanfare. However, in 2005, Arbitron is reviving interest in single-source measurement and has a new model in development.

Using inquiries as a behavioral measure is one of the oldest and easiest ways to evaluate advertising. Adding a coupon to an ad or using 800 phone numbers are two methods of inviting inquiries and providing an easy way of comparing one ad to another, especially through the use of split-run techniques. In a typical example, alternate copies of a single issue of a newspaper or magazine will carry one ad or another that is being tested. The ad that produces the most coupons returned or 800 calls is judged the most effective. Companies may also track which inquiries were later converted into sales.

The major disadvantage of inquiry testing is the difficulty in relating inquiries to sales or communications objectives, particularly when it is uncertain if the coupon clipper or 800 caller is a typical consumer. Inquiry tests are a popular method with industrial advertisers who use the inquiries as a prospect list for their sales forces.

▌EVALUATING OTHER MARKETING COMMUNICATIONS TOOLS

The evaluation of other promotional tools, such as sales promotions, public relations, and direct mail, is a complex but often neglected part of a marketing communications campaign. Measuring the effects of sales promotions should be more than counting coupon redemptions, measuring the value of the public relations program should be more than keeping track of exposures in the media, and evaluating direct mail should be more than checking sales figures. Many of the techniques discussed earlier in this chapter with sometimes only slight modification can be used to evaluate the complete marketing communications plan. Indeed, many of the research companies mentioned in this chapter routinely test other elements of the promotional mix besides advertising. Readers are encouraged to consult publications in the marketing area for more details.

A FINAL NOTE ON EVALUATION

Throughout this book we have stressed the importance of looking ahead and thinking strategically. We recognize that most of the people who read this book will not be using the principles, procedures, and sources discussed in this chapter, at least not in the near future. This information will have applicability in the years ahead. We also believe that a sound system of evaluation should be built into all strategic plans. Such a system should improve efficiency and effectiveness so that a firm can take full advantage of its marketing opportunity in the short run and develop new, market-winning strategies for the future.

CAMPAIGN PROGRESS CHECKLIST

At this point in the campaign you should generally be aware of the following points:

1. Evaluation can be a critical factor in marketing success.
2. Evaluation remains an inexact science because of the difficulty in isolating the effects of a marketing communication campaign on sales.
3. Research activities tend to be divided into developmental research, which is used to develop a campaign, and evaluative research, which is used to evaluate the effectiveness of the marketing communications campaign.
4. There are at least four stages during which evaluative testing commonly takes place.
5. Concept testing is used at the beginning of the creative process.
6. Copy testing is used in the middle and at the end of the creative process.
7. Concurrent testing takes place during the campaign.
8. Posttesting takes place after advertising has appeared in the media.
9. Although the focus of many of the tests in this chapter has been on advertising, many of the tests and procedures work well with other marketing communications tools.
10. A system of evaluation should be built into all strategic plans to improve the campaign's efficiency and effectiveness.

Notes and References

[1] J.J. Burnett, *Promotion Management* (Boston: Houghton Mifflin, 1993), p. 603.

[2] P. Kotler, *Marketing Management* (Englewood Cliffs, NJ: Prentice Hall, 1994), p. xxiv.

[3] G.E. Belch and M.A. Belch, *Advertising and Promotion: An Integrated Marketing Communications Perspective* (Homewood, IL: Irwin, 2004), pp. 621–624.

[4] "100 Leading National Advertisers: Ranked by Total U.S. Advertising Spending in 2001," *Advertising Age Online* (March 31, 2003). http://www.adage.com/page.cms?pageId=913

[5] Belch and Belch, *Advertising and Promotion,* p. 565.

[6] Kotler, *Marketing Management,* p. xxvi.

[7] Some of this material has been adapted from D.J. Curry, *The New Marketing Research Systems* (New York: John Wiley and Sons, 1993), p. 19.

[8] R.I. Haley and A.L. Baldinger, "The ARF Copy Research Validity Project," *Journal of Advertising Research* (April/May 1991), pp. 27–28.

[9] The directions and the statements here were adapted slightly from the ones used in the ARF Copy Research Validity Project.

[10] For more information, see W. Wells et al., *Advertising: Principles and Practice, 4th Ed.* (Upper Saddle River, NJ: Prentice Hall, 1998), pp. 621–622.

[11] C.E. Young and M. Robinson, "Guidelines: Tracking the Commercial Viewer's Wandering Attention," *Journal of Advertising Research* 27 (June–July 1987), pp. 15–16.

[12] C.E. Young and M. Robinson, "Visual Connectedness and Persuasion," *Journal of Advertising Research* 32 (March/April 1992), pp. 51–59.

[13] J. Haskins and A. Kendrick, *Successful Advertising Research Methods* (Lincolnwood, IL: NTC Business Books, 1993), p. 313.

[14] Haley and Baldinger, "The ARF Copy Research Validity Project," p. 18.

[15] Ibid., p. 29.

[16] Ibid., p. 18.

[17] These forms are adapted only slightly from the classification in the survey reported in K.W. King et al., "Pretesting TV Commercials: Method, Measures, and Changing Agency Roles," *Journal of Advertising* 22 (September 1993), p. 91.

[18] PACT-Positioning Advertising Copy Testing (The PACT Agencies Report, 1982), pp. 10–27. Also reprinted in the *Journal of Advertising.*

[19] For more information, see J.J. Davis, *Advertising Research Theory and Practice* (Upper Saddle River, NJ: Prentice Hall, 1997), p. 564.

[20] Ibid., p. 574.

[21] L.D. Gibson, "Not Recall," *Journal of Advertising Research* 23 (February/March 1983), p. 45. For other criticism, see also H.A. Zielske, "Does Day-After-Recall Penalize 'Feeling' Ads?" *Journal of Advertising Research* 22 (February/March 1982), pp. 19–22.

[22] J. McQueen, (1990, August/September). "The Different Ways Ads Work," *Journal of Advertising Research* 30 (August/September 1990), pp. 15–16.

[23] For more information on the early development of these systems, see Curry, *The New Marketing Research Systems,* pp. 66–74.

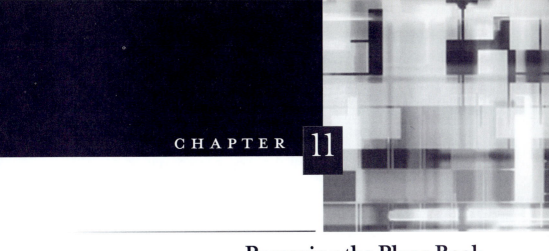

CHAPTER 11

Preparing the Plans Book

APPROACHING THE PLANS BOOK

Putting a plans book together can be a daunting task. Some of you may wonder how you will ever be able to get one finished. Trust us . . . you will. Take our advice, but be sure to leave room for your own way of presenting the material. You want this to be your plan, not ours. When you finish, you'll not only feel a sense of relief, but it will also likely leave you feeling empowered. And you will realize your next campaign is likely to be even *better.*

Approach this task systematically and carefully. Don't be meek about it. Throw yourself into this project with passion. These will be your ideas you're putting on paper. Let them reflect the full measure of your ability. However, profit from the accumulated wisdom of others. Even though this plan should consist of your ideas and work, consider letting it also reflect the procedures, ideas, and concepts we've presented in this book. It can work.

You should begin by thinking about just what it is your plans book is supposed to accomplish. First, think about its purpose. No two advertising situations are exactly alike and, therefore, no two plans books should be either. Your book should reflect who your client is, what the client's problem is, how you are going to solve the problem, and why your recommendations are superior to other possibilities. You want to demonstrate that you have a firm understanding of the client's current situation and the expertise and experience to achieve the objectives set forth in your recommendations.

Although plans books can differ, there is a general form beginners can follow. We provide a general outline in this chapter. Over the course of your career, some of your assignments might call for writing a full-blown plans book for a total marketing communications campaign, whereas others might require that you write only a fragment of a plan for a special project. Clients and situations vary. The people you will be working with will also change over time. Knowing the general form of a plans book will allow you to make adjustments as situations differ. Following are some situations for which you could be asked to write marketing communication recommendations.

- *A Special Project Involving a Small Client with a Limited Budget.* This also could be an issue advocacy campaign. Your plans book should be short, and focus on a smaller number of media and promotional opportunities. The budget will probably be limited, and even though you may not be able to afford a research or evaluation plan, follow the steps of the campaign process as best as you can.
- *The National Student Advertising Competition Sponsored by the American Advertising Federation (AAF's NSAC).* The competitive factor and the AAF's guidelines will dictate a particular type of plans book. This is a textbook situation in which you are expected to demonstrate that you can develop a complete marketing communications program. This competition provides a good opportunity to learn how to balance comprehensiveness with precision in writing a plans book.
- *A New Product Introduction.* Most of the marketing and advertising information will be entirely new. Our book has been designed to handle these situations. You can follow our recommendations from the analysis of primary and secondary research through strategic planning and tactical executions. Your written recommendations are likely to be quite comprehensive for a new product introduction. Appendices or optional fact books can supplement your written plan.
- *A Small Campaign.* Small campaigns are usually narrowly focused in terms of time, budget, and the target to whom the campaign will be directed. These kinds of assignments are quite common in advertising. Advertising agencies often have preprinted covers ready to go for the plans that are written for clients as part of a longer-running business relationship (as opposed to a new business presentation).
- *A Marketing Communication Campaign.* This requires knowledge and use of sales promotion, public relations, or direct marketing, or a combination of these skills, in addition to advertising. This situation is an ideal application for this text because it requires the broadest set of planning abilities.
- *A Local or Regional Campaign or Test Market Effort.* These situations have distinct limits, so be sure not to extend a test market or more limited campaign plan into a national campaign. Recognize the part of the total effort you are being asked to work on.
- *A Trade Campaign Aimed at Building Support among Distributors and Retailers.* This is another specialized situation. Know your client's needs. This is *not* a consumer situation. Chapter 8 on integrated communications provides a discussion of trade considerations and how marketing communications are used to build trade support. Be sure your plans book reflects these differences.

These are but a few possibilities. There are many variations on the above. For example, if the client sells a service, the principles are likely to remain the same, but the terminology will probably differ. The bottom line is that your plans book is the product of your thinking. It is what you say and why you say it that will make the difference. In fact, that has been the point of all the chapters in this text to this point: To provide you with the tools for arriving at your recommendations and developing the reasoning behind them.

PERSPECTIVE ON THE PLANS BOOK

Before you begin, consider how a plans book functions, including its limitations. First, there is no surefire formula for writing the plans book. There are guidelines, but be sure you adapt and extend our guidelines to your particular situation.

Second, your plans book will recommend that the client spend a considerable sum of money. Your thinking and presentation must be well organized and flow logically from problem analysis through strategic and tactical recommendations. Your reasoning should be apparent and well supported. Remember, you are asking for business. You have to establish client confidence in your plan.

Third, if you are pitching an account, the plans book will become the key document through which you will manage the campaign should you win the account. Ultimately, you will be working with a team of people from many departments who have to understand the details of the campaign plan. The plans book will provide the appropriate direction and standards for what needs to be a collaborative effort. Otherwise, the client will take its business elsewhere.

Fourth, a plans book should tell the client what is right and wrong with the current market situation, and what should be done to resolve the problems. *Clients want solutions—not simply ideas.* The plans book should include strategies and tactics recommended to correct the situation, or solve the problems. This approach is analogous to what you want from your doctor when you are ill. You want to know what's wrong and what to do about it. That's what your client wants too.[1]

WRITING THE PLANS BOOK

First, we recommend you defer preparing the cover, title page, table of contents, and executive summary until you have finished writing the body copy of your plan. Next, quickly get started.

INTRODUCTION

This section is optional. If you include an executive summary in your report, you won't need an introduction. Otherwise, the purpose of the introduction is simply to give the reader an overview of what he or she will be reading explained in very general terms, usually no more than a paragraph. Consider including the nature of the assignment (say, a marketing communication campaign for brand X), campaign length, and budgeted amount of money.

THE SITUATION ANALYSIS

Analyses of each of five subparts—company, consumer, market, product, and competition—are covered in the situation analysis. Each of these sections should interrelate with the others. In the event a different individual is assigned to each section, it is important to emphasize the importance of establishing who is covering each aspect of the various analyses. The idea is to avoid redundant information, an all-too-common problem in student group projects. A major question to consider is how to handle primary research.

Company Analysis

In many ways, the company analysis functions as the introduction to the campaign, but this should be kept relatively brief. You will have to gather more information, and understand more about your client than is necessary, to include in the plans book. **Never confuse what you need to know to produce a campaign with what you need to report to the client.** The bottom line is that the client needs to know that you understand the company, its mindset, where it has been, and where it wants to go. You don't want to write about these points extensively, but you do need to establish that you and the company are on the same wavelength. To convince the client that your team is the one it wants to work with, show the client how its problems are the same or different from those incurred by similar companies in the field. You might also include a special section called "Industry Analysis," or "Environmental Analysis." How important is it to set up a special section? It really depends on how much of the company's problems are a reflection of what is going on in the industry. At a minimum, you should refer to what's going on in the industry. In the company analysis, consider addressing the following points, not necessarily in the order listed below:

- The company culture and its mission
- A history of the company's problems
- Industry or generic demand trends
- Miscellaneous trends
- Company opportunities

Company Culture.   It's important to understand the kind of company you are dealing with. If the company has a mission statement, you may get an idea what it stands for and what it wants to pursue in terms of opportunities. Often, however, the mission statement doesn't help very much. Still, you need to understand the type of businesspeople with whom you are working. Are they conservative? Ambitious? Do they have specific ideas about how they want to grow?

   You probably won't put any of this information in your report, but you will want to keep this information in the back of your mind when you reach conclusions. For example, if you believe there is an opportunity for the company to venture out in a new direction, it's helpful to know how receptive the company is likely to be to new ideas. Keep in mind: Clients like to work with agencies they feel comfortable with, not necessarily the agency they feel will deliver the best work.

Company Problems.   Executives lose sleep over problems, even small ones. Your plan, in essence, is recommending that the client spend a significant sum of money. Convince your clients that you are at least aware of the situations that most concern them. Few things are more tiresome for a busy executive than to wade through page after page of material before he or she reaches the company's problems. If you don't convince your client from the get-go that you understand the company's problems, you run the risk that the executive will simply skim the pages until he or she finds the section on problems. Few problems are more serious than those associated with sales or profits. Arrange your plans book so that this material appears early on. It helps if you can show sales trends over a period of four or five years.

Industry or Generic Demand Trends.   Company problems are often influenced by trends that are endemic to the industry. It's important to show whether the company's problems are better or worse than the industry norm. If you can include sales data for either the industry or the generic category, this should provide some perspective on whether the solutions to the company's problems are related more to the industry's or whether the solution lies in what the company can do for itself. When you're reporting on generic trends, remember this material is related to but not quite the same as what you might cover in the competitive analysis. To be sure the information is covered only once, discuss how the material will be covered with whomever will be doing the competitive analysis (in the event more than one person works on this section).

Miscellaneous Trends.   Numerous items can obviously have a strong effect on the company's problems, such as the social, cultural, economic, political, and legal environment. This section takes the broadest view of the marketing environment for a brand by including sales trends, geographical patterns, technological trends, economic trends and influences, regulatory considerations, changes in competitive activity, and changes in consumer attitudes and lifestyles. The important point here is to relate how what's happening in the environment is influencing the company's problems and opportunities. The idea is to focus on *trends*. Charts and graphs are often a good way to present this material.

New Opportunities.   Change generally comes in increments—new customers, styles, colors, sizes, flavors, or line extensions. Chances are the client has already thought of most of these. It may not even be within your discretion to recommend something dramatically different. However, at this point in the plans book you want the reader to believe that your campaign is going to do significant things for the brand. Although we are firm believers in setting realistic goals, as opposed to stretching objectives, painting a rosy picture for the brand is desirable. If you can't demonstrate optimism, the client may feel you are not the right agency for the job. If the plans book is going to be read by a group of judges, this panel is likely to think much like a client. If you want the client to think your report is special, then make sure you describe the opportunities for the brand with some enthusiasm or passion. However, you also want to be sure whatever you suggest in this section can be supported in later sections. This means you should avoid clichés, especially the word *great*, when describing the company's opportunities. The opportunities you describe, along with the problems you suggest the company needs to solve, in part will form the basis of the campaign objectives.

Primary Research

There is no set way on how to handle primary research. One suggestion is to hold off discussing this topic until you encounter a need to discuss your research findings. Typically, this point comes in the consumer analysis, but put your findings in the sections where they best fit. Include consumer research findings in the consumer analysis section and perhaps in the product analysis section. The description of the methods you used to gather your data should be placed immediately before the report of your findings regardless of where in the plans book you include your research results. If you choose to divide up your findings and place them in more than one section, be sure to describe your research methods before the first discussion of the primary research.

Don't elaborate on all your findings at this point; include a brief discussion of your methodology, and only those findings necessary to underline the point you are making. Additional information should be presented only as needed in subsequent analyses. A copy of the questionnaire and a summary of your findings should be included in an appendix at the back of the report. **Just remember clients are looking for insight—not descriptive detail!**

Another somewhat more formal approach is to present your research in a special section called "Primary Research" and place it before the consumer analysis. Describe your research plan as precisely as possible, and include its objectives and methodology. Tell the client what information you wanted to know but did not have. Describe the type of research you decided to conduct, the sampling scheme, the questions asked, and how the data were analyzed. Then provide a summary of your findings as a foundation for your analyses, objectives, and subsequent strategy recommendations.

Research should be performed with a purpose in mind. Do not get caught up in doing research just for the sake of presenting it. Be sure your research is well conceived and clearly presented. Interpret the results for the client. Do not merely present data without explaining exactly what they represent.

Make judicious use of tables and graphs to present your research findings. Also, place your questionnaire and any detailed analysis of your data in an appendix. You do not want to interrupt the flow of your plans book with your research materials. However, you do want these items to be available in your plans book for easy reference.

Consumer Analysis

The consumer analysis is the most important section in the plans book. As a result, it is likely to be two or three times longer than any of the other sections. This section should both describe the consumers in some detail and provide some insight into how they think, feel, and behave. The key word here is *insight.* Can you suggest something about the consumers that will provide some key motive that relates to why they may or may not buy the brand?

Keep in mind: **This is not the section where you determine the target audience.** At this point in the book, you're merely analyzing consumers. Targeting decisions should be presented following all the analyses (usually, that means defining the target audience should follow the competitive analysis). Consider the following questions (discussed in some detail in Chapter 2):

- Who are the consumers?
- What motivates them to buy?
- What do they look for in a product?
- How do they look at life?

Identifying Consumers.   You should at least profile the audience in demographic terms. You want to show who uses the product in absolute and relative terms. Indicate how much of a product is consumed by various population segments, and how this usage varies depending on whether you are talking about light, medium, or heavy usage. Consider using data from all four columns in the *MRI* and *Simmons* volumes on product usage (i.e., the A, B, C, and D columns). Feel free to interpret the index numbers for the reader. If the index number is 189, say that this demo uses "nearly twice as much of the product as the average consumer." Identify product usage for both the product category and the brand, if this information is available. If you can also delineate product usage with psychographic data, put that here. This section is another place where a chart can convey detailed information a lot easier than text.

Identifying Consumer Motivations.   This section is tricky for students to write because it is hard to feel confident about what motivates people to buy, especially considering the limited amount of research students can access. Nonetheless, it is a good idea to go ahead and speculate about what consumers might think or feel about the product or brand. If the researchers or planners don't do this, then the creatives will have to reach conclusions without any insight from the research. Just be careful how you present your ideas. For example, focus groups may or may not be representative of the target audience so what you uncover in this type of research may not be characteristic of the target audience.

Identifying Consumer Needs, Wants, Problems, and Interests.   Why people buy is, of course, related to their needs, wants, and the problems they would like to solve. When presenting this information, remember to discuss needs, wants, and problems in terms of the degree to which they are important. Sometimes people just sort of want something. Try to convey, as carefully as you can, a realistic appraisal of what consumers think and feel. As is often the case, consumers may not *really* need something. If this is so, then evaluate whether the brand is something consumers can get interested in without any degree of difficulty. The information in this section should be based on your research, but some of your conclusions will most likely be intuitive in nature. Don't shy away from giving an opinion because you can't back it up with research findings. Simply be careful how you phrase your opinions so the reader recognizes that your statement is based on personal judgment.

Identifying Consumer Values and Lifestyles. Consumers can be resistant to advertising. Copywriters and artists need detail and insight about the target audience so they can craft ads that motivate consumers. Little details about the target audience's values, activities, passions, or hobbies, how the product fits into their lives, who influences them, may be the tiny aspect of an ad that makes the audience feel you are talking to them. If you have accumulated a great deal of information in this area, display it in a chart.

When you have completed the above, your analysis should provide a precise description of the important consumer segments in terms of demographic factors such as age, gender, income, education, marital status, and occupation. Because demographic profiles only provide part of the picture of a prospective target audience, you should also include any psychographic, lifestyle, and geodemographic data that are available to give a richer picture of how your brand fits into the audience's lives. These factors can be compared to product usage and media usage patterns to determine the characteristics of the prospective consumer targets for your campaign. You are looking for some insight into prospective buyers' behavior that you can effectively use as part of your strategy.

Market Analysis

The market analysis is an extension of the consumer analysis. As such, there may be some practical advantage to doing these two analyses together to avoid redundant information. This section should tell the reader where the consumers are—obviously. But to derive much value out of this information, planners (especially those in media) need to know more than simply the best markets for the brand; they need to know how much better one market is than another. Index numbers are a good way to show how one market compares to an average market. Be careful not to misuse index numbers. A high index number may indicate the market uses more of the brand than the average market. However, if the market is a small percentage of the overall market, it is important to point out that detail as well.

The market analysis section should also include pertinent data on the size of the market in terms of sales, market share, and structural aspects of the market (such as distribution and your client's relationship with the trade). This section should provide an overall sense of market potential, what the viable market segments might be, and where you should focus your marketing communication efforts.

The geographic pattern of sales can be broken down by region, major metropolitan markets, and by comparing rural, urban, and suburban purchase patterns. The market analysis should provide a clear picture of where your brand does best and its market potential in areas where it may not be doing as well as expected. Market potential is evaluated by calculating and reporting the product category development index (CDI) and brand development index (BDI) for the markets in which your brand competes.

Student groups often have an especially difficult time with the market analysis because they usually don't have access to the detailed market-by-market sales information professionals get from ACNielsen, Information

Resources, Inc., and Claritas. Regional product usage can be obtained from *Simmons* and *MRI,* but this information, although helpful, doesn't provide the local market sales data that planners use to determine which markets may need extra emphasis. One approach, albeit of limited value, is to use a local market as an example of the kinds of decisions the student group would make if it had access to local market data on a national basis. This type of information could go in this section or in the section on media.

Product Analysis
Although this may seem obvious to some people, the first thing to get straight is to use the correct terminology for this section. If the assign-ment is for a service or an issue advocacy campaign, then the title of this section should reflect this difference. If it is for a product, avoid the temptation to begin this section by describing the product. This may have some small value if you are preparing the plans book for someone other than the client. However, *the product analysis section should be more than a descriptive presentation of the physical attributes of the product.* Your client is more concerned with how consumers rate, evaluate, and perceive a product than with its tangible characteristics. If this report goes to the advertiser, assume it already knows product detail.

You can begin this section with an assessment of how the product's qualities match up with what consumers want. Do this both qualitatively and quantitatively. Your research should have uncovered what consumers like and dislike about the product and, perhaps, what they think is missing. You'll also need to present how well the product sells and when. This point is also important to the competitive analysis and could instead be included in that section. An argument can also be made that because the client already knows this information, you don't really need to present it until you get to the media section where you might want to allocate media dollars on the basis of seasonal variation in sales.

As we said previously, the client already knows a lot of this information. What the client may not quite know is what the brand has to offer the consumer—something that will set it apart from the competition. Here's where your analysis can provide some insight. Products exist on shelves. Brands exist in the minds of consumers. Brands have an identity based on images, reputation, personalities, and assets—even liabilities. Minute Maid orange juice is made from concentrate, unlike Tropicana, which is not. It's an asset for Tropicana, but a liability for Minute Maid. Copywriters need this kind of information.

Give the client some idea of how much value there is in the brand name. Further, evaluate the opportunity to add value to the brand name—to determine whether it can become a "power" brand. End this section the way you began it—by stating what the brand has that is im-portant to the target audience. Naturally, this means you have presented how the consumer perceives the brand. These consumer perceptions in-fluence the essence of what the brand is. Be sure to point this out with some emphasis.

Competitive Analysis

The competitive analysis is an extension of the product analysis, and the two analyses should be coordinated to avoid overlap. The first step in the competitive analysis is to address how the brand stacks up against the competition. To do that well, you have to identify who or what is the competition. Competition can come from companies within the product category, or from outside the category. Coca-Cola competes against other soft drinks; it also competes against any beverage consumers drink for refreshment. Kroger competes directly against other supermarkets and indirectly against McDonald's. If consumers spent less time at McDonald's, they might buy more groceries.

Still, the most important comparisons should be provided against companies within the product category. Some of the information about the product such as price, distribution, and promotion, can be included here. What's important is not the information per se, but the *evaluation* of the comparison among brands. Comparisons of the advertising, including media expenditures, can be helpful to include in this section. This information can be useful in predicting how the competition may respond to your campaign. Marketing communication strategy is developed specifically to compete against other brands in your category. It is important not only to know them well, but also to specifically point out exactly where they are weak or where they are strong. *Identifying the competition is not nearly as important as an evaluation of how the company or brand stacks up against competitors.*

WRITING THE SITUATION ANALYSIS

There are several ways to make the situation analysis concise to reduce its length.

- *Use Graphs, Charts, and Tables to Present Important Data.* Converting your data into pictures makes it easier to digest, and this will allow you to reference the data without having to describe it at great length in writing. Pie charts work well for illustrating market share, competitive media spending, product usage segments, and budgets. Bar graphs are ideal for comparing data as well as for indicating trends. Line graphs illustrate expenditure and sales trends.
- *Use Bulleted Lists to Highlight or Summarize Key Information.* The following example shows how a bulleted list summarizes key findings on pet ownership in the United States.

EXAMPLE

- More households own dogs than cats.
- Cat owners are more likely than dog owners to have more than one pet.
- Working couples are more likely to own a cat than a dog.
- Cat ownership is on the rise, and dog ownership levels remain constant.

This outline form of writing gives emphasis to important information while presenting it as concisely as possible.

- *Make Good Use of Heads and Subheads.* Heads organize your information, and make it easier to find. Usually, only primary and secondary heads are listed in the table of contents. For example, your creative strategy is typically a subheading under your advertising strategy section. Always give more emphasis to the major sections and successively less emphasis to each subsection in a hierarchical fashion. A quick perusal of this text will illustrate how subheads are used to organize the book's content.

Overuse of heads or subheads can impede the flow of your writing by making it appear choppy. Too many subheads can also make the organization of your chapters appear unnecessarily complicated. However, students generally underuse subheads.

▌PROBLEMS AND OPPORTUNITIES

It is highly recommended that you set up a formal section for problems and opportunities as a bridge from your situation analysis to your objectives and strategies. *Remember, a problem well defined is a problem half-solved.* Your objectives and strategies will be based on problems and opportunities that you uncovered in the situation analysis. This is a necessary part of your thinking whether or not you state the problems and opportunities formally. Stating the problems and opportunities is a good exercise in digging for that insight that will catapult your recommendations forward. Likewise, a good set of problems and opportunities demonstrates to the client how you got from your analysis to the objectives and strategies.

Problems are drawn from weaknesses that you found in your situation analysis. These problems can be derived from a particular piece of information or a set of findings. Put them in any one or all sections of your situation analysis. Exhibit 11-1 illustrates how problems were deduced from various sections of the situation analysis.

The problem statements in the exhibit are conclusions drawn from the situation analysis and state the weakness without offering a solution. *Do not steal the thunder from the rest of your plan by presenting your solutions to the problems in this section—solutions belong in your strategy section.*

As you analyze your marketing situation, aim to find some *opportunities* in addition to problems. An opportunity is something that you discover in the situation analysis that you can exploit. This opportunity may be the result of a particular company or product strength or a competitor's weakness, or a new trend or change in government regulations. There are many places to look for opportunities. Remember, in analyzing your situation, look for opportunities as well as problems. Exhibit 11-2 illustrates how opportunities might be derived from the situation analysis.

Real opportunities translate into expanded sales. Typically, to increase sales you (1) strive to get new users, (2) get current users to use more of

---

EXHIBIT 11-1 DERIVING PROBLEMS FROM THE SITUATION ANALYSIS

Company Analysis

Company X has been changing advertising agencies at a rather frequent rate resulting in inconsistent advertising messages with no recurring and unifying theme. This example is similar to a situation Burger King found itself in for many years before developing quality campaigns in the late 1990s.

Problem

Company X's advertising messages are inconsistent with no recurring and unifying theme.

Consumer Analysis

Consumers in the product category perceive all the major brands to be relatively alike. They tend to buy when a brand is on sale, or they have a coupon, and then repurchase whatever other brand is on sale the next time they buy. Category usage is high but brand repurchase is low. The soft-drink category might exhibit these characteristics for many brands. Home delivered pizza is another example.

Problem

Consumers in category are not brand loyal.

Combined Market, Product, and Competitive Analysis

The company's current models are lagging the competition in technological sophistication. The company is presently working on new models but has to sell its existing inventory. Automotive and computer companies often have to work within the constraints of this type of problem.

Problem

Company X's models do not offer the most current technology available in the market.

---

the product, or (3) find new uses for the product. You will run into situations where it is not clear whether you have found a problem or an opportunity. Many situations are actually hybrid cases where a problem can be turned into an opportunity. Don't assume, however, that you can simply restate any problem as an opportunity. Look also for genuine opportunities that the situation analysis presents apart from the problems you have found.

Your list of problems and opportunities should include only those areas that are relevant to the marketing communication plan. A client may have problems, such as store location, that cannot be resolved by marketing communication; omit those problems from your plans book. If you present a SWOT analysis, handle the information much as suggested above. SWOT analyses lend themselves particularly well to the use of a chart or table. If you do a brand audit, handle the information in a similar

---

$\boxed{\text{EXHIBIT } 11\text{-}1}$ Continued

Market Analysis

The product usage of some product categories and specific brands do especially well in some regions of the country and not well in others. Breakfast sausage in general, and Jimmy Dean's brand in particular, are examples of this situation.

Problem

Consumers are predisposed to prefer brands that have been historically identified with certain regions of the United States.

Product Analysis

The client is operating in a parity product category where there are differences between brands, but these differences are not known to consumers. Furthermore, it is not clear whether or not these differences are important criteria to the purchase decision. Over-the-counter drugs and personal-hygiene-products marketers have to be concerned about consumer understanding of brand differences in their categories.

Problem

Consumers perceive company X's brand to be the same as the competitors' brands.

Competitive Analysis

Company X was the first to enter the growing health-food market and established itself as the category leader. Since then, new competitors have made inroads, and this has altered company X's brand position in the market. These new competitors have also been successful in influencing consumer preferences for the types of foods offered in the category. As new categories grow and mature, consumer preferences for certain attributes and types of products often change. This can be a natural result of new competitors entering the category and offering new benefits to the consumer market.

Problem

Company X's brand has lost its position and image in the category due to changes in consumer preferences and new competition.

---

fashion. Regardless of the format you use to present your analysis, the company still has problems that need solving and opportunities it can exploit. These should be the focus of your attention.

▌TARGET MARKET PROFILE

This section of the plans book tells your client to whom your marketing communication campaign is going to be directed. It sets up the marketing and advertising objectives, in that the underlying assumption is that the objectives are to be achieved against this group.

The target market profile also tells your client where the resources and efforts of the company are going to be focused. The consumer and

---

EXHIBIT 11-2 DERIVING OPPORTUNITIES FROM THE SITUATION ANALYSIS

Company Analysis

Company X has established a strong distribution system and has good trade relationships with its retailers. It would like to use this experience and positive image with the trade to support a new product introduction. This could be a fairly common advantage to a company wishing to extend its product line around an existing brand name.

Opportunity

Company X already has a strong distribution system and good trade relations.

Combined Consumer and Product Analysis

Company X has found that consumers want a particular product attribute that company X's brand has but that attribute has never been advertised. Consumers do not associate company X's brand with this attribute. This may appear to be too good to be true, but 7-UP found itself in this exact position regarding the caffeine in soft drinks. It never had caffeine in 7-UP and was able to take advantage of the fact that consumers were unaware of this.

Opportunity

Company X's brand contains a highly desired attribute that consumers are unaware of.

Combined Consumer and Market Analysis

The increase in two-wage-earner families and the aging of the population have made company X's experience in the service area the foundation for expansion of its business. Lawn and garden services, house painters, snow removal companies, and house cleaning firms are all benefiting from this current trend.

Opportunity

Company X's services are in more demand due to reduced leisure time for people to do chores and the inability of older consumers to do these household jobs.

---

market analysis sections of your plans book set up the selection of the target market by analyzing various potential market segments that might become the focus of your campaign. Therefore, the profile of the target market should come as no surprise.

The target market or target audience for a given brand or product is that segment whose needs and wants are best met by the product and thus provides the best opportunity for business growth. This means that the target market for a brand may not always be the heavy user segment in the category. Still, understanding heavy users is always important because it can show a brand's potential. Heavy users are usually the ones that understand the brand the best—its magic—and thus are worthy of significant study. Your situation analysis should provide the appropriate insight with which to select a target that will best respond to your product and marketing communication campaign. Different brands in many consumer product categories meet different needs.

EXHIBIT 11-2 CONTINUED

Product Analysis

Company X has been focusing on one particular use of its brand and in doing so had marketed to one market segment. Analysis of the product found that it offered other uses that appealed to different market segments. Some readers will recognize this as the classic Arm & Hammer baking soda case where they advertised the product for use as a deodorizer in kitty litter and the refrigerator among other things. The reality is that some companies miss opportunities because they only see their products from one perspective.

Opportunity

Company X's brand has multiple uses, most of which have yet to be marketed to the appropriate market segments.

Competitive Analysis

The analysis uncovered that existing competitors were upgrading their models and by doing so making them more expensive. Their move upward was leaving the lower end of the market open and ripe for entry by a new company willing to sell cheaper models. This has happened in the automobile industry, where companies that entered the market with cheap subcompact cars could not resist the temptation to build bigger and more expensive cars. Often the low end of the market has been abandoned, thus providing an opportunity for another manufacturer to enter the market.

Opportunity

There is no competition for company X in the lower end of the product category.

EXAMPLE

A Typical Target Market Profile for a Manufacturer of Canned Vegetables

Primary Market
- Heavy users (35% of the users and 65% of the total consumption) who normally stock large quantities of inexpensive food for their families
- Female homemakers
- Ages 25 to 49
- Blue-collar occupation
- Household income $25,000 to $40,000
- Resides in size B and C counties
- High school education
- Family size three or more skewing to five or more
- Eastern and Midwest regions

Secondary Market
- Trade
- Buyers for chain supermarkets and independent grocers who cumulatively represent a minimum of 65% of total canned vegetable sales
- Current brokers/wholesalers[2]

In this example there is a secondary target market, the trade, which will have to be sold on carrying the product. These two targets complement each other. Usually, there will not be two or more consumer markets because it is difficult to design a marketing communication campaign that can communicate with equal effectiveness to more than one consumer target. However, as we saw in Chapter 8 on marketing communication, the trade is an important target if an advertiser hopes to gain distribution for the product advertised to the ultimate consumer.

Although it might be simplest to identify one target audience, there will be situations in which you will have to combine several submarkets into a group that is large enough to warrant your marketing communication effort. Or, you might be asked to develop a campaign for a large client that sells to more than one market segment. In these cases, you will find yourself defining more than one audience as the target of your campaign. When this occurs, it makes sense to determine which markets are primary and which are secondary.

A short rationale should be provided for the selection of your target markets. In the example on the previous page, some of this rationale concerning the size of the target markets has been built into the profiles. The rationale should be brief because you have spent some time and space in your consumer analysis supporting this choice.

▌MARKETING AND ADVERTISING OBJECTIVES

Usually, it is not the job of the advertising or marketing communication team to develop the marketing objectives. These are usually provided by the client. However, the marketing objectives are often restated here to demonstrate to your client how the proposed marketing communication campaign supports the total marketing effort. Smaller clients may not have the sophistication to provide marketing objectives to you. You may also want to estimate some sales or share-of-market objectives for smaller clients because they may not have the means to produce these goals themselves. Estimating may not be as difficult as it sounds because smaller clients are likely to be retailers or local businesses for whom there is often much more of a direct link between marketing communication activities and sales than is true for national advertisers.

In Chapter 4 we presented a detailed discussion of how to set objectives. Remember, marketing objectives are best defined in terms of sales; advertising objectives are best set using communication criteria such as awareness or comprehension. (Also, advertising objectives should include a message element—say, awareness—and a media part—say, reach 70% of the target audience.) Your job in the plans book is to present objectives that provide clear direction to your campaign. You should also demonstrate that you understand the interrelationship between the sales goals of marketing and the communication goals of advertising and the other marketing communication elements. You might find that you can skip setting communications and advertising objectives at this stage in favor of presenting them with the appropriate marketing communication elements. This decision depends on how extensive your advertising, sales promotion, public relations, and direct marketing recommendations will be.

Setting advertising objectives at this stage assumes that your marketing communications recommendations are simply the execution part of the plan. However, if you intend to give each marketing communication element a major strategic emphasis, then you should defer your advertising and other objectives for the appropriate section.

BUDGET

There is some discretion as to where the campaign budget should be placed in the plans book. We include it here merely to cause you to think about this section early. Some clients and agencies like to put the budget directly following the marketing objectives so that expenditures can be compared easily to what they are going to achieve. Others (usually agency presenters) do not like to tell the client what a campaign is going to cost until after they have convinced the client's management team that the recommendations are really worth the costs involved. You will have to assess each situation to determine where it makes the most sense.

Another way to look at the budget is in terms of presenting the total figure broken down by major marketing communication elements to illustrate the relative strategic emphasis given to each early in the plans book. Then the budget for each marketing communication element can be further broken down in its section. We prefer to put the budget either after the media section or following the section on integrated communications.

The other approach is to build toward the total budget by placing it at the end of the plans book. Although this approach makes it difficult for the client to remember how the budget relates to objectives and elements of the campaign, it does place the budget closer to the recommendations— the items the client is really paying for in the final analysis.

List all expenditures that will be incurred in the implementation of your campaign, including not only media but also research, production (this is optional depending on the client), and contingencies. The budget presentation should be no more than a page or two and can be presented in both tabular and graphic formats. Tables can be used to break down the budget into all its important items, and pie graphs can be used to illustrate major allocations. Remember to include a small percentage as a reserve, or contingency fund.

MARKETING COMMUNICATION STRATEGY OVERVIEW

The key word in this section is *overview*. This section can be relatively brief. What you want to present here is an indication of how the various marketing communication tools, such as advertising, sales promotions, direct marketing, public relations, and other communication activities, will complement each other to achieve the campaign goals. This overview covers some major strategic decisions. Do not equate a brief section with one that is only of minor importance.

This is the section where you indicate how much money to allocate to the various communication tools, such as advertising and public relations. You can present this information simply enough in a pie chart, table, or graph, but your rationale should be closely argued and well reasoned. Briefly explain how each of the marketing communication elements will fit together to accomplish the campaign objectives. Be sure that your strategies cover all your objectives and at the same time establish the direction for how you are going to use various communication elements.

Each strategy statement should have only one focus. It should state how you are going to employ some promotional element or combination of elements to achieve the campaign's objectives. Keep your strategies broad and directional. Do not let them become tactical. For example, state whether you are going to use advertising to maintain the brand's image during peak sales cycles. But do not state what the ads will look or sound like or what the slogan will be. These explanations are reserved for the actual advertising part of your plan.

A short rationale should be provided for each strategy that links it back to your problems and opportunities, objectives, and key information that have been gleaned from the situation analysis. For example, if you found there are certain times during the year when sales dip and have set an objective to achieve better sales during these periods, you should have a strategy that addresses that problem. Your short rationale should be able to provide the link between the strategy and objectives.[3]

EXAMPLE

Promotion Strategy—Emphasize sales promotions during slow sales periods in July and August to build product categories in which company X is not realizing its full potential.

Rationale—The strategy is based on the realization that sales promotion is required to bolster sales during slow periods and for products that are not reaching their sales potential. Company X should continue to use advertising during peak sales seasons to maximize margins and profit when consumers are buying at higher rates.[4]

ADVERTISING STRATEGY

Your advertising strategy consists of two substrategies: one that addresses what will be said in the advertising messages and one that addresses how media will be used to deliver these messages with the greatest impact. These substrategies are the creative and media strategies that make up the heart of a typical marketing communication campaign. This section should be very brief.

CREATIVE STRATEGY

Creative Objectives and Strategy

The creative strategy section of your plans book tells the client how advertising messages are going to be used to achieve the campaign's objectives. The primary function of this section is to explain your creative objectives, your strategy, and your tactics. You have some discretion as to whether you want to include your creative executions here or instead put them in a special section at the end labeled "Creative Supplement."

You will probably want to restate the target audience, perhaps in creative terms (see Chapter 6). Next, present the objectives of your creative strategy—what you want the strategy to accomplish. These should be couched in communication terms, such as *awareness, comprehension, attitude,* or *image.* Use action words with these objectives, such as *to convince, to establish* in teenagers' minds, *to make aware, to remind, to educate, to persuade, to counter* the impression, and *to demonstrate* how to use. Remember, the creative objective is the message (or content) part of the advertising objective. Think in terms of the response you want to elicit from the target audience. What do you want your target audience to think, feel, or do after being exposed to your ad?

Be ever mindful of what advertising can accomplish by itself. Do not set marketing or sales-oriented objectives here unless direct marketing is a key element and you expect to generate sales.

Consider also using subheads to explain the major components of your creative strategy, such as the message strategy itself, a big unifying idea, or how you want to position the product. Refer back to Chapter 6 for more details. When you discuss the message strategy, be sure to point out how the strategy centers on a strategic focal point. *Distill down to one or two sentences the essence of the message strategy.* Do the same with your big unifying idea and your brand position. Write a paragraph or two to provide rationale for your strategic decisions.

Use subheads and a paragraph of rationale for optional creative elements, such as a theme, slogan, or tactical focal points (also called key copy points). Other strategic elements you might want to include are discussions about the tone, attitude, or appeal (not discussed in this book), which are part of your message strategy.

Creative Tactics

Examples or prototypes of your creative executions should be included in the plans book. If these examples are numerous, you might consider including representative examples here and placing the rest in a creative supplement or appendix. Print ads should be in a semicomprehensive layout form with illustrations and display copy sketched in. Body copy can be ruled in and provided on a separate copy sheet.

Television spots are best presented in storyboard form and radio commercials as scripts. Large-scale ads, such as outdoor and transit ads, should be scaled down but still maintain the proper proportions of the life-size posters. All executions should be copied so that they can fit into the plans book. Sometimes photographs of the ads in their media context can aid a client in seeing how they will look in their real environment. For example, a photograph of an outdoor board in place or transit card on a bus can supplement the scaled-down example of the ad.

To double-check your executions, review the following three sections. If you feel comfortable in your knowledge about copy and layout, especially if you have taken a basic course, you may want to move on to the media section.

Points to Consider When Creating Print Ads

1. Does the headline attract attention and appeal to the reader's self-interest? Does it present news? Arouse curiosity? Offer a benefit? Is the headline believable?

2. Is the illustration or photograph in the advertisement relevant to the headline and body copy? Does it work with the headline to communicate the important part of the message?
3. Does the body copy expand on the headline? Does it substantiate or elaborate on what has been stated or implied in the headline? Does it identify the features of the product? Does it discuss the benefits of these features? Is the copy long enough? Is it easy to read?
4. Does the layout feature unity? Harmony? Does it employ formal balance? Informal balance? Does it employ proportion? Does it contain contrast? Do the physical elements lead the reader's eye from one area to another in a logical sequence?

Points to Consider When Creating Radio Commercials

1. Does the commercial convey the major selling idea?
2. Does the commercial focus on one idea?
3. Does the commercial register the brand name?
4. Can the listener visualize what has been presented (words and sounds)?
5. Does the commercial repeat key terms and/or brand name?
6. Is the choice of music appropriate for the spot?
7. Is the commercial interesting and arresting throughout? Or does it contain weak spots? Does it end with a positive and suggestive statement? (In most cases, you want the consumer to respond to your commercial by purchasing the product.)
8. Is the commercial's message believable?

Points to Consider When Creating Television Commercials

1. Does the commercial focus on a major selling idea?
2. Does the commercial present a situation with which the target can relate?
3. Does the video show as well as tell the story?
4. Does the commercial demonstrate the product's benefits?
5. Are different shots, including close-ups, employed to help maintain interest?
6. Are scene transitions appropriate and not distracting? Are camera directions properly used?
7. Do certain scenes show the brand, package, and logotype clearly?
8. Is the commercial believable?
9. Does the product's promise reflect the product's characteristics?

MEDIA STRATEGY

Media strategy may be the traditional title for this section, but "cutting-edge" media organizations like to refer to this area as communication planning or creative media planning. These expressions convey the idea that there are many different platforms to deliver promotional messages. New or alternative media and promotional activities are used to deliver messages in such a way that consumers *engage* with the message through a clever use of a nontraditional message delivery.

In your plans book, the media or communication strategy can be divided into five subsections: (1) an introductory statement of key media (or communication) implications to be drawn from the situation analysis and marketing communication strategy, (2) media objectives, (3) media strategy, (4) the media vehicles (i.e., the tactics) and schedule, and (5) the media budget summary. Your media recommendations should be based on a thorough understanding of how media can be used to help achieve campaign objectives. This requires a *brief* review of the situation analysis and marketing strategy with an eye toward identifying those problem areas that are specifically the concern of the media planner. The media planner should be looking most closely at data and information concerning the target audience, geographic markets, possible seasonal sales patterns, competitive spending levels, and the nature of the marketing communication and advertising objectives. Here we are looking down the road a bit to get a sense of how difficult (or easy) it is going to be to put enough media exposure directed at the target audience at the right times and in the right places to meet your objectives.

Media Objectives

These objectives provide the direction and standards to be met for the media strategy and tactics. The criteria used in setting media objectives reflect the availability of audience data with which they can be measured. *Usually, media objectives state how much reach, frequency, gross impressions, gross or targeted rating points the plan is expected to achieve.*

You will not need to incorporate all these measures of exposure into your objectives, so consider your selection carefully. If you use reach, then you will also want to use frequency. If you use impressions or rating points, you should indicate that you want to achieve these goals against the target audience or against a specific demo. Campaign continuity is also an important media consideration. Continuity is concerned with the pattern with which the messages will be delivered. Media planning is a game of trade-offs. On a given budget, you can expose your message to many different people (i.e., emphasize reach) or expose it to fewer people more often (i.e., emphasize frequency). Likewise, you can limit your media weight to short periods (flights) for impact, spread it out for continuity (but lose some impact), or combine some of each by varying media weight from one period to the next (pulsing). You determine which of these patterns is best by comparing the alternatives to what the entire campaign has been designed to achieve.

Setting media objectives is no different from setting objectives for other parts of your campaign. They should always include a target audience, a criterion to measure, and a time limit in which they will be achieved. Usually, media objectives are written in terms of reach and frequency. If you recommend nontraditional media and promotional activities, you will also want to set qualitative objectives, usually emphasizing how they enhance the creative message.

Media Strategy Elements

In writing the media strategy section, *avoid the temptation to jump right in and start buying specific media vehicles,* such as *Time, Newsweek,* and *Sports*

Illustrated. First, consider and report the elements that make up a media strategy:

- **Target Audience**—Is this the same as the target for the campaign? If so, indicate that. If not, then carefully explain that.
- **Media Classes**—You need to indicate which media you select, and if you are not using some major medium, sometimes it's appropriate to indicate why.
- **Media Mix**—The amount of emphasis you place on each medium you select is a major strategic decision. It's not enough simply to show a pie chart for the media mix. Explain how you determined the relative weight to place on the various media classes you chose.
- **Media Timing**—Both the pattern you choose to deliver the messages and when you schedule them are major decisions.

Explain and support your decisions; support for your decisions can include both quantitative and qualitative factors.

Decision Criteria

The two primary quantitative criteria that you want to look at closely are the relative cost-efficiency of each media vehicle and its ability to deliver your message to the target audience. Some of these data are available in syndicated media-audience reference sources, some will have to be calculated, and some come from experience. At this point, your calculations or estimations are generalized. Specific information on the relative cost-efficiency of the vehicles that you select should come later in the media section.

It is a good idea to rank order your media alternatives from best to worst in terms of their ability to deliver your audience in a cost-efficient manner. If you have access to a cost-estimating guide used by some of the major agencies (e.g., DDB Needham and Starcom/Leo Burnett), estimating the relative cost-efficiency of media is fairly straightforward. If you do not, then you will have to calculate costs for vehicles that are representative of the type you are likely to select for your plan. When you present your material, consider indicating where the competition is spending its media dollars. Will your recommendations schedule the client in head-to-head competition or will your plan select media that the client can dominate without worrying about competitive activity?

Qualitative factors include creative message requirements, such as the use of sound, motion, product demonstrations, coupon offers, or color. The media environment should be evaluated in terms of its news value, entertainment value, and quality. You are trying to ascertain what the media environment might add or take away from the effectiveness of your ad. Controversial topics, for example, tend to frighten advertisers because they do not know how the controversy will rub off on their advertising. Some media, such as television and newspapers, have a built-in risk in this regard. Media that carry only advertising messages, such as outdoor ads and direct mail, do not possess this characteristic. Qualitative considerations are very important and come from experience with the media.

After you have evaluated the media alternatives, you should decide on the relative weight to be given to each medium in the mix. Some of your media choices should be identified as primary because they are going to carry the major responsibility of delivering your audience; others will be support media. **Support media** typically add something special to the campaign, such as reaching more of the audience, adding synergy in terms of a different way to execute the creative message, providing a vehicle for delivering samples or coupons, or providing a special timing or placement advantage. For example, an owner of a local, upscale specialty shop might put most of the advertising budget into local media. But the owner might add a small-space ad in the *New Yorker* for image and status reasons because many of the shop's customers read that magazine. Consider also discussing how the media you select can enhance the message strategy. Review the figure captioned "Which Media Do It Best" in Chapter 7.

For each media type selected, you should describe how it is going to be used. For example, what dayparts are you recommending for television and radio? Are there special programming considerations? If you are recommending newspapers, be sure to indicate the days of the week and newspaper sections you feel are best. If you are recommending outdoor advertising (be sure to refer to it as outdoor, not simply billboards), indicate the size showing or the gross rating points (GRPs) you would like to see scheduled. If direct mail is recommended, how many pages will the mailing consist of? What about color? How many pieces will you be printing?

Media Tactics

After you have made these strategic decisions, present the specific media vehicles that you are recommending. Obviously, vehicle selection should fit the strategy and rationale that have preceded these choices. You want to describe which TV programs, radio stations, magazines, newspapers, and other media you are including in your schedule. To support your decisions, present at least the cost-efficiency of the vehicles you recommend. Simply presenting the cost per thousand (CPM) next to the vehicles you select helps, but it is more helpful to show comparisons between the vehicles you recommend and those you do not. In the event you are recommending some vehicle with a relatively high CPM, discuss why it is a good choice.

The following statements are not sufficient reasons for choosing a vehicle: "This vehicle reaches more of our target than any other" and "All our program selections have high ratings." You need to evaluate your recommendations in light of a vehicle's cost-efficiency, especially its ability to deliver the target efficiently. Cost per thousand prospects or TRPs (targeted rating points) are always more powerful measures than a CPM based on total audience.

Media Calendar

Your media plan and schedule is easiest to visualize in the form of a media calendar or flowchart (also called a continuity schedule). The media calendar illustrates how you have scheduled your media over time and what weight you have given to your selections. Your scheduling and media mix strategies will be obvious from one look at this calendar. Figure 11-1 provides an example of a media schedule calendar. Note that each medium has its own symbolic code so that you can tell at a glance how each is scheduled.

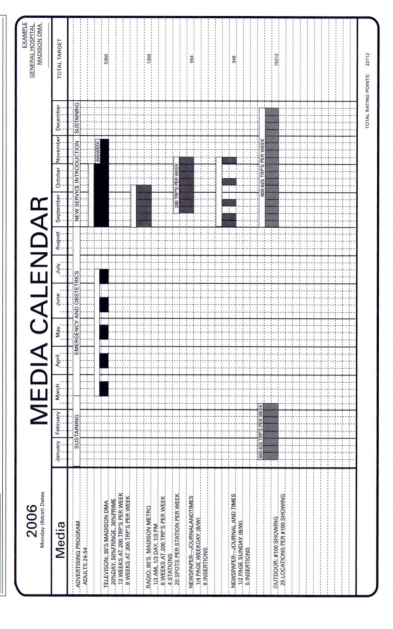

FIGURE 11–1 ADVERTISING CAMPAIGN STRATEGY

MEDIA CALENDAR

EXAMPLE
GENERAL HOSPITAL
MADISON DMA

Media Budget Summary

The last item to include in your media strategy section is a media budget summary. Media budget summaries can take a number of different forms depending on those factors that are most important to your plan. If market coverage is important, then present how much money you allocated to each medium by market. Perhaps scheduling is the most important consideration. In this case, present the budget by each quarter of the campaign year. If product support is important, show how much money you have allocated to support each brand in a product line. If more than one factor is important, do not hesitate to provide more than one table to illustrate how the media budget has been allocated.

INTEGRATED COMMUNICATIONS

Sales promotions, public relations, and direct marketing should be broken out into individual sections in the plans book. Each section should follow the general form of the media section. You should state specific objectives appropriate to what you want these communication elements to accomplish. Likewise, describe the strategies recommended and include the actual activities or techniques you have selected to implement these strategies. Include examples of your tactics, as you did in your creative strategy section. To illustrate how your entire plan fits together, provide a schedule of these activities in each section to demonstrate how they dovetail with your advertising media recommendations. Finally, a brief budget summary should demonstrate how you have allocated your marketing communication dollars to the recommended activities in each area. Pricing some of your recommendations, especially in the area of sales promotions, can be difficult for students. If you use estimates, be sure you label them clearly as such.

Not every plans book has a complete set (sales promotions, public relations, and direct marketing, etc.) of marketing communication recommendations. Some plans may also break out from the media section and include here creative media recommendations, such as viral marketing, buzz marketing, "wild postings," buzz marketing, seeding, and other guerrilla marketing activities. How extensive these sections are will depend on the scope of the marketing communication problem you have been asked to resolve.

CAMPAIGN EVALUATION

The purpose of a campaign evaluation plan is to provide a methodology for determining whether you are achieving your stated objectives. Because you have set objectives for your overall campaign and each substrategy, you have to decide how you want to measure your campaign results.

The nature of the evaluation plan will be influenced by how much money your client wants to invest in monitoring and evaluating the campaign. This plan can run from a simple before-and-after survey of the communication objectives (such as awareness, comprehension, attitude, and image) to an expensive and elaborate controlled experiment (test market) in the marketplace. This plan should answer the question, "Are we getting there?"

You have at your disposal methodologies ranging from focus groups (with all their inherent external validity problems) to surveys to field experiments (which are very expensive). Many clients are removing from their agencies the responsibility for evaluative research. Nonetheless, you should be able to demonstrate to your client how you will judge whether the recommended campaign is being successful.

APPENDICES

You want your plans book to be a clear presentation of your analysis and recommendations unencumbered by unnecessary items. You also want your client to see that you have done your homework. The appendices of a plans book are good places to include research findings, media calculations, extra ad examples, and alternative strategies.

Do not allow your appendices to become catchall sections in which you indiscriminately deposit material. Be sure that the appendices genuinely add something to the impression you want to make. They should serve a purpose.

KEY POINTS TO WRITING THE PLANS BOOK SUMMARIZED

Exhibit 11-3 lists 15 points to remember when writing your plans book. These tips also follow the general logic of campaign planning from your situation analysis through your plans for executing the substrategies of marketing communication. The arrangement of the plans book follows a logical flow. Within this framework you can adjust and adapt to the specific marketing communication problem confronting you.

Advertising and marketing communication demand creative and innovative solutions formed within the discipline demanded by carefully set objectives and strategic thinking. A creative approach to showcase a technique or a special effect will not help you achieve your objectives because often these types of ads are created without regard for the target audience or an understanding of what has to be communicated to them for a campaign to succeed.

The plans book should be a clear presentation of your analysis of the marketing situation, problems and opportunities, objectives, strategies, recommended tactical executions, and evaluation of results. The marketing communication plan should be efficient and effective. Although the process you undertake to put this plan together is dynamic, the final plan should be a carefully crafted set of recommendations that is easy to understand and that pushes for closure in terms of solving the client's problem.

THE COVER

Once you've completed your writing tasks, you can attend to details that will enhance the impression of the plans book. Consider a professional-looking cover. Be sure it contains all the pertinent information, including

---

EXHIBIT 11-3 15 KEY POINTS FOR WRITING MARKETING
COMMUNICATION RECOMMENDATIONS

Develop an outline before writing.

Develop tables, graphs, and visual support before writing.

Make your situation analysis as concise and factual as possible.

Use primary research to support your consumer and product analysis.

Make sure your problems and opportunities reflect each section of your situation analysis.

Be sure your analysis is analytical, not merely descriptive.

Keep all objectives to one sentence.

Aim objectives at a specific target audience. Write objectives that are specific, and measurable, to be achieved within an established time frame.

Make sure strategies describe how objectives will be achieved.

Make sure your advertising and other marketing communication recommendations are on target and on strategy.

Create disruptive ads.

Make sure your media plan will deliver the reach, frequency, and media weight necessary for your campaign to achieve its objectives.

Integrate all promotional recommendations into a unified campaign.

Propose how you plan to measure your results.

Be clear and concise. Not brief.

---

(1) the client's name, (2) your agency's name (in a student competition this should be your school's name), other information optional in a university setting such as (3) the course name, and (4) the competition name. The cover is the first place that sells your campaign. Consider how to make it stand out from the competition. Do not leave your creativity behind after you've completed your campaign work. Extend colors, design approaches, and themes to your plans book cover. Most cover designs incorporate the client's colors and logo at a minimum.

Consider going beyond this minimum standard for the cover in special situations such as the AAF/NSAC competition or a new business pitch. However, ask your instructor or supervisor if putting more effort into the design of the cover is appropriate. In any competitive activity it is better to put in a little extra effort, but the cost of doing so might outweigh the benefits. Your instructor (or supervisor) is the best person to guide you in this regard. If you decide to put a little more into your plans book cover, the next two paragraphs are for you.

The plans book is considered a companion piece to the campaign presentation. It should be designed to look like the presentation. Use similar graphics on the cover and section dividers to establish a team identity. This shared look will help campaign judges and clients make a quick association between your team and the plans book once the presentation is over. A creative design might not be necessary for most class or routine agency projects, but it has become close to a necessity for the AAF National Student Advertising Competition.

Take into consideration how many copies of your plans book are necessary to produce. If you need to make a lot of copies, color graphics and other fancy technological frills will be expensive to reproduce. You might decide to make full-color and comprehensive plans books for judges, instructors, and clients while providing black-and-white copies for others. Once again, you will have to assess your situation and the importance of the use of color in your plans book.

THE TITLE PAGE

The first page inside your plans book should be a title page. Once again, the content of the title page has some optional elements. The title page can include more information than the cover because cover design considerations typically do not have to be considered. Most title pages include (1) the client's name, (2) the agency's name, (3) agency team members' names and titles, (4) advisor's or instructor's name, (5) course title, (6) school name, (7) appropriate dates, and (8) acknowledgments. There is a lot of discretion in how to set up your title page. The best advice is to keep it simple and clean.

You can carry over some of the content from the cover onto the title page. Campaign themes, slogans, and logos add to the continuity of the plans book as you move the reader from the cover to the inside.

TABLE OF CONTENTS

Once you complete the writing of the plans book, it's time to create a table of contents, which should be the second page of your book. List the major headings in your plans book in chronological order, and then indicate the page location of each along the right-hand margin of the page. A typical table of contents is illustrated in Exhibit 11-4.

The general form for a table of contents reflects the outline of a marketing communication plan, as shown in Chapter 1. These are the basic elements of a plans book. These headings will be given different emphases as the marketing and advertising problems you are confronted with change from project to project. Your instructor might ask for a slightly different order, or the client's problem could require other areas to be included. For example, the information in Exhibit 11-1 does not include a section for a test market. If your client's problem requires a test market, then you will include it in a section in your plans book (and in the table of contents).

| EXHIBIT 11-4 | PLANS BOOK TABLE OF CONTENTS |

*The primary research section may not be an official section, but a description of the methods you used to gather data should be included in the plans book. This section will appear in different places in different plans books depending on where the findings fit best. Primary research as an official section is usually placed before the consumer analysis as illustrated in this exhibit.

**The location of the budget can be located at various places in the plans book. We place it in the above position only to remind you of its importance early in the campaign process. In most instances, the budget will be located following the media or the marketing communication section.

THE EXECUTIVE SUMMARY (OPTIONAL)

The first one to three pages of your plans book should include a brief version of the entire marketing communication plan, called the executive summary. This summary should hit the highlights of your campaign recommendations. Your client is most interested in knowing what you plan to do and what it is going to cost. Key elements of an executive summary should include (1) the central thrust of your campaign; (2) whom you are targeting; (3) how much it will cost, or the total budget; (4) the creative strategy (usually expressed in a simple statement); (5) any key elements that will encapsulate the campaign, such as the theme, product position, or slogan; (6) which media you are recommending (including nontraditional activities); and (7) the scheduled time period in which it is going to run. Write this summary after the rest of the plans book has been completed. This will help you know your recommendations in detail and you will be better prepared to write a summary highlighting what you have actually put in the plans book.

The executive summary should be clearly written and organized so that the client's management team can understand the recommendations without having to distill them from the detailed presentation inside the book. Clients can and will look inside the plans book for verification and details to support the recommendations, but typically do not want to read the plans book in depth from cover to cover.

We asked Dennis G. Martin, professor of advertising at Brigham Young University (BYU) and author of *Media Flight Plan*,[5] to give us his impressions on putting together a plans book. Professor Martin is a longtime advisor to student groups in the NSAC competition (AAF). Teams he has advised have won the NSAC competition twice, and a third team took first place for the Best Plans Book. In addition, his teams won first place NSAC district honors 16 out of the 20 years his teams entered. His advice follows:

TOP 10 TIPS FOR WRITING A WINNING PLANS BOOK

A classic advertising maxim might be adapted to the plans book: *I know the client reads only half of the plans book; I just don't know which half.* Here's what I've learned in over 25 years of competition.

1. The plans book is a sales piece disguised as a marketing plan. Every word, every page must move me toward one goal—to accept your branding strategy. Persuade me, sell me, romance me, or lose me.
2. If it's not dangerous, it's not creative. BYU won first place in the Chevy Cavalier competition by persuading the client (supported with convincing primary research) that the case study was wrong. Instead of "following orders" (sell all six Cavalier models), students believed in their primary research and sold it to the client. Research told us the target wanted only one model, the Z-24. We were the only team that challenged the case study. Risky, but it worked.
3. Primary research must break new ground. Clients yearn for new knowledge, but most teams tell clients what they already know. (The familiar is comfortable; clients aren't looking for comfort). If

you don't think you've discovered anything new, keep digging. Winning teams never settle for the superficial.

4. Merchandise your research. Clients won't hunt for genius in your plan—you have to rub their noses in it. Intelligent research usually goes unnoticed because the writers bury it. Put it in bold type. Write subheads to sell the main findings. Use graphics and white space liberally.

5. Executives hate reading plans books. Trey Hall, a former BYU student and now chief marketing officer for Quiznos, said: "I hate reading plans books. If you can't hold my attention with witty, intelligent writing, you'll be flippin' burgers tomorrow." If a sentence or paragraph doesn't move the client closer to accepting your marketing, branding, media or creative strategy, rewrite it. Every sentence counts.

6. The situation analysis is usually the client's first impression of your thinking. Students often gloss over writing Part I, assuming "it's just the situation analysis." Write Part I as if it were the first chapter of a novel. It has to set up the story line for your whole strategy. Lose me in Part I and kiss off any chance of winning.

7. Subheads are vital; write complete, whole sentences. Romance the client with informative, meaningful subheads on every page. Clients should be able to read only the subheads and grasp the essence of your entire campaign. If you expect me to give you the business, convince me you can write. Craft brilliant headlines that compel me to read the paragraph below.

8. Less is more. We took a risk the year Hallmark was the AAF client and edited the plans book down to about half of the normal volume. Tons of white space. Each divider page was limited to about 25 words along with a photo. Hallmark judges loved it and thanked us for getting to the point; they awarded us second in the nation.

9. There is no recipe, no formula. Winning plans books don't follow all of the conventions. If there were a formula, the client wouldn't need you.

10. Media strategy is a big deal. BYU students won "Best Plans Book" in the national AAF Saturn competition, and primary research was the secret. Initial research told us the Saturn story demanded long copy, but this wasn't new knowledge. We went deeper by calling the nation's top four Saturn store owners. They told us our target (young, single women) was hungry for details about the SC1, and that other car brands assumed women were not car savvy. We researched that further, and confirmed women felt ignored. Next, we called 20 women's magazines. We learned that our target spent an average of 30 minutes curled up with their favorite magazine. Supporting our strategy with primary research (clients can tell when you believe in your research), we spent almost half of our budget on magazines, ignored high CPMs, and sold the client on "quality" instead of low cost. A big part of our strategy was "cost be damned." We won because we had an original strategy backed with solid primary research. Original strategies win every time.

Notes and References

[1] R.L. Baumgardner, "Writing Plans and Recommendations," in *What Every Account Executive Should Know About Writing Plans and Recommendations,* eds. American Association of Advertising Agency Committee on Client Service (New York: American Association of Advertising Agencies, 1998), pp. 7–8.

[2] R.G. Hiebing, Jr. and S.W. Cooper, *The Successful Marketing Plan: A Disciplined and Comprehensive Approach* (Lincolnwood, IL: NTC Business Books, 1991), p. 100.

[3] Ibid., pp. 114–115.

[4] Ibid., p. 115.

[5] *Media Flight Plan* (Provo, UT: Deer Creek Publishing, 2002, dennis_martin@byu.edu.)

Preparing a Winning Presentation

Presentations are inherently competitive. The competition may be with another agency, or the presentation may be judged against some vague standard the agency has set. *The key to winning this competition is to take clients somewhere they can't go themselves.*

Clients require insight and information, but what they really *want* are solutions driven by creative ideas. They may feel comfortable with the marketing or strategic direction of the campaign, but they know they have neither the talent nor the experience to think *and* execute creatively. And style does matter, so make your ideas come alive. The way you deliver the presentation could go a long way toward convincing a client that you can take them where they want to go.

Presentations are serious business, but they *are* also performances— a kind of show. Winning presentations excite, enthuse, energize, and empower clients. The right presentation stirs the clients' interest and ramps up their intensity. It can give them the power to take action, and the confidence to move boldly with new ideas. As intimidating as presentations may be to beginners, they can be quite rewarding and intensely satisfying. However, many beginners spend 90% of their time doing research and 10% or less putting together the oral presentation. They are often dismayed when others who do less research win the account or get a better grade. This happens because they underestimated the power of a good presentation. If you are unable to present your ideas orally, no one will understand and appreciate them. Does this mean that substance is less important than style? Certainly not. In today's business world, both are necessary to excel, and the same is true in the classroom.

No matter how hard you've prepared for the presentation, it's natural to feel nervous and concerned. Still, if your nervousness shows, it's probably more apparent to you than it is to the audience. It's best not to worry excessively about things mostly beyond your control. Relax and enjoy yourself.[1]

PRELIMINARY PREPARATIONS

As you begin putting your presentation together, there are four questions you should answer:

1. To whom will you be presenting?
2. Where will you give your presentation?
3. How will you present your material?
4. What is the one thing you want your audience to remember when the presentation is over?

It is important to have answers to these questions before you prepare for your "show."

UNDERSTANDING THE AUDIENCE

Knowing your audience can give you insight on what you should emphasize and what you cover quickly. We'll look at three basic types of audiences: clients, review panels, and faculty.

Clients and Panels

Typically, clients and panel members are working professionals. However, they can differ considerably in the way they will evaluate your presentation. Find out as much as you can about their backgrounds, especially if they have a particular expertise or interest in the area of advertising and marketing.

Generally, clients are interested in how you can help them solve problems. Panels, although they can vary widely, want to see quality advertising. Usually this means a balanced campaign, an expression of a clear point of view, and a few compelling ideas. For clients, getting a well-balanced campaign is nice, but getting something that addresses their problems directly is likely to have greater value. Start by identifying the client's problems. This puts them at ease and helps them be receptive to your analysis and ideas. Later, if you can show them how they can *solve* these problems and, even better, how they can capitalize on some unanticipated opportunities, this is mostly all they want.

If this is a high-level panel or a very competitive presentation, you need a strong presentation with no weaknesses. The creative, however, is generally where campaigns are won and lost. Naturally, you should have great strategy and big ideas. But do not underestimate the value of impressing the panel with *quantity*. It shouldn't make a difference if you have a great strategy—but only a small number of very good ads. Here's why having quantity can work (even though you are unlikely to get a professional to agree with this point). Winning a creative shootout can be like a crapshoot. Some of it is luck—or at least a matter of differing opinions. Consider the annual surveys of the best and worst ads: some campaigns are frequently cited in *both* categories!

Even though you emphasize the importance of strategy, some clients still are captivated by executions. By providing numerous executions, the panel is likely to quickly gloss over the ads they don't like until their eyes catch one they do. If they only have a few to look at, they'll look at all—good and bad—in detail. How many ads should you present? At least three or four more than the other teams have, and at least two or three more than the panel has time to carefully consider.

Faculty
Just as with a client, think hard about what your instructors have said—in class and in the courses they teach. Do they teach creative, media, or management courses? If you are not sure about their expectations, ask their advice. It's no more a good idea for you to surprise your instructor with your work than it would be for a copywriter to show an ad directly to a client. Professionals show their work first to a supervisor—at least, to an account executive. Most instructors naturally have personal biases. One might be strongly impressed with primary research. Another might be impressed with research, but may be skeptical about your data-gathering methods. In the creative area, it helps to know the relative value faculty place on professional-looking executions versus strategic driven ideas. The best advice we can possibly give you is to get advice—not once, but twice. The first time to get the information, and the second time to see if you are interpreting it correctly. (A third time wouldn't hurt either.)

EVALUATING THE PRESENTATION LOCATION

The location of the presentation is very important because it will influence the context in which your ideas and information will be received. A small intimate boardroom lends itself to a warmer, more casual environment than a large classroom. This can influence the style of your presentation. In smaller rooms, clients like to ask questions. Knowing this in advance can help you prepare for answers. You will want to check out the site physically, if possible. Later, we'll give you some tips on what to check out on the day of the presentation. At this point, you want to evaluate how the site will enhance or limit your presentation options. For example, if you ask clients if they are equipped to handle PowerPoint presentations at their facility, be sure you check out what they mean by "equipped." You want to be sure that their idea of a PowerPoint presentation isn't viewing it on a 25-inch TV set while what you have in mind is projecting on a six-by-eight-foot screen.

CHOOSING THE PRESENTATION MEDIUM

There are several media from which you can choose to deliver your presentation. However, your selection will mostly likely come down to one of the following:

- Computer-based media
- Overhead projectors
- Presentation boards and flipcharts

Computer-Based Media
Computers have ushered in new electronic methods that allow users to produce professional-quality slides, overheads, and handouts. Most multimedia software allow you to incorporate audio and video, and to choose

to operate the presentation manually or automatically. Users can also create interactive buttons that allow viewers or presenters to jump, in a nonlinear manner, to other slides with related material. The information can also be linked to the Internet.

In the late 1990s, presenters used a variety of presentation software. After the turn of the century, Microsoft® PowerPoint® is clearly the most popular. Occasionally, a sophisticated user will use Macromedia Director, and occasionally you might find someone using Astound. For those who are unsure which software to use, see the following (or just use PowerPoint).

Microsoft PowerPoint

- **Performance**—By far, this is the most widely used presentation software. When bundled with Microsoft Office, PowerPoint has the ability to execute word processing, spreadsheets, graphs, tables, and illustrations within the application. It can also import specific formats of pictures, movies, and sounds with the click of a mouse. Animation, interactivity, transitions, and narration can be applied automatically. Annotation allows the presenter to draw on the slide during the presentation (notes disappear as soon as you select the next slide). Users can choose from a variety of output formats—on-screen slide shows, 35mm slides, color overheads, handouts, and Web pages.
- **Compatibility**—PowerPoint is available for both Macintosh and PC. "Pack and Go" command allows you to save your presentation as a slide show and play it back on any computer with the free Power-Point Viewer software.
- **Difficulty**—No scripting or programming is required. PowerPoint comes with dozens of predesigned slide and page templates. Pull-down menus add custom animation to text and graphics. Pop-up messages appear automatically to provide tips to new users.

Macromedia Director

- **Performance**—By far, the most powerful and complex multimedia software available. Unlike the others, Director is a true multimedia authoring program. It has too many attributes to list—it is capable of programming almost any trick you desire. Special effects allow 360-degree rotation, horizontal/vertical flipping, object transparency, and blending.
- **Compatibility**—Director can output to either platform, Macintosh or PC. Presentations can be converted for use on the Web or on CD-ROM.
- **Difficulty**—The learning curve for Director is much steeper than for the others. It uses object-oriented scripting (lingo), some of which can be accessed via menus. It has familiar drag-and-drop functions and automated "behaviors" for some events. Director has the power to give professionals a definitive edge, and to virtually humiliate amateurs.

Overhead Projectors
Overhead projectors can be the familiar stand-alone devices that display transparencies directly on the screen, or they can be a visual presenter

(Elmo type) that is wired into a multimedia system and projected on the screen. The Elmo projectors can use transparencies, paper, or 3D objects.

Transparencies are easy to make, inexpensive, portable, and flexible. You can write on them. On the downside, the colors are not as clear or the type as crisp as with other media unless you use a good laser printer. Probably, the biggest disadvantage to using transparencies is that the audience may think you're not as sophisticated as another group. However, if you do use transparencies consider the following tips:

- **Use frames for holding the transparencies in place.** If you need to use tape, don't make it masking tape; instead use drafting tape.
- **Lightly pencil in cues or tips for your presentation on the frame borders of each transparency.** These tips can remind you of script points, or to smile or to hold your hands at your sides.
- **Label each of your transparencies.** This is important because you don't want to have to turn on lights to check which transparency you are showing.

If you use an Elmo visual presenter, **avoid the temptation to copy material directly out of the plans book!** Too often it gives the impression that the group took the easy (lazy) way out. Consider the following tips:

- **Create each sheet of paper for the presentation as you would for a slide.** A sheet of paper can contain many more words than a slide. Resist cramming too many words on the sheet. If the audience reads too many words, they pay less attention to the speaker.
- **Make the size of the typeface appropriate to the room.** Run a test. Have someone stand near the back of the room to check for readability of your material.
- **Personalize each sheet you present.** Put the group name or a border on each sheet. This can give the impression that your group attends to small details and it looks nicer.

Presentation Boards and Flipchart Pads

Boards and flipchart pads shorten the psychological distance between you and the client. You can write on them, handle them, and move them closer. They seem more real and exciting to the client. You can use them extemporaneously to generate ideas and executions. And they are dependable because they have no mechanized parts that can break down as some machinery tends to do at the most inopportune times. If you choose to use presentation boards and flipcharts, consider the following tips:

- **Use bold magic markers to write.** Create contrast with the background.
- **On a flipchart pad, use all capital letters.** Don't be afraid to add or delete on the pads and charts as you present them. Lightly pencil in cues for yourself on the back of the pad or chart.
- **Staple a blank sheet behind each page so that bleeding or fuzzy lettering doesn't show through. If you're concerned about the quality of lettering or art, go to the Yellow Pages or other source for traceable images.** Clip-art books, rub-on letters, and children's coloring books are also helpful.

CREATING A LASTING IMPACT

Professional presenters know that the audience will not remember much of what they say. But this fact is often disheartening to students who may have spent the better part of a semester collecting information to present. After you've assessed your audience, your venue, and your presentation medium, you're ready to answer an important question. If your audience remembers only one thing about your presentation, what would you want that to be? This is often difficult to answer, especially if you are presenting the work of a team. You must all agree on this one point to make a successful presentation. Usually, the answer to this question is that you want the client to remember your solution to their problem.

Make the solution the "hero" of your presentation. Too often, students focus on all the research they have collected. In a client presentation, this is not as important as showing your ideas, your solution to the problem. Develop a theme to your presentation that brings the listeners back again and again to your main idea. If you want your audience to remember your key point, we believe they should hear it at least four times.

▌PLANNING THE PRESENTATION

DETERMINING THE ORDER OF THE PRESENTATION

Much of the discussion about the order in which to present the various areas in the campaign focuses on how to showcase the creative section. Clearly, the ads and the message strategy are the highlights of impressive campaigns. The following are some options:

1. SA → CS → ADS → MP → RMC → RMCE → B
2. SA → MP → RMC → B → CS → ADS → RMCE
3. SA → CS → MP → RMC → B → ADS → RMCE
4. CT → SA → CS → CT → MP → B → RMC → B → ADS → RMCE

Key

SA = situation analysis	CS = creative strategy
ADS = advertising examples	MP = media plan
RMC = related marketing communications	CT = creative teasers
RMCE = related marketing communication examples	B = budget

Is there a preferred order in the above options? Not really. The order in which you deliver your presentation depends a lot on what you think of your creative. It is important to remember that when people leave presentations, they don't usually talk about the media; they talk about the message strategy or the ads. All of the approaches, even the fourth one, basically start out with the situation analysis. The logic of this approach assumes that the analysis forms the foundation upon which subsequent strategy and executions are based.

The **first option** is fairly straightforward and mostly follows the outline of the book. Its advantage is that it is logical. Its disadvantage is that once the ads are shown, anything shown afterward can be anticlimactic. One way to minimize this limitation—don't show much in the way of media or other communication ideas. In the business world, this approach works fine. In fact, frequently the media plan is presented separately, or handled by another agency. In a competition or a class situation, the judging criteria will usually militate against taking this direction. However, as campaigns increasingly use nontraditional media creatively for impact or to create buzz, presenting these media last is one way to leave the audience talking. Clients generally understand marketing and can develop strategic thinking, but for creative and alternative ways to get the message out, they look to the agency for guidance.

The **second option** is sometimes appropriate for established brands for which the media plan is fairly well assumed. The idea here is to get the analysis and the media out of the way and then devote most of the presentation to the creative. The advantages and disadvantages here are similar to the above in that what works well in the business world may not go so well out of it.

The **third option** is highly recommended. You get to talk about your strategy and ideas early, but you still save the executions for the end of the presentation where you hope you will "wow" the audience. By saving your executions until the end, you hope that the last thing the audience remembers about your presentation are the features that are likely to leave the most favorable impression. Although we put the marketing communication examples after the ads, don't take that position literally. You can also consider mixing the marketing communication examples in with the ads. For example, if you had a radio or television spot with music, you might want to put that execution at the end—to leave people humming.

The **fourth option** is the most fluid and potentially creative of all the options. However, it won't work very well unless there is something in the creative plan to weave a thread of excitement throughout the presentation. The idea is to build excitement for the creative ideas by hinting or teasing at what they might be. For example, you could start your presentation off by announcing, "On January first, in the year 2006, Brand X will introduce its advertising idea for the new millennium." Of course, once you have the audience hooked you must deliver on your promise. The new idea could be something serious such as a product promise or a new warranty. It could also be something less serious such as a new trade character like a lizard or a Chihuahua. A variation of this option is to show ads and use them as examples of specific points you want to make in the presentation.

DETERMINING THE CONTENT OF THE PRESENTATION

Depending on the order in which you present your material, what you present can vary considerably. As you go through the plans book, consider the following tips regarding what to present:

Company Analysis

- Keep this section brief. *Avoid covering material that could be covered in the product analysis.*

- Very quickly let the client know you understand their problems.
- Tell the client how you will improve sales or profits.
- Find a gap between what is and what could be.
- Let the client know that you will be telling them how to close the gap.
- Do more than simply identify the problem, expand the client's knowledge of it.
- Use the client's values to understand why they should care about their problems.
- Lay the foundation for your campaign by identifying opportunities your campaign will later address.
- Be sure to relate what is going on with the company to the industry or economy in general.

Consumer Analysis

- Establish who is using both the brand and other products in the generic category.
- At a minimum, delineate users with demographic variables, using other criteria as available.
- Describe usage with terms such as heavy, medium, light, above average, and so on. Indicate *or be prepared to explain* index numbers to give an indication as to what these terms mean.
- If you have done primary research, indicate very briefly a description of what you did, including your methodology.
- Include only the key findings that provide insight into how consumers think or feel about the brand and generic category.
- Indicate what consumers want from either your brand or this type of product.
- Indicate the *degree* to which consumers might be interested in either the brand or the category.
- Briefly, sketch out the consumers' lifestyle, brand loyalty, and other factors that may influence consumers' thoughts or feelings about the brand.
- Provide a detailed understanding of the consumer's buying decision process.
- **Note: Avoid stating the target audience until all the analyses have been presented!**

Market Analysis

- Briefly indicate the relative geographical dispersion both of users and product usage across the United States.
- Indicate the quantity of users with raw numbers or percentiles and the type of usage (i.e., heavy, medium, or above average) with index numbers on a *selective* basis.
- Indicate how brand usage compares to usage in the generic category.
- Use brand development index (BDI) and category development index (CDI) numbers if available, but be sensitive to the audience's understanding of these terms.
- If available, indicate whether usage varies with county size.

Product Analysis

- Tell what the product has that addresses what consumers want. **Avoid merely describing the product.**
- Search hard to find something insightful about the brand that the client doesn't already know.
- Indicate advantages and limitations.
- Include in your appraisal of the product an evaluation of the brand's distribution, price, and past advertising—being careful not to merely describe this information.
- Indicate whether the consumer's perception of the brand reflects real product characteristics or whether it is a result of cultural trends, advertising, competitive efforts, or past experiences with the brand.
- Show how consumers feel about the brand, apart from the way they feel about the product's physical characteristics. How much brand equity does the product have? What is the brand's market position?
- Evaluate the opportunity to build the brand. Can it be a power brand? Give the client hope, but don't overpromise.
- Explain how the consumers' perception of the brand matches, exceeds, or falls short of what consumers want from the product.
- Be willing to talk fluent brand. Make the brand the hero of the presentation. Clearly indicate you know the difference between a brand and a product.

Competitive Analysis

- Evaluate the competition similar to what was done in the product analysis. **Avoid simply describing the competition,** both direct and indirect.
- Compare the competition (and their brands) on the basis of criteria, such as service, image, and quality, not just sales (which the client likely already knows).
- Be sure to indicate where the competition does well.
- Evaluate briefly (no more than a few sentences) the competition's advertising.
- Indicate competitive media expenditures if available.
- Show where your brand falls on a perceptual map vis-à-vis the competition. (Great idea.)
- Compare the competitive brands on basis of how each meets, exceeds, or falls short of consumer expectations for the product category.

Problems and Opportunities

- If you haven't already discussed problems and opportunities at the end of each analysis, sum them up here.
- In your summary, indicate the difference between major and minor problems and opportunities.
- At some point in this section, your discussion of problems and opportunities should converge on your conclusion of the opportunity to expand sales.

- Is there an opportunity to expand sales by getting new users? By getting current users to use more of the product? By promoting new uses of the product?
- Consider a SWOT analysis to summarize problems and opportunities.
- Consider turning problems into opportunities. Even a skeptical client can be converted by optimism.

Profiling the Target Audience

- Upon completion of the previous section, inform the audience that the decision about whom to target comes only after considering the entire situation analysis carefully.
- State the target as simply as possible. Indicate who they are and where they are located. It shouldn't be necessary to provide any justification.
- Prioritize multiple targets by indicating your rationale for selecting primary, secondary, and tertiary markets.

Objectives

- If you have been given marketing objectives, restate them here.
- If you can set realistic marketing objectives, state them here (students generally do not have enough information to do a good job here).
- If you don't have marketing objectives, indicate your sales expectations in a general way, probably without putting them on a slide (or other medium).
- List your campaign objectives. Indicate you will later break down these objectives further in the other sections.

Campaign Budget

- We recommend you put the budget near the end of the presentation with the section on evaluation. However, if you prefer to put it here, show the budget at least two different ways: in percentages allocated to specific items, such as advertising, public relations, and sales promotions; and in terms of the dollar amounts allocated for each item.
- **It's not necessary to read every number that appears in front of the audience.** Give highlights and round off big numbers.
- If you offer this material at the end of the presentation, tie the budget to the achievement of objectives.

Marketing Communication Strategy Overview

- If you present anything from this section, keep it very brief. You may not even want to put anything in a visual aid. If you do, consider a pie chart indicating the breakdown of money spent on the various marketing communications tools.
- Briefly tell how all the marketing communications tools will complement each other to achieve campaign objectives.
- Present strategy and rationale throughout the presentation.
- If you are not using an advertising intensive strategy, then obviously this section should be expanded.

Advertising Strategy

- Remember, in many people's eyes, advertising strategy and the message strategy are the same thing. So if you want to say anything about media here, keep it very brief.

Creative Strategy

- Whatever you show or say, it has to be both special and different. Your visuals, speech, and manner should all convey the feelings of pride, confidence, excitement, and even . . . the love (there we've said it!) that your team has toward the ads.
- Consider quickly reminding the audience of the target audience, perhaps restated in creative terms.
- If you present creative objectives on a visual (although you may not want to), do so briefly. **Resist the urge to read full sentences.**
- **Summarize your creative strategy in a simple statement. For emphasis, we say it again: Summarize your creative strategy in a simple statement.** Consider putting the statement on a visual.
- Present other major elements of your message strategy, such as a big unifying idea or your brand position. Consider visuals for these elements, too.
- Consider presenting other elements of the message strategy, such as the theme, slogan, or tone, but discuss these as you present your executions. Use them to tell the client why the ads will work.
- If you have mounted examples of print ads, take them off the easel and bring them to the client. Show just how special you think they are.
- Read the headline in your print ads. Describe the copy, but don't read all the ads unless the client requests it.
- For television, don't read anything the audience can see. If they can't see your storyboards, briefly describe them.
- When reading the audio for television or radio, inject enthusiasm and personality into each reading. Make it a performance.
- If two females read a spot written for a male and a female, have one lower her voice. If two males read a spot written for male and female, use your judgment.
- If presenters are free to move about, consider moving closer to the client and audience to give them a close look. Use the opportunity to make a more personal connection with the audience.

Remember: Clients want more than just ideas, they want solutions!

Media Strategy

- Move quickly into the media presentation. Media is becoming more and more important and creative. Show original thinking and integrate nontraditional media.
- If you present your media objectives on a visual, don't read them verbatim. If you read your media objectives, don't put the full text on a visual. (Present objectives in terms of reach, frequency, impressions, and rating points.)

- If you are recommending nontraditional media, you might mention how your approach will enhance the message strategy.
- Briefly discuss the major elements of your strategy: the media choices, the media mix, and the timing.
- You can discuss media choices by presenting pictures of media vehicles each selected along with your rationale.
- The media mix can be communicated easily with a pie chart.
- You may want to talk briefly about media timing. You can show a continuity schedule (i.e., a media calendar) after you have discussed media tactics.
- When presenting media vehicles, group them according to media categories and provide both quantitative and qualitative reasons for selecting them.
- **Remember, cost per thousand prospects (CPMP) is usually more relevant than a simple CPM.** Provide CPMs for vehicles you did not select to compare.
- Graphs or maps are quick ways to show how media dollars are allocated on a geographical or seasonal basis.
- End this section with a media calendar and a budget.

Sales Promotion, Public Relations, and Direct Marketing

It's ok to have lots of ideas here, but always relate them to how they will solve the client's problem.

- Briefly state objectives, indicating how they tie into campaign goals.
- Briefly state strategy in a few sentences and be ready to move quickly into your promotion examples.
- Be sure promotional ideas integrate with and complement your advertising.
- Execute prototypes of your promotional ideas. Show them on your slides.
- Talk about the role of promotions in accomplishing your objectives.
- Small ideas that will probably get rejected by the client are no big deal in this area, especially if you preface your ideas by saying, "Here are some additional ideas for you to consider."
- Develop a calendar for your ideas.
- Try to give the impression you are a source of unlimited ideas.
- Include promotions in your budget.
- Indicate how the public relations program will complement the other marketing communications activities.
- Tie PR objectives in with campaign goals.
- Briefly state strategy and give examples of your PR ideas.
- Indicate when the PR activities will take place. Talk about costs.
- Give examples of public relations.
- If you are using direct marketing in the campaign, indicate how it fits in with other marketing communication tools.
- Very briefly state objectives and strategy. Show or pass around examples of what you plan to use in the program.
- Very briefly indicate your costs and a calendar.

Evaluation

- Indicate how you will evaluate the campaign's effectiveness. Include examples of benchmarking surveys, focus groups, or other research.
- If this is the last item in the presentation, use the last tip to segue into a closing statement where the account executive will . . .

Conclusion

- **. . . ask for the account.**

Important Advice for Planning the Presentation

The tips discussed above are only advice. Campaigns are different and so are agencies. Customize your presentation to fit your team and the situation. Moreover, if you are in a competition with other schools and they have read this book, you will want to avoid looking like them. This book has been used by approximately 165 schools in the United States and over 200 schools worldwide. Retain the important principles, but be different.

Presentation Goals for the Individual Presenters

As you think about the individual role you will play in the overall team presentation, there are five points (goals) to keep in mind.

1. **Understand the Presentation.** As you plan your own individual role in the overall presentation, be careful not to lose sight of the team's presentation goals. The team should discuss specifically what impressions they want to leave with the client and the audience. Campaigns are like a product. Telling consumers a product is special for *multiple* reasons makes them less likely to remember what is *really* special about the product. Determine what is special about your campaign. Then be sure team members keep that in mind when they plan their own parts.
2. **Get and Keep Attention.** Whatever you say or show in the presentation will be meaningless unless your audience is paying attention. Thus, the second goal for individuals is to find ways to keep the audience involved. Consider a few surprises at the outset and along the way, the kind that raise eyebrows and pique one's attention. You should also give long and hard consideration to the beginning and end of the presentation. A presentation is like a horse race; it's the beginning and end that count. Possible openings for the beginning of your presentation are featured later in this chapter.
3. **Bond with the Audience.** You need to find common ground with the client. You want them to feel you're on their side, with their best interests at heart. Part of that common ground relates to the personal connection you make with the client. There's nothing wrong with friendliness throughout the presentation, but it's especially important at the beginning. Think of how you can establish some common ground with the client to better promote your ideas.
4. **Establish Credibility.** Product success, reputations, brand equity, and certainly money are at stake for the client, and so doubts inevitably surface. One key doubt relates to your credibility. Your

presentation plan should include pointed strategies for eliminating that doubt.

5. **Be Persuasive.** Plan your presentation so the client feels you are sincere and trustworthy. Project those traits. With your presentation, hook into the prospective client's wish list of needs and wants. What you say and show requires alignment with those needs and wants.

Overall, these five goals should guide your presentation. Consider them as you make the hard decisions centered on what to say and show.

Writing the Presentation

Some people suggest you literally write out everything you say in a presentation. If you will be presenting in a set period, say 20 minutes, there is some merit to this idea. If time is somewhat flexible, it is usually more spontaneous to present from an outline. This spontaneity helps develop credibility as the client sees that you understand the material and are not simply reading from a script. A common suggestion is that you memorize only the beginning and end, and then rely on key words or concepts to guide you through the presentation's middle. It depends somewhat on how you feel most comfortable and confident. But be aware that complete memorization can break down and leave you speechless. It's often better to have a firm grip on the flow of the presentation, with key terms and concepts memorized.

Still, scripting has benefits. Ambitious presentations are often storyboarded in the planning stage in the same way storyboards are used to guide the production of commercials or movies. (Yes, movies. Steven Spielberg, for example, uses highly detailed storyboards before beginning filming, and refers to them constantly during filming.) It can be especially helpful to storyboard ideas using PowerPoint software. You can use the sort option to arrange and rearrange slides until you feel comfortable with the sequence of the points you plan on covering in the presentation.

Decide on Governing Messages or Themes. An advertising presentation usually contains more than one message. Typically, there is a range of information provided, spanning topics such as creative and media. To link together these topics or information, a few governing themes should be threaded throughout the presentation. The themes unify all that you say and show, and they serve to anchor the client's internal responses in a meaningful, easily understood context. The messages presented through the script attach themselves to that theme. Typically, this theme will involve something with the message strategy, but it could center on some new opportunity such as a new product launch.

Unify and Coordinate Sections. Governing themes help unify and coordinate the diverse sections of the presentation, but are not enough by themselves. Within each section, such as creative, media, and promotion, you should strive for consistency of format and structure.

Be consistent with the use of words and terms. Tighten your language to cut down on the amount of material the client is expected to decode or remember. For example, if your creative is introduced through objectives and strategies, then consider introducing all of your media and promotion the same way. This consistency provides symmetry between the sections and makes it easier for the client to follow your presentation, even though you may be moving quickly from one part to another.

In a similar way, keep your wording of terms consistent from one part to another. For example, if you use the word *objectives* in the creative part of the presentation, consider this usage in the media and promotion parts. All language should be consistent.

Keep a Consistency in the Style of Presenting Visual Aids.   As you plan visuals, such as slides and charts, keep what is said about them in the script consistent with what is portrayed on them. There is nothing wrong with saying aloud what is also shown on a slide. (*Just don't read every word.*) Repeating key words or terms from slide to slide or presentation section to section can help unify and coordinate the presentation.

Structural Integrity.   View the presentation both as a whole and as parts and sections within the whole. The structural integrity of the presentation means you give each part and section a strategic and pointed emphasis, rather than giving all of them equal weight.

In the presentation, you will have a limited amount of time to make your case. How much time should you devote to the beginning? The middle? The end? To the research? To the creative or media? In the National Student Advertising Competition (NSAC), the creative section generally receives the most time and is placed closer to the beginning of the presentation than to the end.

As you consider the steps and tips in planning your presentation, be aware that your presentation structure will likely be refined over time.

Think Beginning, Middle, and End

Think of your presentation as having three distinct parts: a beginning, middle, and end. Each of these parts should be tied together, in much the same way that you would tie together the specific sections of the presentation.

The Beginning.   The beginning and end are considered the most important parts of your presentation. Some professional presenters believe you should design the end of your presentation first, before the beginning. We'll take the traditional approach and plan the beginning first. Either way, plan these two parts before you work on the middle.

A good beginning quickly gets the audience's attention and develops an interest in what will follow. As you write the beginning, consider the following points about how a beginning should function.

- It should grab attention.
- It should preview the subject by introducing the main messages or themes.
- It clarifies and emphasizes what's in it (the benefit) for the prospective client.
- It establishes you as a credible source.

By considering these points, you should have an idea about what to say or even what to show at the presentation's beginning. You know, for instance, that before the beginning blends into the presentation's middle or body, the audience should be riveted, clear about the presentation's focus and benefit, and confident in your credibility. The question is, how do you achieve these desired results? The following techniques are some of the tried-and-true methods:

- **Ask a question**—This rivets and focuses audience attention.
- **State an unusual fact**—This raises eyebrows, especially when the fact is in some way central to the client's needs, wants, or problems.
- **Give an illustration, an example, or a story**—This pulls your audience into the presentation.
- **Give a quote**—Why not quote directly from the prospective client or someone the client knows or respects?
- **Tell what's common between you and the client**—If, for example, both your agency and the client were central to furthering a certain business practice or perspective, make that known.
- **Use humor**—Be careful if you decide to inject humor into your presentation because what's funny to one person is not necessarily funny to another. Finally, make certain your humor relates to the client's general business or the situation at hand. Local libraries have books that you can use that contain humorous anecdotes for all occasions and situations.
- **Tell why you're credible**—The key here is understatement and subtlety, not overstatement and boldness.

The Middle.   To be effective, this section often requires a lot of information. This can lead to tedium, if not boredom. You can keep the client interested by embedding the script with elements similar to some of the points we have already discussed in other sections. They include the following:

- Keep words and terms alike or similar.
- Tie concepts to the main messages or themes.
- Get personal. Be sure to use the pronoun *you* in your presentation.
- Simplify complex data or information.
- Summarize frequently.
- Embed minor diversions for strategic purposes. If you have flooded the client with a great deal of information, take a breather and inject some humor or a brief anecdote.
- Avoid "jargon" or confusing concepts without explanations. Don't assume that all clients are familiar with some of the more technical advertising terms. However, assume that they may be able to intuitively figure out some terms, like cost per thousand.

The End.   Like the beginning, the presentation's end, or close, is significant, simply because it will be the last thing the audience will remember about you and your agency. This is why care needs to be taken with the ending. Overall, you should seek to reinforce the presentation's goals and to consolidate the main points around the governing themes that have acted as glue for your presentation. Consider the following possible presentation endings:

- **The happy ending**—End on a positive note. Be upbeat and optimistic.
- **The funnel ending**—Here, you distill numerous points made in the presentation down to a few main points, often centered on the governing themes.
- **The "we're here to help" ending**—Position yourself as a genuine, sincere, and constructive solution to the client's problem.
- **The "predict the future" ending**—Make projections of how your proposal will have an impact on the client's future, obviously in a positive way.
- Emphasize the enthusiasm of your agency for the account.

At the very end, write a note to yourself: **"ASK FOR THE BUSINESS."**

Improve Writing Style

Once you've determined the structural integrity and content of the presentation's main parts and sections, concentrate on stylistic improvements in the script. Consider the following stylistic tips:

- **Write in a conversational tone**—Write like you talk, but with some elaboration at key points.
- **Use action verbs**—Action verbs breathe life into the writing and speaking. They stimulate the listener to imagine and construct scenes, emotions, and meanings. Use action verbs such as *propel, surge, advance,* or *stimulate.*
- **Vary the sentence pacing**—Sound out your script by reading it aloud. If reading it aloud results in a singular rhythmic drone of words, then changes are needed.
- **To add variety to the rhythm, vary sentence lengths**—If you have two long sentences together, then think about following them with a short sentence or phrase. It will help a sentence stand out.
- **Write short paragraphs**—The presenter finds short paragraphs easier to remember and less intimidating. Short paragraphs also force the scriptwriter to focus on organization and embed more transitions.
- **Explain and repeat difficult or knotty concepts**—If a certain concept seems particularly difficult or knotty for the client, elaborate it, perhaps by use of analogy or example.

DESIGNING AND USING VISUALS

Visual aids reinforce and help explain the points you cover while making the presentation. People tend to trust what they see. Moreover, visuals can liven up a presentation.

Although certain principles might change as you move from boards to slides to transparencies, essentially the foundation of basic design principles remains the same.

Using Type in Visual Aids

- **Keep it simple**—Use discretion when emphasizing a point; only stress the most important point.
- **Put words near the top**—Words near the top of the enclosure or page lift the viewers' eyes and are easier to read. So, with flipcharts as well as slides or transparencies, place words or images in the top two-thirds of a page.
- **Limit the number of words**—Don't expect the audience to read too much. Use only key words, especially when the visual field is crowded, as with lists or a number of items.
- **Use uppercase and lowercase letters**—You can use all caps on flipcharts; otherwise use uppercase and lowercase letters, which is what people are generally accustomed to reading.[2]
- **Use large letters**—Don't be misled by how easy something is to read when you're right on top of it. Assume a safe distance from the visual field, and then judge how large the letters should be.
- **Use only one method of emphasis**—If you use boldface, then don't underline. Avoid italics, which read better in print than on visuals.
- **Consider using pictures to represent target audience segments**—People like to look at people. Using pictures for the target can help maintain interest and help the viewer get a better feel for what you're trying to get across.

Using Graphics in Visual Aids

- **Use a single orientation**—Choose either a landscape (horizontal) or portrait (vertical) format for your visuals, not both. As much as possible, you should stick with one orientation or format. Only when you cannot apply that orientation should you change.
- **Color can offer emphasis, mood, distinction, associations**—As with advertising generally, color adds considerable attention-grabbing potential to your visuals. Particularly with slides, color can be used to lead the viewer from one line of words down or up to another. One of the most common of all slide treatments is to highlight in color the item or line of words the presenter is addressing. A rule of thumb is not to use more than three colors. You need to make strategic decisions about the actual choices of color. Contrast works best here, with an understanding that black type or images on a yellow ground shows up well for reading, although the yellow can be a visually nervous color. You may want to consider a cool-color background, such as blue, which tends to recede and not advance. Then your words or images would be a hot color, such as yellow, which tends to advance and not recede. And color choice, like your other choices, should be consistent and continuous throughout.
- **Keep visuals simple and singular**—Don't be tempted to cram as much as humanly possible on one slide or flipchart. Limit what you include; try to keep each visual enclosure limited to one core idea or concept.
- **Condensation is important in your visuals**—Highlight key words or terms and don't feel obliged to abide by rules of grammar, particularly in respect to complete sentences.

- **Use bullets and graphic flourishes**—Consistency is important. If you start with one type of graphic element such as a bullet or a checkmark, you should continue with it.
- **Condense complex numbers into pie charts and bar graphs**—Simplify numbers so that they can be understood in a glance.
- **Reduce the number of curves on a graph to no more than three**—Limit the curves you show on each graph. Simplicity leads to clarity and comprehension.
- **Use charts, graphs, and diagrams appropriately**—Charts, graphs, and diagrams serve various functions. Use bar charts to show comparisons. Use pie charts to show relationships of parts to a whole. Use graphs to show changes and trends. And use diagrams to show complex ideas or concepts. Make simple associations, not clichés.
- **Keep maximum screen time to one minute**—Audiences can get into a rhythm. If a slide remains on-screen longer than a minute, the audience's rhythm can be disrupted.

Visuals for Data and Numbers

A variety of visuals can help you convey data and numbers quickly to the client. All of them can be created on a computer, then enlarged for display or photographed for slides. Duncan and Moriarity suggest the following use of visuals for quantitative material:[3]

- **Tables**—Tables are good for showing extensive data and numbers, but these kinds of detail can drag down a presentation. However, tables may serve your purpose if you need to explain some information in detail. You can always highlight some of the data by using boldface or color.
- **Line graphs**—Line graphs work on two dimensions, showing time horizontally and volume or amounts vertically. Line graphs are effective for showing trends or changes over time.
- **Bar graphs**—Bar graphs show units and are effective for making comparisons. They can also be shown three-dimensionally, creating depth in the visual image and thus highlighting key comparisons.
- **Flowcharts**—One of the most popular uses for a flowchart is to show media uses over time.
- **Pie charts**—Pie charts show the relationship of parts to a whole and are generally appropriate for showing percentages. An interesting and arresting visual adaptation of pie charts is to have them explode, separating one wedge or piece from the others.
- **Diagrams**—Diagrams often are effective for showing how something works. They can also be used to show cross sections or even the flow of one element to another.
- **Pictographs**—Pictographs lend visual excitement to data because the data are captured in an arresting visual field. For example, if you were pitching to an automobile manufacturer, you might be inclined to show data inside the outline of a particular car model.

These data displays shown in Figure 12-1 all simplify within a glance what could be complex data to explain in words.

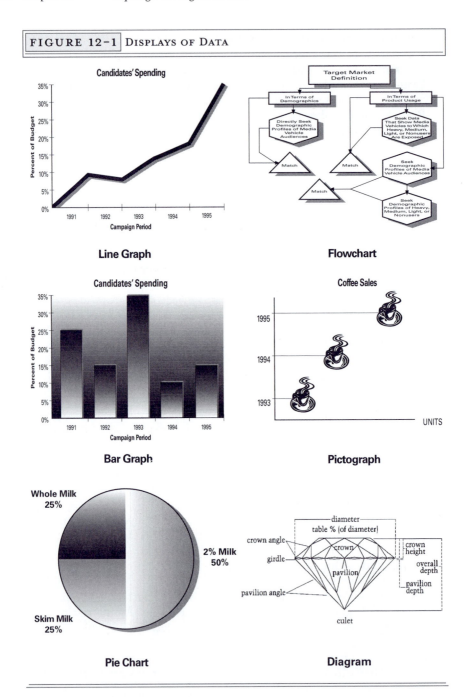

FIGURE 12-1 DISPLAYS OF DATA

Line Graph

Flowchart

Bar Graph

Pictograph

Pie Chart

Diagram

Reinforcing Visual Aids

Another way to add extra interest to the presentation is to give the audience something to look at other than a screen or the presentation. It gives people a momentary rest, especially if they have been watching more than one presentation. Consider the following reinforcements for comprehensives (comps).

- Create comps of actual ads and sales promotion materials. Despite the visual power of slides or transparencies, nothing quite beats comps where clients can lay their hands on the real thing. Comps can also be brought closer for inspection, creating involvement on the part of clients.
- Use acetate overlays for a glossy finish.
- Letter in headlines and subheads. Body copy should be neatly ruled.
- Present comps on boards. Use an easel or wall background.
- Board sizes should be 18 inches, and the type size approximately 60 points if the viewing distance is 12 feet. If the viewing distance is 14 feet, the board size should be 24 inches and the type size approximately 72 points. If the viewing distance is 16 feet, the board size should be 36 inches and the type size 120 points.

Consider using props; they can be valuable for breaking down the walls between you and the client and for creating involvement. Your choice of props might include the following: miniversions of your client's product, product packaging, and product displays.

▉REHEARSING THE PRESENTATION

Everybody understands the value of rehearsing. However, it's not only about the amount of time you devote to rehearsing, but the quality of time as well. Practice won't automatically make things perfect. But perfect practice can get you closer to where you want to be. Consider the following tips to help you rehearse.

- **Be serious about practice**—There's an old saying in sports that applies here. If you practice bad, you'll play bad.
- **Be prepared**—If there are stumbling blocks during rehearsal, they are only going to be bigger obstacles when the time comes to make the final pitch. Knowing your information inside and out can prevent a bad case of the "ums" ("the, um, target audience, um . . .").
- **Attitude**—You may be worn out from producing the campaign. Professionals don't let it show. Be enthusiastic. Sell yourself during the presentation. Vocal resonance, body language, and eye contact can communicate excitement as well as confidence better than anything you say. Practice enthusiastically.
- **Visual aids**—Aids are in the presentation to help you. If they are distracting or irrelevant, then reevaluate their place in your presentation. Simplify wherever you can.
- **Nervous quirks**—Although it's natural to be fidgety, when presenting in front of a group, nervous mannerisms can undermine your ability to persuade the audience (or client) of your good ideas. When rehearsing, be on the lookout for wringing hands, holding elbows, and biting nails.
- **Physical appearance**—It's natural to want to practice in casual clothes. Consider dressing in the type of clothes you will wear in the presentation at least once. (It's called a dress rehearsal.) Practice at the site if possible or create a close simulation.

FINAL CHECKING AT THE SITE

It's always a good idea to do a final check on the site before your presentation. Anticipation, preparation, and attention to detail will go a long way to build confidence. Develop a checklist consisting of the following points.

- **Know the room necessities for making a presentation.** Know all about lights, temperature, chairs, and tables. Be certain they are ready to operate for your benefit.
- **Know whom to call for help.** Wherever you are presenting, the owners or managers are certain to have staff people to help. Know who they are and how you can reach them in a hurry.
- **Know the building's facilities and equipment.** Your presentation room will be in a building. You should know where certain facilities and operations are in that building. For example, know where the restroom is, where the stairs and elevators are, and where the copy machine is.
- **Check the equipment.** Do tests on lecterns, easels, overhead projectors, and computers.
- **Check chairs and tables for positioning and stability.** If permitted, arrange the chairs and tables to suit your presentation's purposes. For informality, avoid lecterns or tables separating you from the client. Leave room to stroll. Check lighting and light switches. Know how to work the dimmers, for instance.

▌MAKING THE PRESENTATION

A lot can go wrong with your presentation. Machinery can break down. The lighting may not be right. Heads can get in the way. All sorts of disastrous and sometimes unimaginable things can happen. It's your job to make sure they don't. The following tips are organized according to two primary concerns, your visual aids and you as a presenter. These tips should guide you in making certain everything goes according to plan.

PRESENTING VISUALS

- **Don't block the audience's view.** Take pains to clear the viewing area before starting. Be certain about audience placement so that heads and arms don't obstruct the view.
- **Direct audience attention.** The audience is watching you. If you cast your eyes to the visual, the audience's eyes will follow. At key words use a pointer, especially for emphasis.
- **Round off big numbers.** Though you may be speaking of millions of dollars, don't be tempted to show the entire figure. Abbreviate and round off big numbers so that they are easily read and understood.
- **Use circles, arrows, and other directional devices.** Help your audience direct its attention by use of such devices.
- **Keep transparencies in a binder.** Avoid shuffling your visuals about or keeping them loose.

- **Project images straight on the screen.** Before you begin the presentation, make certain slides and transparencies are aligned properly on your screen.
- **Show and remove visuals at the right time.** The general formula is to introduce, show, and comment. For example, introduce the slide, show it, and then comment on it.
- **Cover parts of some visuals at times.** You can cover all but one line on a flip pad or transparency, then show each of the next lines one at a time. You can do this easily in a PowerPoint presentation. Progressively disclosing information helps control what the audience is watching and thinking.
- **Begin and end with lights full bright.** Don't upstage yourself with a visual. You take the lead and direct the audience, and when your use of a visual is over, take the lead again.
- **Use visuals to help other parts of the presentation.** As mentioned previously, keep cues or notes on transparency frames or on flipcharts (front or back). Write key words from the script lightly on the palm of your hand.
- **Make certain the first of everything is in place and in working order.** Stretch a rubber band around the flipchart pad.
- **Check the equipment.** Check the sound level if you're using audio. Clean fingerprints from overheads. Check the focus on overhead projectors.
- **Bring spare everything.** Bring as much as you can to the presentation—not that you'll use it—that can bail you out of a jam: binders, extra flipchart paper, magic markers, pens, a screwdriver or good Swiss army knife, and an extension cord. Make a checklist before leaving for the presentation, and then check off the items as they're readied for transport.

YOU AS PRESENTER

Many items on the previous two lists go beyond the use of your visuals. They begin to move into another sensitive area in your presentation's success: **you.** All the best visuals will come to nothing if you don't present well. Consider the following tips to help you do a winning presentation:

- **Rehearse.** Rehearse. Rehearse—as a team and alone.
- **Leave cues in handy places.** Leave them around the presentation area and on your own hand.
- **Make eye contact.** This is one of the most important considerations in nonverbal communication. Look for one person first, then make eye contact every three to five seconds with different people. Or, make eye contact in a Z direction around the room.
- **Smile.** A smile helps put your audience at ease. Draw happy faces on your notes or in secret places to remind you to smile.
- **Don't drink before a presentation (especially the stuff that is supposed to make you relax; it won't).** Drinking any liquid may make things more difficult for you. If you need to refresh yourself, moisten your mouth or lips or use Vaseline. Try biting your tongue.

- **Use talcum powder.** Talcum powder will help keep you dry. As the saying goes, "Never let them see you sweat."
- **Face your audience head-on.** This will suggest your confidence and sincerity.
- **Practice gestures beforehand.** Make pointed gestures during highlights in the presentation. Don't cross your arms. Keep your arms and hands at your side, but use them for emphasis when the time is right.
- **Vary the distance and movement in relationship to the audience.** Don't just stand in one place. Move around. Be comfortable. At key points shorten the distance, literally and figuratively, between you and the audience.
- **Practice vocal tone, pitch, and pace variations.** Use pauses to emphasize key points. Deepen your pitch by speaking from the diaphragm. Punch certain words or concepts. Vary your volume and rate of speaking so you speed up in some places and slow down in other places.
- **Lean forward, not backward, and hold yourself erect.** By leaning forward you'll seem eager and enthusiastic. By holding yourself erect you'll seem confident and sure.
- **Coordinate with the team the entrance and exit of the presentation.** These can be the two most unorganized times (getting things set up or cleaned up), but they are also the most remembered moments. In fact, coordinate as much as possible with team members.
- **Relax.** This Should Be Fun.

▊ NATIONAL STUDENT ADVERTISING COMPETITION (NSAC)

Each year around 200 schools enter a national advertising competition sponsored by the American Advertising Federation.

For over 30 years, AAF's National Student Advertising Competition (NSAC) has been the testing ground for advertising student knowledge, insight, and creative problem solving in a real-world environment. Arguably the most prestigious, difficult, and comprehensive of all student advertising competitions, the NSAC features a different corporate sponsor each year. Competing teams solve a case study developed by the client. Each team produces a 32-page plans book and a 20-minute oral presentation that includes all aspects of an advertising and integrated marketing communications plan.

Winners at the 15 AAF regional competitions compete at "Nationals" for the coveted first place prize. The judges for both the plans books and the presentations include distinguished persons from the sponsoring company as well as advertising agencies and the media. They are consistently amazed and impressed at the quality of the student presentations, likening them to major ad agency pitches. Moreover, AAF-sponsoring clients actually use the students' ideas and may even hire some team members.

LYNDA MADDOX

Professor Lynda Maddox of George Washington University (GW) was asked to give her impressions (for the second edition) about what it takes to create a winning presentation at the AAF.

Professor Maddox has been involved with the National Student Advertising Competition for most of its 30-year history, as both a student and a faculty advisor. In 1998, her school won in both district and Nationals. A key component of the competition is a winning presentation. Her advice follows.

The following tips are similar to what has been presented above, but are especially relevant for a winning presentation at the national competition.

Getting Started

- **Start thinking early about the presentation.** You should spend at least as much time putting the presentation together as you spent collecting the information. Many teams wait until the plans book is finished to begin thinking about it. This is too late. Read the presentation score sheet so you get a handle on the relative importance of various aspects. Remember that the judges will be using this to score you.
- **Take pictures throughout the semester to include in your presentation.** Record each stage of the campaign. For example, take pictures of your focus groups or of one of your team members conducting a survey. These pictures will add clout and interest to your presentation.
- **Include some humorous shots.** One year the GW team went on a road trip to conduct surveys in another city. On the way, they got a speeding ticket. The picture of the team members posing with the Pennsylvania State policeman brought a chuckle from the judges and expressed the dedication of this team! You'll also find that these pictures bond the team and are cherished memories after everything is finished.
- **Before you begin writing the presentation, ask yourself, "If there was only one thing that the judges could remember after my presentation, what would I want that to be?"** Be sure the team agrees on this point, because it will serve as the theme or focal point of the presentation. It will help you organize large amounts of information.
- **Reread the case and your plans book to be sure you know what to communicate.** Set objectives and build your presentation around them. Do not think, "What can I say in 20 minutes?" Think, "What do I need to say?" You can edit your speech once you have included all that you need to express.

Selecting Presenters

- **Throughout the semester, schedule various interim presentations to allow each class member to practice presenting.** Sometimes an individual who does not think he or she is a good presenter will become the star after receiving feedback from the class and the advisor.

- **Develop a procedure for selecting presenters.** Set criteria early so that each student in the class has a chance to develop the skills necessary to be selected as a presenter. This helps improve learning and maintain fairness. It reduces the chance that the selecting of presenters will become a popularity contest.
- **Some teams opt to use formal auditions, and this can certainly work.** At GW, each team member will have had at least three "auditions" throughout the semester because each student participates in interim presentations.
- **It is usually best to select presenters who have been intimately involved in the development of the campaign *and* who have developed excellent presentation skills.** A skilled presenter without an emotional attachment to the material will sound stilted and unconvincing. This is especially important because presenters must also perform well in the all-important Question and Answer (Q&A) session.
- **To give each student an opportunity to learn and to meet advertising professionals, the GW team usually opts to have the maximum five presenters.** Judges respond well to this format, but it requires careful choreography.
- **Each team member also has a "coach."** The coach's job is to encourage and support the presenter and to work with them one-on-one. If need be, the coach is fully prepared to step in and become a presenter.

Crafting the Presentation

- **Know whom your judges are and remember your objectives as you begin writing your presentation.** Learn as much as you can about the judges ahead of time. This will help you feel more comfortable and help you connect with them when you get to the presentation.
- **Make *your ideas* the hero of your presentation.** The judges do not want to hear each team regurgitate the information the company gave to you. They are there to hear the fresh, creative insight that can only come from unbiased creative thinkers like you.
- **Start fresh when crafting your presentation.** Do not follow the linear format of the plans book. As you make your ideas the focal point of the presentation, use your primary and secondary research, as well as the information from the case, as the supporting rationale.
- **Your creative executions are usually the most influential part of your presentation.** Build your presentation around your creative ideas. Show your strategic thinking.
- **Answer the question, "Why does this ad work?"** Demonstrate that you believe in your creative, and tell the judges the supporting research. Let them know that you are proud of your work and even that you have favorites among your ads.
- **Show ads on the screen and on storyboards.** Display promotional ideas on slides and create prototypes. The more the judges can see and interact with the creative executions, the more they will remember them.

- **Remember that oral speech differs from written.** Because you have a strict 20-minute time limit, it is too dangerous to speak extemporaneously. You must script your presentation and memorize it, but you should do this so well that you will seem as if you are speaking to the judges one on one.
- **Script the presentation, then edit and rewrite it until it is short, concise, and conversational.**
- **Be creative in your presentation style and format.** Be sure your presentation has an element of surprise that makes it stand out. This can mean using a different audio visual aid, unique slides, or presentation styles. Avoid standing behind podiums and robotic-type presentations.
- **Make it easy for the judges to follow your presentation.** Provide an agenda and follow it. Remind judges periodically throughout the presentation about where you are on your agenda.
- **Give your team an identity.** Name your "agency" and be sure to repeat your name throughout the presentation. The name of your agency and the name of the client should be on every slide.
- **Slides should be interesting and creative.** Intersperse text, photographs, graphs, charts, and other visuals. Interact with your visuals. Do not operate in the dark. The judges want to see you as well as your visuals.
- **Have a point of view and stick with it.** Your campaign theme should connect all aspects of your presentation.
- **Each presentation should have a strong introduction and a strong close.** Tell the judges what you will present and why it is important. At the end, summarize what you have presented, tell how it accomplishes the goals of the assignment, and ask for the business.
- **Practice, practice, practice.** Practice in front of friends, classmates, and faculty. Consider criticisms constructive even if they sometimes seem harsh. Watch facial expressions as you present. The feedback you receive at this point will allow you to craft an excellent presentation.
- **Practice until you sound natural and conversational.** Practice until you do not need notes. Practice gestures, intonation, and timing. You should run through your presentation at least three times exactly the way you want it to be before the big day.

Making the Presentation

- **Above all, remember that your judges are the audience you should be addressing.** As you stand on the stage facing an audience, you may be tempted to talk to the room. Resist this temptation and talk to the people who matter—the judges.
- *Connect* **with the judges.** Talk to them in a conversational style. Shake their hands. Make eye contact. Come out from behind the podium. Get down off the stage. Walk up to them. Show them your work. Feed off their reactions. Smile with them. Tell them your names. Wear name tags. Make them like you as individuals, and as a team.

- **Be sure the judges remember the key aspects of your presentation.** Think back to the one thing you want them to remember. Keep in mind that in order for a judge to remember something you've said, he or she must see or hear it at least four times. So say it, say it again in another way, show it, and then repeat it again. You will not bore the judges. You will make your point.
- **Do not worry too much about your randomly selected order of presentation.** You cannot do anything about it. If you try to use a particular slot to your advantage, this may backfire on you because the judges are concerned about fairness.
- **If you're first or immediately after lunch, keep in mind that it takes the judges a minute or two to warm up.** Pay special attention to greeting them and acclimating them to your presentation format. If you're toward the end, be especially careful not to repeat the case information because many teams before you will have already done this.
- **Show the judges that you are a team and that you enjoy working together.** This is not easy to fake, so work on building team spirit and camaraderie throughout the project. Research shows that wanting to work with a team is the number-one criterion for selecting an agency.
- **Show the judges that you work and think well together.** Feed off one another in a conversational style throughout the presentation. When a team member is speaking, nod affirmatively to support key ideas. Do not fidget or look bored. Let the personality of the team members and the team shine through.
- **Ask for the business.** At the end of the presentation, tell the judges why the campaign will work and why you're the best team to work with.
- **Confidently invite the judges to ask you questions.**

Doing Well on the Q&A Session

- **If you've done a good job on your presentation, the judges will have a lot of questions!** Welcome them. Students often think that judges ask questions to trip them up, and they respond defensively. This is rarely the case.
- **Judges want to know more about your thinking and want to see how committed you are to your ideas.** They are not looking for right or wrong answers. Use this as an opportunity to connect with the judges and to show them how well you can work together as a team. The Q&A session is often where the competition is won or lost.
- **Prepare for the Q&A session ahead of time by having team members and others ask questions.** Rehearse answers to questions just as you rehearse your presentation.
- **Address any controversial issues in the regular presentation where you have control of it.** Never assume that you will answer a major question only if it comes up in Q&A.
- **The Q&A session is a good opportunity for you to "roll up your sleeves" with the judges.** They will often ask you to move toward them or to sit down. You may want to do this at the beginning of the

Q&A. At the Nationals for Hallmark, University of Texas received high marks for pulling up their chairs to the judges' table and looking them in the eyes.

- **If you do not know the answer to a question, let the judges see you think.** Use your research and your insight to show the judges that you can think on your feet. Team members should avoid "piling on." Give team members a chance to answer. Then team members can assist or elaborate.

- **Answer the questions clearly and succinctly.** Although it is a good idea to feed off one another, do not "overanswer" a question. Because judges have only 10 minutes of Q&A, they want you to answer concisely so they can have all of their questions answered.

Conclusion

- **Good presentations do not just happen.** They are carefully planned and orchestrated performances that affect whether the information is remembered, retained, and believed.

THOMAS GROTH

For the third edition, we talked with Thomas Groth, an advertising professor at the University of West Florida. Professor Groth has led student "agencies" to 11 district championships, winning the national championship a record four times, and placing second and third once each. He has led "agencies" from two different schools: Iowa State University and the University of West Florida. His ideas follow.

Twenty Ideas on the NSAC

Nothing here is new. Everything here has been tested under fire. They are some ideas that have worked for teams I've advised over the years. Enjoy the trip.

1. The answer is in the question.

Many agencies answer the "question" correctly—it's just the wrong question. *For example, they answered the question of how to attract prospects to a Web site when the question was, "How do we relaunch a fading brand?"*

- Corollary A: First, understand the client challenge.

The client wants your agency to do something for it. Often the client wants you to solve a problem. You absolutely must understand what it expects.

Suggestion: Put the complete case study on the overhead and literally go through every word and every chart, everything as a group—probe and mine and think. What is the client asking you to do? Often, the obvious answer is the wrong answer.

- Corollary B: Then redefine the challenge for the client.

Establish what your campaign will do for the company. In the end, go back to *the challenge* and note how you achieved the goal. Sale made!

2. Good enough, isn't good enough.

Thank you Chiat Day.
The goal is to astonish the client. My goal is to get the students to astonish themselves.

3. The NSAC is not a competition.

The goal is not to win the competition. The goal is to create the most wonderful, powerful advertising campaign possible. Winning is the *result* not the goal.

4. The brand is everything.

Every assignment is a branding assignment.
Define your brand. Define your brand's personality.

* Corollary: Brands are people too.

People choose brands like they choose their friends. Always define your brand's personality as if it were a human. Then work that personality throughout every execution. It affects everything from the choice of type to media selection.

5. Creativity is king.

Every aspect of the campaign is a creative one—media, direct response, promotions, public relations, research, and so forth.
The quality of the idea is the name of the game. The breakthrough answer is not in the research or on the Internet—it is within the student.
The slogan for West Florida's advertising program is "brilliant ideas—well executed."

6. Funny business.

Have fun! People like to work with people who have a sense of humor. Clients hire people they like. A sense of humor wins accounts.

7. It's a team sport.

Dilettantes don't win.

What type of student tends to thrive in an NSAC agency situation? DDB/Needham had a checklist to evaluate an intern many years ago. The qualities listed are the qualities that count. It works!

8. Where is your business coming from?

Although many teams identify the competition, they rarely identify where the money (brand share) will come from. There are only three places, and each requires a different marketing approach.

1. Convince current users to use more or spend more.
2. Steal competitive users.
3. Convince nonusers to use your brand.

9. The key fact, please.

Always identify the one thing that will make or break the case. That fact might be as simple as having a new brand that nobody has ever heard of, or as complex as having a brand that is caught in an unexpected cultural swing.

10. Advertising is easy.

It's all about matching products to people. John Caples said it all, "A great ad is a believable promise to the right audience."
It is too easy to get caught up in the details and forget what it's all about.

11. Birds of a feather flock together.

Birds of feather not only flock together, but they like similar media, buy for similar motives, and care about similar issues.
Instead of just using traditional market segmentation (e.g., 18–34 males making $35,000), cluster prospects intelligently. For example, group by lifestage (newlyweds, first jobs, empty nesters).

12. Competitively benefit segment.

Use a **perceptual map.** It lets everyone clearly see where your brand is in your prospect's mind relative to your competition. It can also clearly show where you are, and where you plan on going.
Example: If most of your competitive set is clustered in one quadrant, it might prove successful to differentiate your brand by moving to a less crowded neighborhood.

13. Take a risk.

Your advertising and your presentation must demonstrate *intelligent daring.* Break the boredom barrier. Take a shot and don't merely play it safe. **Warning:** taking a risk is just that—a risk. A conservative client may frown on your breakthrough approach, but savvy clients will welcome your efforts. Furthermore, your originality will help the client remember your agency.
Not taking a risk is taking a risk.

14. The media is the message.

Where your advertising *hangs out* is hyperimportant. Rethink all obvious media choices. You can always return to the "tried-and-true," but ask yourself, "What if we . . ."
*What if we placed a cereal advertisement in a business journal? Often merely appearing in an unexpected place will increase relevance and impact at a better CPM. Oh, and there are **no** pesky competitive ads to crash your party.*

15. K.I.S.S.

An old line says "Keep It Simple, Stupid." Thirty pages, 20 minutes, and complexity don't mix. The client has to "get it" quickly. When in doubt—throw it out. Eliminate anything that doesn't contribute to your core plan.

This doesn't mean your ideas and presentation should be "simplistic," just simple.

16. Strategies that have worked.

There is no one best strategy but these are some approaches that we have used:
1. Lifestage (transition) marketing
2. Value-added tactics
3. Relationship marketing
4. Associative marketing
5. Transformation advertising
6. Paradigm shift
7. Lifetime consumer value (LTV)
8. Personal media network
9. "Laddering" (Brand feature→Consumer benefit→Consumer value)

17. Structure campaign year by phases.

This outline will add a simplified structure to a campaign plan.

It can be used to link integrated marketing elements such as advertising, promotions, media, and so forth.

<u>Phase</u>   <u>Target</u>   <u>Goal</u>   <u>Timing</u>   <u>Strategy</u>   <u>Response sought</u>

18. Understand the consumer's "sweet spots."

What is *really, really, really* important to your target? Link your brand with these *hot buttons,* and you'll increase the chances for a home run.

Use your research and all the empathy you can muster to write a first-person, personal monologue "by your prospect." Perform this monologue for your agency so that everybody has a relationship with the prospect.

19. Presentation.

- Don't merely entertain—"infotain."
- Enthusiasm makes up for many defects. You should be hungry to present your work—the feeling: *"I can't wait to show 'em."*
- Be professional, but not so professional that the client feels you aren't students.
- Do lots and lots and lots of killer ads. (Every ad could win a One Show Pencil—You have no excuses.)
- Be realistic.
- It's all about selling.
- When you win, win with graciousness.
- When you lose, lose with graciousness.

The ad business is small. Memories are long.

20. Plans book.

Think of a judge as a *viewer,* not a *reader.* Therefore:

- Design the book so that the significance shines through.
- Break the book into bite-sized, easily digestible pieces.
- Write and design the publication so it is unified.
- Make the book easy and fun to view and read.
- Use a summary for each section. This can be done as a "prologue" or a "review."
- Overwrite, then edit.
- Use real headlines that make sense.
- It's all about selling.
- Upon completion, I test over the plans book to make sure everybody understands not only their section, but the entire campaign as well.

ONE FINAL NOTE

For many advertising students, a presentation in a campaigns class is one of the last academic assignments you will have. Look forward to doing it. Doing it well. And enjoying it.

Notes and References

[1]This chapter has been developed and written in part by Dr. Lynda M. Maddox, a professor of marketing and advertising at The George Washington University.

[2]Some material in this section is based on Joyce Kupsh and Pat R. Graves, *High Impact Business Presentations* (Lincolnwood, IL: NTC Books, 1994), pp. 27–48.

[3]T. Duncan and S. Moriarity, *How to Create and Deliver Winning Advertising Presentations* (Lincolnwood, IL: NTC Business Books, 1989), pp. 62–72.